Teachers Discovering and Integrating Microsoft

Office

Essential Concepts and Techniques

WORD   POWERPOINT   EXCEL   ACCESS

Teachers Discovering and Integrating Microsoft

Office

Essential Concepts and Techniques

WORD   POWERPOINT   EXCEL   ACCESS

Gary B. Shelly
Thomas J. Cashman
Randolph E. Gunter
Glenda A. Gunter

Contributing Authors
Mary Z. Last
Philip J. Pratt
James S. Quasney
Victoria O. Rath
Susan L. Sebok
Misty E. Vermaat

THOMSON
COURSE TECHNOLOGY

COURSE TECHNOLOGY
25 THOMSON PLACE
BOSTON MA 02210

SHELLY
CASHMAN
SERIES®

Australia • Canada • Denmark • Japan • Mexico • New Zealand • Philippines • Puerto Rico • Singapore
South Africa • Spain • United Kingdom • United States

THOMSON
COURSE TECHNOLOGY

COPYRIGHT © 2003 Course Technology, a division of Thomson Learning.
Printed in the United States of America

Asia (excluding Japan)
Thomson Learning
5 Shenton Way #01-01
UIC Building
Singapore 068808

Japan
Thomson Learning
Nihonjisyo Brooks Bldg 3-F
1-4-1 Kudankita, Chiyoda-Ku
Tokyo 102-0073 Japan

Australia/New Zealand
Nelson/Thomson Learning
102 Dodds Street
South Melbourne, Victoria 3205
Australia

Latin America
Thomson Learning
Seneca, 53
Colonia Polanco
11560 Mexico D.F. Mexico

South Africa
Thomson Learning
Zonnebloem Building,
Constantia Square
526 Sixteenth Road
P.O. Box 2459
Halfway House, 1685
South Africa

Canada
Nelson/Thomson Learning
1120 Birchmount Road
Scarborough, Ontario
Canada M1K 5G4

UK/Europe/Middle East
Thomson Learning
Berkshire House
168-173 High Holborn
London, WC1V 7AA United Kingdom

Spain
Thomson Learning
Calle Magallanes, 25
28015-MADRID
ESPANA

PHOTO CREDITS: Microsoft Word *Project 1, pages WD 1.04-05* Shakespeare, book, Hamlet, Romeo and Juliet, MacBeth, line art monitor, Courtesy of ArtToday; computer, mouse, monitor, Courtesy of PhotoDisc, Inc.; **Microsoft PowerPoint** *Project 1, pages PP 1.04-05* COMDEX, COMDEX audience, Courtesy of COMDEX; Bill Gates, Courtesy of Microsoft; notebook, palm PC, Courtesy of Toshiba; cell phone, Courtesy of Ericcson; Michael Dell, Courtesy of Dell Computers; **Microsoft Excel** *Project 1, pages E 1.04-05* Stopwatch, girls sitting, man standing, Courtesy of PhotoDisc, Inc.; child with checkbook, police officer, kids in computer lab, graduate, Courtesy of ArtToday; **Microsoft Access** *Project 1, pages A 1.04-05* Man and girl, senior citizen and teenagers, woman and two boys, phone operators, man, woman, and girl, teacher, Courtesy of PhotoDisc, Inc.

ISBN 0-7895-6733-4

2 3 4 5 6 7 8 9 10   BC   06 05 04 03

Teachers Discovering and Integrating

Microsoft

Office

Essential Concepts and Techniques
WORD   POWERPOINT   EXCEL   ACCESS

Contents

Microsoft **PowerPoint**

---

1 PROJECT ONE

USING A DESIGN TEMPLATE AND TEXT SLIDE LAYOUT TO CREATE A PRESENTATION

Microsoft Excel

Microsoft Access

Preface

The Shelly Cashman Series® offers the finest textbooks in computer education. We are proud of the fact that our series of *Microsoft Office 4.3, Microsoft Office 95, Microsoft Office 97, Microsoft Office 2000*, and *Microsoft Office XP* textbooks have been the most widely used books in education. With each new edition of our Office books, we have made improvements based on the software and comments made by the instructors and students who use our textbooks.

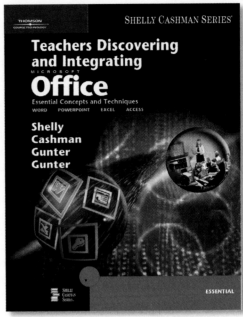

We are pleased to announce the publication of *Teachers Discovering and Integrating Microsoft Office*, the latest in a series of textbooks created specifically for pre-service and in-service teachers and K-12 administrators. The *Teachers Discovering and Integrating Microsoft Office* book continues with the innovation, quality, and reliability that educators have come to expect from the Shelly Cashman Series.

In this *Teachers Discovering and Integrating Microsoft Office* book, you will find an educationally sound and easy-to-follow pedagogy that combines a step-by-step approach with corresponding screens. All projects and exercises in this book are designed to take full advantage of the Office enhancements. The popular Other Ways and More About features offer in-depth knowledge of Office. The In the Lab page presents a wealth of additional exercises to ensure your students have all the reinforcement they need. The Productivity in the Classroom and Integration in the Classroom activities allow your students to learn how to use and more importantly integrate Office applications into the K-12 environment. The project openers provide a fascinating perspective of the subject covered in the project. The project material is developed carefully to ensure that educators will see the importance of learning Office both as a classroom productivity tool and as an integration tool to enhance student learning.

Objectives of This Textbook

Teachers Discovering and Integrating Microsoft Office: Essential Concepts and Techniques is intended for a course that includes a concise introduction to Microsoft Office. No experience with a computer is assumed, and no mathematics beyond the high school freshman level is required. The objectives of this book are:

- To teach the fundamentals of Microsoft Office
- To provide educators with practical examples of how to use Microsoft Office as a classroom productivity tool
- To provide educators with practical examples of how to integrate Microsoft Office in elementary school, middle school, high school, and special education classrooms

- To acquaint educators with the proper procedures to create documents, worksheets, databases, and presentations suitable for coursework, professional purposes, and personal use
- To expose educators to how Microsoft Office is used in business and industry
- To help students discover the underlying functionality of Microsoft Office so they can become more productive
- To develop an exercise-oriented approach that allows learning by doing
- To introduce students to new input technologies
- To encourage independent study and help those who are working alone

The Shelly Cashman Approach

Features of the Shelly Cashman Series *Teachers Discovering and Integrating Microsoft Office* books include:

- **Project Orientation:** Each project in the book presents a practical problem and complete solution in an easy-to-understand approach.
- **Step-by-Step, Screen-by-Screen Instructions:** Each of the tasks required to complete a project is identified throughout the development of the project. Full-color screens accompany the steps.
- **Thoroughly Tested Projects:** Every screen in the book is correct because it is produced by the author only after performing a step, resulting in unprecedented quality.
- **Other Ways Boxes and Quick Reference Summary:** Office provides a variety of ways to carry out a given task. The Other Ways boxes displayed at the end of most of the step-by-step sequences specify the other ways to do the task completed in the steps. Thus, the steps and the Other Ways box make a comprehensive reference unit. A Quick Reference Summary that summarizes the way specific tasks can be completed can be found at the back of this book.
- **More About Feature:** These marginal annotations provide background information and tips that complement the topics covered, adding depth and perspective.
- **Integration of the Microsoft Teaching and Learning CDs and World Wide Web:** Included with this textbook is a set of two Microsoft CDs that provides educators with extensive resources for both learning how to use Microsoft Office and how to integrate Microsoft Office in K-12 educational settings. Many of the activities in this textbook have students access and use resources from these CDs. In addition, the World Wide Web is integrated into the Office learning experience in many ways including the In The Lab page at the end of each project, which has project reinforcement exercises, learning games, and other types of student activities.

Other Ways

1. Press ALT+O, A
2. In Voice Command mode say, "Format, AutoFormat, [desired AutoFormat], OK"

More About

Scrolling

Computer users frequently switch between the keyboard and the mouse during a word processing session, which strains the wrist. To help prevent wrist injury, minimize switching. If your fingers are already on the keyboard, use keyboard keys to scroll. If your hand is already on the mouse, use the mouse to scroll.

Organization of This Textbook

Teachers Discovering and Integrating Microsoft Office: Essential Concepts and Techniques provides basic instruction on how to use and integrate Office applications. The material is divided into an introduction, four projects, five appendices, and a Quick Reference Summary.

An Introduction – Using and Integrating Microsoft Office

Students will learn about Microsoft Office and how Microsoft Office is used in business and education. Topics include the differences between Office XP and Office 2000 and a brief explanation of the different versions of Microsoft Windows being used in K-12 schools. Students are introduced to the importance of using Microsoft Office both as a productivity tool and an integration tool. In addition, students are provided with step-by-step instructions and associated screens so they can learn how to use the Microsoft Teaching and Learning CDs that are included with this textbook.

Microsoft Word – Creating and Editing a Word Document

Students are introduced to Word terminology and the Word window by preparing an announcement. Topics include starting and quitting Word; entering text; checking spelling while typing; saving a document; selecting characters, words, lines, and paragraphs; changing the font and font size of text; centering, right-aligning, applying bold and italic to text; undoing commands and actions; inserting clip art into a document; resizing a graphic; printing a document; opening a document; correcting errors; and using the Word Help system.

Microsoft PowerPoint – Using a Design Template and Text Slide Layout to Create a Presentation

Students are introduced to PowerPoint terminology, the PowerPoint window, and the basics of creating a bulleted list presentation. Topics include choosing a design template by using a task pane; creating a title slide and text slides; changing the font size and font style; ending a slide show with a black slide; saving a presentation; viewing the slides in a presentation; checking a presentation for spelling errors; printing copies of the slides; and using the PowerPoint Help system.

Microsoft Excel – Creating a Worksheet and Embedded Chart

Students are introduced to Excel terminology, the Excel window, speech recognition and speech playback, and the basic characteristics of a worksheet and workbook. Topics include starting and quitting Excel; customizing Excel, entering text and numbers; selecting a range; using the AutoSum button; copying using the fill handle; changing font size and color; formatting in bold; centering across columns; using the AutoFormat command; charting using the Chart Wizard; saving and opening a workbook; editing a worksheet; using the AutoCalculate area; and using the Excel Help system.

Microsoft Access – Creating a Database Using Design and Datasheet Views

Students are introduced to the concept of a database and shown how to use Access to create a database. Topics include creating a database; creating a table; defining the fields in a table; opening a table; adding records to a table; closing a table; and previewing and printing the contents of a table. Other topics in this project include using a form to view data; using the Report Wizard to create a report; and using the Access Help system. Students also learn how to design a database to eliminate redundancy.

Appendices

The book includes five appendices. Appendix A presents a detailed step-by-step introduction to the Microsoft Office XP Help system. Appendix B describes how to use the speech and handwriting recognition features of Office XP. Appendix C explains how to publish Office Web pages to a Web server. Appendix D shows students how to reset the menus and toolbars. Appendix E introduces students to the Microsoft Office User Specialist (MOUS) Certification program.

Microsoft Office Quick Reference Summary

This book concludes with a detailed Quick Reference Summary. In the Microsoft Office applications, you can accomplish a task in a number of ways, such as using the mouse, menu, shortcut menu, and keyboard. The Quick Reference Summary provides a quick reference to each task presented in this textbook.

End-of-Project Student Activities

A notable strength of the Shelly Cashman Series *Microsoft Office* books is the extensive student activities at the end of each project. Well-structured student activities can make the difference between students merely participating in a class and students retaining the information they learn. The activities in the Shelly Cashman Series *Teachers Discovering and Integrating Microsoft Office* book include the following.

- **What You Should Know** A listing of the tasks completed within a project together with the pages on which the step-by-step, screen-by-screen explanations appear. This section provides a perfect study review for students.
- **In the Lab** Every project features an In the Lab page comprised of two sets of exercises. The first set of exercises, Learn It Online, utilizes the Web to offer project-related reinforcement activities that will help students gain confidence in their Office abilities. These exercises include True/False, Multiple Choice, Short Answer, Flash Cards, Practice Test, Learning Games, and Crossword Puzzle Challenges. The second set of exercises, Using the Microsoft Office Training CD, utilizes the Microsoft Training CD and provides students with hundreds of resources tailored for educators that they can use to enhance their understanding and use of Microsoft Office applications.
  - **Productivity in the Classroom** Three in-depth assignments per project require students to apply the knowledge gained in the project to create Office products specifically for use in K-12 educational settings.
  - **Integration in the Classroom** Eight unique integration ideas per project allow students to integrate Microsoft Office into their classroom-specific curriculum. Included are integration ideas for elementary, middle school, high school, and special education teachers.

Shelly Cashman Series Teaching Tools

Teachers Discovering and Integrating Microsoft Office is accompanied by the Instructor's Manual, available for download by instructors at `course.com`.

- **Instructor's Manual** The Instructor's Manual is made up of Microsoft Word files. The files include lecture notes, solutions to laboratory assignments, and a large test bank. The files allow you to modify the lecture notes or generate quizzes and exams from the test bank using your own word processing software. Where appropriate, solutions to laboratory assignments are embedded as icons in the files. When an icon appears, double-click it and the application will start and the solution will display on the screen. The Instructor's Manual includes the following for each project: project objectives; project overview; detailed lesson plans with page number references; teacher notes and activities; answers to the end-of-project exercises; and a test bank of 110 questions for every project (25 multiple-choice, 50 true/false, and 35 fill-in-the-blank).

Shelly Cashman Series Microsoft Office User Specialist (MOUS) Web Page

The Shelly Cashman Series MOUS Web Page has links to Web pages you can visit to obtain additional information on the MOUS Certification program. The Web page (scsite.com/tdoff/cert) includes links to general information on certification, choosing an application for certification, preparing for the certification exam, and taking and passing the certification exam.

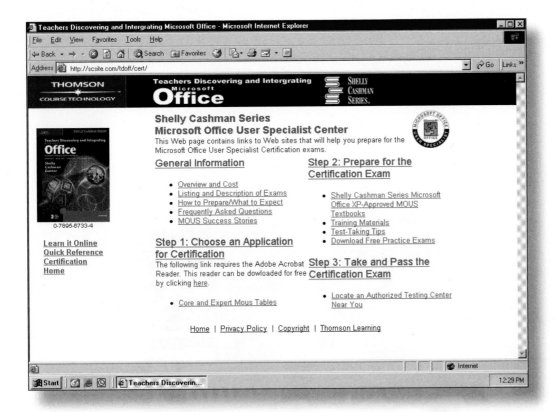

Acknowledgments

The Shelly Cashman Series would not be the leading computer education series without the contributions of outstanding publishing professionals. First, and foremost, among them is Becky Herrington, director of production and designer. She is the heart and soul of the Shelly Cashman Series, and it is only through her leadership, dedication, and tireless efforts that superior products are made possible. Under Becky's direction, the following individuals made significant contributions to these books: Doug Cowley, production manager; Ginny Harvey, series specialist and developmental editor; Ken Russo, senior Web and graphic designer; Michelle French, cover designer; Christy Pardini, graphic artist; Jeanne Black and Betty Hopkins, QuarkXPress compositors; Rich Hansberger, proofreader; Nancy Lamm, copy editor/proofreader; and Cristina Haley, indexer.

Finally, we would like to thank Richard Keaveny, associate publisher; Cheryl Ouellette, managing editor; Jim Quasney, series consulting editor; Alexandra Arnold and Erin Runyon, product managers; Reed Cotter, associate product manager; Emilie Perreault, editorial assistant; Marc Ouellette, Web product manager; and Katie McAllister, marketing manager.

Gary B. Shelly
Thomas J. Cashman
Randolph E. Gunter
Glenda A. Gunter

Shelly Cashman Series – Traditionally Bound Textbooks

The Shelly Cashman Series presents the following computer subjects in a variety of traditionally bound textbooks. For more information, see your Course Technology representative or call 1-800-648-7450. For Shelly Cashman Series information, visit Shelly Cashman Online at course.com/shellycashman

COMPUTERS	
Computers	Discovering Computers 2003: Concepts for a Digital World, Web Enhanced, Complete Edition
	Discovering Computers 2003: Concepts for a Digital World, Web Enhanced, Introductory Edition
	Discovering Computers 2003: Concepts for a Digital World, Web Enhanced, Brief Edition
	Teachers Discovering Computers: Integrating Technology in the Classroom 2e
	Exploring Computers: A Record of Discovery 4e
	Study Guide for Discovering Computers 2003: Concepts for a Digital World, Web Enhanced
	Essential Introduction to Computers 4e (32-page)

WINDOWS APPLICATIONS	
Microsoft Office	Microsoft Office XP: Essential Concepts and Techniques (5 projects)
	Microsoft Office XP: Brief Concepts and Techniques (9 projects)
	Microsoft Office XP: Introductory Concepts and Techniques (15 projects)
	Microsoft Office XP: Advanced Concepts and Techniques (11 projects)
	Microsoft Office XP: Post Advanced Concepts and Techniques (11 projects)
	Microsoft Office 2000: Essential Concepts and Techniques (5 projects)
	Microsoft Office 2000: Brief Concepts and Techniques (9 projects)
	Microsoft Office 2000: Introductory Concepts and Techniques, Enhanced Edition (15 projects)
	Microsoft Office 2000: Advanced Concepts and Techniques (11 projects)
	Microsoft Office 2000: Post Advanced Concepts and Techniques (11 projects)
Integration	Integrating Microsoft Office XP Applications and the World Wide Web: Essential Concepts and Techniques
PIM	Microsoft Outlook 2002: Essential Concepts and Techniques
Microsoft Works	Microsoft Works 6: Complete Concepts and Techniques[1] • Microsoft Works 2000: Complete Concepts and Techniques[1] • Microsoft Works 4.5[1]
Microsoft Windows	Microsoft Windows XP: Complete Concepts and Techniques[2]
	Microsoft Windows XP: Brief Concepts and Techniques
	Microsoft Windows 2000: Complete Concepts and Techniques (6 projects)[2]
	Microsoft Windows 2000: Brief Concepts and Techniques (2 projects)
	Microsoft Windows 98: Essential Concepts and Techniques (2 projects)
	Microsoft Windows 98: Complete Concepts and Techniques (6 projects)[2]
	Introduction to Microsoft Windows NT Workstation 4
Word Processing	Microsoft Word 2002[2] • Microsoft Word 2000[2] • Microsoft Word 97[1] • Microsoft Word 7[1]
Spreadsheets	Microsoft Excel 2002[2] • Microsoft Excel 2000[2] • Microsoft Excel 97[1] • Microsoft Excel 7[1]Microsoft Excel 5[1]
Database	Microsoft Access 2002[2] • Microsoft Access 2000[2] • Microsoft Access 97[1] • Microsoft Access 7[1]
Presentation Graphics	Microsoft PowerPoint 2002[2] • Microsoft PowerPoint 2000[2] • Microsoft PowerPoint 97[1]
	Microsoft PowerPoint 7[1]
Desktop Publishing	Microsoft Publisher 2002[1] • Microsoft Publisher 2000[1]

PROGRAMMING	
Programming	Microsoft Visual Basic.NET: Complete Concepts and Techniques[2] • Microsoft Visual Basic 6: Complete Concepts and Techniques[1] • Programming in QBasic • Java Programming: Complete Concepts and Techniques[1] • Structured COBOL Programming 2e

INTERNET	
Browser	Microsoft Internet Explorer 6: Introductory Concepts and Techniques • Microsoft Internet Explorer 5: An Introduction • Microsoft Internet Explorer 4: An Introduction • Netscape Navigator 6: An Introduction Netscape Navigator 4: An Introduction
Web Page Creation and Design	Web Design: Introductory Concepts and Techniques • HTML: Complete Concepts and Techniques 2e[2] Microsoft FrontPage 2002: Essential Concepts and Techniques • Microsoft FrontPage 2002[2] Microsoft FrontPage 2000[1] • JavaScript: Complete Concepts and Techniques 2e[1]

SYSTEMS ANALYSIS	
Systems Analysis	Systems Analysis and Design 4e

DATA COMMUNICATIONS	
Data Communications	Business Data Communications: Introductory Concepts and Techniques 3e

[1]Also available as an Introductory Edition, which is a shortened version of the complete book
[2]Also available as an Introductory Edition, which is a shortened version of the complete book and also as a Comprehensive Edition, which is an extended version of the complete book

Teachers Discovering and Integrating Microsoft

Office

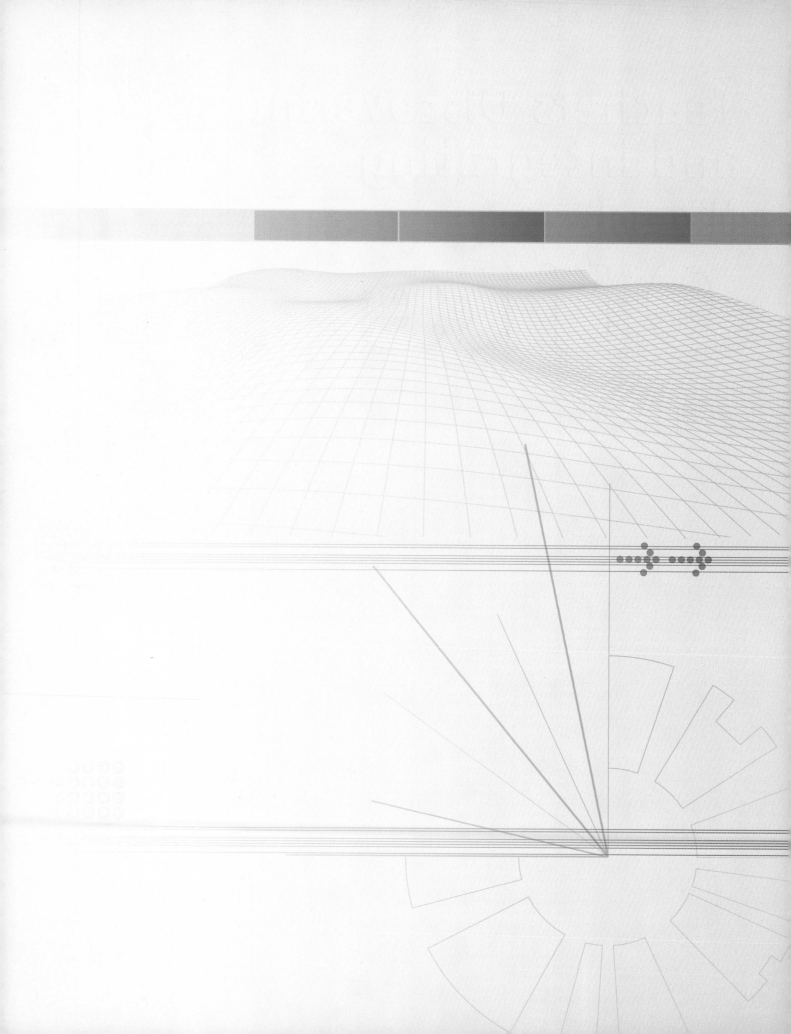

Using and Integrating
Microsoft Office

Teachers Discovering and Integrating
Microsoft Office

Using and Integrating Microsoft Office

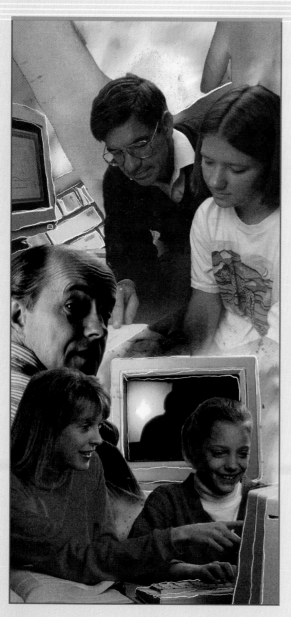

Introduction

Teachers Discovering and Integrating Microsoft Office is an innovative introductory textbook for you to learn how to use and more importantly how to integrate Microsoft Word, Microsoft PowerPoint, Microsoft Excel, and Microsoft Access into your classroom-specific curriculum. This book offers you opportunities to become more proficient in using Microsoft Office as a daily productivity tool, however, you also will learn new and innovative ideas for using and integrating Microsoft Office into your classroom instruction and student projects.

Teachers Discovering and Integrating Microsoft Office can be used by educators regardless if they are using Office XP or Office 2000. Because many schools have either or both versions of Office, the content of this textbook is written to be flexible and user-friendly by addressing the features in both versions. Office XP and Office 2000 applications are very similar (in most cases identical) in both appearance and operation. The projects in this textbook were created in Office XP; however, to prevent any confusion, differences between the two versions are noted both in the text and in the step-by-step instructions.

If you are using Office 2000, Office 2000 differences in the step-by-step instruction will be preceded by the following Office 2000 icon, 2000 .

What Is Microsoft Office?

Microsoft Office is the world's best-selling office suite and is a collection of the more popular Microsoft application software products. Microsoft Office allows you and your students to work and communicate more effectively, and improve the appearance of each document, presentation, spreadsheet, or database you

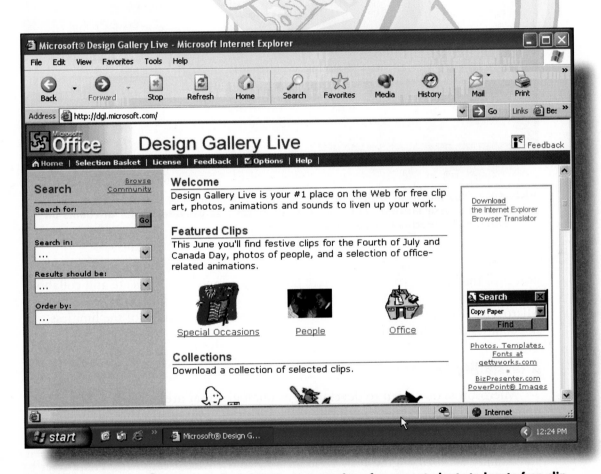

FIGURE I-1 Microsoft® Design Gallery Live is a great place for your students to locate free clip art, photos, animations, sounds, and more to liven up their work.

and your students create. For example, Microsoft Office contains a collection of media files (art, sound, animation, and movies) that you can use to enhance your and your student's projects. In addition, **Microsoft Office Design Gallery Live** is accessible from the Microsoft Web site and contains thousands of additional media files (Figure I-1).

Microsoft also maintains a Web site dedicated to communicating the latest information about their products, tutorials, innovative assistive technologies, articles, events, a monthly newsletter, and more (Figure I-2 on the next page). These resources allow Microsoft Office to be used and integrated into all learning environments.

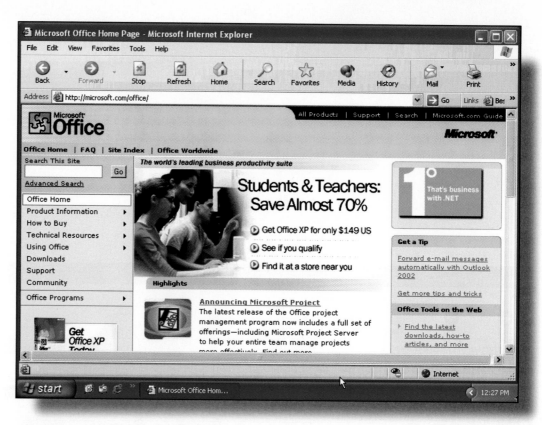

FIGURE I-2 The Microsoft Office Web site contains a multitude of resources that you can use to enhance your teaching and learning. Microsoft also provides major discounts on their products for teachers and students.

To further the possibilities, Microsoft Office integrates its applications with the power of the Internet so you can share information, and communicate and collaborate on projects at a distance. Students even can learn to conduct online meetings. Microsoft Office allows you and your students to take advantage of the limitless possibilities of the Internet and World Wide Web.

Accessibility Features

Microsoft is dedicated to developing technologies that are usable and accessible to everyone, including those with physical challenges. Microsoft Office has many accessibility features built right into the software without the need for additional accessibility aids. Use Microsoft Office Help to learn more about Microsoft Office accessibility features (Figure I-3). To learn how to use Microsoft Office Help, refer to Appendix A.

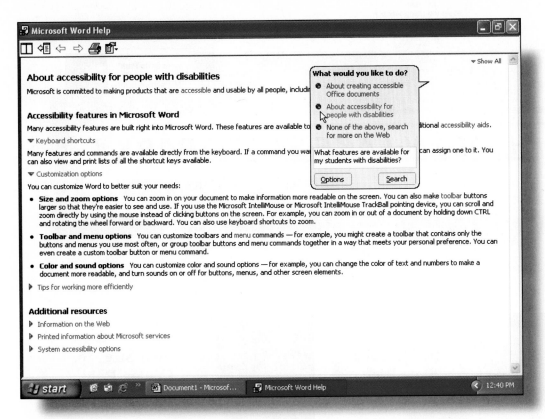

FIGURE I-3 Many accessibility features are built into Microsoft Office applications.

What Is Microsoft Office XP?

Microsoft Office XP (**eXPerience**) is the latest edition of the Office suite. Microsoft Office XP is available in Standard, Professional, and Developer editions. The **Microsoft Office XP Professional Edition** includes Word 2002, Excel 2002, Access 2002, PowerPoint 2002, Outlook 2002, and Internet Explorer 6. Major Office XP enhancements include: (1) streamlined user interface, (2) smart tags and task panes to help simplify the way people work, (3) speech and handwriting recognition, (4) improved Help system, and (5) enhanced Web capabilities.

With a new feature of Office XP, Office Speech Recognition, and a microphone, you can speak the names of toolbar buttons, menus and menu commands, list items, screen alerts, and dialog box controls, such as OK and Cancel. You also can dictate text and numbers to insert as well as delete. If you have speakers, you can instruct the computer to speak a document or worksheet to you. For students with disabilities these features can be extremely helpful (Figure I-4 on the next page).

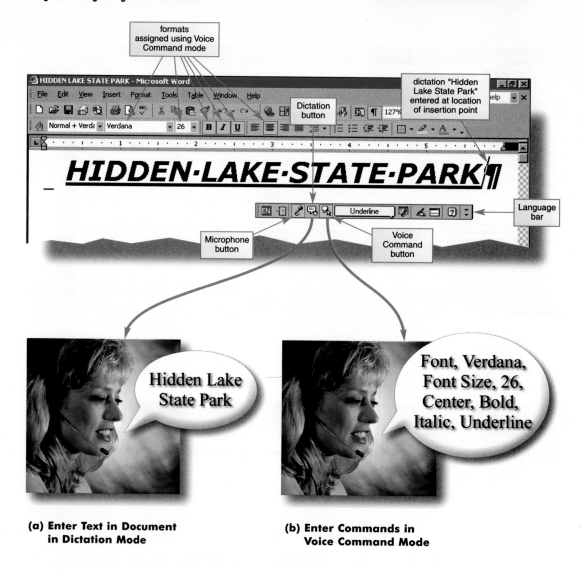

(a) Enter Text in Document in Dictation Mode

(b) Enter Commands in Voice Command Mode

FIGURE I-4 Teachers and students will find many uses for the speech and handwriting recognition capabilities of Office XP.

In addition, you can translate a word, phrase, or an entire document from English to Japanese, Chinese, French, Spanish, or German. Due to the extended languages available and working with students with English as a Second Language (ESL), Office is a great tool to use to bridge the language barrier. For more information on the Speech and Handwriting Recognition and Speech Playback, refer to Appendix B.

Each of the Microsoft Office XP applications makes publishing documents on a Web server as simple as saving a file on a hard disk. Once the file is placed on the Web server, users can view and edit the documents, and conduct Web discussions and live online meetings. For information and instructions on publishing Office Web pages to a Web server, refer to Appendix C.

What Is Microsoft Office 2000?

Microsoft Office 2000 is available in Standard, Small Business, Professional, Premium, and Developer editions. The **Microsoft Office Premium Edition** includes Word 2000, Excel 2000, Access 2000, PowerPoint 2000, Publisher 2000, FrontPage 2000, PhotoDraw 2000, Outlook 2000, and Internet Explorer.

Using Different Versions of Microsoft Windows

A number of different versions of Microsoft Windows currently are being used on school and home computers and networks because schools and home users often do not upgrade their computers every time a new version of an operating system is released. Each new version contains new features and offers increased ease of operation. In addition, recent upgrades increase the integration of the World Wide Web and enhance the multimedia capabilities of computers.

Microsoft Windows is the most used operating system in the world. Windows XP is the latest Windows operating system and is installed on most new computers purchased for home and business use. Over time, many K–12 schools will upgrade to Windows XP. The following is a brief summary of the evolution of the various versions of Microsoft Windows that are in use today.

Windows XP

Windows XP, released in late 2001, is a significant upgrade to the Windows operating system and is available in two main versions: Windows XP Home Edition and **Windows XP Professional**, for businesses and schools (Figure I-5). Included with this latest version are significant multimedia and movie-making enhancements, increased ease of use, and Internet Explorer 6. All of the screen shots used in this introduction were taken while using Windows XP.

FIGURE I-5   Windows XP, with its new simplified look, is the fastest and most reliable Windows operating system to date.

Windows 2000

Windows 2000 was marketed by Microsoft in two main versions: Windows Millennium Edition, or Windows Me, for home users and **Windows 2000 Professional**, which is a network version for businesses and schools. Windows 2000 is similar in appearance to Windows 98. Because Windows 2000 Professional is the dominate operating system used in K–12 schools that use Windows-based PCs, all of the screen shots used in the four projects in this book were taken while using Windows 2000 Professional.

Windows 98

Windows 98 was an upgrade to an earlier version of Windows, Windows 95, and still is a commonly used version of Windows found on many school and home computers. Many schools use a networked version of Windows 95/98 called **Windows NT**. Windows 98 appears and operates similar to Windows 2000.

Using and Integrating Microsoft Office

Educators in our nation's schools are tasked with teaching students who will spend all of their lives in a technology driven society. The ability to use and, more importantly, to integrate technology into the curriculum is a necessity in the teaching profession. Teachers and classrooms no longer can afford to be left behind when it comes to technology integration. In a world increasingly dependent on technology whether it is in the home or the workplace, students and teachers must be technology literate.

Teachers must have the technology skills to prepare students with the skills they need to succeed in a digital society. We must have teachers, administrators, and students who meet the national standards developed by the **International Society for Technology in Education** (**ISTE**), which is a non-profit group that promotes the use of technology with the **National Educational Technology Standards for Teachers** (**NETS-T**), the **Technology Standards for School Administrators** (**TSSA**), and the **National Educational Technology Standards for Students** (**NETS-S**) (Figure I-6). These standards define the fundamental concepts, knowledge, skills, and aptitudes for applying technology in K–12 educational settings.

As you teach students the basic skills you also must prepare them to enter society and the workforce. Students must be prepared to work and use technology successfully and to enter a technology rich society with the skills necessary to change, adapt, and learn continuously. For example, two of the NETS for students states under technology productivity tools that:

▶ Students use technology tools to enhance learning, increase productivity, and promote creativity.

▶ Students use productivity tools to collaborate in constructing technology-enhanced models, prepare publications, and produce other creative works.

Office as a Business, Productivity, and Integration Tool

Educators should understand what their K–12 students need to know about Office applications, in other words you need to have a working knowledge of how Microsoft Office applications are used in the workplace. Second, you need to be able to use the various Office applications as productivity tools both in your classroom and your professional life. Third, you should be proficient at integrating Microsoft applications in your classroom specific curriculum. The textbook projects and end-of-chapter materials support learning in these three areas.

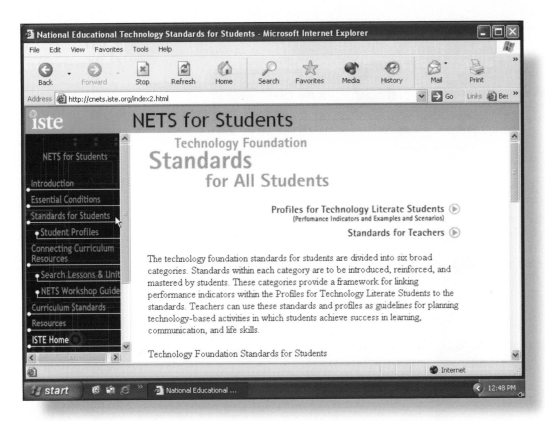

FIGURE I-6   Many states have adopted ISTE's Technology Foundation Standards for All Students.

OFFICE USE IN BUSINESS   By completing the Word, PowerPoint, Excel, and Access projects, you not only will learn important Office related skills, you also will see examples of how these tools are used in the workplace.

OFFICE PRODUCTIVITY IN THE CLASSROOM   At the end of each project is an In the Lab section that provides exercises that utilize the Web to offer project-related reinforcement activities that will help you gain confidence in your Office abilities. In addition, three in-depth Productivity in the Classroom assignments allow you to learn how to use Office as a productivity tool with your students.

OFFICE INTEGRATION IN THE CLASSROOM   At the end of each project is an In the Lab section that allows you to interact with resources provided by Microsoft so you can use and integrate the latest technology into your classroom curriculum. In addition, eight Integration in the Classroom assignments allow you to learn how to use Office as an integration tool with your students. Included are integration ideas and projects for elementary, middle school, high school, and special education teachers (Figure I-7 on the next page).

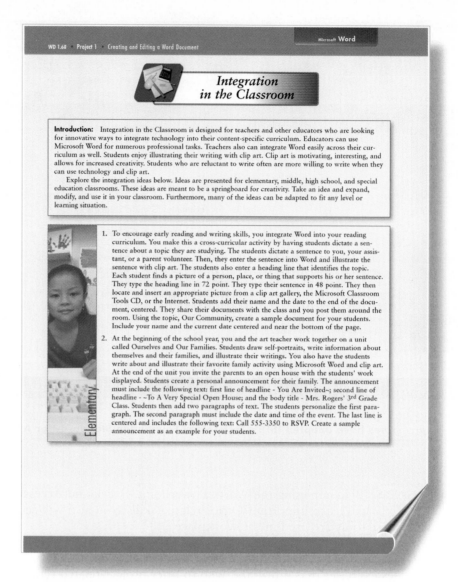

FIGURE I-7 Shown is the first page of the Integration in the Classroom end-of-chapter section for the Word project.

Teaching and Learning with Microsoft Office CDs

Included with this textbook is a Teaching and Learning with Microsoft Office set of two CDs created and distributed by Microsoft: a Microsoft Office Training CD and a Microsoft Office Classroom Tools CD. These CDs can be used on personal computers with Windows and on Macintosh computers. This special two-CD set, created for K–12 educators, is designed to give you the resources you need to take advantage of Microsoft Office applications and integrate the latest technology into your classroom. When you access these CDs, Internet Explorer or your default browser displays the initial information. The CDs also contain links to a vast array of additional information available at the Microsoft Web site.

Using the resources on these CDs, you will discover new timesaving ways to use technology in your classroom and create new learning opportunities for your students.

What's On the Microsoft Office Training CD?

The Microsoft Office Training CD is all about helping you get the most out of Microsoft Office in your classroom. This CD includes the following educator training resources.

IN & OUT OF THE CLASSROOM   A series of practical tutorial guides for teachers, students, and administrators to learn how to use Microsoft Office software in the classroom.

TIPS & TRICKS   Ready-to-use ideas for integrating Office applications, including Word, PowerPoint, Excel, and Access into a variety of different subject areas like math, science, and language arts.

TUTORIAL PACKS AND ONLINE TUTORIALS   These step-by-step tutorials provide in-depth, practical educational applications of Microsoft products, including tools such as downloadable Word documents and PowerPoint presentations that make training teachers easier.

OFFICE XP DEMO   Created just for educators, this demo introduces you to the advanced capabilities and Web integration that make Office XP the smarter tool for learning.

Using the Microsoft Office Training CD

When you insert the Microsoft Office Training CD with the label side up in your CD-ROM drive, your computer should access the CD automatically and display the Microsoft Welcome to Teaching and Leaning with Microsoft® Office home page in Internet Explorer (see Figure I-8 on the next page) or you default browser. If the Welcome home page does not display automatically, refer to the setup instructions if AutoPlay is not enabled in the booklet that is packaged with the CDs under the section, For PCs with Microsoft Windows. If you are using a Macintosh computer, refer to the setup instructions under the section, For Macintosh Computers. Perform the steps on the next page to use the Microsoft Office Training CD.

To Use the Microsoft Office Training CD

1 **Insert the Microsoft Office Training CD with the label side up in your CD-ROM drive. When the Welcome to Teaching and Learning with Microsoft® Office home page displays, point to the Get Started link.**

The Welcome to Teaching & Leaning with Microsoft® Office home page displays in Internet Explorer (Figure I-8). In addition to important information, this page also contains a link to the companion Teaching and Learning site. Note: You must be connected to the Internet to access the Teaching and Learning site.

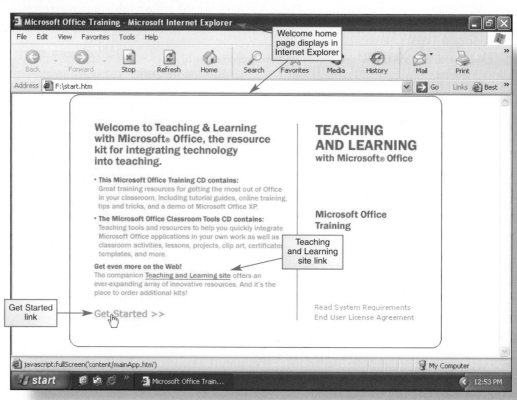

FIGURE I-8

2 **Click Get Started.**

The browser displays the Teaching and Learning with Microsoft Office main page (Figure I-9). This page contains links to the available resources and an EXIT button.

FIGURE I-9

Exploring the Microsoft Office Training CD Resources

As mentioned earlier, the Microsoft Office Training CD contains information in five categories, In & Out of the Classroom, Tips & Tricks, Tutorial Packs, Online Tutorials, and Office XP Demo.

Perform the following steps to explore briefly the various resources available on the Microsoft Office Training CD. You can explore these resources in greater detail at this time or at a future date.

 To Explore the Microsoft Office Training CD Resources

1 **Click the In & Out of the Classroom tab. When the browser displays the In and Out of the Classroom A Practical Guide for Teachers page, point to the Office XP link.** **00 If you are using Office 2000, point to the Office 2000 link.**

The browser displays A Practical Guide for Teachers page (Figure I-10). This page contains links to eight tutorial guides. Also included is a link to the Microsoft Education site. Note: You must be connected to the Internet to access this site.

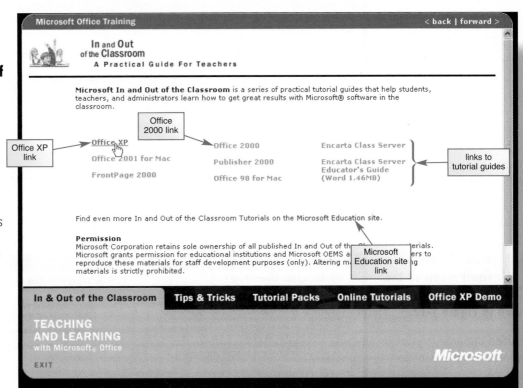

FIGURE I-10

2 **Click Office XP.
If using
Office 2000, click Office
2000. Point to the down
scroll arrow.**

*The browser displays
the Office XP page
(Figure I-11). Note: Both the
Office XP and Office 2000
screens display similar information and links.*

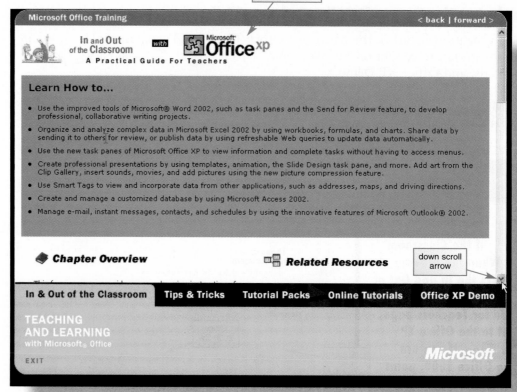

FIGURE I-11

3 **Click the down
scroll arrow so the
information displays as
shown in Figure I-12.**

*Included are links to com-
prehensive instructions for
using the powerful features
of Microsoft Office XP
effectively in the
classroom
(Figure I-12).
Clicking any of the links will
open the chapter files in
Internet Explorer. Also
included are links to the
Microsoft Classroom
Teacher Network and the In
and Out of the Classroom
Tutorials. Scroll further down
the page for links to information on PowerPoint,
Excel, and Access.*

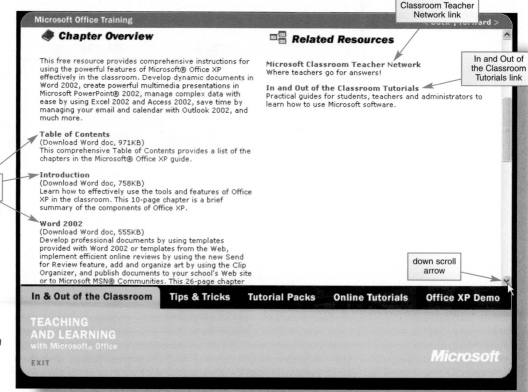

FIGURE I-12

4 Click the Tips & Tricks tab.

The browser displays the Office Tips for Teachers page (Figure I-13). Included are links to dozens of ready-to-use ideas that integrate Office applications like Word, Excel, PowerPoint, and Access into a variety of different subject areas like math, science, and language arts. Scroll down to access additional Office tips and tricks.

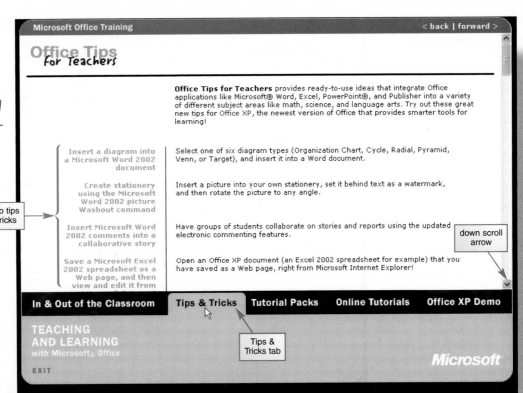

FIGURE I-13

5 Click the Tutorial Packs tab.

The browser displays the Tutorials page (Figure I-14). Included are step-by-step tutorials to enhance teaching and learning using Office products. Scroll down to access additional teaching and learning tutorials.

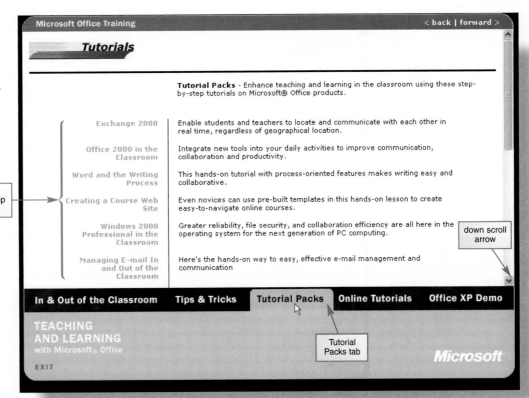

FIGURE I-14

6 **Click the Online Tutorials tab.**

The browser displays the Online Tutorials page (Figure I-15). Included are links to easy-to-use online tutorials that will show you how to put Microsoft software to work in your classroom. Included is a link to the Microsoft Education site.

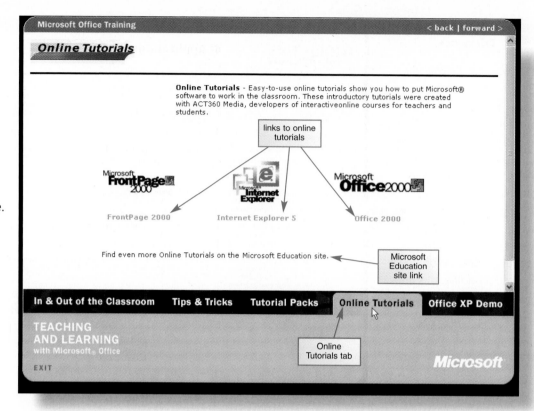

FIGURE I-15

7 **Click the Office XP Demo tab.**

The browser displays the Office XP Demo page (Figure I-16). Click the Start Presentation here link to see how students and teachers use Office XP in an automated demonstration.

8 **When you are finished reviewing the CD, click the EXIT button and remove the Microsoft Office Training CD from your CD-ROM drive.**

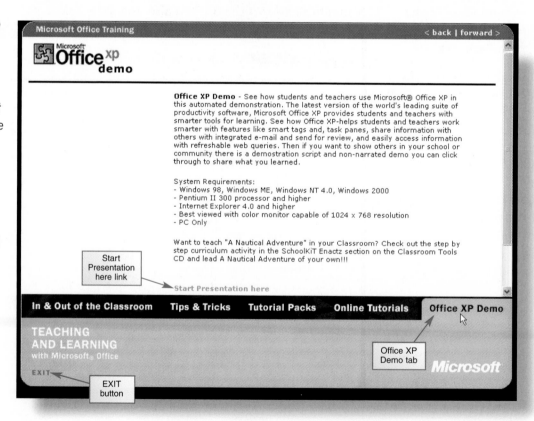

FIGURE I-16

What's On the Microsoft Office Classroom Tools CD?

Now that you are off and running with Microsoft applications, here are the tools and resources to help you quickly integrate Office into your own work and classroom activities. This CD includes:

SCHOOLKIT SchoolKiT Enactz helps turn Microsoft Office into an exciting activity center for student learning. Each curriculum-based activity presents a challenge with step-by-step instructions for students to explore. With simple ways to add and share activities, managing classroom computing activities has never been easier.

TEMPLATES These 66 school-smart templates include calendars and lesson plans as well as templates for overdue book notices, parent bulletins, class directories, and more. The templates get you off to a great start to begin using Office for class projects or for changing administrative forms into electronic versions. Additional templates are available at the Microsoft Web site.

PRODUCTIVITY IN THE CLASSROOM These themed lessons are designed to help students communicate and collaborate by using new technologies, including Microsoft Office XP Professional, Office 2000, Office 2001 for Mac, Encarta Encyclopedia 2001, and the Internet. Each lesson is grade- and subject-specific and includes a teaching guide and student activities that will make using computers more effective and fun. Themes include High-Energy Science, Reading on the Edge, and Census Math.

CERTIFICATE OF THE MONTH Reward your students with a school-year's worth of certificates in honor of such occasions as National Safety Month, National Poetry Month, and National Nutrition Month. All 12 include guides with teaching suggestions and ideas related to that month's national theme. You also will get a link to a Web site to get updated certificates for the coming year.

COOL PROJECTS These projects used in real classrooms show you how creative teachers nationwide are enhancing the learning experience for their students by integrating technologies into teaching activities.

CLIP ART Nothing attracts attention to a document more quickly than great clip art! Add polish with 2,500 new images for Windows and Macintosh — animals, cartoons, flags, maps, and others. Plus, get directed to online resources for thousands more!

Using the Microsoft Office Classroom Tools CD

When you insert the Microsoft Office Classroom Tools CD with the label side up in your CD-ROM drive, your computer should access the CD-ROM automatically and display the Welcome to Teaching & Leaning with Microsoft® Office home page in Internet Explorer (see Figure I-17 on the next page) or you default browser. If the Welcome home page does not display automatically, refer to the setup instructions if AutoPlay is not enabled in the booklet that is packaged with the CDs under the section, For PCs with Microsoft Windows. If you are using a Macintosh computer, refer to the setup instructions under the section, For Macintosh Computers. Perform the steps on the next page to setup and then use the Microsoft Office Classroom Tools CD.

Steps | **To Use the Microsoft Office Classroom Tools CD**

1 **Insert the Microsoft Office Classroom Tools CD with the label side up in your CD-ROM drive. When the browser displays the Welcome home page, point to the Get Started link.**

The browser displays the Welcome home page (Figure I-17). Besides important information, this page also contains a link to the companion Teaching and Learning site. Note: You must be connected to the Internet to access the Teaching and Learning site.

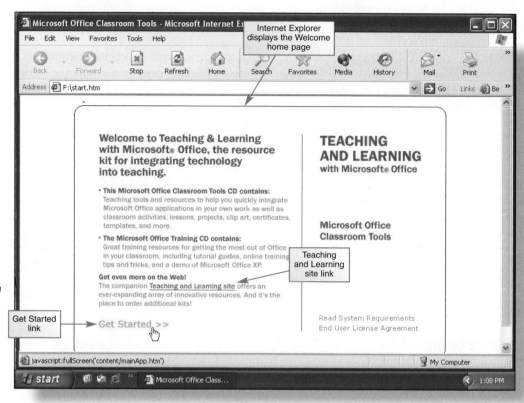

FIGURE I-17

2 **Click Get Started.**

The Microsoft Office Teaching and Learning Training with Microsoft Office Classroom Tools home page displays (Figure I-18). This page contains tabs that provide links to the available resources and an EXIT button.

3 **Using the procedures on pages MO I.15 through MO I.18, explore the various resources available on the Microsoft Office Classroom Tools CD. Included are links to thousands of additional classroom resources, clip art, and tutorials available at the Microsoft Web site. When you are finished reviewing the CD, click the EXIT button and remove the Office Training CD from your CD-ROM drive.**

FIGURE I-18

Using Additional Microsoft Educational Tools

More is available — Microsoft also provides tools and activities for administrators, teachers, and students that are installed on a computer's hard drive when Microsoft Office XP or Office 2000 is installed. Perform the following step to access these tools.

TO USE ADDITIONAL MICROSOFT EDUCATIONAL TOOLS INSTALLED ON YOUR HARD DRIVE

1 Click the Start button on the Windows XP taskbar, point to All Programs (Programs if using Windows 2000/98) on the Start menu, point to Microsoft Office Classroom tools and then click one of the four options, Admin Tools, Classroom Activities, Student Tools, or Teacher Tools.

The tools available in each area are displayed (Figure I-19 on the next page).

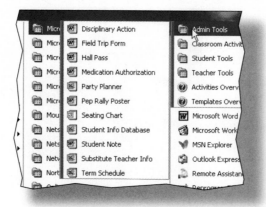

(a) Admin Tools

(b) Classroom Activities

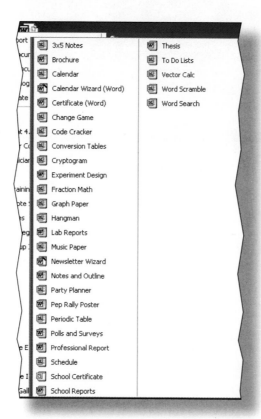

(c) Student Tools

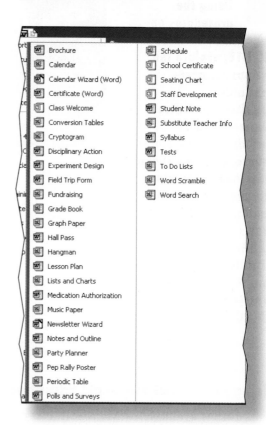

(d) Teacher Tools

FIGURE I-19   The four available categories of tools are shown.

In addition, Microsoft provides extensive resources at the Microsoft Education Web site, including instructional resources, tutorials, lesson plans, laptop learning, e-learning, Microsoft Classroom Teacher Network, and much more. Perform the following step to access the Microsoft Education Web site.

TO ACCESS THE MICROSOFT EDUCATION WEB SITE

1 Start your browser, type www.microsoft.com/education in the Address text box, and then press the ENTER key.

The browser displays the Microsoft Education home page (Figure I-20).

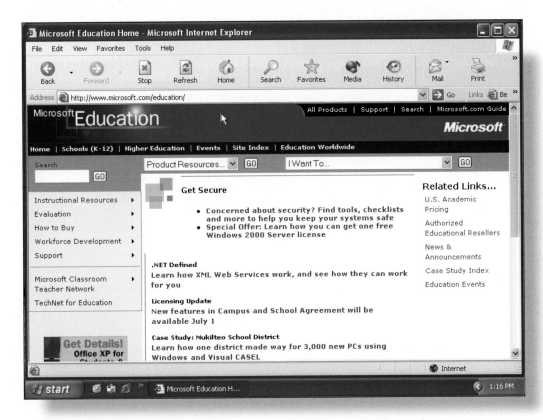

FIGURE I-20 The Microsoft Education Web site provides thousands of resources for educators.

Microsoft
WORD

Microsoft Word

Creating and Editing a Word Document

You will have mastered the material in this project when you can:

O B J E C T I V E S

- Start Word
- Describe the Word window
- Describe the speech and handwriting recognition capabilities of Word
- Zoom page width
- Change the default font size of all text
- Enter text into a document
- Scroll through a document
- Check spelling as you type
- Save a document
- Select text
- Change the font size of selected text
- Change the font of selected text
- Right-align a paragraph
- Center a paragraph
- Undo commands or actions
- Italicize selected text
- Underline selected text
- Bold selected text
- Insert clip art into a document
- Resize a graphic
- Print a document
- Open a document
- Correct errors in a document
- Use Word Help
- Quit Word

To Be or Not To Be...
Word Word Processor Provides Options

How many words did William Shakespeare add to the English language? Guesses range from a few hundred terms to more than 10,000, with the most likely estimate approximately 1,500 words. Other English Renaissance writers also added words to the English language. The dramatist Ben Jonson is credited with coining words such as *analytic* and *antagonist*. But it is Shakespeare's inventiveness and imaginative wordplay that created words such as *puppy dog, watchdog,* and *zany*. He used them in hundreds of plays and poems to enrich the arts.

Imagine the possibilities if Shakespeare would have had Word. In many ways, twenty-first century writers are more fortunate than Shakespeare. Even if you don't plan on writing as many literary masterpieces as he, the Microsoft Word with its built-in Task Wizards for letters, resumes, and other documents gives anyone a running start.

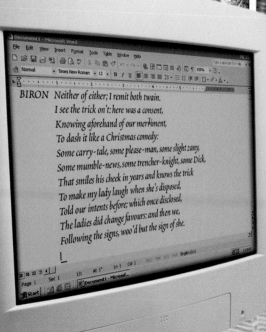

BIRON Neither of either; I remit both twain.
I see the trick on't: here was a consent,
Knowing aforehand of our merriment,
To dash it like a Christmas comedy:
Some carry-tale, some please-man, some slight zany,
Some mumble-news, some trencher-knight, some Dick,
That smiles his cheek in years and knows the trick
To make my lady laugh when she's disposed,
Told our intents before; which once disclosed,
The ladies did change favours: and then we,
Following the signs, woo'd but the sign of she.

While in college and during virtually any career thereafter your education career, it is essential that you present the ideas and products of your work in clear, accurate written form. In fact, just getting a start in a chosen profession may depend on how well you are represented by your stand-in: a well-prepared resume. Making a favorable first impression is not only important, it is vital.

Fortunately, technology has risen to the challenge. During Shakespeare's days of quill pens and inkwells, every change and every mistake meant rewriting the entire page or sometimes the whole document. Today's innovations enable words, sentences, paragraphs, and even whole pages of text to be added, deleted, or reordered with the click of a mouse before using a single page of printer paper. The built-in spelling checker and thesaurus are included for finding spelling errors and finding hard to pin down synonyms.

Accuracy is important. The reason is simple. Consider *TIME* magazine's $100,000 missing

"r." The presses had already begun rolling out the cover of the March 2, 1983 issue when someone discovered the letter r missing from the word "Control" in the headline: "A New Plan for Arms Contol." The mistake cost the publication $100,000 and a day's delay to add the letter r. Spelling checker would have spotted this.

Written errors also can become legends. In 1631, an authorized edition of the Holy Bible came off the presses in London with the "not" missing from the seventh of the Ten Commandments. The result: "Thou shalt commit adultery." The book's publishers were fined 3,000 English pounds and went down in history as the creators of the *Wicked Bible*. This illustrates that even the best tools cannot replace careful proofing.

Although Word is not a substitute for careful review or original thought, even Shakespeare would agree that it can remove many of the barriers that might stand in the way of getting a quality education and a quality job.

Microsoft Word

Creating and Editing a Word Document

Tara Stellenbach is the Activities chairperson for the Student Government Association (SGA). One of her responsibilities is to coordinate student discount programs with local businesses. She then prepares fliers announcing the discount programs.

Tara's favorite pastime is sailing on beautiful Hidden Lake. The large lake has crystal clear water and is located in a mountainous area just 15 miles from campus. Because no motors are allowed on Hidden Lake, it is peaceful and often scattered with sailboats. Tara decides to contact Hidden Lake State Park to inquire about student discounts for sailboat rentals. After meeting with the marketing director, Tara is elated. The marketing director agrees to give all students a 30 percent discount on sailboat rentals!

As a marketing major, Tara has learned the guidelines for designing announcements. She will use large, bold characters for the headline and title. To attract attention to the announcement, she will include a large graphic of a sailboat. When complete, she will recruit you and other members of the SGA to distribute the flier.

What Is Microsoft Word?

Microsoft Word is a full-featured word processing program that allows you to create and revise professional looking documents such as announcements, letters, resumes, and reports. You can use Word's desktop publishing features to create high-quality brochures, advertisements, and newsletters. Word also provides many tools that enable you to create Web pages with ease. From within Word, you even can place these Web pages directly on a Web server.

Word has many features designed to simplify the production of documents. With Word, you easily can include borders, shading, tables, graphics, pictures, and Web addresses in your documents. You can instruct Word to create a template, which is a form you can use and customize to meet your needs. When using Word, you even can dictate or handwrite text instead of typing it into Word. You also can speak instructions to Word.

While you are typing, Word can perform tasks automatically. For example, Word can detect and correct spelling and grammar errors in a variety of languages. Word's thesaurus allows you to add variety and precision to your writing. Word also can format text such as headings, lists, fractions, borders, and Web addresses as you type them. Within Word, you also can e-mail a copy of your Word document to an e-mail address.

Project One — Hidden Lake Announcement

To illustrate the features of Word, Project 1 uses Word to produce the announcement shown in Figure 1-1.

The announcement informs students about student discounts on sailboat rentals at Hidden Lake State Park. The announcement begins with a headline that is followed by a graphic of a sailboat. Below the graphic of the sailboat is the body title, HIDDEN LAKE STATE PARK, followed by the body copy that consists of a brief paragraph about the park and another paragraph about the discount. Finally, the last line of the announcement lists the park's telephone number.

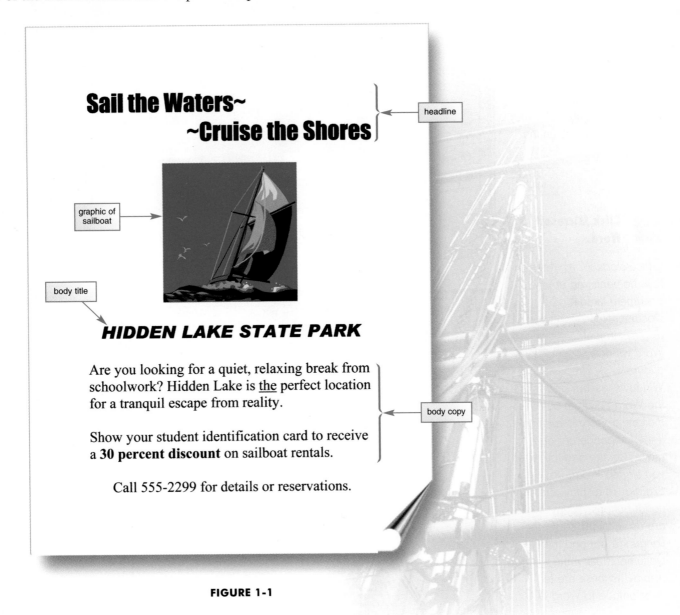

Sail the Waters~
~Cruise the Shores

headline

graphic of sailboat

body title

HIDDEN LAKE STATE PARK

Are you looking for a quiet, relaxing break from schoolwork? Hidden Lake is <u>the</u> perfect location for a tranquil escape from reality.

body copy

Show your student identification card to receive a **30 percent discount** on sailboat rentals.

Call 555-2299 for details or reservations.

FIGURE 1-1

Starting and Customizing Word

To start Word, Windows must be running. Perform the steps on the next page to start Word, or ask your instructor how to start Word for your system.

Microsoft **Word**

Steps To Start Word

1 **Click the Start button on the Windows taskbar, point to Programs on the Start menu, and then point to Microsoft Word on the Programs submenu.**

The commands on the Start menu display above the Start button and the Programs submenu displays (Figure 1-2). If the Office XP Speech Recognition software is installed on your computer, the Language bar may display somewhere on the desktop.

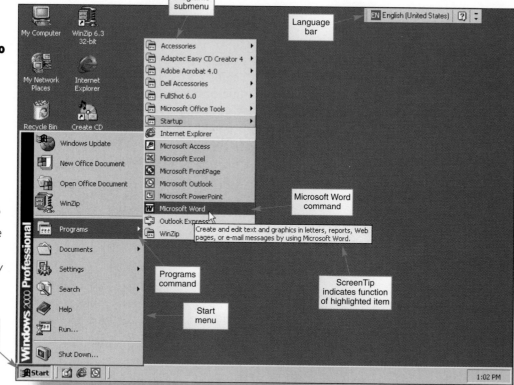

FIGURE 1-2

2 **Click Microsoft Word.**

Office starts Word. After a few moments, an empty document titled Document1 displays in the Word window (Figure 1-3). The Windows taskbar displays the Word program button, indicating Word is running. If the Language bar displayed on the desktop when you started Word, it expands to display additional buttons. **2000** If you are using Word 2000, the Language bar and the New Document task pane will not display as these are features unique to Word 2002.

3 **If the Word window is not maximized, double-click its title bar to maximize it.**

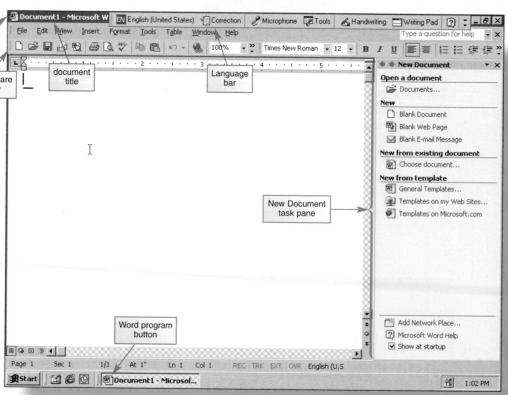

FIGURE 1-3

The screen in Figure 1-3 shows how the Word 2002 window looks the first time you start Word after installation on most computers. If the Office Speech Recognition software is installed on your computer, then when you start Word either the Language bar displays somewhere on the desktop (shown at the top of Figure 1-3) or the Language Indicator button displays on the right side of the Windows taskbar (Figure 1-5 on the next page). In this project, the Language bar will be kept minimized. For additional information about the Language bar, see page WD 1.17 and Appendix B.

Also, if you are using Word 2002, the New Document task pane displays on the screen, and the buttons on the toolbars display on a single row. A **task pane** is a separate window that enables users to carry out some Word tasks more efficiently. In this project, to allow the maximum typing area in Word, a task pane should not display when you start Word. For more efficient use of the buttons on the toolbars, they should display on two separate rows instead of sharing a single row.

 If you are using Word 2000, perform the following steps to display the toolbars on two rows, if necessary and then skip to the bottom of page WD 1.11 and the text that begins after Figure 1-8.

Other Ways

1. Double-click Word icon on desktop
2. Click Start button, click New Office Document, click General tab, double-click Blank Document icon

TO DISPLAY THE TOOLBARS ON TWO ROWS WHEN USING WORD 2000

1 Click View on the menu bar, point to Toolbars, and then click Customize.

2 When the Customize dialog box displays, click the Options tab, click the Standard and Formatting toolbars share one row check box to remove the check mark, and then click the Close button.

If using Word 2002, perform the following steps to minimize the Language bar, close the New Document task pane, and display the toolbars on two separate rows.

Steps **To Customize the Word Window**

1 If the Language bar displays, point to its Minimize button (Figure 1-4).

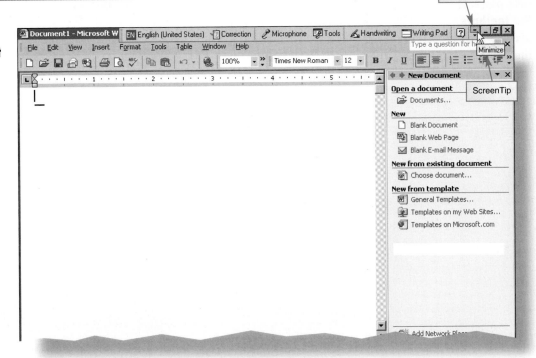

FIGURE 1-4

2 **Click the Minimize button on the Language bar. If the New Document task pane displays, click the Show at startup check box to remove the check mark and then point to the Close button in the upper-right corner of the task pane title bar.**

Word minimizes the Language bar (Figure 1-5). With the check mark removed from the Show at startup check box, Word will not display the New Document task pane the next time Word starts.

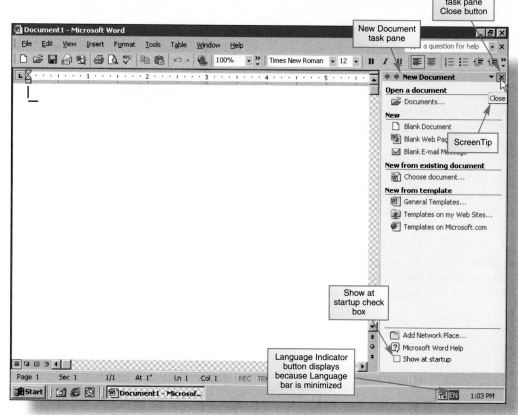

FIGURE 1-5

3 **Click the Close button on the New Document task pane. If the toolbars display positioned on the same row, point to the Toolbar Options button.**

The New Document task pane closes (Figure 1-6).

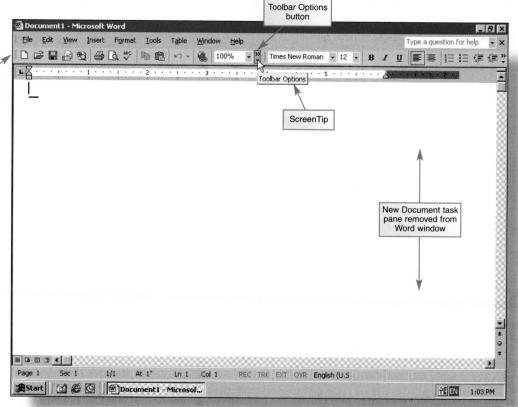

FIGURE 1-6

4 Click the Toolbar Options button and then point to Show Buttons on Two Rows.

Word displays the Toolbar Options list (Figure 1-7). The Toolbar Options list contains buttons that do not fit on the toolbars when the toolbars display on one row.

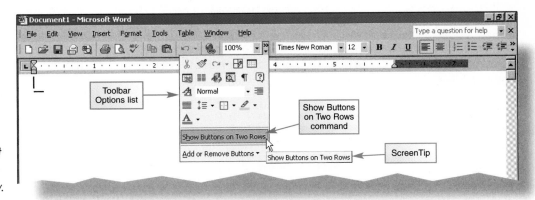

FIGURE 1-7

5 Click Show Buttons on Two Rows. If your screen differs from Figure 1-8, click View on the menu bar and then click Normal.

Word displays the toolbars on two separate rows (Figure 1-8). The Toolbar Options list is empty because all of the buttons fit on the toolbars when they display on two rows.

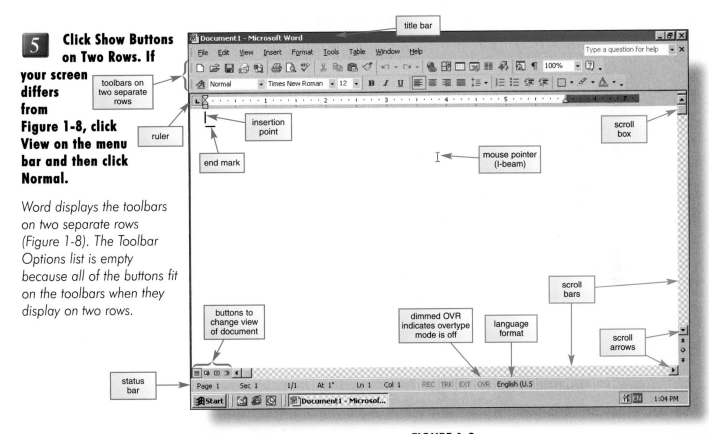

FIGURE 1-8

As an alternative to Steps 4 and 5 above, you can point to the left edge of the Formatting toolbar, and when the mouse pointer changes to a four-headed arrow, drag the toolbar down below the Standard toolbar to create two rows.

When you point to many objects in the Word window, such as a button or command, Word displays a ScreenTip. A **ScreenTip** is a short on-screen note associated with the object to which you are pointing. Examples of ScreenTips are shown in Figures 1-2, 1-4, 1-5, 1-6, and 1-7 on this and the previous pages.

Each time you start Word, the Word window displays the same way it did the last time you used Word. If the toolbars displayed on one row, then they will display on one row the next time you start Word. Similarly, if the Show at startup check box in the New Document task pane contains a check mark, then this task pane will display the next time you start Word.

More About

The Office Assistant

The Office Assistant is an animated object that can answer questions for you. On some installations, the Office Assistant may display when Word starts. If the Office Assistant displays on your screen, right-click it and then click Hide on the shortcut menu.

Microsoft **Word**

As you work through creating a document, you will find that certain Word operations automatically display the task pane. In addition to the New Document task pane, Word provides seven other task panes: Clipboard, Search, Insert Clip Art, Styles and Formatting, Reveal Formatting, Mail Merge, and Translate. These task panes will be discussed as they are used in the projects.

The Word Window

The **Word window** (Figure 1-8 on the previous page) consists of a variety of components to make your work more efficient and documents more professional. The following sections discuss these components.

Document Window

The **document window** displays text, tables, graphics, and other items as you type or insert them into a document. Only a portion of your document, however, displays on the screen at one time. You view the portion of the document displayed on the screen through the document window (Figure 1-9).

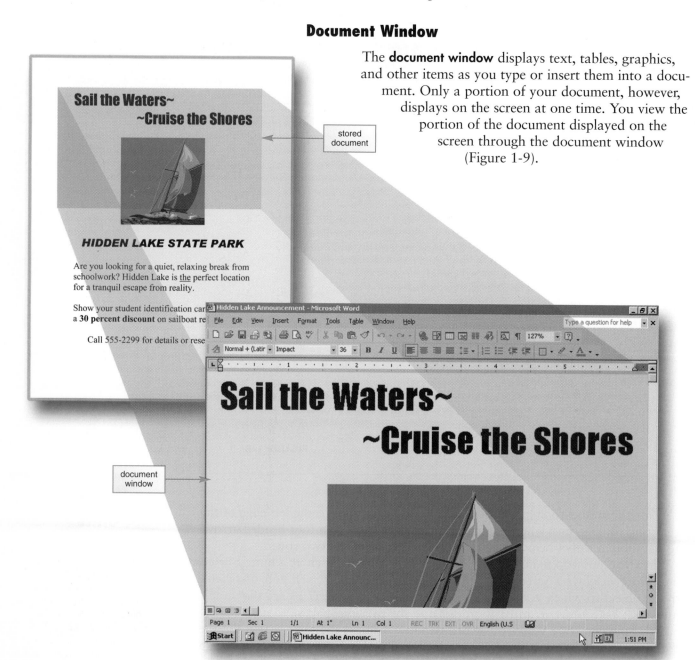

FIGURE 1-9

The document window contains several elements commonly found in other applications, as well as some elements unique to Word. The main elements of the Word document window are the insertion point, end mark, mouse pointer, rulers, scroll bars, and status bar (Figure 1-8 on page WD 1.11).

INSERTION POINT The **insertion point** is a blinking vertical bar that indicates where text will be inserted as you type. As you type, the insertion point moves to the right and, when you reach the end of a line, it moves downward to the beginning of the next line. You also can insert graphics, tables, and other items at the location of the insertion point.

END MARK The **end mark** is a short horizontal line that indicates the end of your document. Each time you begin a new line, the end mark moves downward.

MOUSE POINTER The **mouse pointer** becomes different shapes depending on the task you are performing in Word and the pointer's location on the screen. The mouse pointer in Figure 1-8 has the shape of an I-beam. Other mouse pointer shapes are described as they appear on the screen during this and subsequent projects.

RULERS At the top edge of the document window is the **horizontal ruler.** You use the horizontal ruler, usually simply called the ruler, to set tab stops, indent paragraphs, adjust column widths, and change page margins.

An additional ruler, called the vertical ruler, sometimes displays at the left edge of the Word window when you perform certain tasks. The purpose of the vertical ruler is discussed as it displays on the screen in a later project. If your screen displays a vertical ruler, click View on the menu bar and then click Normal.

SCROLL BARS By using the **scroll bars**, you can display different portions of your document in the document window. At the right edge of the document window is a vertical scroll bar. At the bottom of the document window is a horizontal scroll bar. On both the vertical and horizontal scroll bars, the position of the **scroll box** reflects the location of the portion of the document displaying in the document window.

On the left edge of the horizontal scroll bar are four buttons you can use to change the view of a document. On the bottom of the vertical scroll bar are three buttons you can use to scroll through a document. These buttons are discussed as they are used in later projects.

STATUS BAR The status bar displays at the bottom of the document window, above the Windows taskbar. The **status bar** presents information about the location of the insertion point and the progress of current tasks, as well as the status of certain commands, keys, and buttons.

From left to right, the following information displays on the status bar in Figure 1-9: the page number, the section number, the page containing the insertion point followed by the total number of pages in the document, the position of the insertion point in inches from the top of the page, the line number and column number of the insertion point, followed by several status indicators.

You use the **status indicators** to turn certain keys or modes on or off. The first four status indicators (REC, TRK, EXT, and OVR) display darkened when on and dimmed when off. For example, the dimmed OVR indicates overtype mode is off. To turn these four status indicators on or off, double-click the status indicator. These status indicators are discussed as they are used in the projects.

More About

The Horizontal Ruler

If the horizontal ruler does not display on your screen, click View on the menu bar and then click Ruler. To hide the ruler, also click View on the menu bar and then click Ruler.

More About

Scroll Bars

You can use the vertical scroll bar to scroll through multi-page documents. As you drag the scroll box up or down the scroll bar, Word displays a page indicator to the left of the scroll box. When you release the mouse button, the document window displays the page shown in the page indicator.

The next status indicator displays the name of the language that appears at the location of the insertion point. In Figure 1-9 on page WD 1.12, the indicated language is English (U.S.). Word automatically detects the language as you type. Most installations of Word can detect more than 60 languages, including Chinese, Dutch, English, French, German, Italian, Japanese, and Russian. This means Word can check the spelling, grammar, and punctuation in each of these languages.

The remaining status indicators display icons as you perform certain tasks. When you begin typing in the document window, a Spelling and Grammar Status icon displays. When Word is saving your document, a Background Save icon displays. When you print a document, a Background Print icon displays. If you perform a task that requires several seconds (such as saving a document), the status bar displays a message informing you of the progress of the task.

Menu Bar and Toolbars

The menu bar and toolbars display at the top of the screen just below the title bar (Figure 1-10).

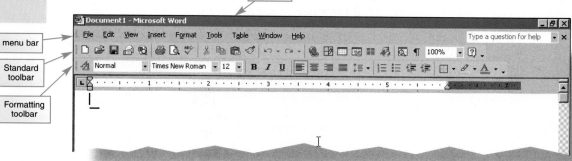

FIGURE 1-10

MENU BAR The **menu bar** is a special toolbar that displays the Word menu names. Each **menu** contains a list of commands you can use to perform tasks such as retrieving, storing, printing, and formatting data in your document. When you point to a menu name on the menu bar, the area of the menu bar containing the name changes to a button. To display a menu, such as the Edit menu, click the Edit menu name on the menu bar. If you point to a command on a menu that has an arrow to its right edge, a **submenu** displays another list of commands.

When you click a menu name on the menu bar, a **short menu** displays that lists your most recently used commands, as shown in Figure 1-11a.

If you wait a few seconds or click the arrows at the bottom of the short menu, it expands into a full menu. A **full menu** lists all the commands associated with a menu, as shown in Figure 1-11b. You immediately can display a full menu by double-clicking the menu name on the menu bar. In this book, when you display a menu, always display the full menu using one of these techniques:

1. Click the menu name on the menu bar and then wait a few seconds.
2. Click the menu name on the menu bar and then click the arrows at the bottom of the short menu.
3. Click the menu name on the menu bar and then point to the arrows at the bottom of the short menu.
4. Double-click the menu name on the menu bar.

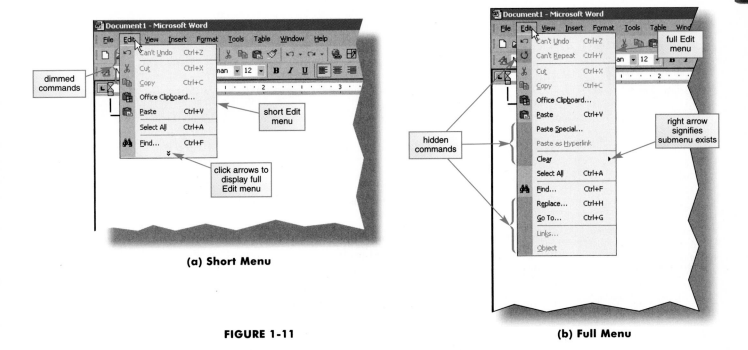

FIGURE 1-11

(a) Short Menu

(b) Full Menu

Both short and full menus display some **dimmed commands** that appear gray, or dimmed, instead of black, which indicates they are not available for the current selection. A command with a dark gray shading in the rectangle to the left of it on a full menu is called a **hidden command** because it does not display on a short menu. As you use Word, it automatically personalizes the short menus for you based on how often you use commands. That is, as you use hidden commands on the full menu, Word *unhides* them and places them on the short menu.

TOOLBARS Word has many pre-defined, or built-in, toolbars. A **toolbar** contains buttons, boxes, and menus that allow you to perform tasks more quickly than using the menu bar and related menus. For example, to print a document, you click the Print button on a toolbar. Each button on a toolbar displays an image to help you remember its function. Also, when you point to a button or box on a toolbar, a ScreenTip displays below the mouse pointer (Figure 1-6 on page WD 1.10).

Two built-in toolbars are the Standard toolbar and the Formatting toolbar. Figure 1-12a illustrates the **Standard toolbar** and identifies its buttons and boxes. Figure 1-12b on the next page illustrates the **Formatting toolbar**. Each button and box is explained in detail as it is used in the projects throughout the book.

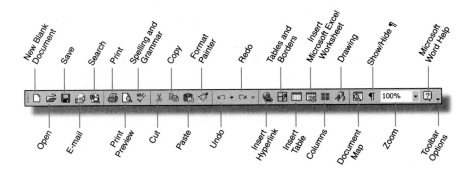

FIGURE 1-12a Standard Toolbar

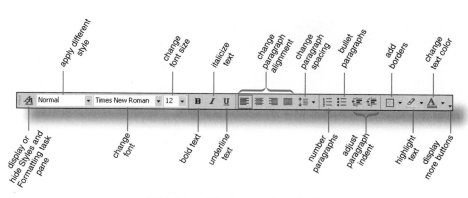

FIGURE 1-12b Formatting Toolbar

When you first install Word, the Standard and Formatting toolbars are preset to display on the same row immediately below the menu bar (Figure 1-13a). Unless the resolution of your display device is greater than 800 × 600, many of the buttons that belong to these toolbars do not display when the two toolbars share one row. The buttons that display on the toolbar are the more frequently used buttons. Hidden buttons display in the Toolbar Options list. When you click the Toolbar Options button on a toolbar, Word displays a Toolbar Options list that contains the toolbar's hidden buttons (Figure 1-13b). In this mode, you also can display all the buttons on either toolbar by double-clicking the **move handle** on the left of each toolbar.

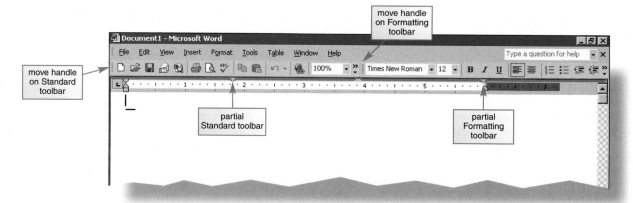

FIGURE 1-13a

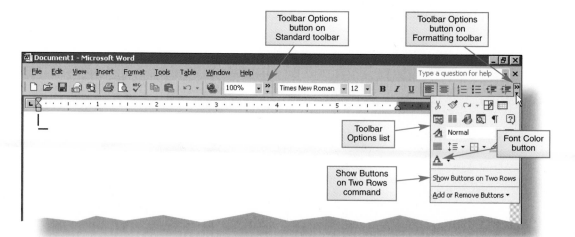

FIGURE 1-13b

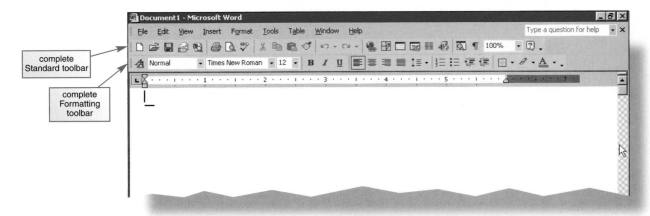

complete Standard toolbar

complete Formatting toolbar

FIGURE 1-13c

In this project, the Standard and Formatting toolbars are shown on separate rows, one below the other so that all buttons display (Figure 1-13c). You show the two toolbars on two rows by clicking the Show Buttons on Two Rows command in the Toolbar Options list (Figure 1-13b).

In the previous figures, the Standard and Formatting toolbars are docked. A **docked toolbar** is one that is attached to the edge of the Word window. Depending on the task you are performing, additional toolbars may display on the Word screen. These additional toolbars display either docked or floating in the Word window. A **floating toolbar** is not attached to an edge of the Word window; that is, it displays in the middle of the Word window. You can rearrange the order of docked toolbars and can move floating toolbars anywhere in the Word window. Later in this book, steps are presented that show you how to float a docked toolbar or dock a floating toolbar.

Resetting Menus and Toolbars

Each project in this book begins with the menus and toolbars appearing as they did at the initial installation of the software. To reset your menus and toolbars so they appear exactly as shown in this book, follow the steps in Appendix D.

Speech Recognition and Handwriting Recognition (Not Available in Word 2000)

With the **Office Speech Recognition software** installed and a microphone, you can speak the names of toolbar buttons, menus, menu commands, list items, alerts, and dialog box controls, such as OK and Cancel. You also can dictate text, such as words and sentences.

To indicate whether you want to speak commands or dictate text, you use the **Language bar** (Figure 1-14a). You can display the Language bar in two ways: (1) click the Language Indicator button in the taskbar tray status area by the clock and then click Show the Language bar on the menu (Figure 1-14b on the next page), or (2) click Tools on the menu bar and then click Speech.

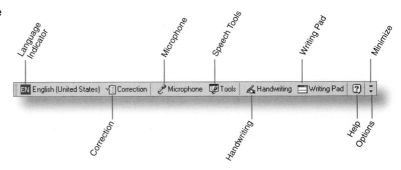

FIGURE 1-14a Language Bar

Speech Recognition

If Office Speech Recognition software is installed on your computer, you can speak instructions to Word including toolbar button names, menu names and commands, and items in dialog boxes and task panes. You also can dictate so Word writes exactly what you say. The microphone picks up others' voices and background sounds, so speech recognition is most effective when used in a quiet environment.

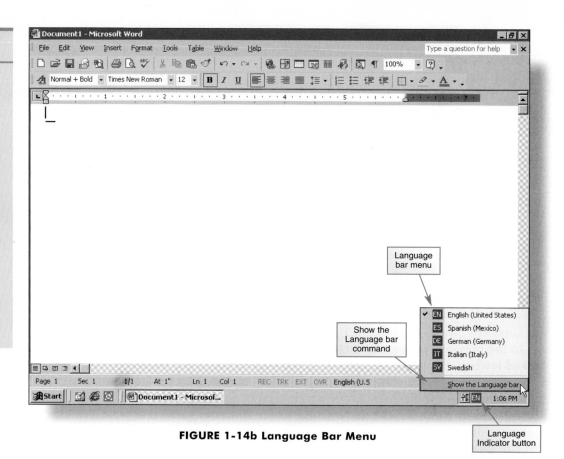

FIGURE 1-14b Language Bar Menu

If the Language Indicator button does not display in the taskbar tray status area, the Office Speech Recognition software may not be installed. To install the software, you first must start Word and then click Speech on the Tools menu.

You can use the speech recognition and handwriting recognition capabilities of Office XP to enter text into Word by speaking or writing, instead of typing. Additional information on the Office Speech Recognition, Handwriting Recognition, and other text services is available in Appendix B.

Zooming Page Width

Depending on your Windows and Word settings, the horizontal ruler at the top of the document window may show more inches or fewer inches than the ruler shown in Figure 1-15. The more inches of ruler that display, the smaller the text will be on the screen. The fewer inches of ruler that display, the larger the text will be on the screen. To minimize eyestrain, the projects in this book display the text as large as possible without extending the right margin beyond the right edge of the document window.

Two factors that affect how much of the ruler displays in the document window are the Windows screen resolution and the Word zoom percentage. The screens in this book use a resolution of 800 × 600. With this resolution, you can increase the preset zoom percentage beyond 100% so that the right margin extends to the edge of the document window. To increase or decrease the size of the displayed characters to a point where both the left and right margins are at the edges of the document window, use the **zoom page width** command as shown in the following steps.

Handwriting Recognition

If Handwriting Recognition software is installed on your computer, Word can recognize text as you write it on a handwriting input device, such as a graphics tablet, or with the mouse. To use the mouse, you drag the mouse to form the cursive characters. If you have a handheld computer, or PDA, you also can convert the handheld computer's handwritten notes into text in Word.

Steps **To Zoom Page Width**

1 **Click the Zoom box arrow on the Standard toolbar and then point to Page Width.**

Word displays a list of available zoom percentages and the Page Width option in the Zoom list (Figure 1-15).

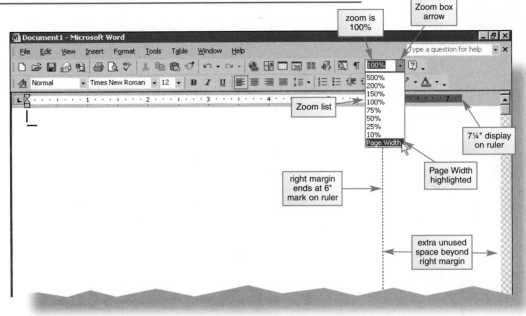

FIGURE 1-15

2 **Click Page Width.**

Word extends the right margin to the right edge of the document window (Figure 1-16).

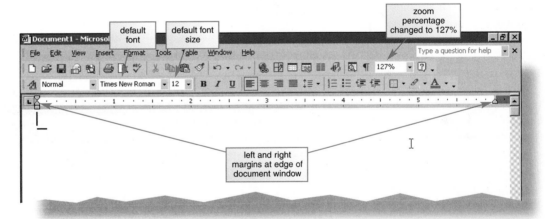

FIGURE 1-16

If your Zoom list (Figure 1-15) displayed additional options, click View on the menu bar and then click Normal.

The Zoom box in Figure 1-16 displays 127%, which Word computes based on a variety of settings. Your percentage may be different depending on your computer configuration.

Changing the Default Font Size

Characters that display on the screen are a specific shape, size, and style. The **font**, or typeface, defines the appearance and shape of the letters, numbers, and special characters. The preset, or **default**, font is Times New Roman (Figure 1-16). **Font size** specifies the size of the characters and is determined by a measurement system called

Other Ways

1. On View menu click Zoom, select Page Width, click OK button
2. In Voice Command mode, say "Zoom, Page Width"

More About

Zooming

If you want to zoom to a percentage not in the Zoom list, click the Zoom box on the Standard toolbar, type the desired percentage, then press the ENTER key.

More *About*

Font Size

An announcement usually is posted on a wall. Thus, its font size should be as large as possible so that all potential readers easily can see it.

points. A single **point** is about 1/72 of one inch in height. Thus, a character with a font size of 12 is about 12/72 or 1/6 of one inch in height. On most computers, the default font size in Word is 12.

2000 If you are using Word 2000, the default font size is 10.

If more of the characters in your document require a larger font size than the default, you easily can change the default font size before you type. In Project 1, many of the characters in the body of the announcement are a font size of 22. Perform the following steps to increase the font size before you begin entering text.

Steps **To Increase the Default Font Size Before Typing**

1 **Click the Font Size box arrow on the Formatting toolbar and then point to 22.**

A list of available font sizes displays in the Font Size list (Figure 1-17). The available font sizes depend on the current font, which is Times New Roman.

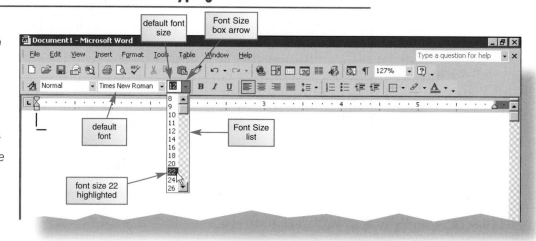

FIGURE 1-17

2 **Click 22.**

The font size for characters entered in this document changes to 22 (Figure 1-18). The size of the insertion point increases to reflect the new font size.

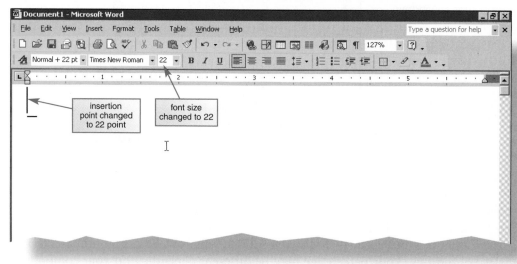

FIGURE 1-18

Other **Ways**

1. Right-click paragraph mark above end mark, click Font on shortcut menu, click Font tab, select desired font size in Size list, click OK button
2. On Format menu click Font, click Font tab, select desired font size in Size list, click OK button
3. Press CTRL+SHIFT+P, type desired font size, press ENTER
4. In Voice Command mode, say "Font Size, [select font size]"

The new font size takes effect immediately in your document. Word uses this font size for characters you type into this announcement.

Entering Text

To enter text into a document, you type on the keyboard or speak into the microphone. The following example illustrates the steps required to type both lines in the headline of the announcement. These lines will be positioned at the left margin. Later in this project, you will format the headline so that both lines are bold and enlarged and the second line is positioned at the right margin.

Perform the following steps to begin entering the document text.

More About

The Tilde Key

On most keyboards, the TILDE (~) key is located just below the ESCAPE key and just above the TAB key. The tilde is the top character on the key. Thus, to display the tilde character on the screen, press the SHIFT key while pressing the TILDE key.

Steps **To Enter Text**

1 **Type** Sail the Waters **and while holding the SHIFT key, press the TILDE (~) key. If you make an error while typing, press the BACKSPACE key until you have deleted the text in error and then retype the text correctly.**

As you type, the insertion point moves to the right (Figure 1-19). On most keyboards, the TILDE (~) key is immediately below the ESCAPE key.

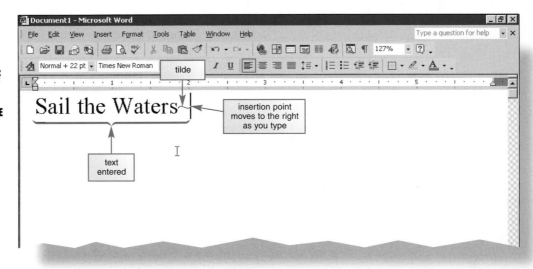

FIGURE 1-19

2 **Press the ENTER key.**

Word moves the insertion point to the beginning of the next line (Figure 1-20). Notice the status bar indicates the current position of the insertion point. That is, the insertion point currently is on line 2 column 1.

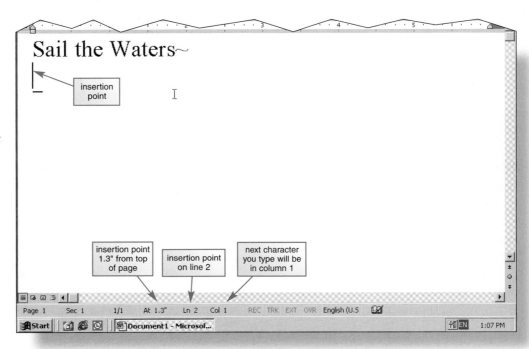

FIGURE 1-20

Microsoft **Word**

3 Press the TILDE (~) key. Type Cruise the Shores and then press the ENTER key.

The headline is complete (Figure 1-21). The insertion point is on line 3.

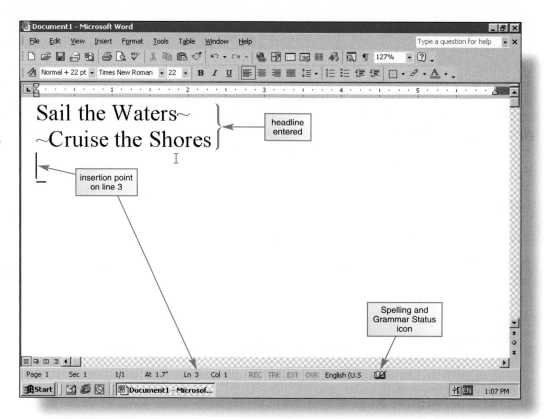

FIGURE 1-21

When you begin entering text into a document, the **Spelling and Grammar Status icon** displays at the right of the status bar (Figure 1-21). As you type, the Spelling and Grammar Status icon shows an animated pencil writing on paper, which indicates Word is checking for possible errors. When you stop typing, the pencil changes to either a red check mark or a red X. In Figure 1-21, the Spelling and Grammar Status icon displays a red check mark.

In general, if all of the words you have typed are in Word's dictionary and your grammar is correct, a red check mark displays on the Spelling and Grammar Status icon. If you type a word not in the dictionary (because it is a proper name or misspelled), a red wavy underline displays below the word. If you type text that may be incorrect grammatically, a green wavy underline displays below the text. When Word flags a possible spelling or grammar error, it also changes the red check mark on the Spelling and Grammar Status icon to a red X. As you enter text into the announcement, your Spelling and Grammar Status icon may show a red X instead of a red check mark. Later in this project, you will check the spelling of these words. At that time, the red X will return to a red check mark.

Entering Blank Lines into a Document

To enter a blank line into a document, press the ENTER key without typing any text on the line. The following example explains how to enter three blank lines below the headline.

 Steps **To Enter Blank Lines into a Document**

1 **Press the ENTER key three times.**

Word inserts three blank lines into your document below the headline (Figure 1-22).

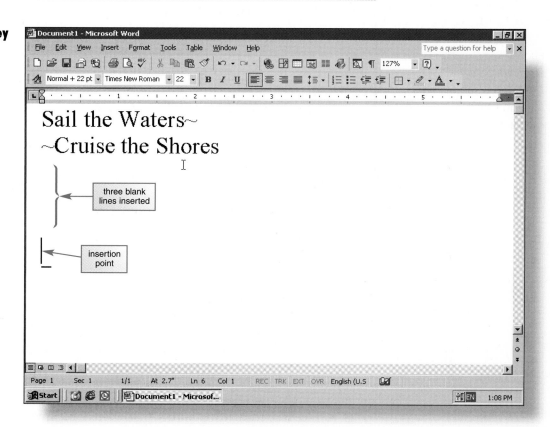

Sail the Waters~
~Cruise the Shores

three blank lines inserted

insertion point

FIGURE 1-22

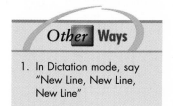

Other **Ways**

1. In Dictation mode, say "New Line, New Line, New Line"

Displaying Formatting Marks

To indicate where in the document you press the ENTER key or SPACEBAR, you may find it helpful to display formatting marks. A **formatting mark**, sometimes called a **nonprinting character**, is a character that displays on the screen but is not visible on a printed document. For example, the paragraph mark (¶) is a formatting mark that indicates where you pressed the ENTER key. A raised dot (•) shows where you pressed the SPACEBAR. Other formatting marks are discussed as they display on the screen.

Depending on settings made during previous Word sessions, your screen already may display formatting marks (Figure 1-23 on the next page). If the formatting marks do not display already on your screen, follow the step on the next page to display them.

Steps **To Display Formatting Marks**

1 **If it is not already selected, click the Show/Hide ¶ button on the Standard toolbar.**

Word displays formatting marks on the screen (Figure 1-23). The Show/Hide ¶ button is selected. Selected toolbar buttons are shaded light blue and surrounded with a blue outline.

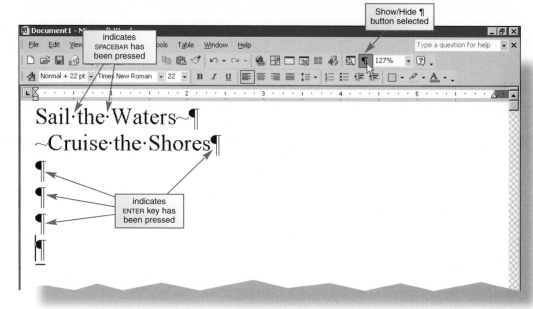

FIGURE 1-23

Notice several changes to the Word document window (Figure 1-23). A paragraph mark displays at the end of each line to indicate you pressed the ENTER key. Each time you press the ENTER key, Word creates a new paragraph. Because you changed the font size, the paragraph marks are 22 point. Notice Word places a paragraph mark above the end mark; you cannot delete this paragraph mark. Between each word, a raised dot appears, indicating you pressed the SPACEBAR. Finally, the Show/Hide ¶ button is shaded light blue and surrounded with a blue outline to indicate it is selected.

If you feel the formatting marks clutter the screen, you can hide them by clicking the Show/Hide ¶ button again. It is recommended that you display formatting marks; therefore, the document windows presented in this book show the formatting marks.

Entering More Text

Every character of the body title (HIDDEN LAKE STATE PARK) in the announcement is capitalized. The next step is to enter this body title in all capital letters into the document window as explained below.

TO ENTER MORE TEXT

1 Press the CAPS LOCK key on the keyboard to turn on capital letters. Verify the CAPS LOCK indicator is lit on your keyboard.

2 Type HIDDEN LAKE STATE PARK and then press the CAPS LOCK key to turn off capital letters.

3 Press the ENTER key twice.

The body title displays on line 6 as shown in Figure 1-24.

Using Wordwrap

Wordwrap allows you to type words in a paragraph continually without pressing the ENTER key at the end of each line. When the insertion point reaches the right margin, Word automatically positions it at the beginning of the next line. As you type, if a word extends beyond the right margin, Word also positions that word automatically on the next line with the insertion point.

As you enter text using Word, do not press the ENTER key when the insertion point reaches the right margin. Word creates a new paragraph each time you press the ENTER key. Thus, press the ENTER key only in these circumstances:

1. To insert blank lines into a document
2. To begin a new paragraph
3. To terminate a short line of text and advance to the next line
4. In response to certain Word commands

Perform the following step to familiarize yourself with wordwrap.

More About

Wordwrap

Your printer controls where wordwrap occurs for each line in your document. For this reason, it is possible that the same document could wordwrap differently if printed on different printers.

Steps **To Wordwrap Text as You Type**

---

1 **Type** Are you looking for a quiet, relaxing break from schoolwork?

Word wraps the word, schoolwork, to the beginning of line 9 because it is too long to fit on line 8 (Figure 1-24). Your document may wordwrap differently depending on the type of printer you are using.

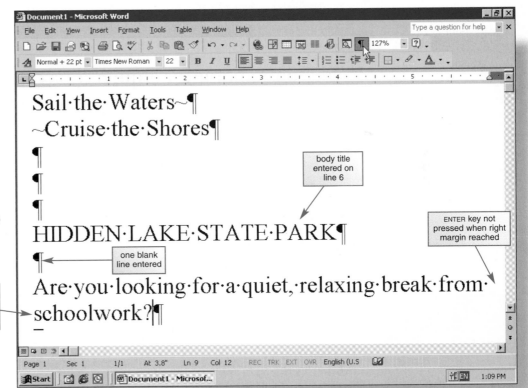

FIGURE 1-24

Other **Ways**

1. In Dictation mode, say "Are you looking for a quiet Comma relaxing break from schoolwork Question Mark"

Entering Text that Scrolls the Document Window

As you type more lines of text than Word can display in the document window, Word **scrolls** the top portion of the document upward off the screen. Although you cannot see the text once it scrolls off the screen, it remains in the document. As previously discussed, the document window allows you to view only a portion of your document at one time (Figure 1-9 on page WD 1.12).

Perform the following step to enter text that scrolls the document window.

Steps **To Enter Text that Scrolls the Document Window**

1 **Press the SPACEBAR.**
Type Hidden Lake is the perfect location for a tranquil escape from reality. **Press the ENTER key twice.**

Word scrolls the headline off the top of the screen (Figure 1-25). Your screen may scroll differently depending on the type of monitor you are using.

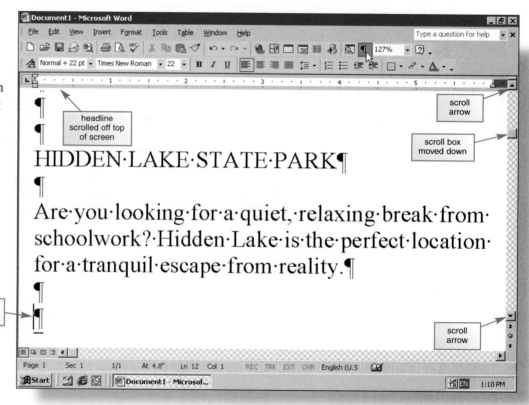

FIGURE 1-25

Other **Ways**

1. In Dictation mode, say "Hidden Lake is the perfect location for a tranquil escape from reality Period, New Line, New Line"

When Word scrolls text off the top of the screen, the scroll box on the vertical scroll bar at the right edge of the document window moves downward (Figure 1-25). The **scroll box** indicates the current relative location of the insertion point in the document. You may use either the mouse or the keyboard to move the insertion point to a different location in a document.

With the mouse, you use the scroll arrows or the scroll box to display a different portion of the document in the document window, and then click the mouse to move the insertion point to that location. Table 1-1 explains various techniques for scrolling vertically with the mouse.

Table 1-1 Techniques for Scrolling with the Mouse	
SCROLL DIRECTION	*MOUSE ACTION*
Up	Drag the scroll box upward.
Down	Drag the scroll box downward.
Up one screen	Click anywhere above the scroll box on the vertical scroll bar.
Down one screen	Click anywhere below the scroll box on the vertical scroll bar.
Up one line	Click the scroll arrow at the top of the vertical scroll bar.
Down one line	Click the scroll arrow at the bottom of the vertical scroll bar.

More About

Scrolling

Computer users frequently switch between the keyboard and the mouse during a word processing session, which strains the wrist. To help prevent wrist injury, minimize switching. If your fingers are already on the keyboard, use keyboard keys to scroll. If your hand is already on the mouse, use the mouse to scroll.

When you use the keyboard to scroll, the insertion point automatically moves when you press the appropriate keys. Table 1-2 outlines various techniques to scroll through a document using the keyboard.

Table 1-2 Techniques for Scrolling with the Keyboard			
SCROLL DIRECTION	*KEY(S) TO PRESS*	*SCROLL DIRECTION*	*KEY(S) TO PRESS*
Left one character	LEFT ARROW	Down one paragraph	CTRL+DOWN ARROW
Right one character	RIGHT ARROW	Up one screen	PAGE UP
Left one word	CTRL+LEFT ARROW	Down one screen	PAGE DOWN
Right one word	CTRL+RIGHT ARROW	To top of document window	ALT+CTRL+PAGE UP
Up one line	UP ARROW	To bottom of document window	ALT+CTRL+PAGE DOWN
Down one line	DOWN ARROW	Previous page	CTRL+PAGE UP
To end of a line	END	Next page	CTRL+PAGE DOWN
To beginning of a line	HOME	To the beginning of a document	CTRL+HOME
Up one paragraph	CTRL+UP ARROW	To the end of a document	CTRL+END

Checking Spelling as You Type

As you type text into the document window, Word checks your typing for possible spelling and grammar errors. If a word you type is not in the dictionary, a red wavy underline displays below it. Similarly, if text you type contains possible grammar errors, a green wavy underline displays below the text. In both cases, the Spelling and Grammar Status icon on the status bar displays a red X, instead of a check mark. Although you can check the entire document for spelling and grammar errors at once, you also can check these errors immediately.

To verify that the Check spelling as you type feature is enabled, right-click the Spelling and Grammar Status icon on the status bar and then click Options on the shortcut menu. When the Spelling & Grammar dialog box displays, be sure Check spelling as you type has a check mark and Hide spelling errors in this document does not have a check mark.

When a word is flagged with a red wavy underline, it is not in Word's dictionary. To display a list of suggested corrections for a flagged word, you right-click the word. A flagged word, however, is not necessarily misspelled. For example, many names, abbreviations, and specialized terms are not in Word's main dictionary. In these cases, you tell Word to ignore the flagged word. As you type, Word also detects duplicate words. For example, if your document contains the phrase, to the the store, Word places a red wavy underline below the second occurrence of the word, the.

More About

Correcting Spelling

As you type, Word corrects some misspelled words automatically. For example, if you type recieve, Word automatically fixes the misspelling and displays the word, receive, when you press the SPACEBAR or type a punctuation mark. To see a complete list of automatically corrected words, click Tools on the menu bar, click AutoCorrect Options on the Tools menu, click the AutoCorrect tab, and then scroll through the list of words near the bottom of the dialog box.

In the following example, the word, identification, has been misspelled intentionally as indentification to illustrate Word's check spelling as you type feature. If you are doing this project on a personal computer, your announcement may contain different misspelled words, depending on the accuracy of your typing.

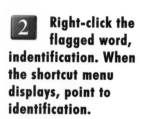 **To Check Spelling as You Type**

1 **Type** Show your student indentification **and then press the SPACEBAR. Position the mouse pointer in the flagged word (indentification, in this case).**

Word flags the misspelled word, indentification, by placing a red wavy underline below it (Figure 1-26). The Spelling and Grammar Status icon on the status bar now displays a red X, indicating Word has detected a possible spelling or grammar error.

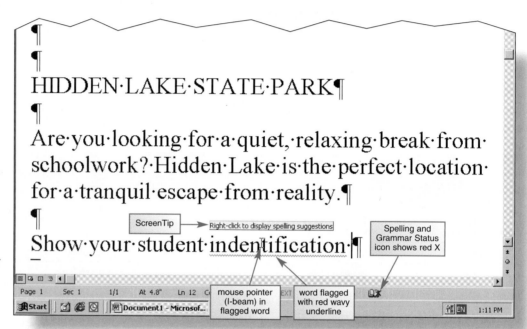

FIGURE 1-26

2 **Right-click the flagged word, indentification. When the shortcut menu displays, point to identification.**

Word displays a shortcut menu that lists suggested spelling corrections for the flagged word (Figure 1-27).

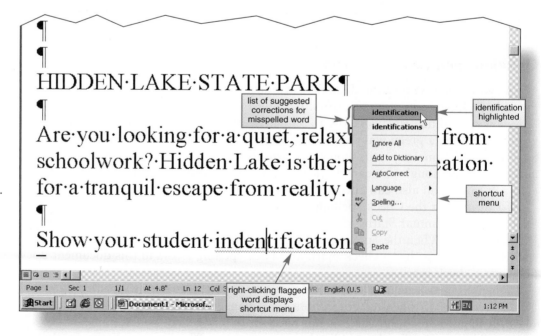

FIGURE 1-27

3 **Click identification.**

Word replaces the misspelled word with the selected word on the shortcut menu. The Spelling and Grammar Status icon once again displays a red check mark.

4 **Press the END key to move the insertion point to the end of the line and then type** card to receive a 30 percent discount on sailboat rentals. **Press the ENTER key twice. Type** Call 555-2299 for details or reservations.

The text of the announcement is complete (Figure 1-28).

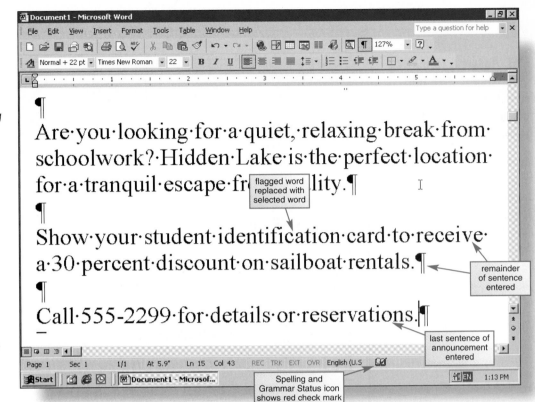

FIGURE 1-28

If a flagged word actually is spelled correctly and, for example, is a proper name, you can right-click it and then click Ignore All on the shortcut menu (Figure 1-27). If, when you right-click the misspelled word, your desired correction is not in the list on the shortcut menu, you can click outside the shortcut menu to make the menu disappear and then retype the correct word, or you can click Spelling on the shortcut menu to display the Spelling dialog box.

If you feel the wavy underlines clutter your document window, you can hide them temporarily until you are ready to check for spelling errors. To hide spelling errors, right-click the Spelling and Grammar Status icon on the status bar and then click Hide Spelling Errors on the shortcut menu. To hide grammar errors, right-click the Spelling and Grammar Status icon on the status bar and then click Hide Grammatical Errors on the shortcut menu.

Saving a Document

As you create a document in Word, the computer stores it in memory. If you turn off the computer or if you lose electrical power, the document in memory is lost. Hence, it is mandatory to save on disk any document that you will use later. The steps on the following pages illustrate how to save a document on a floppy disk inserted in drive A using the Save button on the Standard toolbar.

You will save the document using the file name, Hidden Lake Announcement. Depending on your Windows settings, the file type .doc may display immediately after the file name. The file type .doc indicates the file is a Word document.

Other Ways

1. Double-click Spelling and Grammar Status icon on status bar, click correct word on shortcut menu
2. In Voice Command mode, say "Spelling and Grammar"

More About

Saving

When you save a document, use meaningful file names. A file name can be up to 255 characters, including spaces. The only invalid characters are the backslash (\), slash (/), colon (:), asterisk (*), question mark (?), quotation mark ("), less than symbol (<), greater than symbol (>), and vertical bar (|).

Steps **To Save a New Document**

1 **Insert a formatted floppy disk into drive A. Click the Save button on the Standard toolbar.**

Word displays the Save As dialog box (Figure 1-29). The first line from the document (Sail the Waters) displays selected in the File name text box as the default file name. With this file name selected, you can change it by immediately typing the new name.

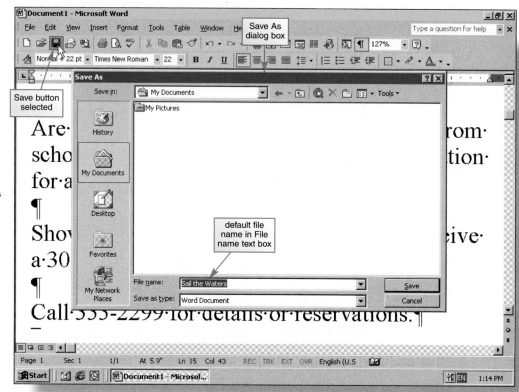

FIGURE 1-29

2 **Type** Hidden Lake Announcement **in the File name text box. Do not press the ENTER key after typing the file name.**

*The file name, Hidden Lake Announcement, displays in the File name text box (Figure 1-30). Notice that the current save location is the My Documents folder. A **folder** is a specific location on a disk. To change to a different save location, use the Save in box.*

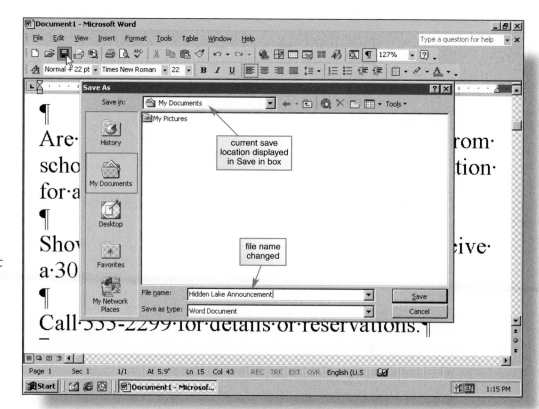

FIGURE 1-30

3 **Click the Save in box arrow and then point to 3½ Floppy (A:).**

A list of the available save locations displays (Figure 1-31). Your list may differ depending on your system configuration.

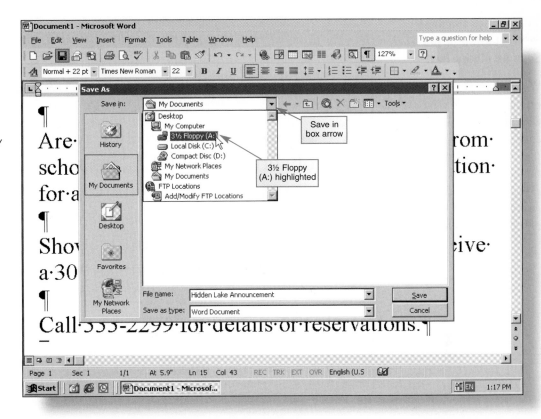

FIGURE 1-31

4 **Click 3½ Floppy (A:) and then point to the Save button in the Save As dialog box.**

The 3½ Floppy (A:) drive becomes the save location (Figure 1-32). The names of existing files stored on the floppy disk in drive A display. In Figure 1-32, the list is empty because no Word files currently are stored on the floppy disk in drive A.

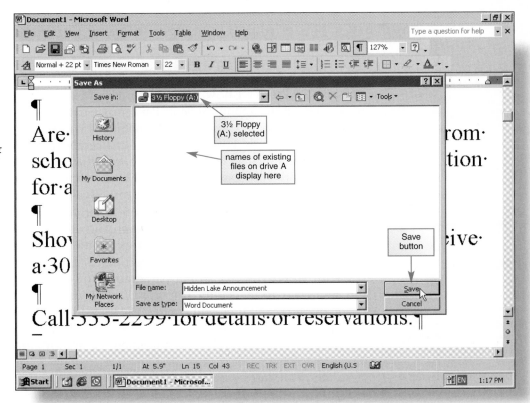

FIGURE 1-32

5 **Click the Save button in the Save As dialog box.**

Word saves the document on the floppy disk in drive A with the file name Hidden Lake Announcement (Figure 1-33). Although the announcement is saved on a floppy disk, it also remains in main memory and displays on the screen.

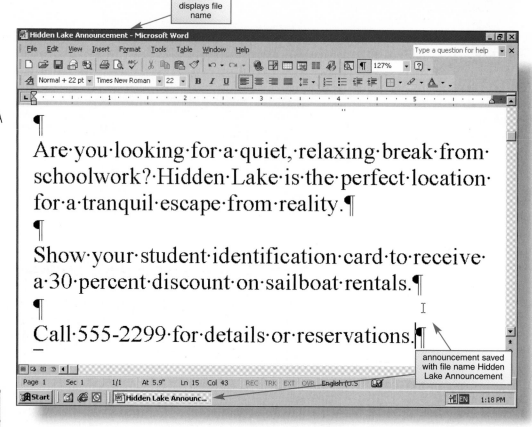

FIGURE 1-33

Formatting

Character formatting includes changing the font, font style, font size; adding an underline, color, strikethrough, or shadow; embossing; engraving; making a superscript or subscript; and changing the case of the letters. Paragraph formatting includes alignment; indentation; and spacing above, below, and between lines.

Formatting Paragraphs and Characters in a Document

The text for Project 1 now is complete. The next step is to format the characters and paragraphs in the announcement. Paragraphs encompass the text up to and including a paragraph mark (¶). **Paragraph formatting** is the process of changing the appearance of a paragraph. For example, you can center or indent a paragraph.

Characters include letters, numbers, punctuation marks, and symbols. **Character formatting** is the process of changing the way characters appear on the screen and in print. You use character formatting to emphasize certain words and improve readability of a document. For example, you can italicize or underline characters.

Very often, you apply both paragraph and character formatting to the same text. For example, you may center a paragraph (paragraph formatting) and bold the characters in a paragraph (character formatting).

With Word, you can format paragraphs and characters before you type, or you can apply new formats after you type. Earlier, you changed the font size before you typed any text, and then you entered the text. In this section, you format existing text.

Figure 1-34a shows the announcement before formatting the paragraphs and characters. Figure 1-34b shows the announcement after formatting. As you can see from the two figures, a document that is formatted not only is easier to read, but it looks more professional.

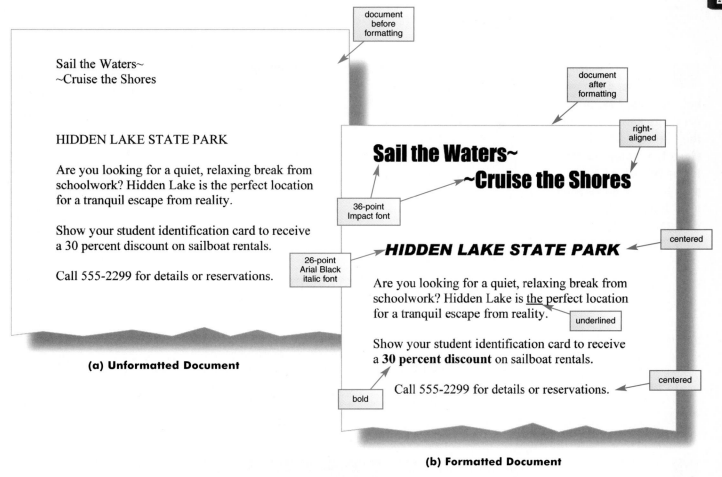

FIGURE 1-34

Selecting and Formatting Paragraphs and Characters

To format a single paragraph, move the insertion point into the paragraph and then format the paragraph. Thus, you do not need to select a paragraph to format it. To format *multiple* paragraphs, however, you first must select the paragraphs you want to format and then format them. In the same manner, to format characters, a word, or words, you first must select the characters, word, or words to be formatted and then format your selection.

Selected text is highlighted text. That is, if your screen normally displays dark letters on a light background, then selected text displays light letters on a dark background.

Selecting Multiple Paragraphs

The first formatting step in this project is to change the font size of the characters in the headline. The headline consists of two separate lines, each ending with a paragraph mark. As previously discussed, Word creates a new paragraph each time you press the ENTER key. Thus, the headline actually is two separate paragraphs.

To change the font size of the characters in the headline, you first must **select**, or highlight, both paragraphs in the headline as shown in the steps on the next page.

More *About*

Spacing

Word processing documents use variable character fonts; for example, the letter w takes up more space than the letter i. With these fonts, it often is difficult to determine how many times someone has pressed the SPACEBAR between sentences. Thus, the rule is to press the SPACEBAR only once after periods, colons, and other punctuation marks. Notice in Figure 1-34b that only one space exists between the ? and the H in Hidden.

Microsoft **Word**

Steps **To Select Multiple Paragraphs**

1 Press CTRL+HOME; that is, press and hold the CTRL key, then press the HOME key, and then release both keys. Move the mouse pointer to the left of the first paragraph to be selected until the mouse pointer changes to a right-pointing block arrow.

CTRL+HOME positions the insertion point at the top of the document (Figure 1-35). The mouse pointer changes to a right-pointing block arrow when positioned to the left of a paragraph.

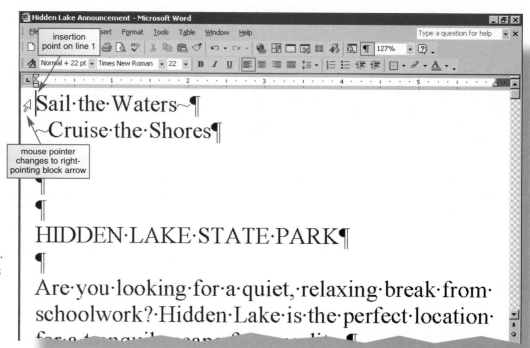

FIGURE 1-35

2 Drag downward until both paragraphs are selected.

Word selects (highlights) both of the paragraphs (Figure 1-36). Recall that dragging is the process of holding down the mouse button while moving the mouse and then releasing the mouse button.

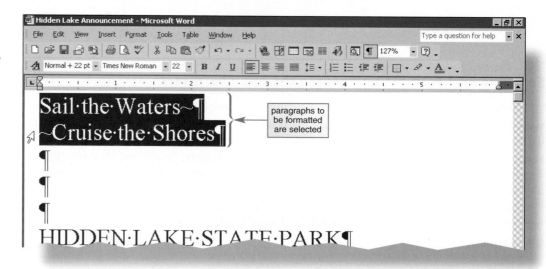

FIGURE 1-36

Other **Ways**

1. With insertion point at beginning of first paragraph, press CTRL+SHIFT+DOWN ARROW

Changing the Font Size of Selected Text

The next step is to increase the font size of the characters in the selected headline. Recall that the font size specifies the size of the characters. Earlier in this project, you changed the font size for characters in the entire announcement to 22. To give the headline more impact, it has a font size larger than the body copy. Perform the following steps to increase the font size of the headline from 22 to 36 point.

To Change the Font Size of Selected Text

1 **While the text is selected, click the Font Size box arrow on the Formatting toolbar and then point to the down scroll arrow on the Font Size scroll bar.**

Word displays a list of the available font sizes (Figure 1-37). Available font sizes vary depending on the font and printer driver.

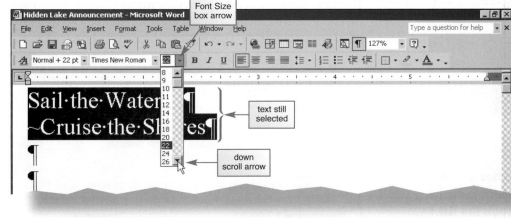

FIGURE 1-37

2 **Click the down scroll arrow on the Font Size scroll bar until 36 displays in the list and then point to 36.**

Word selects 36 in the list (Figure 1-38).

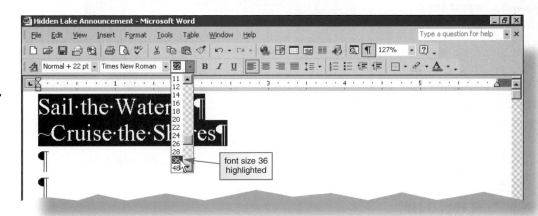

FIGURE 1-38

3 **Click 36.**

Word increases the font size of the headline to 36 (Figure 1-39). The Font Size box on the Formatting toolbar displays 36, indicating the selected text has a font size of 36.

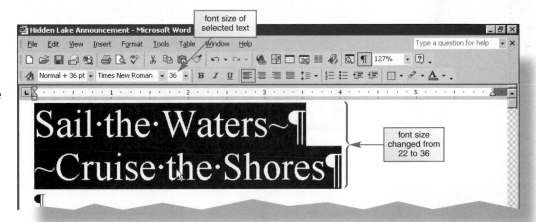

FIGURE 1-39

Other Ways

1. Right-click selected text, click Font on shortcut menu, click Font tab, select font size in Size list, click OK button
2. See Other Ways on page WD 1.20

Changing the Font of Selected Text

As mentioned earlier in this project, the default font in Word is Times New Roman. Word, however, provides many other fonts to add variety to your documents. Perform the following steps to change the font of the headline in the announcement from Times New Roman to Impact (or a similar font).

Steps **To Change the Font of Selected Text**

1 **While the text is selected, click the Font box arrow on the Formatting toolbar, scroll through the list until Impact displays, and then point to Impact (or a similar font).**

Word displays a list of available fonts (Figure 1-40). Your list of available fonts may differ, depending on the type of printer you are using.

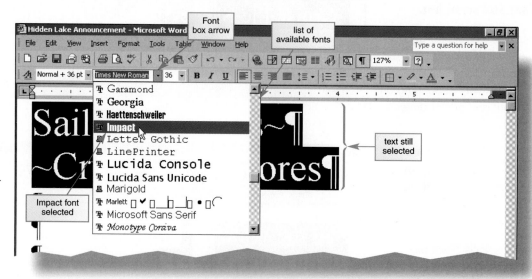

FIGURE 1-40

2 **Click Impact (or a similar font).**

Word changes the font of the selected text to Impact (Figure 1-41).

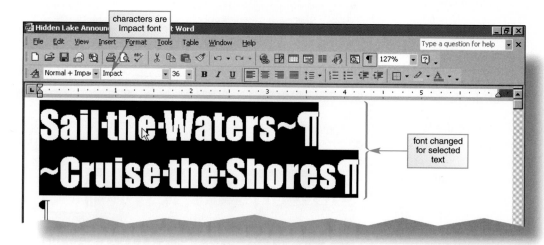

FIGURE 1-41

Other **Ways**

1. On Format menu click Font, click Font tab, click font name in Font list, click OK button
2. Press CTRL+SHIFT+F, press DOWN ARROW to font name, press ENTER
3. In Voice Command mode, say "Font, [select font name]"

Right-Align a Paragraph

The default alignment for paragraphs is **left-aligned**, that is, flush at the left margin of the document with uneven right edges. In Figure 1-42, the Align Left button is selected to indicate the current paragraph is left-aligned.

The second line of the headline, however, is to be **right-aligned**, that is, flush at the right margin of the document with uneven left edges. Recall that the second line of the headline is a paragraph, and paragraph formatting does not require you to select the paragraph prior to formatting. Just position the insertion point in the paragraph to be formatted and then format it accordingly.

Perform the following steps to right-align the second line of the headline.

Steps **To Right-Align a Paragraph**

1 **Click somewhere in the paragraph to be right-aligned. Point to the Align Right button on the Formatting toolbar.**

Word positions the insertion point at the location you clicked (Figure 1-42).

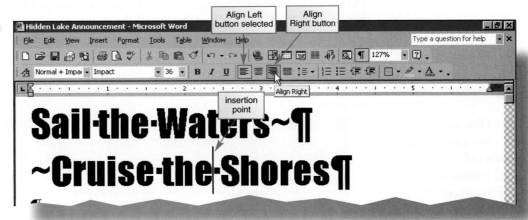

FIGURE 1-42

2 **Click the Align Right button.**

The second line of the headline is right-aligned (Figure 1-43). Notice that you did not have to select the paragraph before right-aligning it. Paragraph formatting requires only that the insertion point be positioned somewhere in the paragraph.

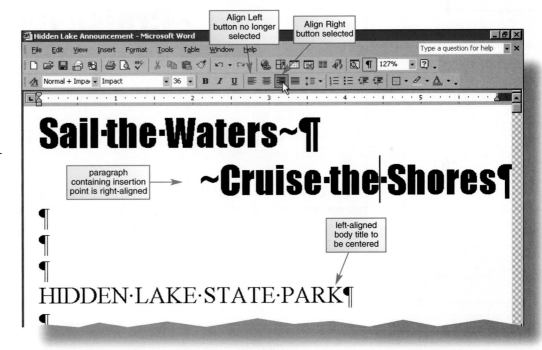

FIGURE 1-43

Other **Ways**

1. On Format menu click Paragraph, click Indents and Spacing tab, click Alignment box arrow, click Right, click OK button
2. Press CTRL+R
3. In Voice Command mode, say "Align Right"

When a paragraph is right-aligned, the Align Right button on the Formatting toolbar is selected. If, for some reason, you wanted to return the paragraph to left-aligned, you would click the Align Left button on the Formatting toolbar.

Center a Paragraph

The body title currently is left-aligned (Figure 1-43 on the previous page). Perform the following step to **center** it; that is, position the body title horizontally between the left and right margins on the page.

To Center a Paragraph

1 **Click somewhere in the paragraph to be centered. Click the Center button on the Formatting toolbar.**

Word centers the body title between the left and right margins (Figure 1-44). The Center button on the Formatting toolbar is selected, which indicates the paragraph containing the insertion point is centered.

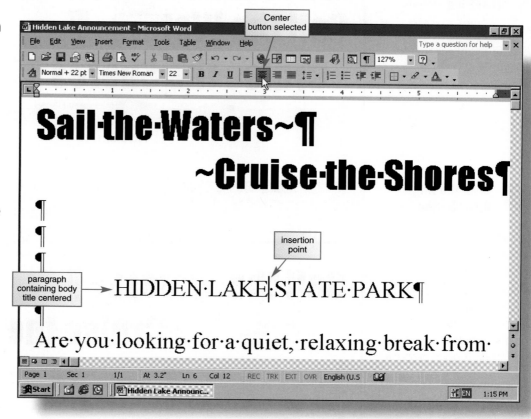

FIGURE 1-44

Other Ways

1. On Format menu click Paragraph, click Indents and Spacing tab, click Alignment box arrow, click Centered, click OK button
2. Right-click paragraph, click Paragraph on shortcut menu, click Indents and Spacing tab, click Alignment box arrow, click Centered, click OK button
3. Press CTRL+E
4. In Voice Command mode, say "Center"

When a paragraph is centered, the Center button on the Formatting toolbar is selected. If, for some reason, you wanted to return the paragraph to left-aligned, you would click the Align Left button on the Formatting toolbar.

Undoing Commands or Actions

Word provides an **Undo button** on the Standard toolbar that you can use to cancel your recent command(s) or action(s). For example, if you format text incorrectly, you can undo the format and try it again. If, after you undo an action, you decide you did not want to perform the undo, you can use the **Redo button** to undo the undo. Word prevents you from undoing or redoing some actions, such as saving or printing a document.

Perform the following steps to undo the center format to the body title using the Undo button and then re-center it using the Redo button.

 Steps **To Undo an Action**

1 **Click the Undo button on the Standard toolbar.**

Word returns the body title to its formatting before you issued the center command (Figure 1-45). That is, Word left-aligns the body title.

2 **Click the Redo button on the Standard toolbar.**

Word reapplies the center format to the body title (shown in Figure 1-44).

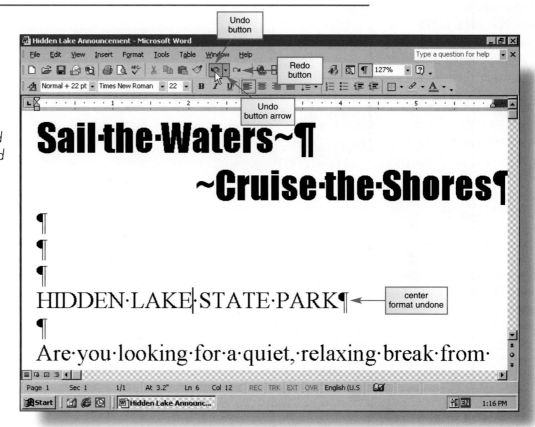

FIGURE 1-45

You also can cancel a series of prior actions by clicking the Undo button arrow (Figure 1-45) to display the list of undo actions and then dragging through the actions you wish to undo.

Whereas the Undo command cancels an action you did not want to perform, Word also provides a **Repeat command**, which duplicates your last command so you can perform it again. The word(s) listed after Repeat vary, depending on your most recent command. For example, if you centered a paragraph and wish to format another paragraph the exact same way, you could click in the second paragraph to format and then click Repeat Paragraph Alignment on the Edit menu.

Selecting a Line and Formatting It

The characters in the body title, HIDDEN LAKE STATE PARK, are to be a different font, larger font size, and italicized. To make these changes, you must select the line of text containing the body title. Perform the step on the next page to select the body title.

Other Ways

1. On Edit menu click Undo
2. Press CTRL+Z
3. In Voice Command mode, say "Undo"

More About

Centering

The Center button on the Formatting toolbar centers text horizontally. You also can center text vertically between the top and bottom margins. To do this, click File on the menu bar, click Page Setup, click the Layout tab, click the Vertical alignment box arrow, click Center in the list, and then click the OK button.

Steps **To Select a Line**

1 **Move the mouse pointer to the left of the line to be selected (HIDDEN LAKE STATE PARK) until it changes to a right-pointing block arrow and then click.**

The entire line to the right of the mouse pointer is selected (Figure 1-46).

FIGURE 1-46

The next step is to change the font of the selected characters from Times New Roman to Arial Black and increase the font size of the selected characters from 22 to 26 point, as explained below.

TO FORMAT A LINE OF TEXT

1 While the text is selected, click the Font box arrow and then scroll to Arial Black, or a similar font, in the list. Click Arial Black, or a similar font.

2 While the text is selected, click the Font Size box arrow on the Formatting toolbar and then scroll to 26 in the list. Click 26.

The characters in the body title are 26-point Arial Black (Figure 1-47).

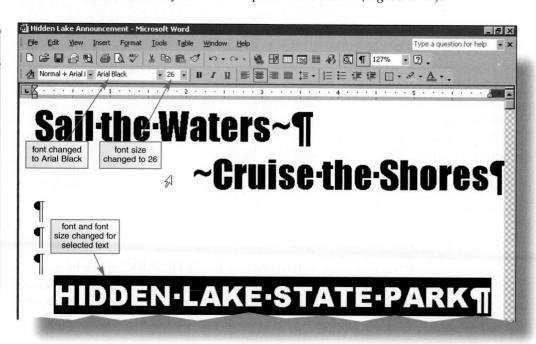

FIGURE 1-47

Italicize Selected Text

Italicized text has a slanted appearance. Perform the following step to italicize the selected characters in the body title.

 Steps **To Italicize Selected Text**

1 **With the text still selected, click the Italic button on the Formatting toolbar.**

Word italicizes the text (Figure 1-48). The Italic button on the Formatting toolbar is selected.

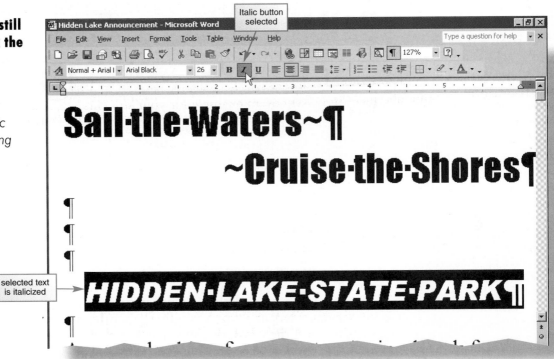

FIGURE 1-48

When the selected text is italicized, the Italic button on the Formatting toolbar is selected. If, for some reason, you wanted to remove the italics from the selected text, you would click the Italic button a second time, or you immediately could click the Undo button on the Standard toolbar.

Scrolling

The next text to format is in the lower portion of the announcement, which does not display in the document window. To continue formatting the document, perform the steps on the next page to scroll down one screen so the lower portion of the announcement displays in the document window.

Other Ways

1. On Format menu click Font, click Font tab, click Italic in Font style list, click OK button
2. Right-click selected text, click Font on shortcut menu, click Font tab, click Italic in Font style list, click OK button
3. Press CTRL+I
4. In Voice Command mode, say "Italic"

More About

Toolbar Buttons

Many of the buttons on the toolbars are toggles; that is, click them once to format the selected text and click them again to remove the format from the selected text.

Steps To Scroll through the Document

1 **Position the mouse pointer below the scroll box on the vertical scroll bar (Figure 1-49).**

2 **Click below the scroll box on the vertical scroll bar.**

Word scrolls down one screen in the document (shown in Figure 1-50 below). Depending on your monitor type, your screen may scroll differently.

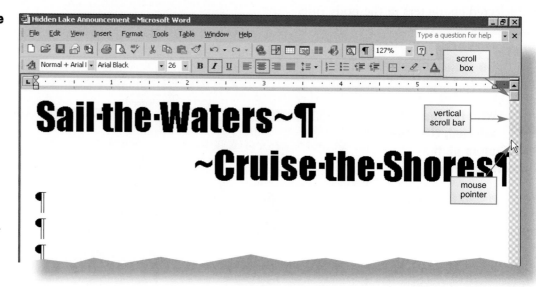

FIGURE 1-49

Other Ways

1. Press PAGE DOWN or PAGE UP
2. See Tables 1-1 and 1-2 on page WD 1.27
3. In Dictation mode, say key name(s) in Table 1-2

Selecting a Word

The next step is to underline a word in the first paragraph below the body title. To format characters in a word, you first select the entire word. Perform the following steps to select the word, the, so you can underline it.

Steps To Select a Word

1 **Position the mouse pointer somewhere in the word to be formatted (the, in this case).**

The mouse pointer's shape is an I-beam when you position it in unselected text in the document window (Figure 1-50).

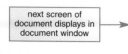

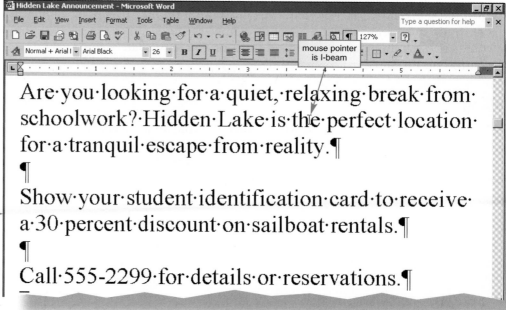

FIGURE 1-50

2 **Double-click the word to be selected.**

The word, the, is selected (Figure 1-51). Notice that when the mouse pointer is positioned in a selected word, its shape is a left-pointing block arrow.

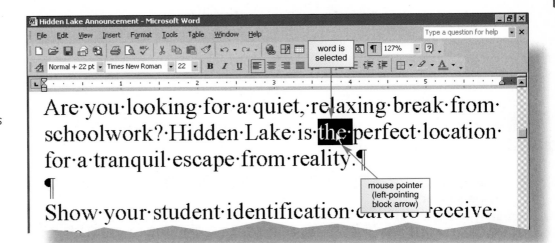

FIGURE 1-51

Other Ways

1. Drag through the word
2. With insertion point at beginning of desired word, press CTRL+SHIFT+RIGHT ARROW
3. With insertion point at beginning of desired word, in Voice Command mode, say "Select Word"

Underlining Selected Text

Underlined text prints with an underscore (_) below each character. Underlining is used to emphasize or draw attention to specific text. Perform the following step to underline the selected word.

Steps **To Underline Selected Text**

1 **With the text still selected, click the Underline button on the Formatting toolbar.**

Word underlines the text (Figure 1-52). The Underline button on the Formatting toolbar is selected.

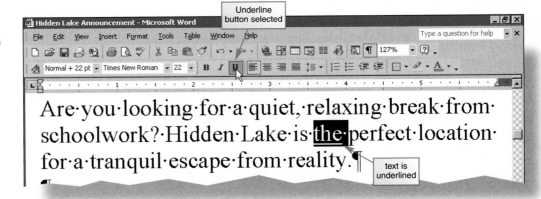

FIGURE 1-52

Other Ways

1. On Format menu click Font, click Font tab, click Underline style box arrow, click desired underline style, click OK button
2. Press CTRL+U
3. In Voice Command mode, say "Underline"

When the selected text is underlined, the Underline button on the Formatting toolbar is selected. If, for some reason, you wanted to remove the underline from the selected text, you would click the Underline button a second time, or you immediately could click the Undo button on the Standard toolbar.

In addition to the basic underline shown in Figure 1-52, Word has many decorative underlines that are available in the Font dialog box. For example, you can use double underlines, dotted underlines, and wavy underlines. In the Font dialog box, you also can change the color of an underline and instruct Word to underline only the words and not the spaces between the words. To display the Font dialog box, click Format on the menu bar and then click Font.

Microsoft **Word**

Selecting a Group of Words

The next step is to bold the words, 30 percent discount, in the announcement. To do this, you first must select this group of words. Perform the following steps to select a group of words.

Steps **To Select a Group of Words**

1 **Position the mouse pointer immediately to the left of the first character of the text to be selected.**

The mouse pointer, an I-beam, is to the left of the 3 in 30 (Figure 1-53).

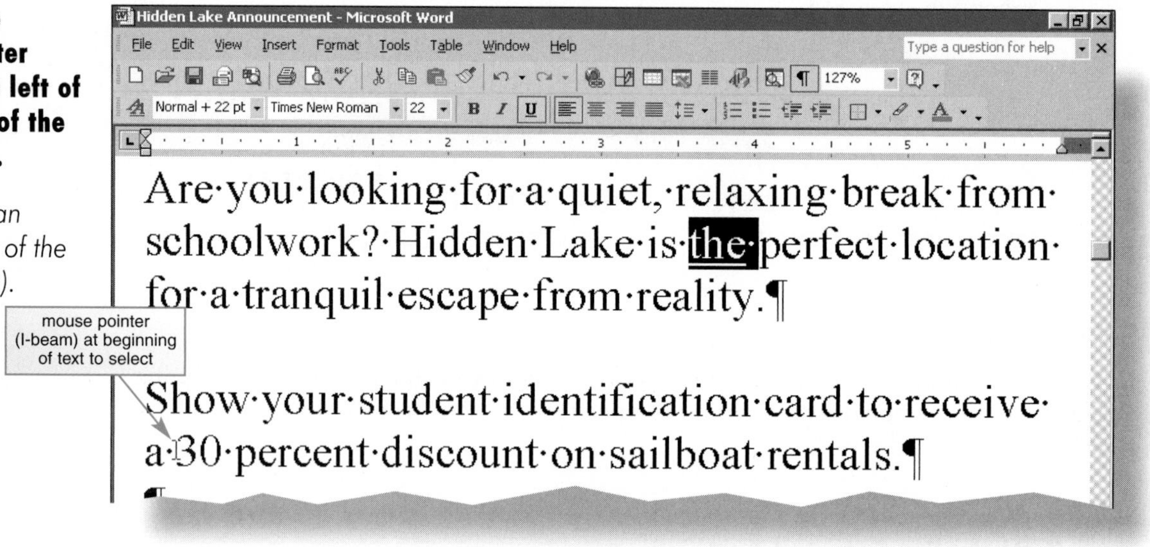

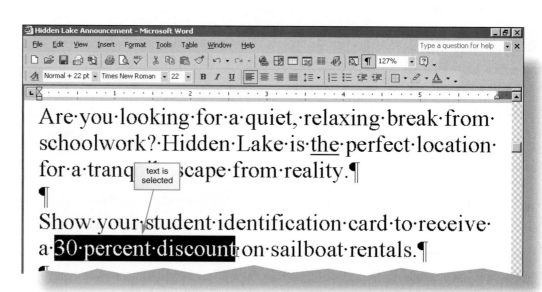

FIGURE 1-53

2 **Drag the mouse pointer through the last character of the text to be selected.**

Word selects the phrase, 30 percent discount (Figure 1-54).

FIGURE 1-54

Other Ways

1. With insertion point at beginning of first word in the group, press CTRL+SHIFT+RIGHT ARROW until words are selected

Bold Selected Text

Bold characters display somewhat thicker and darker than those that are not bold. Perform the following step to bold the phrase, 30 percent discount.

Steps **To Bold Selected Text**

1 **While the text is selected, click the Bold button on the Formatting toolbar. Click inside the selected text, which removes the selection (highlight) and positions the insertion point in the bold text.**

Word formats the selected text in bold and positions the insertion point inside the bold text (Figure 1-55). The Bold button is selected.

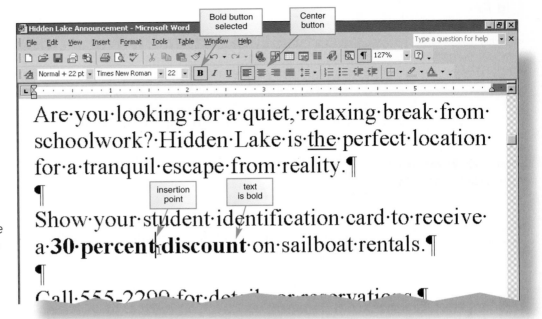

FIGURE 1-55

To remove a selection (highlight), click the mouse. If you click inside the selection, the Formatting toolbar displays the formatting characteristics of the characters and paragraphs containing the insertion point. For example, at the location of the insertion point, the characters are a 22-point Times New Roman bold font. The paragraph is left-aligned.

When the selected text is bold, the Bold button on the Formatting toolbar is selected. If, for some reason, you wanted to remove the bold format of the selected text, you would click the Bold button a second time.

The next step is to center the last line of the announcement, as described in the following steps.

Other **Ways**

1. On Format menu click Font, click Font tab, click Bold in Font style list, click OK button
2. Right-click selected text, click Font on shortcut menu, click Font tab, click Bold in Font style list, click OK button
3. Press CTRL+B
4. In Voice Command mode, say "Bold"

TO CENTER A PARAGRAPH

1 Click somewhere in the paragraph to be centered.

2 Click the Center button on the Formatting toolbar (shown in Figure 1-55).

Word centers the last line of the announcement (Figure 1-56).

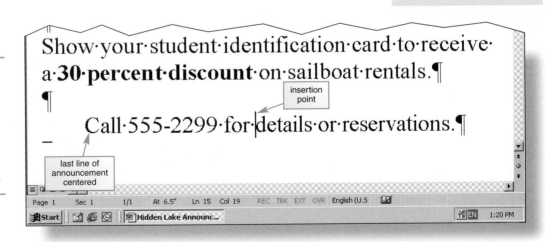

FIGURE 1-56

Microsoft Word

More About

Clip Art

If Word displays a dialog box when you issue the command to display clip art, click the Now button to catalog all media files. If you are not connected to the Web, Word displays clip art from your hard disk. If you are connected to the Web, Word displays clip art from your hard disk and also from Microsoft's Web site. When clip art images display in the Insert Clip Art task pane, Web clips are identified by a small globe displayed in their lower-left corner.

The formatting for the announcement now is complete. The next step is to insert a graphical image into the document and then resize the image.

Inserting Clip Art into a Word Document

Files containing graphical images, also called **graphics**, are available from a variety of sources. Word 2002 includes a series of predefined graphics called **clip art** that you can insert into a Word document. Clip art is located in the **Clip Organizer**, which contains a collection of clips, including clip art, as well as photographs, sounds, and video clips. The Clip Organizer contains its own Help system to assist you in locating clips suited to your application.

Inserting Clip Art

The next step in the project is to insert a clip art image into the announcement between the headline and the body title. Perform the following steps to use the Insert Clip Art task pane to insert clip art into the document.

Steps **To Insert Clip Art into a Document**

1 **To position the insertion point where you want the clip art to be located, press CTRL+HOME and then press the DOWN ARROW key three times. Click Insert on the menu bar.**

The insertion point is positioned on the second paragraph mark below the headline, and the Insert menu displays (Figure 1-57). Remember that a short menu initially displays, which expands into a full menu after a few seconds.

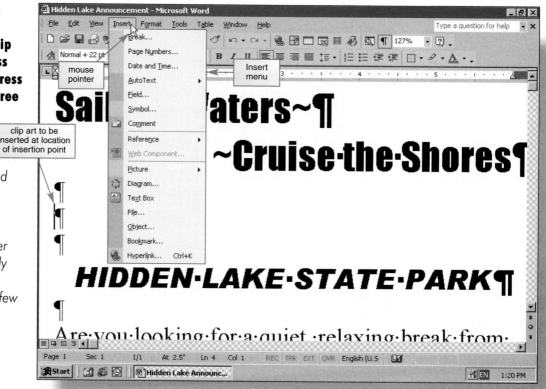

FIGURE 1-57

2 **Point to Picture and then point to Clip Art.** *2000* **If you are using Word 2000, click Insert on the menu bar, point to Picture, and then click Clip Art. When the Insert ClipArt dialog box displays, scroll down and click the Transportation category, scroll down and right-click the sailboat graphic, and then click Insert on the pop-up menu. Close the Insert Clip Art dialog box and then skip to the bottom of page WD 1.49 to center a paragraph containing a graphic and then resize a graphic.**

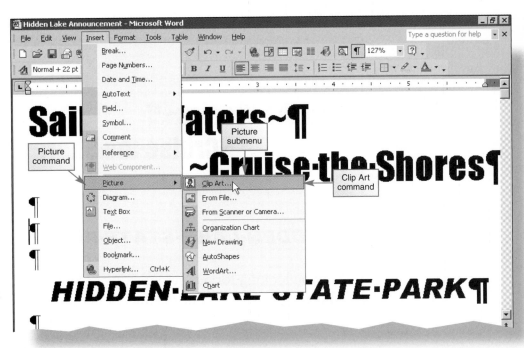

FIGURE 1-58

The Picture submenu displays (Figure 1-58). As discussed earlier, when you point to a command that has a small arrow to its right, Word displays a submenu associated with that command. The graphic may display larger than the sailboat shown in Figure 1-62 on page WD 1.49.

3 **Click Clip Art. If the Search text text box contains text, drag through the text to select it. Type** sailboat **and then point to the Search button.**

Word displays the Insert Clip Art task pane at the right edge of the Word window (Figure 1-59). Recall that a task pane is a separate window that enables you to carry out some Word tasks more efficiently. When you enter a description of the desired graphic in the Search text text box, Word searches the Clip Organizer for clips that match the description.

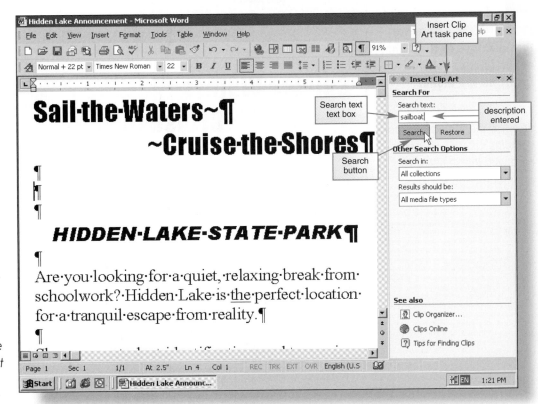

FIGURE 1-59

Microsoft **Word**

4 **Click the Search button.**

A list of clips that match the description, sailboat, displays (Figure 1-60). If you are connected to the Web, the Insert Clip Art task pane will display clips from the Web, as well as those installed on your hard disk.

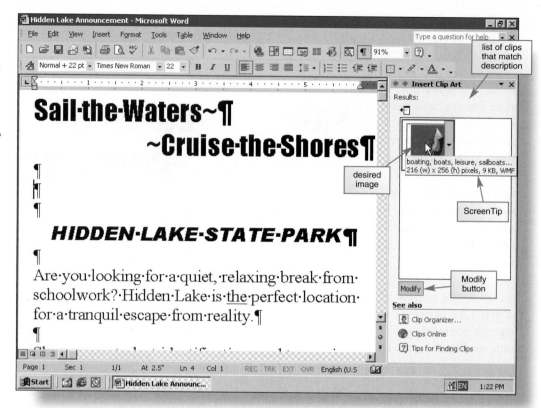

FIGURE 1-60

5 **Point to the desired image and then click the box arrow that displays to the right of the image. Point to Insert on the menu.**

When you click the box arrow, a menu displays that contains commands associated with the selected clip art image (Figure 1-61).

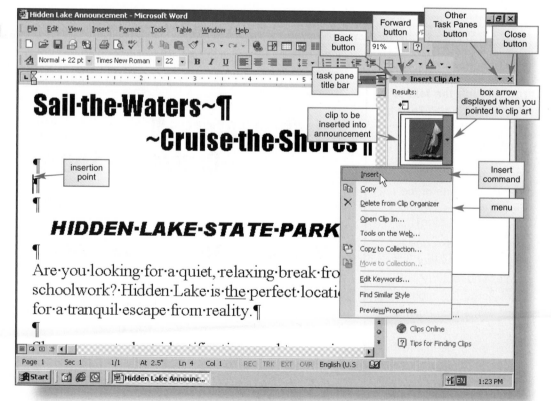

FIGURE 1-61

6 **Click Insert. Click the Close button on the Insert Clip Art task pane title bar.**

Word inserts the clip art into the document at the location of the insertion point (Figure 1-62). The image of the sailboat displays below the headline in the announcement.

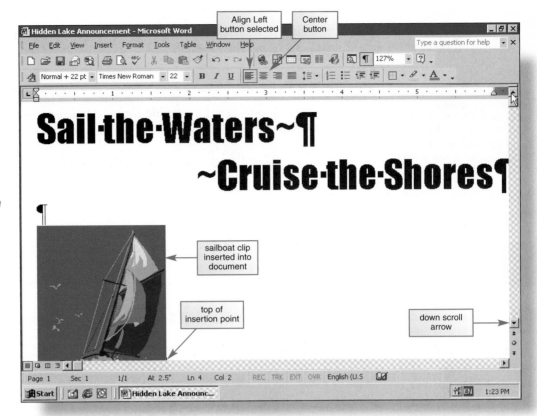

FIGURE 1-62

After you enter a description of a desired image in the Search text text box, you may want to enter a different description to locate additional or different clip art. To redisplay the Search text text box in the Insert Clip Art task pane, click the Modify button in the task pane (Figure 1-60). This will redisplay the screen shown in Figure 1-59 on page WD 1.47.

Recall that Word has eight task panes that automatically display as you perform certain operations. You also can display a task pane by clicking View on the menu bar and then clicking Task Pane. When you do this, the task pane you most recently used displays in the Word window. To display a different task pane, click the Other Task Panes button (Figure 1-61) to the left of the Close button on the task pane title bar. If you have displayed multiple task panes during a Word session, you can click the Back and Forward buttons at the left edge of the task pane title bar to scroll through the various task panes.

The clip art in the announcement is part of a paragraph. Because that paragraph is left-aligned, the clip art also is left-aligned. Notice the Align Left button on the Formatting toolbar is selected (Figure 1-62). You can use any of the paragraph alignment buttons on the Formatting toolbar to reposition the clip art. Perform the following step to center a graphic that is part of a paragraph.

TO CENTER A PARAGRAPH CONTAINING A GRAPHIC

1 If necessary, click the down scroll arrow on the scroll bar to display the entire graphic in the document window. With the insertion point on the paragraph mark containing the image, click the Center button on the Formatting toolbar.

Word centers the paragraph, which also centers the graphic in the paragraph (Figure 1-63 on the next page).

Other Ways

1. In Voice Command mode, say "Insert, Picture, Clip Art"

More About

Positioning Graphics

Emphasize a graphic by placing it at the optical center of the page. To determine optical center, divide the page in half horizontally and vertically. The optical center is located one third of the way up the vertical line from the point of intersection of the two lines.

Microsoft **Word**

More About

Graphics

If you have a scanner or digital camera attached to your computer, Word can insert a graphic directly from these devices. You also can scan a graphic into a file and then insert the scanned file into the Word document.

You would like the clip art in this announcement to be a little larger. Thus, the next step is to resize the graphic.

Resizing a Graphic

Once you have inserted a graphic into a document, you easily can change its size. **Resizing** includes both enlarging and reducing the size of a graphic. To resize a graphic, you first must select it.

Perform the following step to select a graphic.

Steps To Select a Graphic

1 **Click anywhere in the graphic. If your screen does not display the Picture toolbar, click View on the menu bar, point to Toolbars, and then click Picture.**

Word selects the graphic (Figure 1-63). A selected graphic displays surrounded by a selection rectangle that has small squares, called sizing handles, at each corner and middle location. You use the sizing handles to change the size of the graphic. When a graphic is selected, the Picture toolbar automatically displays on the screen.

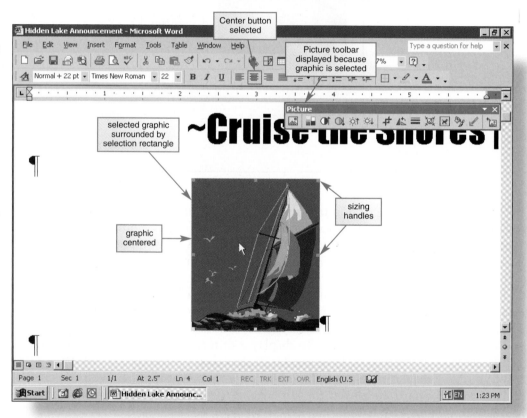

FIGURE 1-63

More About

The Picture Toolbar

The Picture toolbar is a floating toolbar. Thus, you can drag its title bar to move the toolbar to a different location on the screen. You also can double-click the toolbar's title bar to dock the toolbar at the top of the screen.

The following steps show how to resize the graphic you just inserted and selected.

To Resize a Graphic

1 **With the graphic still selected, point to the upper-left corner sizing handle.**

The mouse pointer shape changes to a two-headed arrow when it is on a sizing handle (Figure 1-64). To resize a graphic, you drag the sizing handle(s) until the graphic is the desired size.

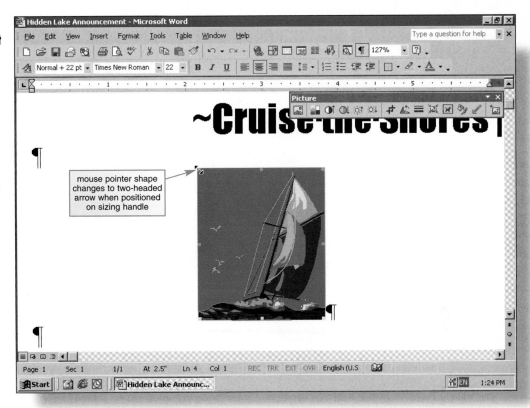

FIGURE 1-64

2 **Drag the sizing handle diagonally outward until the dotted selection rectangle is positioned approximately as shown in Figure 1-65.**

The graphic has a rectangular shape. When you drag a corner sizing handle, this shape remains intact. In this announcement, the graphic is to have a square shape. **2000** *If the graphic displays larger than the one shown, drag the sizing handle diagonally downward until the graphic is reduced to the approximate size shown.*

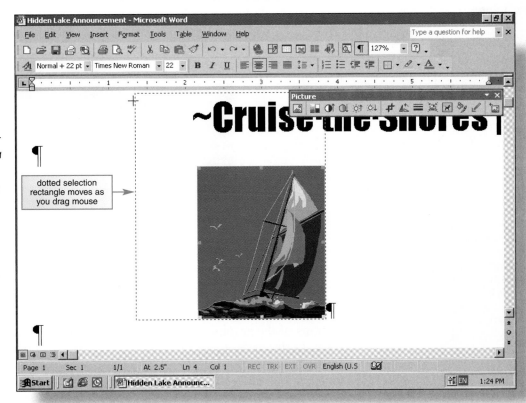

FIGURE 1-65

3 Release the mouse button. Point to the right-middle sizing handle on the graphic (Figure 1-66).

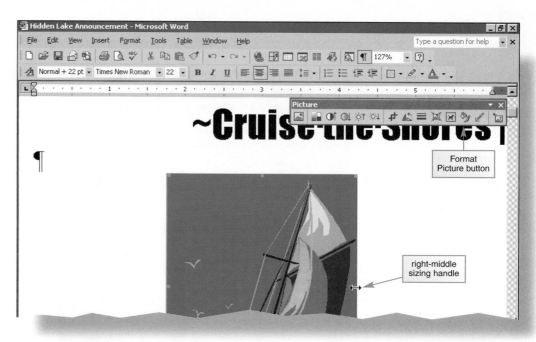

FIGURE 1-66

4 Drag the sizing handle to the right until the dotted selection rectangle is about the size of a square. Release the mouse button. Press CTRL+HOME.

Word resizes the graphic (Figure 1-67). When you click outside of a graphic or press a key to scroll through a document, Word deselects the graphic. The Picture toolbar disappears from the screen when you deselect the graphic.

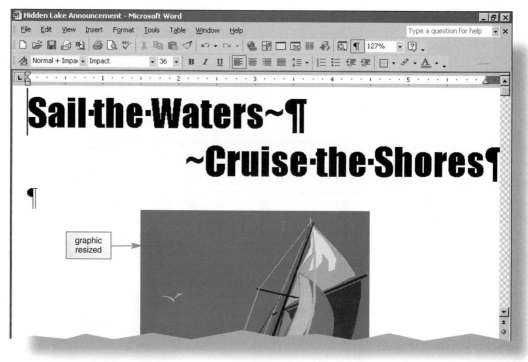

FIGURE 1-67

When you drag a middle sizing handle instead of a corner sizing handle, the proportions of the graphic change, which sometimes causes the graphic to look distorted. In this case, it gives the sail on the sailboat a windblown effect.

Instead of resizing a selected graphic by dragging with the mouse, you also can use the Format Picture dialog box to resize a graphic by clicking the Format Picture button (Figure 1-66) on the Picture toolbar and then clicking the Size tab. Using the

Size sheet, you can enter exact height and width measurements. If you have a precise measurement for a graphic, use the Format Picture dialog box; otherwise, drag the sizing handles to resize a graphic.

Sometimes, you might resize a graphic and realize it is the wrong size. In these cases, you may want to return the graphic to its original size and start again. You could drag the sizing handle until the graphic resembles its original size. To restore a resized graphic to its exact original size, click the graphic to select it and then click the Format Picture button on the Picture toolbar to display the Format Picture dialog box. Click the Size tab and then click the Reset button. Finally, click the OK button.

More About

Resizing Graphics

To maintain the proportions of a graphic, press the SHIFT key while you drag a corner sizing handle.

Saving an Existing Document with the Same File Name

The announcement for Project 1 now is complete. To transfer the modified document with the formatting changes and graphic to your floppy disk in drive A, you must save the document again. When you saved the document the first time, you assigned a file name to it (Hidden Lake Announcement). If you use the following procedure, Word automatically assigns the same file name to the document each time you subsequently save it.

Steps **To Save an Existing Document with the Same File Name**

1 **Click the Save button on the Standard toolbar.**

Word saves the document on a floppy disk inserted in drive A using the currently assigned file name, Hidden Lake Announcement (Figure 1-68).

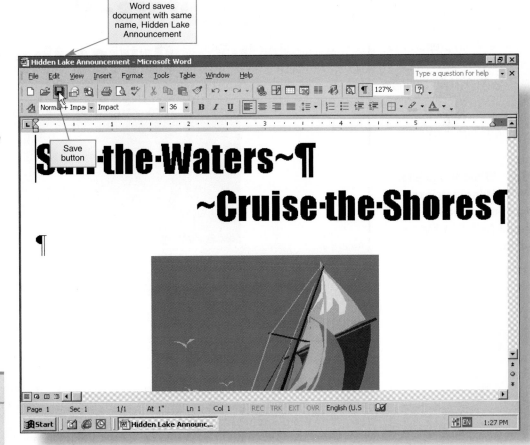

Word saves document with same name, Hidden Lake Announcement

Save button

FIGURE 1-68

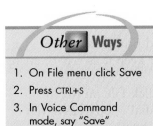

Microsoft **Word**

Printing

If you want to save ink, print faster, or decease printer overrun errors, print a draft. Click File on the menu bar and then click Print. Click the Options button, place a check mark in the Draft output check box, and then click the OK button in each dialog box.

While Word is saving the document, the Background Save icon displays near the right edge of the status bar. When the save is complete, the document remains in memory and on the screen.

If, for some reason, you want to save an existing document with a different file name, click Save As on the File menu to display the Save As dialog box. Then, fill in the Save As dialog box as discussed in Steps 2 through 5 on pages WD 1.30 through WD 1.32.

Printing a Document

The next step is to print the document you created. A printed version of the document is called a **hard copy** or **printout**. Perform the following steps to print the announcement created in Project 1.

 To Print a Document

1 **Ready the printer according to the printer instructions. Click the Print button on the Standard toolbar.**

The mouse pointer briefly changes to an hourglass shape as Word prepares to print the document. While the document is printing, a printer icon displays in the tray status area on the taskbar (Figure 1-69).

2 **When the printer stops, retrieve the printout, which should look like Figure 1-1 on page WD 1.07.**

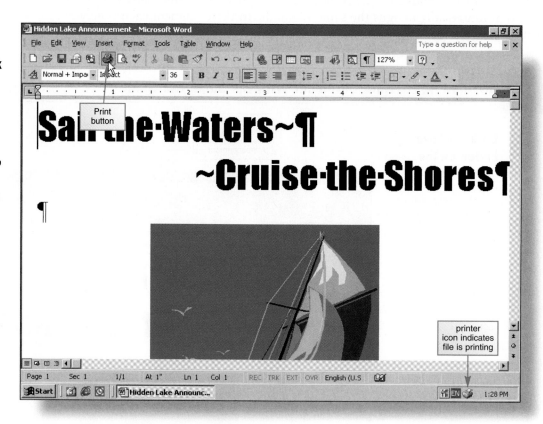

FIGURE 1-69

When you use the Print button to print a document, Word prints the entire document automatically. You then may distribute the hard copy or keep it as a permanent record of the document.

If you wanted to print multiple copies of the document, click File on the menu bar and then click Print to display the Print dialog box. This dialog box has several printing options, including specifying the number of copies to print.

If you wanted to cancel your job that is printing or one you have waiting to be printed, double-click the printer icon on the taskbar (Figure 1-69). In the printer window, click the job to be canceled and then click Cancel on the Document menu.

Quitting Word

After you create, save, and print the announcement, Project 1 is complete. To quit Word and return control to Windows, perform the following steps.

 To Quit Word

1 **Point to the Close button in the upper-right corner of the title bar (Figure 1-70).**

2 **Click the Close button.**

The Word window closes.

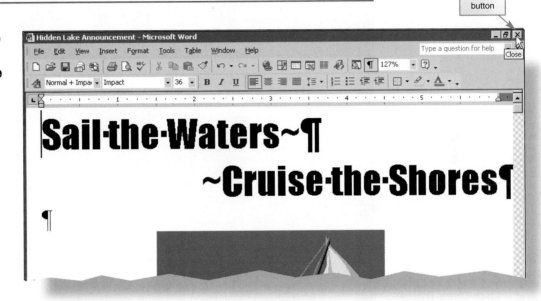

FIGURE 1-70

When you quit Word, a dialog box may display that asks if you want to save the changes. This occurs if you made changes to the document since the last save. Clicking the Yes button in the dialog box saves the changes; clicking the No button ignores the changes; and clicking the Cancel button returns to the document. If you did not make any changes since you saved the document, this dialog box usually does not display.

Opening a Document

Once you have created and saved a document, you often will have reason to retrieve it from disk. For example, you might want to revise the document or print it again. Earlier, you saved the Word document created in Project 1 on a floppy disk using the file name Hidden Lake Announcement.

The steps on the next page illustrate how to open the file Hidden Lake Announcement from a floppy disk in drive A.

Steps To Open a Document

1 **Click the Start button on the taskbar and then point to Open Office Document (Figure 1-71).**

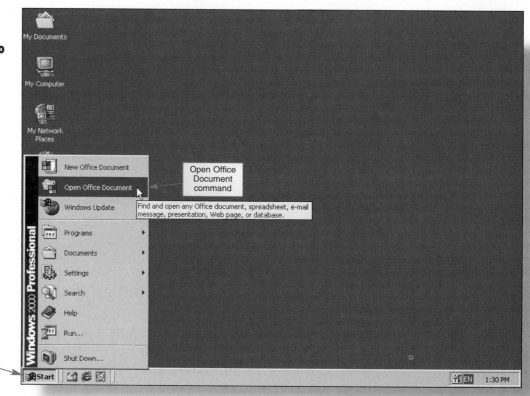

FIGURE 1-71

2 **Click Open Office Document. If necessary, click the Look in box arrow and then click 3½ Floppy (A:). If it is not selected already, click the file name Hidden Lake Announcement. Point to the Open button.**

Office displays the Open Office Document dialog box (Figure 1-72). The names of files on the floppy disk in drive A display in the dialog box.

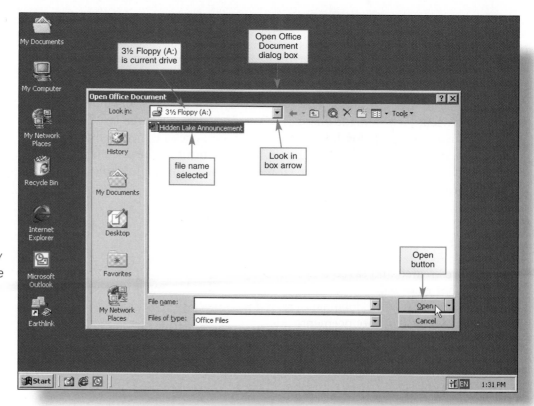

FIGURE 1-72

3 **Click the Open button.**

Office starts Word, and then Word opens the document, Hidden Lake Announcement, from the floppy disk in drive A. The document displays in the Word document window (Figure 1-73).

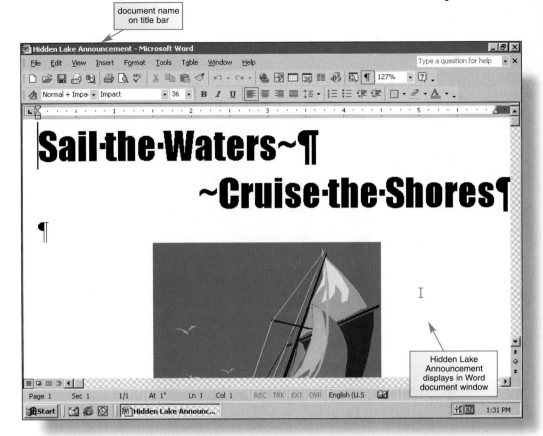

document name on title bar

Hidden Lake Announcement displays in Word document window

FIGURE 1-73

Correcting Errors

After creating a document, you often will find you must make changes to it. Changes can be required because the document contains an error or because of new circumstances.

Types of Changes Made to Documents

The types of changes made to documents normally fall into one of the three following categories: additions, deletions, or modifications.

ADDITIONS Additional words, sentences, or paragraphs may be required in a document. Additions occur when you omit text from a document and want to insert it later. For example, you may want to insert the word, all, in front of sailboat rentals in the Hidden Lake Announcement.

DELETIONS Sometimes, text in a document is incorrect or is no longer needed. For example, the state park may stop taking reservations. In this case, you would delete the words, or reservations, from the last line of the announcement.

MODIFICATIONS If an error is made in a document or changes take place that affect the document, you might have to revise the word(s) in the text. For example, the state park might change the discount from 30 to 35 percent; thus, you would change the number from 30 to 35.

Other Ways

1. Right-click Start button, click Open All Users, double-click Open Office Document, select file name, click Open button in dialog box
2. Click Open button on Standard toolbar, select file name, click Open button in dialog box
3. On File menu click Open, select file name, click Open button in dialog box
4. In Voice Command mode, say "Open, [select file name], Open"

More *About*

Overtype

As you type, if existing text is overwritten with new text, you probably are in overtype mode. Double-click the OVR status indicator to turn overtype mode off. You also can press the INSERT key on the keyboard to turn off overtype mode.

Word provides several methods for correcting errors in a document. For each of the error correction techniques, you first must move the insertion point to the error.

Inserting Text into an Existing Document

Word inserts text to the left of the insertion point. The text to the right of the insertion point moves to the right and downward to fit the new text.

TO INSERT TEXT INTO AN EXISTING DOCUMENT

1 Click to the left of the location of text to be inserted.

2 Type the new text.

In Word, the default typing mode is insert mode. In **insert mode**, as you type a character, Word inserts the character and moves all the characters to the right of the typed character one position to the right. You can change to overtype mode by double-clicking the **OVR status indicator** on the status bar (Figure 1-8 on page WD 1.11). In **overtype mode**, Word replaces characters to the right of the insertion point. Double-clicking the OVR status indicator again returns you to insert mode.

Deleting Text from an Existing Document

It is not unusual to type incorrect characters or words in a document. As discussed earlier in this project, you can click the Undo button on the Standard toolbar to immediately undo a command or action — this includes typing. Word also provides other methods of correcting typing errors.

TO DELETE AN INCORRECT CHARACTER IN A DOCUMENT

1 Click next to the incorrect character.

2 Press the BACKSPACE key to erase to the left of the insertion point; or press the DELETE key to erase to the right of the insertion point.

TO DELETE (CUT) AN INCORRECT WORD OR PHRASE IN A DOCUMENT

1 Select the word or phrase you want to erase.

2 Right-click the selected word or phrase, and then click Cut on the shortcut menu; or click the Cut button on the Standard toolbar (Figure 1-12a on page WD 1.15); or press the DELETE key.

Closing the Entire Document

Sometimes, everything goes wrong. If this happens, you may want to close the document entirely and start over. You also may want to close a document when you are finished with it so you can begin your next document.

TO CLOSE THE ENTIRE DOCUMENT AND START OVER

1 Click File on the menu bar and then click Close. If Word displays a dialog box, click the No button to ignore the changes since the last time you saved the document.

2 Click the New Blank Document button (Figure 1-12a on page WD 1.15) on the Standard toolbar.

More *About*

The Clipboard Task Pane

If you click the Cut button (or Copy button) twice in a row, Word displays the Clipboard task pane. You use the Clipboard task pane to copy and paste items within a document or from one Office document to another. To close the Clipboard task pane, click the Close button on the task pane title bar.

You also can close the document by clicking the Close button at the right edge of the menu bar.

Word Help System

More About

The Word 2002 Help System

The best way to become familiar with the Word Help system is to use it. Appendix A includes detailed information on the Word 2002 Help system as well as exercises that will help you gain confidence in using it.

At anytime while you are using Word, you can get answers to questions by using the **Word Help system**. Used properly, this form of online assistance can increase your productivity and reduce your frustrations by minimizing the time you spend learning how to use Word.

The following section shows how to obtain answers to your questions using the Ask a Question box. For additional information on using help, see Appendix A and Table 1-3 on page WD 1.61.

Obtaining Help Using the Ask a Question Box on the Menu Bar

The **Ask a Question box** on the right side of the menu bar lets you type free-form questions, such as *how do I save* or *how do I create a Web page*, or you can type terms, such as *copy, save,* or *format*. Word responds by displaying a list of topics related to the word or phrase you entered. The following steps show how to use the Ask a Question box to obtain information on handwriting recognition.

Steps **To Obtain Help Using the Ask a Question Box**

1 **Click the Ask a Question box on the right side of the menu bar and then type** handwriting recognition **(Figure 1-74).**

2000 *If you are using Word 2000, click the Microsoft Word Help button on the right side of the Standard toolbar. Type your question or short phrase in the What would you like to do? text box and then click the Search button.*

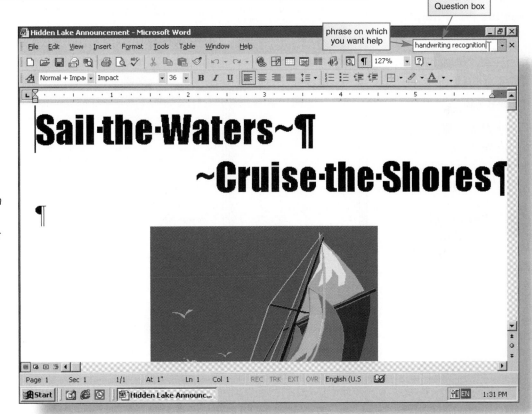

FIGURE 1-74

2 **Press the ENTER key. When the list of topics displays below the Ask a Question box, point to the topic, About handwriting recognition.**

A list of topics displays relating to the phrase, handwriting recognition. The shape of the mouse pointer changes to a hand, which indicates it is pointing to a link (Figure 1-75).

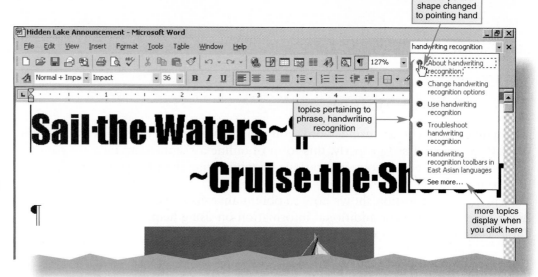

FIGURE 1-75

3 **Click About handwriting recognition. When the Word Help window opens, double-click its title bar to maximize it. If necessary, click the Contents tab.**

A Word Help window opens and provides Help information about handwriting recognition (Figure 1-76).

4 **Click the Close button on the Word Help window title bar.**

The Word Help window closes and the Word document window again is active.

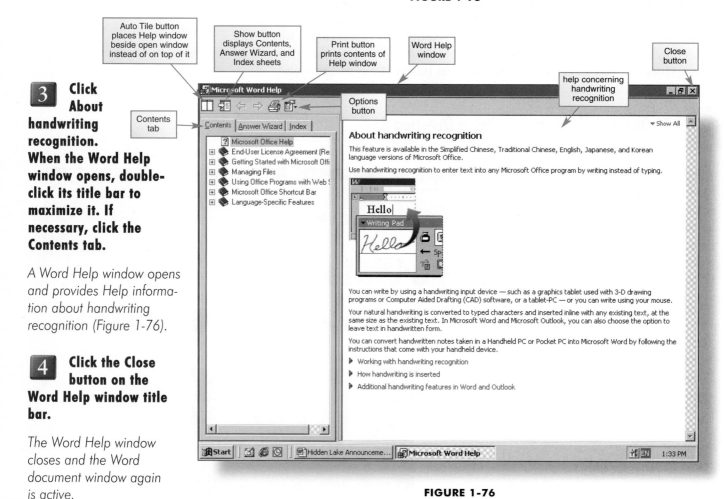

FIGURE 1-76

Use the buttons in the upper-left corner of the Word Help window (Figure 1-76) to navigate through the Help system, change the display, or print the contents of the window.

You can use the Ask a Question box to search for Help on any topic concerning Word. As you enter questions and terms in the Ask a Question box, Word adds them to the Ask a Question list. Thus, if you click the Ask a Question box arrow, a list of previously asked questions and terms will display.

Table 1-3 summarizes the eleven categories of help available to you. This table assumes the Office Assistant is off. See Appendix A for more information.

Table 1-3	Word Help System	
TYPE	*DESCRIPTION*	*HOW TO ACTIVATE*
Answer Wizard	Answers questions or searches for terms that you type in your own words.	Click the Microsoft Word Help button on the Standard toolbar. Click the Answer Wizard tab.
Ask a Question box	Answers questions or searches for terms that you type in your own words.	Type a question or term in the Ask a Question box on the menu bar and then press the ENTER key.
Contents sheet	Groups Help topics by general categories. Use when you know only the general category of the topic in question. Similar to a table of contents in a book.	Click the Microsoft Word Help button on the Standard toolbar. Click the Contents tab.
Detect and Repair	Automatically finds and fixes errors in the application.	Click Detect and Repair on the Help menu.
Hardware and Software Information	Shows product ID and allows access to system information and technical support information.	Click About Microsoft Word on the Help menu and then click the appropriate button.
Index sheet	Similar to an index in a book. Use when you know exactly what you want.	Click the Microsoft Word Help button on the Standard toolbar. Click the Index tab.
Office Assistant	Similar to the Ask a Question box in that the Office Assistant answers questions that you type in your own words, offers tips, and provides help for a variety of Word features.	Click the Office Assistant icon. If the Office Assistant does not display, click Show the Office Assistant on the Help menu.
Office on the Web	Provides access to technical resources on the Web and allows you to download free product enhancements from the Web.	Click Office on the Web on the Help menu.
Question Mark button	Identifies unfamiliar items in a dialog box.	Click the Question Mark button on the title bar of a dialog box and then click an item in the dialog box.
What's This? command	Identifies unfamiliar items on the screen.	Click What's This? on the Help menu, and then click an item on the screen.
WordPerfect Help	Assists WordPerfect users who are learning Microsoft Word.	Click WordPerfect Help on the Help menu.

The final step in this project is to quit Word.

TO QUIT WORD

1 Click the Close button in the Word window.

The Word window closes.

C A S E   P E R S P E C T I V E   S U M M A R Y

Tara is thrilled with the completed announcement. The characters in the headline and body title are large enough so students can read them from a distance, and the image of the sailboat is quite eye-catching. She takes the announcement to the school's Promotions Department and receives approval to post it in several locations around campus, mail it to each student's home, print it in the school newspaper, and publish it on the Web. As a member of the SGA, you assist Tara with these activities.

Project Summary

Project 1 introduced you to starting Word and creating a document. Before entering any text in the document, you learned how to change the font size. You also learned how to save and print a document. You used Word's check spelling as you type feature. Once you saved the document, you learned how to format its paragraphs and characters. Then, you inserted and resized a clip art image. You learned how to insert, delete, and modify text. Finally, you learned one way to use the Word Help system.

What You Should Know

Having completed this project, you now should be able to perform the following tasks:

- Bold Selected Text *(WD 1.45)*
- Center a Paragraph *(WD 1.38, WD 1.45)*
- Center a Paragraph Containing a Graphic *(WD 1.49)*
- Change the Font of Selected Text *(WD 1.36)*
- Change the Font Size of Selected Text *(WD 1.35)*
- Check Spelling as You Type *(WD 1.28)*
- Close the Entire Document and Start Over *(WD 1.58)*
- Customize the Word Window *(WD 1.09)*
- Delete an Incorrect Character in a Document *(WD 1.58)*
- Delete (Cut) an Incorrect Word or Phrase in a Document *(WD 1.58)*
- Display Formatting Marks *(WD 1.24)*
- Display the Toolbars on Two Rows When Using Word 2000 *(WD 1.09)*
- Enter Blank Lines into a Document *(WD 1.23)*
- Enter More Text *(WD 1.24)*
- Enter Text *(WD 1.21)*
- Enter Text that Scrolls the Document Window *(WD 1.26)*
- Format a Line of Text *(WD 1.40)*
- Increase the Default Font Size Before Typing *(WD 1.20)*
- Insert Clip Art into a Document *(WD 1.46)*
- Insert Text into an Existing Document *(WD 1.58)*
- Italicize Selected Text *(WD 1.41)*
- Obtain Help Using the Ask a Question Box *(WD 1.59)*
- Open a Document *(WD 1.56)*
- Print a Document *(WD 1.54)*
- Quit Word *(WD 1.55, WD 1.61)*
- Resize a Graphic *(WD 1.51)*
- Right-Align a Paragraph *(WD 1.37)*
- Save a New Document *(WD 1.30)*
- Save an Existing Document with the Same File Name *(WD 1.53)*
- Scroll through the Document *(WD 1.42)*
- Select a Graphic *(WD 1.50)*
- Select a Group of Words *(WD 1.44)*
- Select a Line *(WD 1.40)*
- Select a Word *(WD 1.42)*
- Select Multiple Paragraphs *(WD 1.34)*
- Start Word *(WD 1.08)*
- Underline Selected Text *(WD 1.43)*
- Undo an Action *(WD 1.39)*
- Wordwrap Text as You Type *(WD 1.25)*
- Zoom Page Width *(WD 1.19)*

More *About*

Microsoft Certification

The Microsoft Office User Specialist (MOUS) Certification program provides an opportunity for you to obtain a valuable industry credential — proof that you have the Word skills required by employers. For more information, see Appendix E or visit the Shelly Cashman Series MOUS Web page at scsite.com/tdoff/cert.

In the Lab

Instructions: To complete the Learn It Online exercises, start your browser, click the Address bar, and then enter scsite.com/tdoff/exs. When the Teachers Discovering Office Learn It Online page displays, follow the instructions in the exercises below. To complete the Using the Office Training CD exercises, insert the Microsoft Office Training CD in your CD drive and access the appropriate section. Refer to the introduction chapter of this book to review step-by-step instructions for both installing and using the Microsoft Office Training CD.

Learn It online

1 Project Reinforcement – TF, MC, and SA

Below Word Project 1, click the Project Reinforcement link. Print the quiz by clicking Print on the File menu. Answer each question. Write your first and last name at the top of each page, and then hand in the printout to your instructor.

2 Flash Cards

Below Word Project 1, click the Flash Cards link. When Flash Cards displays, read the instructions. Type 20 (or a number specified by your instructor) in the Number of Playing Cards text box, type your name in the Name text box, and then click the Flip Card button. When the flash card displays, read the question and then click the Answer box arrow to select an answer. Flip through Flash Cards. Click Print on the File menu to print the last flash card if your score is 15 (75%) correct or greater and then hand it in to your instructor. If your score is less than 15 (75%) correct, then redo this exercise by clicking the Replay button.

3 Practice Test

Below Word Project 1, click the Practice Test link. Answer each question, enter your first and last name at the bottom of the page, and then click the Grade Test button. When the graded practice test displays on your screen, click Print on the File menu to print a hard copy. Continue to take practice tests until you score 80% or better. Hand in a printout of the final practice test to your instructor.

4 Who Wants to Be a Computer Genius?

Below Word Project 1, click the Computer Genius link. Read the instructions, enter your first and last name at the bottom of the page, and then click the Play button. Hand in your score to your instructor.

5 Wheel of Terms

Below Word Project 1, click the Wheel of Terms link. Read the instructions, and then enter your first and last name and your school name. Click the Play button. Hand in your score to your instructor.

6 Crossword Puzzle Challenge

Below Word Project 1, click the Crossword Puzzle Challenge link. Read the instructions, and then enter your first and last name. Click the Play button. Work the crossword puzzle. When you are finished, click the Submit button. When the crossword puzzle redisplays, click the Print button. Hand in the printout.

Using the Microsoft Office Training CD

1 In and Out of the Classroom

With the Microsoft Office Training CD in your CD drive, click the In and Out of the Classroom tab. Review one of the Word tutorials that will help you learn how to use and integrate Microsoft Word in your classroom. The Word tutorials are available in the Office XP, Office 2000, or Office 2001 for the Mac links.

2 Tips and Tricks

With the Microsoft Office Training CD in your CD drive, click the Tips and Tricks tab. Review one of the Word tips and tricks that includes creating stationary, inserting comments into a collaborative story, using tables, and more.

3 Tutorial Packs

With the Microsoft Office Training CD in your CD drive, click the Tutorial Packs tab. Review one of the step-by-step tutorials on using Microsoft Word to enhance your teaching and learning process.

*Productivity
in the Classroom*

1 Creating an Announcement with Clip Art

Problem: You are the sponsor of the garden club at your school. As a year-end culminating activity, the club will go on a field trip to Cypress Gardens. You prepare the announcement shown in Figure 1-77. *Hint*: Remember, if you make a mistake while formatting the announcement, you can click the Undo button on the Standard toolbar to undo your last action.

Instructions:

1. Start Microsoft Word. When the empty document titled Document 1 displays in the Word window, change the font size from 12 to 20 by clicking the Font Size box arrow on the Formatting toolbar and then clicking 20.

2. If necessary, click the Show/Hide ¶ button on the Standard toolbar to display formatting marks.

3. Create the announcement shown in Figure 1-77. Enter the document first without clip art and unformatted; that is, without any bold, underlined, italicized, right-aligned, or centered text. If Word flags any misspelled words as you type, check the spelling of these words and correct them.

4. Save the document on a floppy disk with Garden Club Announcement as the file name.

5. Select the two lines of the headline. Change their font to Albertus Extra Bold, or a similar font. Change their font size from 20 to 36.

6. Click somewhere in the second line of the headline and right-align the headline.

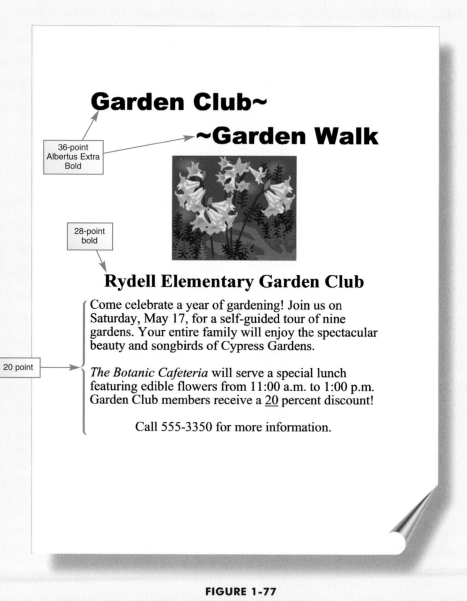

FIGURE 1-77

7. Click somewhere in the body title line and center the body title.
8. Select the body title line. Increase its font size from 20 to 28 and bold the body title.
9. In the second paragraph of the body copy, select the restaurant name: The Botanic Cafeteria. Italicize the name.

Productivity in the Classroom

10. In the same paragraph, select the number 20 and underline the number.
11. Click somewhere in the last line of the announcement and center the last line.
12. Insert the graphic from the Microsoft Classroom Tools CD located in the Nature folder, or any appropriate graphic, between the headline and the body title line.
13. Center the selected graphic by centering the paragraph and then if necessary, resize.
14. Save the announcement again with the same file name.
15. Print the announcement.

2 Creating an Announcement with Resized Clip Art

Problem: You want your students to apply their math skills to every day situations. There- fore, in cooperation with the social studies teacher, students research a location and plan a trip within budget constraints. They select one place of interest and create an announcement. You prepare the announcement shown in Figure 1-78 as an example. *Hint:* Remember, if you make a mistake while formatting the announcement, you can click the Undo button on the Standard toolbar to undo your last action.

Instructions:

1. Start Microsoft Word. When the empty document titled Document 1 displays in the Word window, change the font size from 12 to 22 by clicking the Font Size box arrow on the Formatting toolbar and then clicking 22.
2. If it is not already selected, click the Show/Hide ¶ button on the Standard toolbar to display formatting marks.

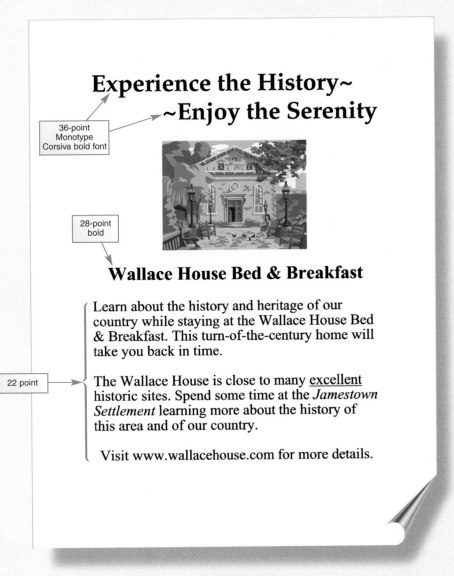

FIGURE 1-78

(continued)

*Productivity
in the Classroom*

Creating an Announcement with Resized Clip Art (*continued*)

3. Create the announcement shown in Figure 1-78 on the previous page. Enter the document first without the clip art and unformatted; that is, without any bold, underlined, italicized, right-aligned, or centered text. If Word flags any misspelled words as you type, check the spelling of these words and correct them.

4. Save the document on a floppy disk with Wallace House Announcement as the file name.

5. Select the two lines of the headline. Change the font to Monotype Corsiva, or a similar font. Change the font size from 22 to 36. Bold both lines.

6. Click somewhere in the second line of the headline and right-align the headline.

7. Click somewhere in the body title line and center the body title.

8. Select the body title line. Increase its font size from 22 to 28 and bold the body title.

9. Select the word, excellent, in the second paragraph of the body copy and underline the word.

10. In the same paragraph, select the words, Jamestown Settlement. Italicize the words.

11. Click somewhere in the last line of the announcement and center the line.

12. Insert the graphic from the Microsoft Classroom Tools CD located in the Buildings folder, or any appropriate graphic, between the headline and the body title line.

13. Enlarge the graphic. If you make the graphic too large, the announcement may flow onto two pages. If this occurs, reduce the size of the graphic so the announcement fits on a single page. *Hint:* Use Help to learn about print preview, which is a way to see the page before you print it. To exit print preview and return to the document window, click the Close button on the Print Preview toolbar.

14. Save the announcement again with the same file name.

15. Print the announcement.

3 Creating an Announcement with Resized Clip Art and a Bulleted List

Problem: You are planning a field trip to the Hannah Village Zoo. To inform parents and recruit chaperones you prepare the announcement shown in Figure 1-79. *Hint:* Remember, if you make a mistake while formatting the announcement, you can click the Undo button on the Standard toolbar to undo your last action.

Instructions:

1. Start Microsoft Word. When the empty document titled Document 1 displays in the Word window, change the font size from 12 to 18.

2. If they are not already, display formatting marks.

3. Create the announcement shown in Figure 1-79. Enter the document first without the clip art and unformatted; that is, without any bulleted, bold, underlined, italicized, right-aligned, or centered text. Check spelling as you type.

4. Save the document on a floppy disk with Hannah Village Announcement as the file name.

5. Format the first line of the headline to 36-point Clarendon Condensed or a similar font. Format the second line of the headline to 36-point Comic Sans MS bold or a similar font.

6. Center both lines of the headline.

7. Center the body title line. Format the body title line to 36-point Verdana bold, or a similar font.

8. Add bullets to the three paragraphs in the body of the announcement. A **bullet** is a symbol positioned at the beginning of a paragraph. In Word, the default bullet symbol is a small darkened circle. A list of paragraphs with bullets is called a **bulleted list**. *Hint:* Use Help to learn how to add bullets to a list of paragraphs.

Productivity in the Classroom

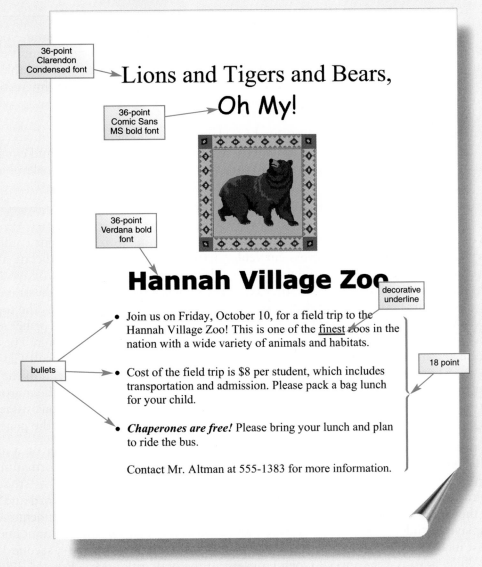

36-point Clarendon Condensed font → Lions and Tigers and Bears,

36-point Comic Sans MS bold font → Oh My!

36-point Verdana bold font → **Hannah Village Zoo**

decorative underline

bullets →

- Join us on Friday, October 10, for a field trip to the Hannah Village Zoo! This is one of the <u>finest</u> zoos in the nation with a wide variety of animals and habitats.

- Cost of the field trip is $8 per student, which includes transportation and admission. Please pack a bag lunch for your child.

- ***Chaperones are free!*** Please bring your lunch and plan to ride the bus.

18 point

Contact Mr. Altman at 555-1383 for more information.

FIGURE 1-79

9. Underline the word, finest, in the first paragraph of the body copy using a decorative underline. ***Hint:*** Use Help to learn how to add a decorative underline to text.
10. Bold and italicize the sentence, Chaperones are free!, in the third paragraph of the body copy.
11. Center the last line of the announcement.
12. Insert the graphic from the Microsoft Classroom Tools CD, or any appropriate image, between the headline and the body title line.
13. Enlarge the graphic. If you make the graphic too large, the announcement may flow onto two pages. If this occurs, reduce the size of the graphic so the announcement fits on a single page. ***Hint:*** Use Help to learn about print preview, which is a way to see the page before you print it. To exit print preview and return to the document window, click the Close button on the Print Preview toolbar.
14. Save the announcement again with the same file name.
15. Print the announcement.

Integration
in the Classroom

Introduction: Integration in the Classroom is designed for teachers and other educators who are looking for innovative ways to integrate technology into their content-specific curriculum. Educators can use Microsoft Word for numerous professional tasks. Teachers also can integrate Word easily across their curriculum as well. Students enjoy illustrating their writing with clip art. Clip art is motivating, interesting, and allows for increased creativity. Students who are reluctant to write often are more willing to write when they can use technology and clip art.

Explore the integration ideas below. Ideas are presented for elementary, middle, high school, and special education classrooms. These ideas are meant to be a springboard for creativity. Take an idea and expand, modify, and use it in your classroom. Furthermore, many of the ideas can be adapted to fit any level or learning situation.

Elementary

1. To encourage early reading and writing skills, you integrate Word into your reading curriculum. You make this a cross-curricular activity by having students dictate a sentence about a topic they are studying. The students dictate a sentence to you, your assistant, or a parent volunteer. Then, they enter the sentence into Word and illustrate the sentence with clip art. The students also enter a heading line that identifies the topic. Each student finds a picture of a person, place, or thing that supports his or her sentence. They type the heading line in 72 point. They type their sentence in 48 point. They then locate and insert an appropriate picture from a clip art gallery, the Microsoft Classroom Tools CD, or the Internet. Students add their name and the date to the end of the document, centered. They share their documents with the class and you post them around the room. Using the topic, Our Community, create a sample document for your students. Include your name and the current date centered and near the bottom of the page.

2. At the beginning of the school year, you and the art teacher work together on a unit called Ourselves and Our Families. Students draw self-portraits, write information about themselves and their families, and illustrate their writings. You also have the students write about and illustrate their favorite family activity using Microsoft Word and clip art. At the end of the unit you invite the parents to an open house with the students' work displayed. Students create a personal announcement for their family. The announcement must include the following text: first line of headline - You Are Invited~; second line of headline - ~To A Very Special Open House; and the body title - Mrs. Rogers' 3rd Grade Class. Students then add two paragraphs of text. The students personalize the first paragraph. The second paragraph must include the date and time of the event. The last line is centered and includes the following text: Call 555-3350 to RSVP. Create a sample announcement as an example for your students.

Integration in the Classroom

3. Your middle school students are studying the election process (see Figure 1-80). Students work in groups to design a mock campaign for a local office. They research the history of the election process and current policies and laws using print and Internet resources. They also interview local government officials about their campaign strategies. One of the projects is to create a campaign announcement with clip art and a bulleted list. Their campaign announcements need to have two lines of text in the headline, a clip art image, a body title, and a bulleted list. Students also need to have bolded, italicized text and use a decorative underline in the announcement. Their name and contact information should appear centered in the last line. They need to check spelling and grammar in the announcement. Using the techniques presented in this project, create an announcement to present as an example for your students. Include your name and e-mail address on the last line of the announcement.

Middle School

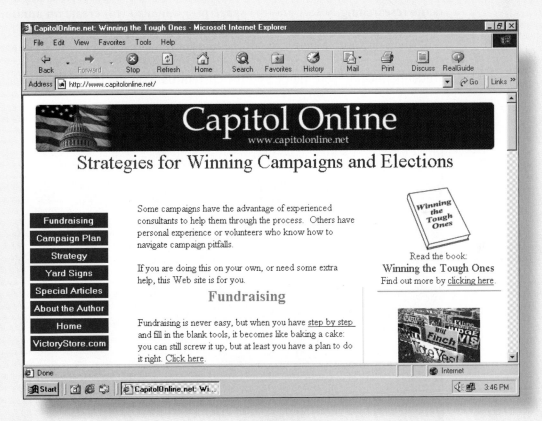

FIGURE 1-80

(continued)

Integration in the Classroom

Integration in the Classroom *(continued)*

4. Your 6th grade science class is studying space and the space program (see Figure 1-81). One of your activities is to have students work in pairs and teach part of a class session. Each pair is assigned a planet and the remaining pairs research NASA and the space program. They will use print resources and the Internet to research their topic or planet. The students will use Word to create an announcement with clip art sharing their research as a learning tool. They will give a copy of their announcement to other students to use as a study tool for the final unit exam. Announcements about the planet must include both the common name and the scientific name and three paragraphs with factual information about the planet (climate, size, distance from the sun, rotation patterns, etc.). In addition, students will include an image of the planet from the Internet or a clip art gallery. Students researching NASA and the space program also will create an announcement that includes a heading, clip art, and three paragraphs of pertinent information. Students also will use a decorative underline in the announcement. Using the techniques presented in this project, select a planet and create an announcement to present as an example for your students. Include your name and the current date on the last line of the announcement.

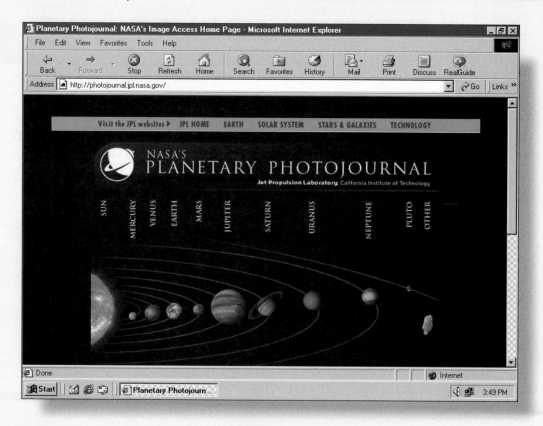

FIGURE 1-81

Middle School

Integration in the Classroom

5. You are teaching your Health and Consumer Science classes about comparison shopping. You have your students bring in a variety of name brand products and then the equivalent store brand product. Students then conduct a "taste test" on the products and determine which has the better flavor and value. They compare the quantity, quality, and price of the two items. Once they have determined which product is preferred, they create an announcement about their chosen product. The announcement includes information about the product as well as reasons why others should choose it and a suitable clip art image. Using the techniques presented in this project, create an announcement to present as an example for your students. Format the announcement effectively and include a bulleted list. Use a decorative underline in the announcement. Include your name and the current date on the last line of the announcement.

6. Your class is studying the stock market (see Figure 1-82). Students create a small company, receive a dollar amount to invest in the stock market, and select three stocks

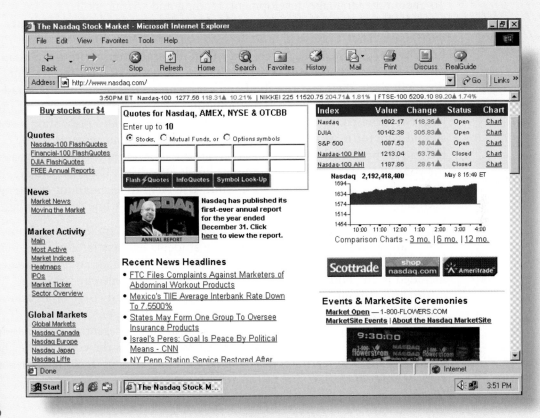

FIGURE 1-82

High School

(continued)

Integration
in the Classroom

Integration in the Classroom *(continued)*

to invest in for a two-week period. At the end of the two weeks, the students will share their stock portfolio with the class. To assist with their presentations, the students will create an announcement. The announcement will include their company name, a suitable graphic, information about the stocks they invested in, and information about their success or failure in the market. Using the techniques presented in this project, create an announcement to present as an example for your students. Format the announcement effectively and include a bulleted list. Select a different bullet style in place of the default symbol. *Hint:* Use Help to learn about changing the bullet style. Include your name and the current date on the last line of the announcement.

7. To encourage language development, reading and writing skills, you cook with your special education students every week. After the cooking activity, students write about the experience. They begin with a topic sentence, add a few sentences about the activity, and finish with a summary sentence. They then illustrate their writing with clip art. To determine what to cook the following week, you are going to have the students vote. Each student will select their favorite food and create an announcement to persuade the rest of the class to vote for their choice. Their announcement will include a clip art image and at least two brief paragraphs describing their food choice and presenting a reason others should vote for it. Students then will present their announcements to the class. Using the techniques presented in this project, create an announcement to present as an example for your students. Format the announcement effectively. Use a decorative underline and change the color of the characters. *Hint:* Use Help to learn about changing the color of text. Include your name and the current date on the last line of the announcement.

8. Your first and second grade hearing impaired students are learning about farm animals. You want to create a class book that the students can use later as a reference tool. You have the students select their favorite animal and create an announcement that will be included in the book. Students will have a title, a suitable clip art image, and include information about what the animal eats, typical size and color of an adult, and what products they produce (i.e., eggs, ham, bacon, hamburger, etc.). Using the techniques presented in this project, create an announcement to present as an example for your students. Format the announcement effectively. Change the color of the characters. *Hint:* Use Help to learn about changing the color of text. Include your name and the current date on the last line of the announcement.

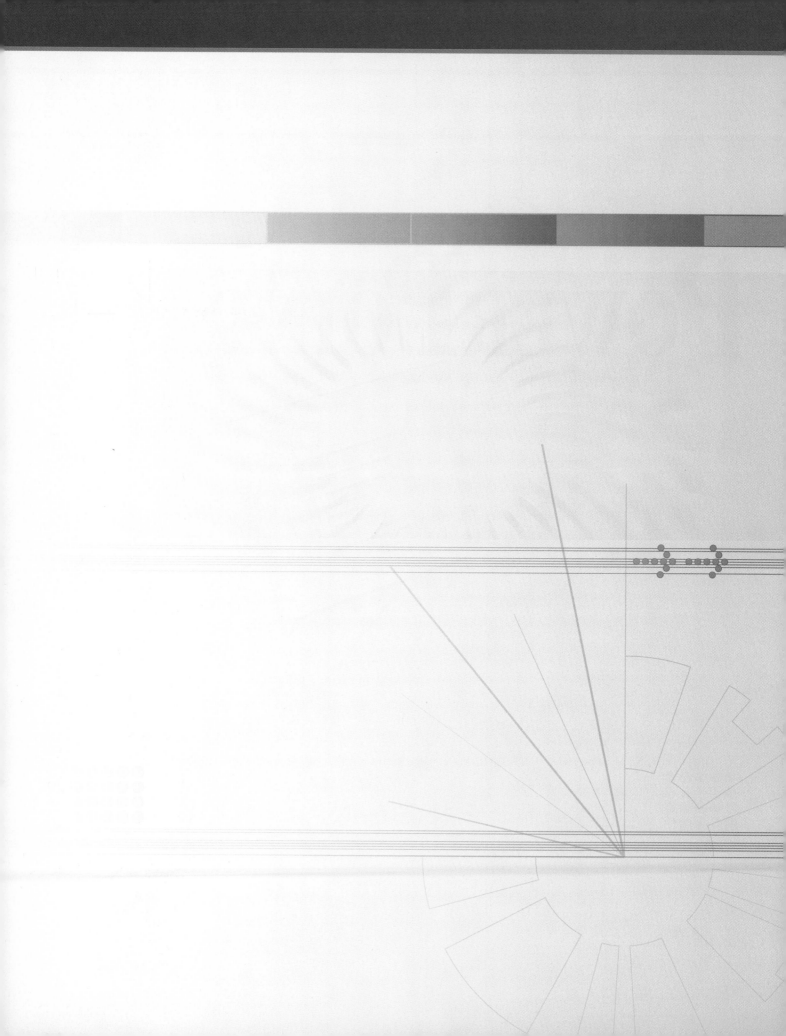

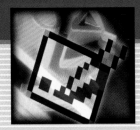

Microsoft PowerPoint

Using a Design Template and Text Slide Layout to Create a Presentation

You will have mastered the material in this project when you can:

O B J E C T I V E S

- Start and customize PowerPoint
- Describe the PowerPoint window
- Describe the speech recognition capabilities of PowerPoint
- Select a design template
- Create a title slide
- Change the font size and font style
- Save a presentation
- Add a new slide
- Create a text slide with a single-level bulleted list
- Create a text slide with a multi-level bulleted list
- End a slide show with a black slide
- Move to another slide in normal view
- View a presentation in slide show view
- Quit PowerPoint
- Open a presentation
- Check spelling and consistency, correct errors, and edit a presentation
- Display a presentation in black and white
- Print a presentation in black and white
- Use the PowerPoint Help system to answer your questions

COMDEX Glitz

Presentations Dazzle the Masses

Thousands of the world's computer industry executives attend, including keynote speakers, Bill Gates, Andy Grove, and Michael Dell. They are joined by hundreds of thousands of technology enthusiasts, industry professionals, and curious spectators seeking the latest trends in hardware, software, and the Internet, as well as the hottest new gizmos, gadgets, and games.

They will be attending COMDEX, North America's largest trade show. COMDEX/Fall is held in Las Vegas each November, and COMDEX/Spring is held in Chicago in April. Both shows feature speeches by industry leaders, tutorials on the latest technologies, and thousands of square feet of exhibits showcasing the latest in computer technology.

Information technology (IT) experts headline COMDEX as the premier IT event in the world. Indeed, more than 10,000 new products are unveiled at the Fall show. Since COMDEX's inception in 1979, some of the more notable product launches have been the IBM PC in 1981, COMPAQ's suitcase-sized portable computer, Microsoft's first version of Windows, Apple's original Macintosh computer, and CD-ROM drives, and the promise of wireless technology utilizing the Bluetooth™ standard.

Attendance and industry representation have grown steadily. The first show featured 150 exhibitions seen by 4,000 curious visitors. Six years later, more than 1,000 companies displayed their wares for more than 100,000 techies. Recent shows have produced as many as 2,400 booths visited by 250,000-plus attendees.

Computer companies realize their sales forces need to capture their audiences' attention, so they add sensory cues to their exhibits. They treat the trade show visitors to a multimedia blitz of sound, visuals, and action with the help of presentation software such as Microsoft PowerPoint. This program enhances the presenters' speeches by highlighting keywords in the presentation, displaying graphs, pictures, and diagrams, and playing sound and video clips.

In this project, you will learn to use PowerPoint 2002 to create a presentation (also called a slide show) for a Westview College counselors' orientation using a design template and one of PowerPoint's layouts. Then, you will run the slide show and print audience handouts.

PowerPoint's roots stem from the innovative work performed by a small company called Forethought, Inc. Programmers at this pioneering business coined the phrase, desktop presentation graphics, for formal slide shows and created a complete software package that automated creating slides containing text, charts, and graphics. Microsoft liked the visual appeal of the software and acquired Forethought in 1987. Company executives decided to market the software to Apple Macintosh users because Mac computers were considered clearly superior to IBM-based personal computers for graphics applications.

Microsoft PowerPoint became a favorite among Mac users. Meanwhile, Lotus Freelance Graphics and Software Publishing Harvard Graphics were popular within the PC community. This division ceased, however, when Microsoft released Windows 3.0 in 1990 and subsequently developed a Windows version of PowerPoint to run on PCs.

Since that time, Macintosh and PC users alike have utilized the presentation power of PowerPoint. The package has grown to include animation, audio and video clips, and Internet integration. Certainly the technology gurus at COMDEX have realized PowerPoint's dazzling visual appeal. So will you as you complete the exercises in this textbook.

Microsoft PowerPoint

Using a Design Template and Text Slide Layout to Create a Presentation

As a receptionist in your college's counseling office, you meet students who are waiting for their scheduled appointments. You have noticed that many of them seem sad. They sit silently and do not make eye contact or speak with their fellow students.

Because of your concern, you mention this observation to Jennifer Williams, the dean of counseling. She tells you that most college students are lonely. In fact, a Carnegie study finds that only 36 percent of college students participate in student activities other than sports. Consequently, they are self-absorbed and miss the joys of college. She says that Intro to Loneliness would be one class that would fill quickly because loneliness is one of college students' worst enemies. Many of these students do not adjust well to the initial move from home, which makes it difficult for them to meet new people and make friends. Therefore, they play it safe and stay by themselves.

You suggest that counselors discuss this loneliness at freshmen orientation, and Jennifer agrees. She knows you are proficient at PowerPoint and asks you to develop a presentation focusing on how to make friends on campus.

What Is Microsoft PowerPoint?

Microsoft PowerPoint is a complete presentation graphics program that allows you to produce professional looking presentations. A PowerPoint **presentation** also is called a **slide show**. PowerPoint gives you the flexibility to make presentations using a projection device attached to a personal computer (Figure 1-1a) and using overhead transparencies (Figure 1-1b). In addition, you can take advantage of the World Wide Web and run virtual presentations on the Internet (Figure 1-1c). PowerPoint also can create paper printouts of the individual slides, outlines, and speaker notes.

PowerPoint contains several features to simplify creating a slide show. For example, you can instruct PowerPoint to create a predesigned presentation, and then you can modify the presentation to fulfill your requirements. You quickly can format a slide show using one of the professionally designed presentation design templates. To make your presentation more impressive, you can add tables, charts, pictures, video, sound, and animation effects. You also can check the spelling or style of your slide show as you type or after you have completed designing the presentation. For example, you can instruct PowerPoint to restrict the number of bulleted items on a slide or limit the number of words in each paragraph. Additional PowerPoint features include the following:

▶ **Word processing** — create bulleted lists, combine words and images, find and replace text, and use multiple fonts and type sizes.

▶ **Outlining** — develop your presentation using an outline format. You also can import outlines from Microsoft Word or other word processing programs.

▶ **Charting** — create and insert charts into your presentations. The two chart types are: standard, which includes bar, line, pie, and xy (scatter) charts; and custom, which displays such objects as floating bars, colored lines, and three-dimensional cones.

(a) Projection Device Connected to a Personal Computer

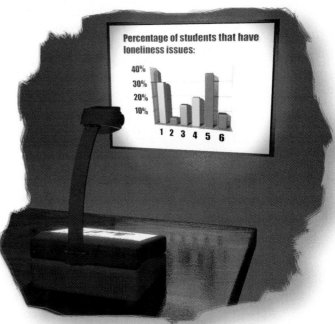

(b) Overhead Transparencies

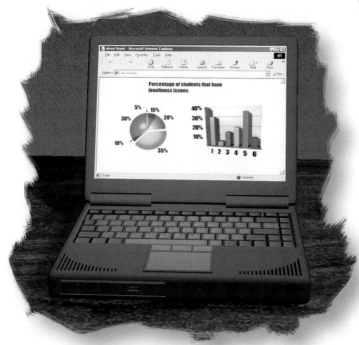

(c) PowerPoint Presentation on the World Wide Web

FIGURE 1-1

> **Drawing** — form and modify diagrams using shapes such as arcs, arrows, cubes, rectangles, stars, and triangles.

> **Inserting multimedia** — insert artwork and multimedia effects into your slide show. The Microsoft Media Gallery contains hundreds of clip art images, pictures, photos, sounds, and video clips. You can search for clips by entering words or phrases that describe the subject you want by looking for clips with similar artistic styles, colors, or shapes, or by connecting to a special Web site just for clip art. You also can import art from other applications.

> **Web support** — save presentations or parts of a presentation in HTML format so they can be viewed and manipulated using a browser. You can publish your slide show to the Internet or to an intranet. You also can insert action buttons and hyperlinks to create a self-running or interactive Web presentation.

> **E-mailing** — send your entire slide show as an attachment to an e-mail message.

> **Using Wizards** — create a presentation quickly and efficiently by answering prompts for specific content criteria. For example, the **AutoContent Wizard** gives prompts for the type of slide show you are planning, such as communicating serious news or motivating a team, and the type of output, such as an on-screen presentation or black and white overheads. If you are planning to run your presentation on another computer, the **Pack and Go Wizard** helps you bundle everything you need, including any objects associated with that presentation. If you cannot confirm that this other computer has PowerPoint installed, you also can include the **PowerPoint Viewer**, a program that allows you to run, but not edit, a PowerPoint slide show.

Project One — Time to Start Making Friends

PowerPoint allows you to produce slides similar to those you would develop in an academic or business environment. In Project 1, you create the presentation shown in Figures 1-2a through 1-2d. The objective is to produce a presentation, called Time to Start Making Friends, to display using a projection device. As an introduction to PowerPoint, this project steps you through the most common type of presentation, which is a **text slide** consisting of a bulleted list. A **bulleted list** is a list of paragraphs, each preceded by a bullet. A **bullet** is a symbol such as a heavy dot (•) or other character that precedes text when the text warrants special emphasis.

Starting and Customizing PowerPoint

To start PowerPoint, Windows must be running. The quickest way to begin a new presentation is to use the **Start button** on the **Windows taskbar** at the bottom of the screen. Perform the steps on page PP 1.10 to start PowerPoint and a new presentation, or ask your instructor how to start PowerPoint for your system.

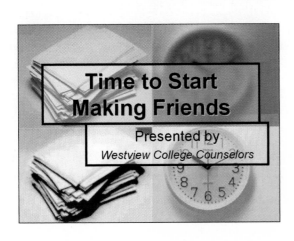

Time to Start Making Friends

Presented by
Westview College Counselors

(a) Slide 1

Meet People

- Develop confidence to introduce yourself to others
- Make eye contact
- Smile and say, "Hi"
- Do not wait; start early in the semester

(b) Slide 2

Find the Right Places

- Go where people congregate
  - Student union, sports events
- Get involved in extracurricular activities
  - Participate in intramurals
  - Join Student Government

(c) Slide 3

Start a Conversation

- Talk about almost anything
  - Comment on what is going on
    - Long lines, class assignments
- Ask questions
  - Get people to discuss their lives
    - Hobbies, classes, and work

(d) Slide 4

FIGURE 1-2

Steps **To Start PowerPoint**

1 **Click the Start button on the Windows taskbar, point to Programs on the Start menu, and then point to Microsoft PowerPoint on the Programs submenu.**

The commands on the Start menu display above the Start button and the Programs submenu displays (Figure 1-3). If the Office XP Speech Recognition software is installed on your computer, then the Language bar may display somewhere on the desktop.

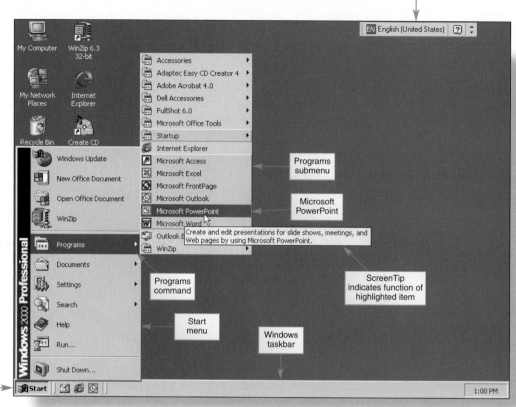

FIGURE 1-3

2 **Click PowerPoint.** **2000** **If using PowerPoint 2000, see the PowerPoint 2000 Users section at the top of the next page.**

PowerPoint starts. While PowerPoint is starting, the mouse pointer changes to the shape of an hourglass. After a few moments, a blank presentation titled Presentation1 displays in the PowerPoint window (Figure 1-4).

3 **If the PowerPoint window is not maximized, double-click its title bar to maximize it.**

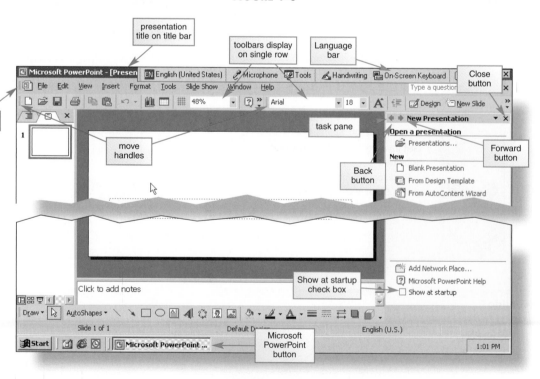

FIGURE 1-4

PowerPoint 2000 Users

2000 If using PowerPoint 2000, when PowerPoint starts a PowerPoint dialog box displays that allows you to create a new presentation using an AutoContent Wizard, a Design Template, or a Blank Presentation. Select the Blank presentation option button and then click the OK button. When the New Slide dialog box displays, select the Title Slide option, if necessary, and then click the OK button. The Language bar and the New Document task pane will not display as these are features unique to PowerPoint 2002.

In addition, if using PowerPoint 2000, slide thumbnails will not display in the tabs pane. Instead, as you enter text, the text displays to the right of an icon of each slide in the outline pane.

PowerPoint 2000 users should perform the following steps to display the toolbars on two rows, if necessary, and then skip to the bottom of page PP 1.13 and the text that begins under the heading, The PowerPoint Window.

TO DISPLAY THE TOOLBARS ON TWO ROWS WHEN USING POWERPOINT 2000

1 Click View on the menu bar, point to Toolbars, and then click Customize.

2 When the Customize dialog box displays, click the Options tab if necessary, click the Standard and Formatting toolbars share one row check box to remove the check mark, and then click the Close button.

PowerPoint 2002 Users

The screen in Figure 1-4 shows how the PowerPoint 2002 window looks the first time you start PowerPoint 2002 after installation on most computers. Notice that a task pane displays on the screen and the toolbars display on a single row. A **task pane** is a separate window within the application that provides commonly used commands and enables users to carry out some PowerPoint tasks efficiently. By default, both toolbars display on the same row immediately below the menu bar. Unless the resolution of your display device is greater than 800 × 600, many of the buttons that belong on these toolbars do not display. Hidden buttons display on the **Toolbar Options list**.

In this book, to allow the maximum slide space in the PowerPoint window, the New Presentation task pane that displays at startup is closed. For the most efficient use of the toolbars, the buttons are displayed on two separate rows instead of sharing a single row. You show the toolbar buttons on two rows by clicking the **Show Buttons on Two Rows command** in the Toolbar Options list. You also may display all the buttons on either toolbar by double-clicking the **move handle** on the left side of each toolbar (Figure 1-4).

Perform the steps on the next page to customize the PowerPoint window at startup by removing the task pane from the startup instructions and displaying the toolbar buttons on two rows, instead of one.

Other Ways

1. Double-click PowerPoint icon on desktop
2. Right-click Start button, click Open All Users, double-click New Office Document, click General tab, double-click Blank Presentation icon
3. On Start menu click New Office Document, click General tab, click New Presentation icon
4. Click New Office Document button on Microsoft Office Shortcut Bar, click General tab, double-click Blank Presentation icon, point to Programs, click Microsoft PowerPoint

Steps **To Customize the PowerPoint Window**

1 **If the New Presentation task pane displays in your PowerPoint window, click the Show at startup check box to remove the check mark, and then click the Close button in the upper-right corner of the task pane title bar (Figure 1-4 on page PP 1.10). If the Language bar displays, point to its Minimize button.**

PowerPoint removes the check mark from the Show at startup check box. PowerPoint will not display the New Presentation task pane the next time PowerPoint starts. The New Presentation task pane closes (Figure 1-5).

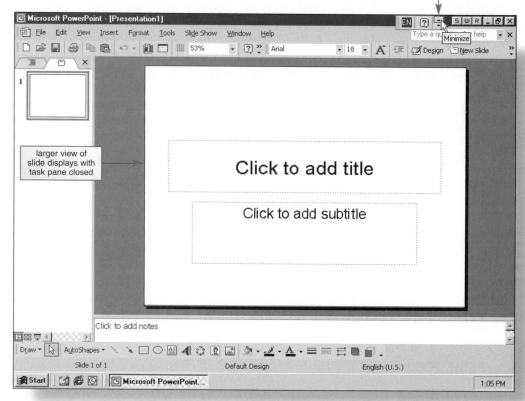

FIGURE 1-5

2 **Click the Minimize button on the Language bar. If the toolbars display positioned on the same row, click the Toolbar Options button on the Standard toolbar and then point to Show Buttons on Two Rows.**

The Toolbar Options list displays showing the buttons that do not fit on the toolbars when the buttons display on one row (Figure 1-6).

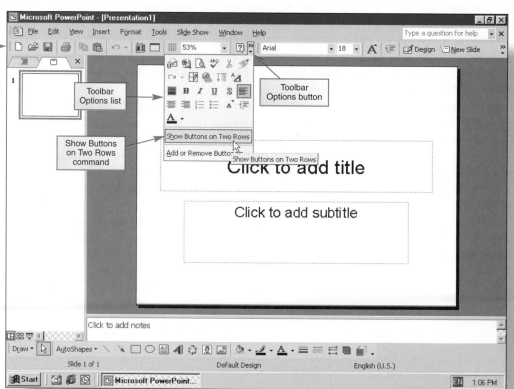

FIGURE 1-6

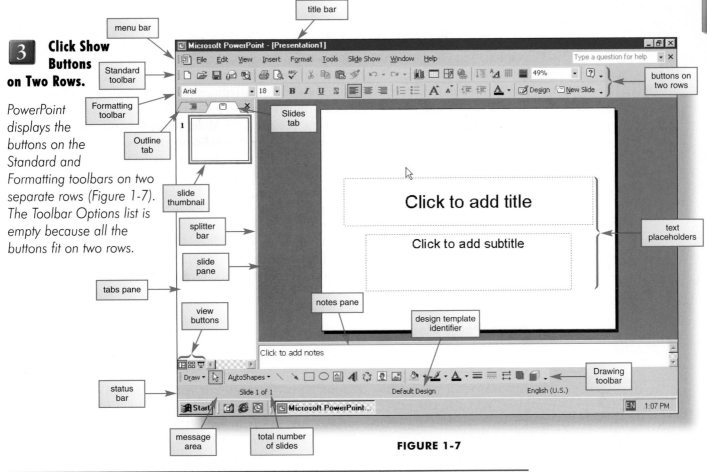

3 **Click Show Buttons on Two Rows.**

PowerPoint displays the buttons on the Standard and Formatting toolbars on two separate rows (Figure 1-7). The Toolbar Options list is empty because all the buttons fit on two rows.

FIGURE 1-7

When you point to a button or other areas on a toolbar, PowerPoint displays a ScreenTip. A **ScreenTip** is a short on-screen note associated with the object to which you are pointing, such as the name of the button. For examples of ScreenTips, see Figure 1-3 on page PP 1.10 and Figure 1-5.

As you work through creating a presentation, you will find that certain PowerPoint operations result in displaying a task pane. Besides the New Presentation task pane shown in Figure 1-4 on page 1.10, PowerPoint provides nine additional task panes: Clipboard, Basic Search, Advanced Search, Slide Layout, Slide Design – Design Templates, Slide Design – Color Schemes, Slide Design – Animation Schemes, Custom Animation, and Slide Transition. These task panes are discussed as they are used. You can display or hide a task pane by clicking the **Task Pane command** on the View menu. You can activate additional task panes by clicking the down arrow to the left of the Close button on the task pane title bar and then selecting a task pane in the list. To switch between task panes, use the Back and Forward buttons on the left side of the task pane title bar.

The PowerPoint Window

The basic unit of a PowerPoint presentation is a **slide**. A slide contains one or many **objects**, such as a title, text, graphics, tables, charts, and drawings. An object is the building block for a PowerPoint slide. PowerPoint assumes the first slide in a new presentation is the **title slide**. The title slide's purpose is to introduce the presentation to the audience.

More About

Task Panes

When you first start PowerPoint, a small window called a task pane may display docked on the right side of the screen. You can drag a task pane title bar to float the pane in your work area or dock it on either the left or right side of a screen, depending on your personal preference.

In PowerPoint, you have the option of using the PowerPoint default settings or establishing your own. A **default setting** is a particular value for a variable that PowerPoint assigns initially. It controls the placement of objects, the color scheme, the transition between slides, and other slide attributes, and it remains in effect unless you cancel or override it. **Attributes** are the properties or characteristics of an object. For example, if you underline the title of a slide, the title is the object, and the underline is the attribute. When you start PowerPoint, the default **slide layout** is **landscape orientation**, where the slide width is greater than its height. In landscape orientation, the slide size is preset to 10 inches wide and 7.5 inches high. You can change the slide layout to **portrait orientation**, so the slide height is greater than its width, by clicking Page Setup on the File menu. In portrait orientation, the slide width is 7.5 inches, and the height is 10 inches.

When a PowerPoint window is open, its name displays in an icon on the Windows taskbar. The **active application** is the one displaying in the foreground of the desktop. That application's corresponding icon on the Windows taskbar displays recessed.

PowerPoint Views

PowerPoint has three main views: normal view, slide sorter view, and slide show view. A **view** is the mode in which the presentation displays on the screen. You may use any or all views when creating a presentation, but you can use only one at a time. You also can select one of these views to be the default view. Change views by clicking one of the view buttons located at the lower-left of the PowerPoint window above the Drawing toolbar (Figure 1-7 on the previous page). The PowerPoint window display varies depending on the view. Some views are graphical while others are textual.

You generally will use normal view and slide sorter view when you are creating a presentation. **Normal view** is composed of three working areas that allow you to work on various aspects of a presentation simultaneously (Figure 1-7). The left side of the screen has a tabs pane that consists of an **Outline tab** and a **Slides tab** that alternate between views of the presentation in an outline of the slide text and a thumbnail, or miniature, view of the slides. You can type the text of the presentation on the Outline tab and easily rearrange bulleted lists, paragraphs, and individual slides. As you type, you can view this text in the **slide pane**, which displays a large view of the current slide on the right side of the window. You also can enter text, graphics, animations, and hyperlinks directly in the slide pane. The **notes pane** at the bottom of the window is an area where you can type notes and additional information. This text can consist of notes to yourself or remarks to share with your audience.

In normal view, you can adjust the width of the slide pane by dragging the **splitter bar** and the height of the notes pane by dragging the pane borders. After you have created at least two slides, **scroll bars**, **scroll arrows**, and **scroll boxes** will display below and to the right of the windows, and you can use them to view different parts of the panes.

Slide sorter view is helpful when you want to see all the slides in the presentation simultaneously. A thumbnail version of each slide displays, and you can rearrange their order, add transitions and timings to switch from one slide to the next in a presentation, add and delete slides, and preview animations.

Slide show view fills the entire screen and allows you to see the slide show just as your audience will view it. Transition effects, animation, graphics, movies, and timings display as they will during an actual presentation.

Table 1-1 identifies the view buttons and provides an explanation of each view.

Sizing Panes

The three panes in normal view allow you to work on all aspects of your presentation simultaneously. You can drag the splitter bar and the pane borders to make each area larger or smaller.

Table 1-1   View Buttons and Functions

BUTTON	BUTTON NAME	FUNCTION
	Normal View	Displays three panes: the tabs pane with either the Outline tab or the Slides tab, the slide pane, and the notes pane.
	Slide Sorter View	Displays thumbnail versions of all slides in a presentation. You then can copy, cut, paste, or otherwise change the slide position to modify the presentation. Slide sorter view also is used to add timings, to select animated transitions, and to preview animations.
	Slide Show View	Displays the slides as an electronic presentation on the full screen of your computer's monitor. Looking much like a slide projector display, you can see the effect of transitions, build effects, slide timings, and animations.

Placeholders, Text Areas, Mouse Pointer, and Scroll Bars

The PowerPoint window contains elements similar to the document windows in other Microsoft Office applications. Other features are unique to PowerPoint. The main elements are the text placeholders, the mouse pointer, and scroll bars.

PLACEHOLDERS Placeholders are boxes that display when you create a new slide. All layouts except the Blank slide layout contain placeholders. Depending on the particular slide layout selected, placeholders display for the slide title, body text, charts, tables, organization charts, media clips, and clip art. You type titles, body text, and bulleted lists in **text placeholders**; you place graphic elements in chart placeholders, table placeholders, organizational chart placeholders, and clip art placeholders. A placeholder is considered an **object**, which is a single element of a slide.

TEXT AREAS Text areas are surrounded by a dotted outline. The title slide in Figure 1-7 on page PP 1.13 has two text areas that contain the text placeholders where you will type the main heading, or title, of a new slide and the subtitle, or other object. Other slides in a presentation may use a layout that contains text areas for a title and bulleted lists.

MOUSE POINTER   The **mouse pointer** can become one of several different shapes depending on the task you are performing in PowerPoint and the pointer's location on the screen. The different shapes are discussed when they display.

SCROLL BARS   When you add a second slide to a presentation, a **vertical scroll bar** displays on the right side of the slide pane. PowerPoint allows you to use the scroll bar to move forward or backward through the presentation.

The **horizontal scroll bar** may display. It is located on the bottom of the slide pane and allows you to display a portion of the slide when the entire slide does not fit on the screen.

Status Bar, Menu Bar, Standard Toolbar, Formatting Toolbar, and Drawing Toolbar

The status bar displays at the bottom of the screen above the Windows taskbar (Figure 1-7). The menu bar, Standard toolbar, and Formatting toolbar display at the top of the screen just below the title bar. The Drawing toolbar displays above the status bar.

The Default Design Template

Some PowerPoint slide show designers create presentations using the Default Design template. This blank design allows them to concentrate on the words being used to convey the message and does not distract them with colors and various text attributes. Once the text is entered, the designers then select an appropriate design template.

STATUS BAR   Immediately above the Windows taskbar at the bottom of the screen is the status bar. The **status bar** consists of a message area and a presentation design template identifier (Figure 1-7 on page PP 1.13). Generally, the message area displays the current slide number and the total number of slides in the slide show. For example, in Figure 1-7 the message area displays Slide 1 of 1. Slide 1 is the current slide, and of 1 indicates the slide show contains only 1 slide. The template identifier displays Default Design, which is the template PowerPoint uses initially.

MENU BAR   The **menu bar** is a special toolbar that includes the PowerPoint menu names (Figure 1-8a). Each **menu name** represents a menu of commands that you can use to perform tasks such as retrieving, storing, printing, and manipulating objects in a presentation. When you point to a menu name on the menu bar, the area of the menu bar containing the name changes to a button. To display a menu, such as the Edit menu, click the Edit menu name on the menu bar. A **menu** is a list of commands. If you point to a command on a menu that has an arrow to its right edge, a **submenu** displays another list of commands.

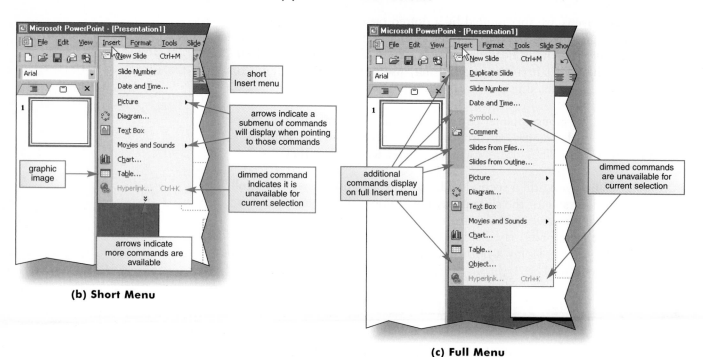

(a) Menu Bar and Toolbars

(b) Short Menu

(c) Full Menu

FIGURE 1-8

When you click a menu name on the menu bar, a short menu displays that lists your most recently used commands (Figure 1-8b).

If you wait a few seconds or click the arrows at the bottom of the short menu, it expands into a full menu. A **full menu** lists all the commands associated with a menu (Figure 1-8c). You immediately can display a full menu by double-clicking the menu name on the menu bar. In this book, when you display a menu, always display the full menu using one of these techniques:

1. Click the menu name on the menu bar and then wait a few seconds.
2. Click the menu name on the menu bar and then click the arrows at the bottom of the short menu.
3. Click the menu name on the menu bar and then point to the arrows at the bottom of the short menu.
4. Double-click the menu name on the menu bar.

Both short and full menus display some commands with an image to the left, which associates the command with a graphic image and dimmed commands that appear gray, or dimmed, instead of black, which indicates they are not available for the current selection. A command with a dark gray shading to the left of it on a full menu is called a hidden command because it does not display on a short menu. As you use PowerPoint, it automatically personalizes the short menus for you based on how often you use commands. That is, as you use hidden commands, PowerPoint *unhides* them and places them on the short menu.

The menu bar can change to include other menu names depending on the type of work you are doing in PowerPoint. For example, if you are adding a chart to a slide, Data and Chart menu names are added to the menu bar with commands that reflect charting options.

More About

Hiding Toolbars

To display more of the PowerPoint window, you can hide a toolbar you no longer need. To hide a toolbar, right-click any toolbar and then click the check mark next to the tool-bar you want to hide on the shortcut menu.

STANDARD, FORMATTING, AND DRAWING TOOLBARS The Standard toolbar (Figure 1-9a), Formatting toolbar (Figure 1-9b), and Drawing toolbar (Figure 1-9c on the next page) contain buttons and boxes that allow you to perform frequent tasks more quickly than when using the menu bar. For example, to print a slide show, you click the Print button on the Standard toolbar. Each button has an image on the button and a ScreenTip that help you remember the button's function.

Figure 1-9 illustrates the Standard, Formatting, and Drawing toolbars and describes the functions of the buttons. Each of the buttons and boxes are explained in detail when they are used.

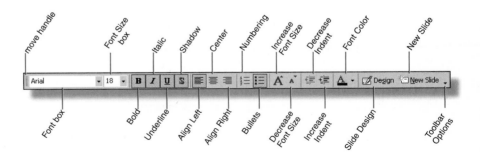

FIGURE 1-9a Standard Toolbar

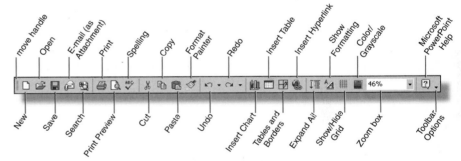

FIGURE 1-9b Formatting Toolbar

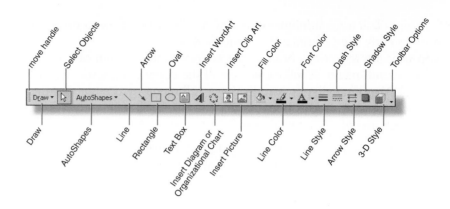

FIGURE 1-9c Drawing Toolbar

PowerPoint has several additional toolbars you can display by pointing to Toolbars on the View menu and then clicking the respective name on the Toolbars submenu. You also may display a toolbar by pointing to a toolbar and right-clicking to display a shortcut menu, which lists the available toolbars. A **shortcut menu** contains a list of commands or items that relate to the item to which you are pointing when you right-click.

Speech Recognition (Not Available in PowerPoint 2000)

With the **Office Speech Recognition software** installed and a microphone, you can speak the names of toolbar buttons, menus, menu commands, list items, alerts, and dialog box controls, such as OK and Cancel. You also can dictate cell entries, such as text and numbers. To indicate whether you want to speak commands or dictate cell entries, you use the **Language bar** (Figure 1-10a), which also is used for handwriting recognition and for Input Method Editors (IME) that convert keystrokes to East Asian characters. You can display the Language bar in two ways: (1) click the Language Indicator button in the Windows taskbar tray status area by the clock, and then click Show the Language bar on the Language bar menu (Figure 1-10b); or (2) click the **Speech command** on the **Tools menu**.

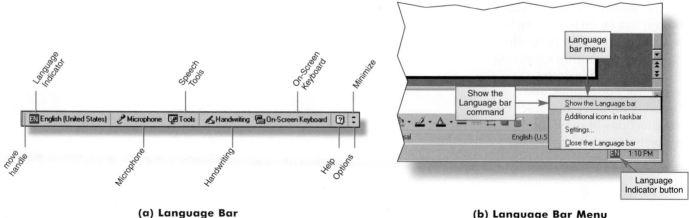

(a) Language Bar

(b) Language Bar Menu

FIGURE 1-10

If the Language Indicator button does not display in the tray status area, and if the Speech command is not displayed or is dimmed on the Tools menu, the Office Speech Recognition software is not installed. To install the software, you first must start Word and then click Speech on the Tools menu.

If you have speakers, you can instruct the computer to read a slide show to you. By selecting the appropriate option, you can have the slides read in a male or female voice.

Additional information on the Office speech and handwriting recognition capabilities is available in Appendix B.

More *About*

Additional Templates

While the Slide Design task pane displays a wide variety of templates, more are available in the Microsoft Office Template Gallery at the Microsoft Web site. These templates are arranged in various categories according to the type of presentation.

Choosing a Design Template

A **design template** provides consistency in design and color throughout the entire presentation. It determines the color scheme, font and font size, and layout of a presentation. PowerPoint has three Slide Design task panes that allow you to choose and change the appearance of slides in your presentation. The **Slide Design – Design Templates task pane** displays a variety of styles. You can alter the colors used in the design templates by using the **Slide Design – Color Schemes task pane**. In addition, you can animate elements of your presentation by using the **Slide Design – Animation Schemes task pane**.

In this project, you will select a particular design template by using the Slide Design – Design Templates task pane. The top section of the task pane, labeled Used in This Presentation, displays the template currently used in the slide show. PowerPoint uses the **Default Design** template until you select a different style. When you place your mouse over a template, the name of the template displays. The next section of the task pane is the Recently Used templates. This area displays the four templates you have used in your newest slide shows. The Available For Use area shows additional templates. The templates display in alphabetical order in the two columns. You want to change the template for this presentation from the Default Design to Proposal. Perform the following steps to apply the Proposal design template.

Steps **To Choose a Design Template**

1 **Point to the Slide Design button on the Formatting toolbar (Figure 1-11).** 2000 **If using PowerPoint 2000, click the Common Tasks button on the Formatting toolbar and then click Apply Design Template. When the Apply Design Template dialog box displays, scroll down the list of design templates until Straight Edge appears. Click Straight Edge, click the Apply button, and then skip to the top of page PP 1.22 and the text that begins under the heading, Creating a Title Slide.**

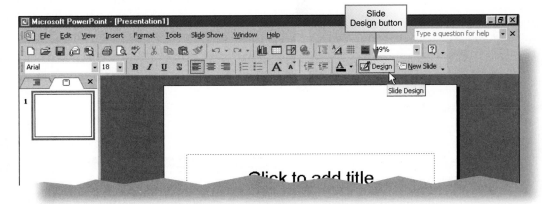

FIGURE 1-11

2 **Click the Slide Design button and then point to the down scroll arrow in the Apply a design template list.**

The Slide Design task pane displays (Figure 1-12). The Apply a design template list displays thumbnail views of numerous design templates. Your list may look different depending on your computer. The Default Design template is highlighted in the Used in This Presentation area. Other templates display in the Available For Use area and possibly in the Recently Used area. The Close button in the Slide Design task pane can be used to close the task pane if you do not want to apply a new template.

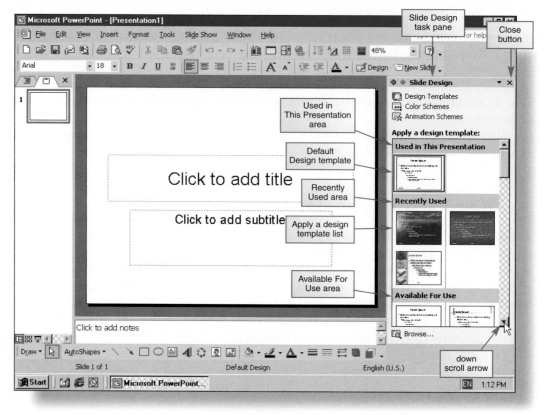

FIGURE 1-12

3 **Click the down scroll arrow to scroll through the list of design templates until Proposal displays in the Available For Use area. Point to the Proposal template.**

The Proposal template is selected, as indicated by the blue box around the template and the arrow button on the right side (Figure 1-13). PowerPoint provides 45 templates in the Available For Use area. Their names are listed in alphabetical order. A ScreenTip displays the template's name. Your system may display the ScreenTip, Proposal.pot, which indicates the design template's file extension (.pot).

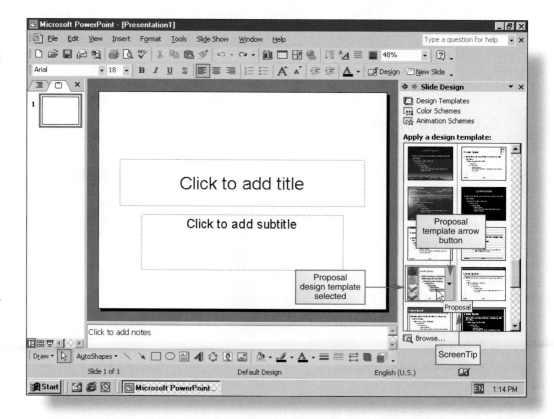

FIGURE 1-13

4 **Click Proposal. Point to the Close button in the Slide Design task pane.**

The template is applied to Slide 1, as shown in the slide pane and Slides tab (Figure 1-14).

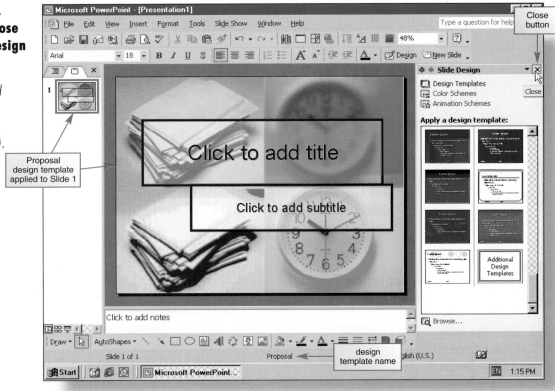

FIGURE 1-14

5 **Click the Close button.**

Slide 1 displays in normal view with the Proposal design template (Figure 1-15).

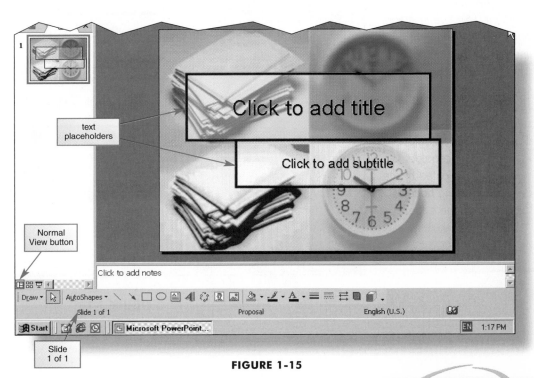

FIGURE 1-15

Other **Ways**

1. Double-click Proposal in list

Creating a Title Slide

With the exception of a blank slide, PowerPoint assumes every new slide has a title. To make creating a presentation easier, any text you type after a new slide displays becomes title text in the title text placeholder.

Entering the Presentation Title

The presentation title for Project 1 is Time to Start Making Friends. To enter text in your slide, you type on the keyboard or speak into the microphone. As you begin entering text in the title text placeholder, the title text displays immediately in the Slide 1 thumbnail in the Slides tab. Perform the following steps to create the title slide for this presentation.

Steps To Enter the Presentation Title

1 **Click the label, Click to add title, located inside the title text placeholder.**

*The insertion point is in the title text placeholder (Figure 1-16). The **insertion point** is a blinking vertical line (|), which indicates where the next character will display. The mouse pointer changes to an I-beam. A **selection rectangle** displays around the title text place-holder. The placeholder is selected as indicated by the border and sizing handles displaying on the edges.*

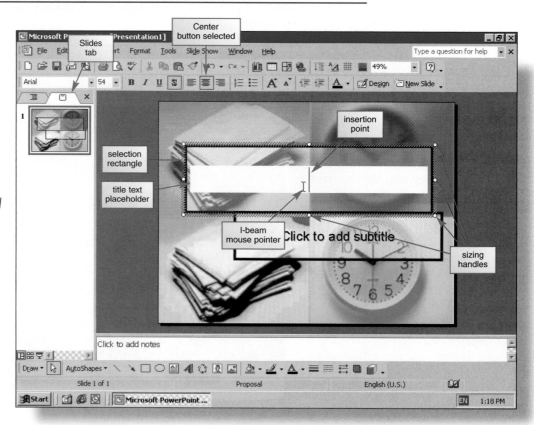

FIGURE 1-16

2 **In the title text placeholder type** Time to Start **and then press the ENTER key. Type** Making Friends **but do not press the ENTER key.**

The title text, Time to Start Making Friends, displays on two lines in the title text placeholder and in the Slides tab (Figure 1-17). The insertion point displays after the letter s in Friends. The title text displays centered in the placeholder

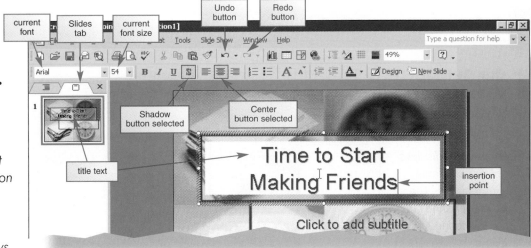

FIGURE 1-17

with the default text attributes: Arial font, font size 54, and shadow effect. **2000** *If using the Straight Edge design, the default text attributes are: Times New Roman 40 No Shadow.*

PowerPoint **line wraps** text that exceeds the width of the placeholder. One of PowerPoint's features is **text AutoFit**. If you are creating a slide and need to squeeze an extra line in the text placeholder, PowerPoint will prompt you to resize the existing text in the placeholder so the spillover text will fit on the slide.

Correcting a Mistake When Typing

If you type the wrong letter, press the BACKSPACE key to erase all the characters back to and including the one that is incorrect. If you mistakenly press the ENTER key after typing the title and the insertion point is on the new line, simply press the BACKSPACE key to return the insertion point to the right of the letter s in the word Friends.

When you install PowerPoint, the default setting allows you to reverse up to the last 20 changes by clicking the **Undo button** on the Standard toolbar. The ScreenTip that displays when you point to the Undo button changes to indicate the type of change just made. For example, if you type text in the title text placeholder and then point to the Undo button, the ScreenTip that displays is Undo Typing. For clarity, when referencing the Undo button in this project, the name displaying in the ScreenTip is referenced. Another way to reverse changes is to click the **Undo command** on the Edit menu. As with the Undo button, the Undo command reflects the last type of change made to the presentation.

You can reapply a change that you reversed with the Undo button by clicking the **Redo button** on the Standard toolbar. Clicking the Redo button reverses the last undo action. The ScreenTip name reflects the type of reversal last preformed.

Entering the Presentation Subtitle

The next step in creating the title slide is to enter the subtitle text into the subtitle text placeholder. Complete the steps on the next page to enter the presentation subtitle.

Other Ways

1. In Dictation mode, say "Time to Start, New Line, Making Friends"

More About

The 7 × 7 Rule

All slide shows in the projects and exercises in this book follow the 7 × 7 rule. This guideline states that each slide should have a maximum of seven lines, and each of these lines should have a maximum of seven words. This rule requires PowerPoint designers to choose their words carefully and, in turn, helps viewers read the slides easily.

Steps To Enter the Presentation Subtitle

1 **Click the label, Click to add subtitle, located inside the subtitle text placeholder.**

The insertion point displays in the subtitle text placeholder (Figure 1-18). The mouse pointer changes to an I-beam indicating the mouse is in a text placeholder. The selection rectangle indicates the placeholder is selected.

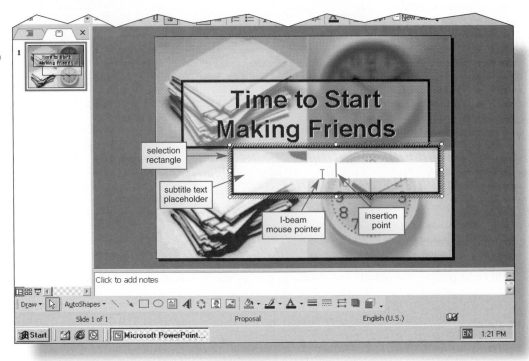

FIGURE 1-18

2 **Type** Presented by **and then press the ENTER key. Type** Westview College Counselors **but do not press the ENTER key.**

The subtitle text displays in the subtitle text placeholder and the Slides tab (Figure 1-19). The insertion point displays after the letter s in Counselors. A red wavy line displays below the word, Westview, to indicate a possible spelling error.

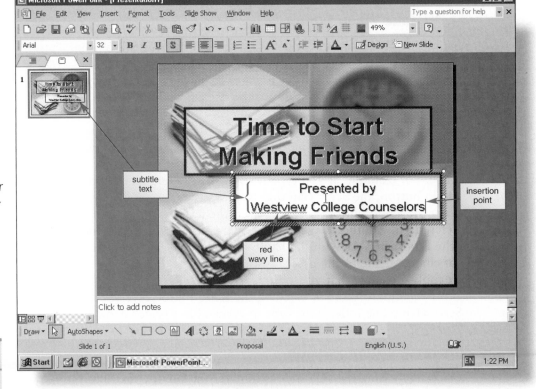

FIGURE 1-19

Other Ways

1. In Dictation mode, say "Presented by, New Line, Westview College Counselors"

After pressing the ENTER key in Step 2, PowerPoint created a new line, which is the second paragraph in the placeholder. A **paragraph** is a segment of text with the same format that begins when you press the ENTER key and ends when you press the ENTER key again.

Text Attributes

This presentation uses the Proposal design template. Each design template has its own text attributes. A **text attribute** is a characteristic of the text, such as font, font size, font style, or text color. You can adjust text attributes any time before, during, or after you type the text. Recall that a design template determines the color scheme, font and font size, and layout of a presentation. Most of the time, you use the design template's text attributes and color scheme. Occasionally, you may want to change the way a presentation looks, however, and still keep a particular design template. PowerPoint gives you that flexibility. You can use the design template and change the font and the font's color, effects, size, and style. Text may have one or more font styles and effects simultaneously. Table 1-2 explains the different text attributes available in PowerPoint.

The next two sections explain how to change the font size and font style attributes.

More About

Modifying Fonts

Designers recommend using a maximum of two fonts and two font styles or effects in a slide show. This design philosophy maintains balance and simplicity.

Table 1-2 Design Template Text Attributes	
ATTRIBUTE	**DESCRIPTION**
Color	Defines the color of text. Displaying text in color requires a color monitor. Printing text in color requires a color printer or plotter.
Effects	Effects include underline, shadow, emboss, superscript, and subscript. Effects can be applied to most fonts.
Font	Defines the appearance and shape of letters, numbers, and special characters.
Size	Specifies the height of characters on the screen. Character size is gauged by a measurement system called points. A single point is about 1/72 of an inch in height. Thus, a character with a point size of 18 is about 18/72 (or 1/4) of an inch in height.
Style	Font styles include regular, bold, italic, and bold italic.

Changing the Style of Text to Italic

Text font styles include plain, italic, bold, shadowed, and underlined. PowerPoint allows you to use one or more text font styles in a presentation. Perform the steps on the next page to add emphasis to the first line of the subtitle text by changing regular text to italic text.

Steps **To Change the Text Font Style to Italic**

1 **Triple-click the paragraph, Westview College Counselors, in the subtitle text placeholder, and then point to the Italic button on the Formatting toolbar.**

The paragraph, Westview College Counselors, is high-lighted (Figure 1-20). The Italic button is surrounded by a blue box. You select an entire paragraph quickly by triple-clicking any text within the paragraph.

FIGURE 1-20

2 **Click the Italic button.**

The text is italicized on the slide and the slide thumb-nail (Figure 1-21).

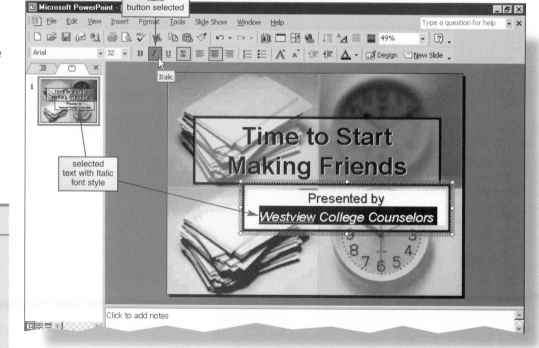

FIGURE 1-21

To remove the italic style from text, select the italicized text and then click the Italic button. As a result, the Italic button is not selected, and the text does not have the italic font style.

Changing the Font Size

The Proposal design template default font size is 54 point for title text and 32 point for body text. A point is 1/72 of an inch in height. Thus, a character with a point size of 54 is 54/72 (or 3/4) of an inch in height. Slide 1 requires you to increase the font size for the paragraph, Presented by. Perform the following steps to increase the font size.

Steps **To Increase Font Size**

1 **Position the mouse pointer in the paragraph, Presented by, and then triple-click.**

PowerPoint selects the entire paragraph (Figure 1-22).

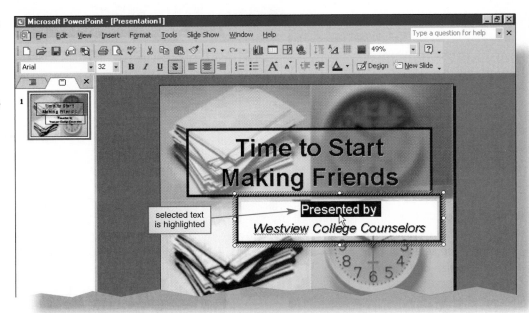

FIGURE 1-22

2 **Point to the Font Size box arrow on the Formatting toolbar.**

*The ScreenTip displays the words, Font Size (Figure 1-23). The **Font Size box** is surrounded by a blue box and indicates that the subtitle text is 32 point.*

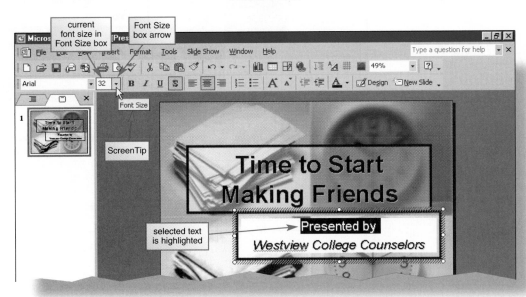

FIGURE 1-23

3 **Click the Font Size box arrow, click the Font Size box scroll bar one time, and then point to 40 in the Font Size list.**

When you click the *Font Size box arrow*, a list of available font sizes displays in the Font Size list (Figure 1-24). The font sizes displayed depend on the current font, which is Arial. Font size 40 is highlighted.

FIGURE 1-24

4 **Click 40.**

The font size of the subtitle text, *Presented by*, increases to 40 point (Figure 1-25). The Font Size box on the Formatting toolbar displays 40, indicating the selected text has a font size of 40.

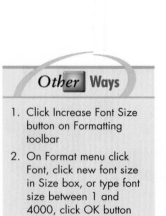

Other Ways

1. Click Increase Font Size button on Formatting toolbar

2. On Format menu click Font, click new font size in Size box, or type font size between 1 and 4000, click OK button

3. Right-click selected text, click Font on shortcut menu, type new font size in Size box, click OK button

4. In Voice Command mode, say "Font Size, [font size]"

FIGURE 1-25

The **Increase Font Size button** on the Formatting toolbar (Figure 1-25) increases the font size in preset increments each time you click the button. If you need to decrease the font size, click the Font Size box arrow and then select a size smaller than 32. The **Decrease Font Size button** on the Formatting toolbar (Figure 1-25) also decreases the font size in preset increments each time you click the button.

Saving the Presentation on a Floppy Disk

While you are building a presentation, the computer stores it in memory. It is important to save the presentation frequently because the presentation will be lost if the computer is turned off or you lose electrical power. Another reason to save your work is that if you run out of lab time before completing your project, you may finish the project later without starting over. Therefore, always save any presentation you will use later. Before you continue with Project 1, save the work completed thus far. Perform the following steps to save a presentation on a floppy disk using the Save button on the Standard toolbar.

 To Save a Presentation on a Floppy Disk

1 **Insert a formatted floppy disk in drive A. Click the Save button on the Standard toolbar.**

The Save As dialog box displays (Figure 1-26). The default folder, My Documents, displays in the Save in box. Time to Start displays highlighted in the File name text box because PowerPoint uses the words in the title text placeholder as the default file name. Presentation displays in the Save as type box. Clicking the Cancel button closes the Save As dialog box.

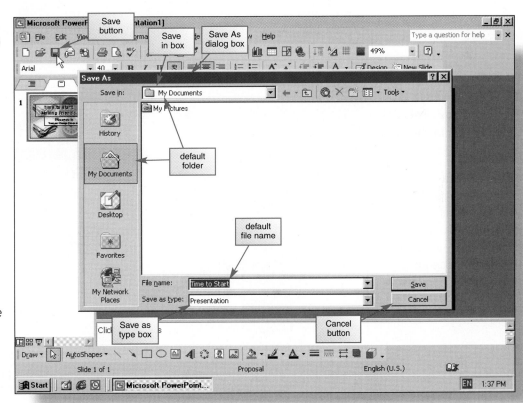

FIGURE 1-26

2 **Type** Make
Friends **in the**
File name text box. Do not
press the ENTER key after
typing the file name.
Point to the Save in box
arrow.

The name, Make Friends,
displays in the File name
text box (Figure 1-27).

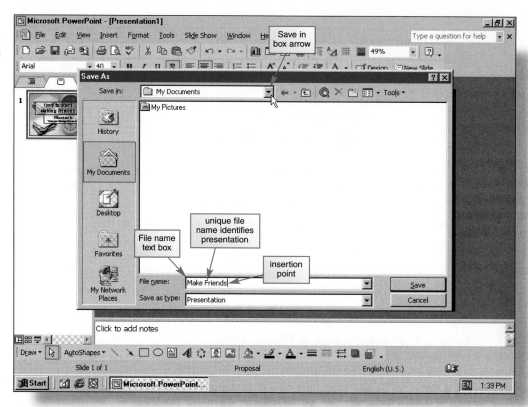

FIGURE 1-27

3 **Click the Save in**
box arrow. Point to
3½ Floppy (A:) in the Save
in list.

The Save in list displays a
list of locations in which to
save a presentation; 3½
Floppy (A:) is highlighted
(Figure 1-28). Your list may
look different depending
on the configuration of your
system.

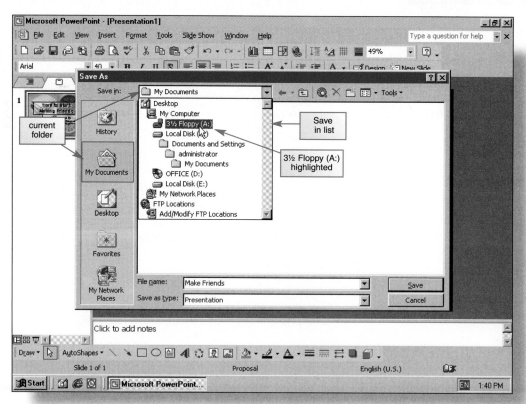

FIGURE 1-28

4 **Click 3½ Floppy (A:) and then point to the Save button in the Save As dialog box.**

Drive A becomes the current drive (Figure 1-29).

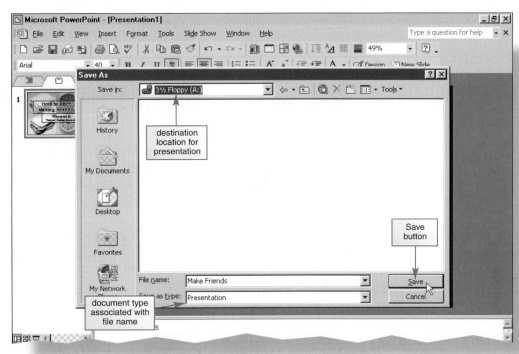

FIGURE 1-29

5 **Click the Save button.**

PowerPoint saves the presentation on the floppy disk in drive A. The title bar displays the file name used to save the presentation, Make Friends (Figure 1-30).

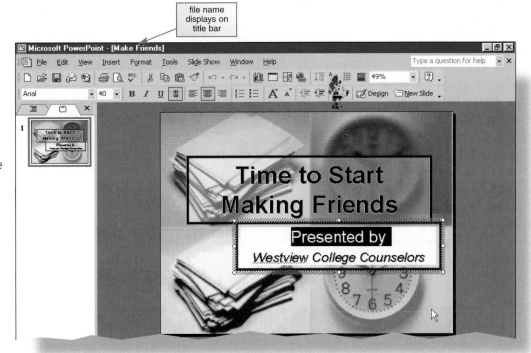

FIGURE 1-30

PowerPoint automatically appends the extension .ppt to the file name, Make Friends. The **.ppt** extension stands for **P**ower**P**oin**t**. Although the slide show, Make Friends, is saved on a floppy disk, it also remains in memory and displays on the screen.

Other Ways

1. On File menu click Save As
2. Press CTRL+S or press SHIFT+F12
3. In Voice Command mode, say "File, Save As, [type file name], Save"

It is a good practice to save periodically while you are working on a project. By doing so, you protect yourself from losing all the work you have done since the last time you saved.

Adding a New Slide to a Presentation

With the title slide for the presentation created, the next step is to add the first text slide immediately after the title slide. Usually, when you create a presentation, you add slides with text, graphics, or charts. When you add a new slide, PowerPoint uses the Title and Text slide layout. Some placeholders allow you to double-click the placeholder and then access other objects, such as media clips, charts, diagrams, and organization charts.

Perform the following steps to add a new Text slide layout with a bulleted list.

Steps **To Add a New Text Slide with a Bulleted List**

1 **Click the New Slide button on the Formatting toolbar (Figure 1-31). 2000** **If using PowerPoint 2000, click the Common Tasks button on the Formatting toolbar and then click New Slide. When the New Slide dialog box displays, click the Bulleted List option, if necessary, and then click the OK button. Then skip to the bottom of page PP 1.33 and the text that begins under the heading, Creating a Text Slide with a Single-Level Bulleted List.**

The Slide Layout task pane opens. The Title and Text slide layout is selected. Slide 2 of 2 displays on the status bar.

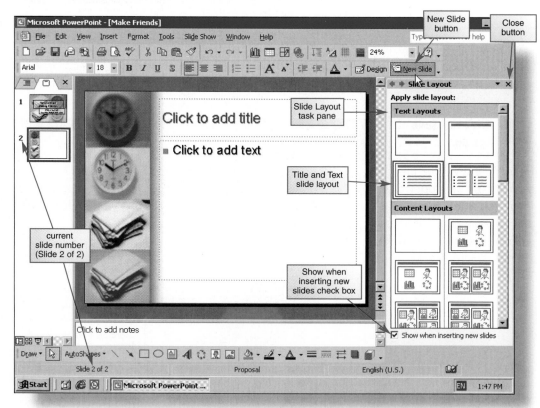

FIGURE 1-31

2 **Click the Show when inserting new slides check box to remove the check mark. Click the Close button on the Slide Layout task pane.**

Slide 2 displays in both the slide pane and Slides tab retaining the attributes of the Proposal design template (Figure 1-32). The vertical scroll bar displays in the slide pane. The bullet displays as a square.

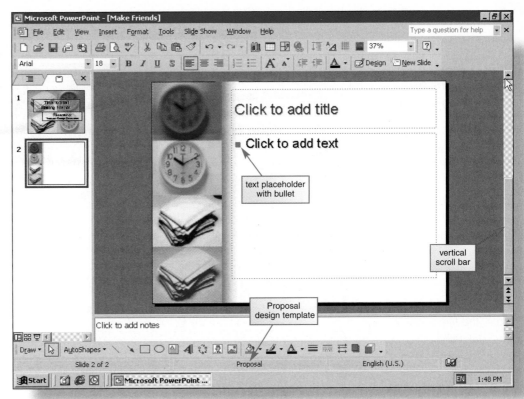

FIGURE 1-32

Slide 2 displays with a title text placeholder and a text placeholder with a bullet. You can change the layout for a slide at any time during the creation of a presentation by clicking Format on the menu bar and then clicking Slide Layout. You also can click View on the menu bar and then click Task Pane. You then can double-click the slide layout of your choice from the Slide Layout task pane.

Other **Ways**

1. On Insert menu click New Slide
2. Press CTRL+M
3. In Voice Command mode, say "New Slide"

Creating a Text Slide with a Single-Level Bulleted List

The information in the Slide 2 text placeholder is presented in a bulleted list. All the bullets display on one level. A **level** is a position within a structure, such as an outline, that indicates the magnitude of importance. PowerPoint allows for five paragraph levels. Each paragraph level has an associated bullet. The bullet font is dependent on the design template and will display differently than shown if you are using the Straight Edge design template.

Entering a Slide Title

PowerPoint assumes every new slide has a title. The title for Slide 2 is Meet People. Perform the step on the next page to enter this title.

Steps **To Enter a Slide Title**

1 **Type** Meet People **in the title text placeholder. Do not press the ENTER key.**

The title, Meet People, displays in the title text placeholder and in the Slides tab (Figure 1-33). The insertion point displays after the e in People. The selection rectangle indicates the title text placeholder is selected. Note: If using the Straight Edge design template, the title text will display centered.

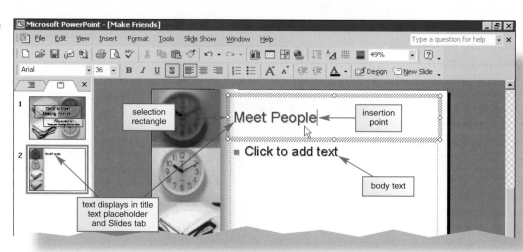

FIGURE 1-33

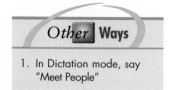

Selecting a Text Placeholder

Before you can type text into the text placeholder, you first must select it. Perform the following step to select the text placeholder on Slide 2.

Steps **To Select a Text Placeholder**

1 **Click the bulleted paragraph labeled, Click to add text.**

The insertion point displays immediately to the right of the bullet on Slide 2 (Figure 1-34). The mouse pointer may change shape if you move it away from the bullet. The selection rectangle indicates the text placeholder is selected. Note: If using the Straight Edge design template, the first-level bullet will display as a blue diamond.

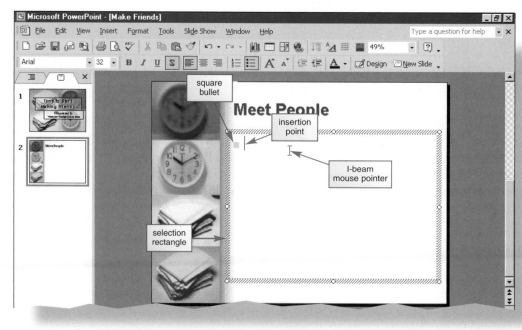

FIGURE 1-34

Typing a Single-Level Bulleted List

As discussed previously, a bulleted list is a list of paragraphs, each of which is preceded by a bullet. A paragraph is a segment of text ended by pressing the ENTER key. The next step is to type the single-level bulleted list, which consists of four entries (Figure 1-2b on page PP 1.09). Perform the following steps to type a single-level bulleted list.

Steps ## To Type a Single-Level Bulleted List

1 **Type** Develop confidence to introduce yourself to others **and then press the ENTER key.**

The paragraph, Develop confidence to introduce yourself to others, displays (Figure 1-35). The font size is 32. The insertion point displays after the second bullet. When you press the ENTER key, PowerPoint ends one paragraph and begins a new paragraph. With the Text slide layout, PowerPoint places a red square bullet in front of the new paragraph.

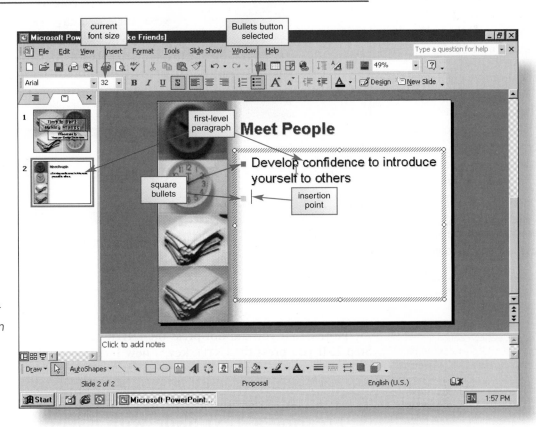

FIGURE 1-35

2 **Type** Make eye contact **and then press the ENTER key. Type** Smile and say, "Hi" **and then press the ENTER key. Type** Do not wait; start early in the semester **but do not press the ENTER key. Point to the New Slide button on the Formatting toolbar (Common Tasks button in PowerPoint 2000).**

The insertion point displays after the r in semester (Figure 1-36). Three new first-level paragraphs display with square bullets in both the text placeholder and the Slides tab. When you press the ENTER key, PowerPoint adds a new paragraph at the same level as the previous paragraph.

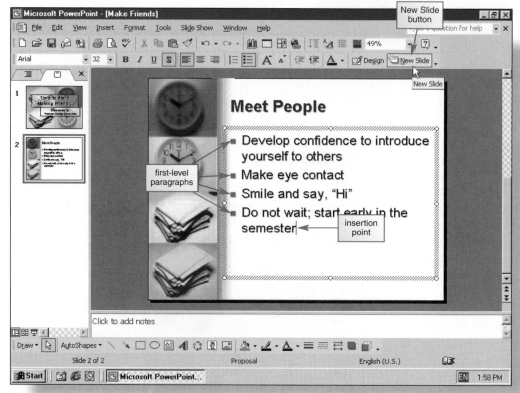

FIGURE 1-36

Other Ways

1. In Dictation mode, say "Develop confidence to introduce yourself to others, New Line, Make eye contact, New Line, Smile and say, Comma, Open Quote, Hi, Close Quote, New Line, Do not wait semicolon start early in the semester"

Notice that you did not press the ENTER key after typing the last paragraph in Step 2. If you press the ENTER key, a new bullet displays after the last entry on this slide. To remove an extra bullet, press the BACKSPACE key.

Creating a Text Slide with a Multi-Level Bulleted List

Slides 3 and 4 in Figures 1-2c and 1-2d on page PP 1.09 contain more than one level of bulleted text. A slide that consists of more than one level of bulleted text is called a **multi-level bulleted list slide**. Beginning with the second level, each paragraph indents to the right of the preceding level and is pushed down to a lower level. For example, if you increase the indent of a first-level paragraph, it becomes a second-level paragraph. This lower-level paragraph is a subset of the higher-level paragraph. It usually contains information that supports the topic in the paragraph immediately above it. You increase the indent of a paragraph by clicking the **Increase Indent button** on the Formatting toolbar.

When you want to raise a paragraph from a lower level to a higher level, you click the **Decrease Indent button** on the Formatting toolbar.

Creating a text slide with a multi-level bulleted list requires several steps. Initially, you enter a slide title in the title text placeholder. Next, you select the body text placeholder. Then, you type the text for the multi-level bulleted list, increasing and decreasing the indents as needed. The next several sections explain how to add a slide with a multi-level bulleted list.

Adding New Slides and Entering Slide Titles

When you add a new slide to a presentation, PowerPoint keeps the same layout used on the previous slide. PowerPoint assumes every new slide has a title. The title for Slide 3 is Find the Right Places. Perform the following steps to add a new slide (Slide 3) and enter a title.

Steps **To Add a New Slide and Enter a Slide Title**

1 **Click the New Slide button.** ![2000] **If using PowerPoint 2000, click the Common Tasks button on the Formatting toolbar and then click New Slide. When the New Slide dialog box displays, click the Bulleted List option, if necessary, and then click the OK button.**

Slide 3 of 3 displays in the slide pane and Slides tab (Figure 1-37).

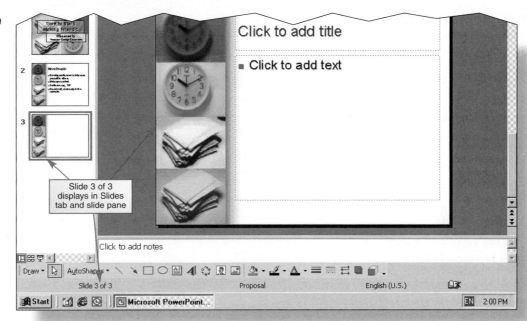

FIGURE 1-37

2 **Type** Find the Right Places **in the title text placeholder. Do not press the ENTER key.**

Slide 3 displays the Text slide layout with the title, Find the Right Places, in the title text placeholder and in the Slides tab (Figure 1-38). The insertion point displays after the s in Places.

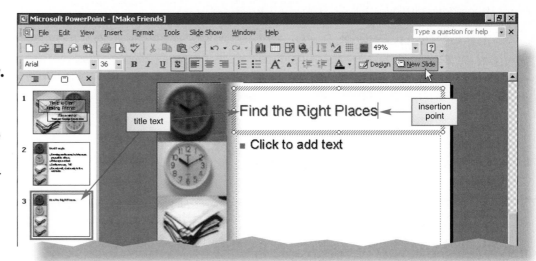

FIGURE 1-38

Slide 3 is added to the presentation with the desired title.

Other **Ways**

1. Press SHIFT+CTRL+M
2. In Dictation mode, say "New Slide, Find the Right Places"

Typing a Multi-Level Bulleted List

The next step is to select the body text placeholder and then type the multi-level bulleted list, which consists of five entries (Figure 1-2c on page PP 1.09). Perform the following steps to create a list consisting of three levels.

Steps **To Type a Multi-Level Bulleted List**

1 **Click the bulleted paragraph labeled, Click to add text.**

The insertion point displays immediately to the right of the bullet on Slide 3. The mouse pointer may change shape if you move it away from the bullet.

2 **Type** Go where people congregate **and then press the ENTER key. Point to the Increase Indent button (Demote button in PowerPoint 2000) on the Formatting toolbar.**

The paragraph, Go where people congregate, displays (Figure 1-39). The font size is 32. The insertion point displays to the right of the second bullet.

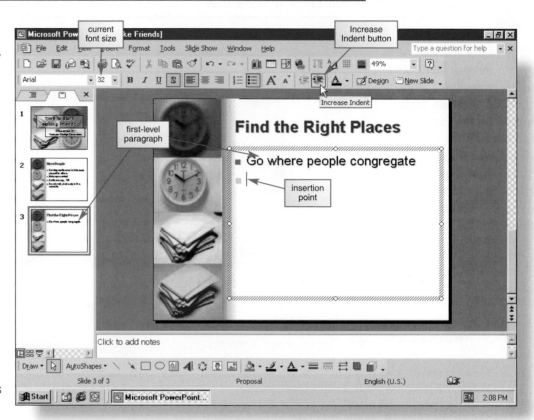

FIGURE 1-39

3 **Click the Increase Indent button (Demote button in PowerPoint 2000).**

The second paragraph indents below the first and becomes a second-level paragraph (Figure 1-40). The bullet to the left of the second paragraph changes from a square to a circle, and the font size for the paragraph now is 28. The insertion point displays to the right of the circle.

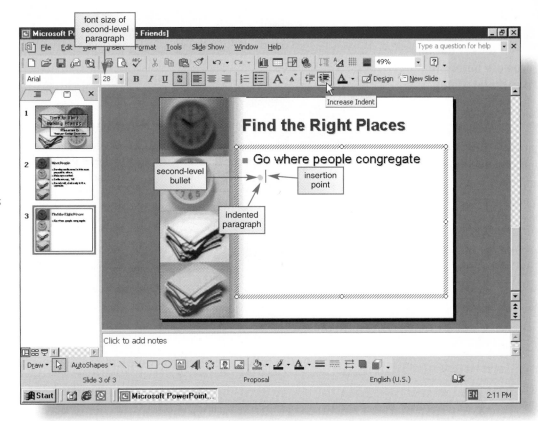

FIGURE 1-40

4 **Type** Student union, sports events **and then press the ENTER key. Point to the Decrease Indent button (Promote button in PowerPoint 2000) on the Formatting toolbar.**

The first second-level paragraph displays with a brown circle bullet in both the slide pane and the Slides tab (Figure 1-41). When you press the ENTER key, PowerPoint adds a new paragraph at the same level as the previous paragraph. Note: If using the Straight Edge design template, the second-level bullet will display as a square.

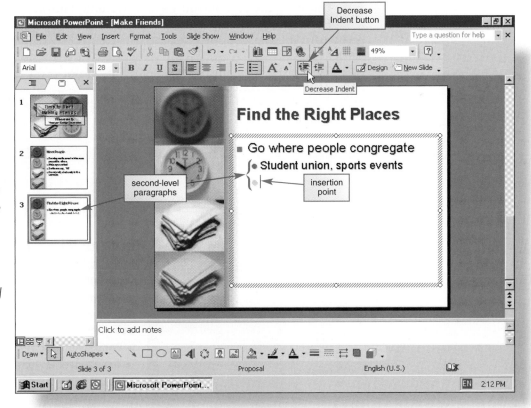

FIGURE 1-41

5 **Click the Decrease Indent button (Promote button in PowerPoint 2000).**

The second-level paragraph becomes a first-level paragraph (Figure 1-42). The bullet of the new paragraph changes from a circle to a square, and the font size for the paragraph is 32. The insertion point displays to the right of the square bullet.

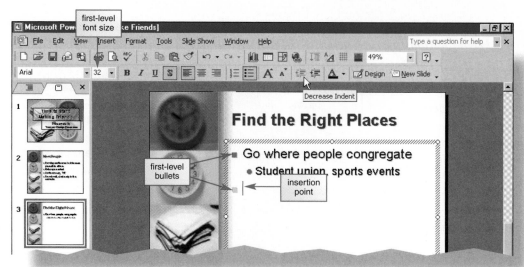

FIGURE 1-42

Perform the following steps to complete the text for Slide 3.

TO TYPE THE REMAINING TEXT FOR SLIDE 3

1 Type `Get involved in extracurricular activities` and then press the ENTER key.

2 Click the Increase Indent button (Demote button in PowerPoint 2000) on the Formatting toolbar.

3 Type `Participate in intramurals` and then press the ENTER key.

4 Type `Join Student Government` but do not press the ENTER key.

Slide 3 displays as shown in Figure 1-43. The insertion point displays after the t in Government.

FIGURE 1-43

In Step 4 above, you did not press the ENTER key after typing the last paragraph. If you press the ENTER key, a new bullet displays after the last entry on this slide. To remove an extra bullet, press the BACKSPACE key.

Slide 4 is the last slide in this presentation. It also is a multi-level bulleted list and has three levels. Perform the following steps to create Slide 4.

TO CREATE SLIDE 4

1 Click the New Slide button on the Formatting toolbar. 🔲**2000** If using PowerPoint 2000, click the Common Tasks button on the Formatting toolbar and then click New Slide. When the New Slide dialog box displays, click the Bulleted List option, if necessary, and then click the OK button.

2 Type Start a Conversation in the title text placeholder.

3 Press CTRL+ENTER to move the insertion point to the body text placeholder.

4 Type Talk about almost anything and then press the ENTER key.

5 Click the Increase Indent button (Demote button in PowerPoint 2000) on the Formatting toolbar. Type Comment on what is going on and then press the ENTER key.

The title and first two levels of bullets are added to Slide 4 (Figure 1-44).

Creating a Third-Level Paragraph

The next line in Slide 4 is indented an additional level to the third level. Perform the following steps to create an additional level.

Steps **To Create a Third-Level Paragraph**

1 **Click the Increase Indent button (Demote button in PowerPoint 2000) on the Formatting toolbar.**

The second-level paragraph becomes a third-level paragraph (Figure 1-44). The bullet to the left of the new paragraph changes from a circle to a square, and the font size for the paragraph is 24. The insertion point displays after the square bullet. Note: If using the Straight Edge design template, the third-level bullet will display as a circle.

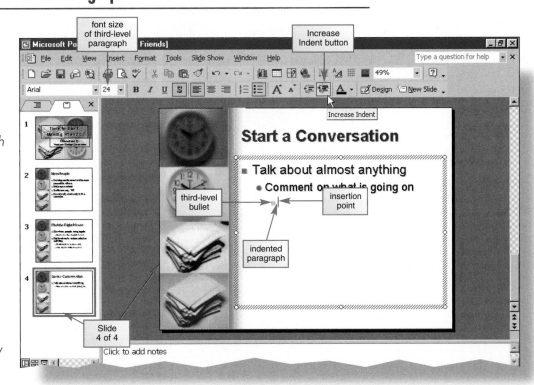

FIGURE 1-44

2 **Type** Long lines, class assignments **and then press the ENTER key. Point to the Decrease Indent button (Promote button in PowerPoint 2000) on the Formatting toolbar.**

The first third-level paragraph, Long lines, class assignments, displays with the bullet for a second third-level paragraph (Figure 1-45).

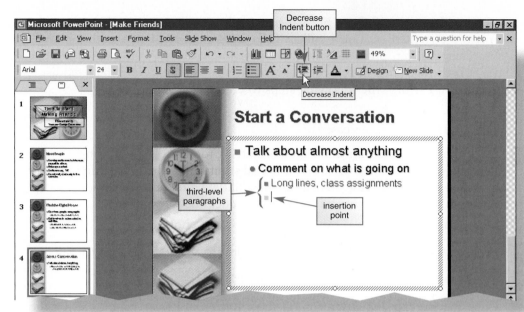

FIGURE 1-45

3 **Click the Decrease Indent button (Promote button in PowerPoint 2000) two times.**

The insertion point displays at the first level (Figure 1-46).

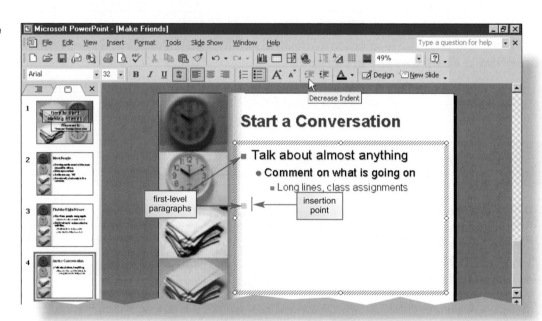

FIGURE 1-46

Other **Ways**

1. In Dictation mode, say "Tab, Long lines comma class assignments, New Line, [type Backspace]"

The title text and three levels of paragraphs discussing conversation topics are complete. The next three paragraphs concern the types of questions to ask. As an alternative to clicking the Increase Indent button, you can press the TAB key. Likewise, instead of clicking the Decrease Indent button, you can press the SHIFT+TAB keys. Perform the following steps to type the remaining text for Slide 4.

TO TYPE THE REMAINING TEXT FOR SLIDE 4

1 Type Ask questions and then press the ENTER key.

2 Press the TAB key to increase the indent to the second level.

3 Type Get people to discuss their lives and then press the ENTER key.

4 Press the TAB key to increase the indent to the third level.

5 Type Hobbies, classes, and work but do not press the ENTER key.

Other Ways

1. In Dictation mode, say "Ask questions, New Line, Tab, Get people to discuss their lives, New Line, Tab, Hobbies comma classes comma and work"

The Slide 4 title text and body text display in the slide pane and Slides tabs (Figure 1-47). The insertion point displays after the k in work.

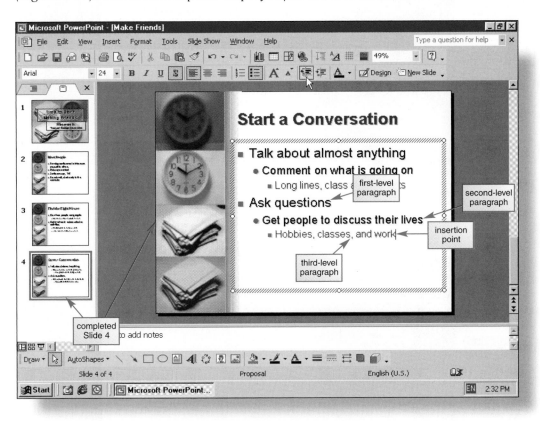

FIGURE 1-47

All the slides are created for the Make Friends slide show. This presentation consists of a title slide and three text slides with a multi-level bulleted list.

Ending a Slide Show with a Black Slide

After the last slide in the slide show displays, the default PowerPoint setting is to end the presentation with a black slide. This black slide displays only when the slide show is running and concludes the slide show gracefully so your audience never sees the PowerPoint window. A **black slide** ends all slide shows unless the option setting is deselected. Perform the steps on the next page to verify the End with black slide option is activated.

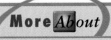

More About

Black Slides

Black slides can be used effectively to end a presentation, to pause for discussion, or to separate sections of a large presentation. The black slide focuses the audience's attention on you, the speaker, and away from the screen display.

Steps **To End a Slide Show with a Black Slide**

1 **Click Tools on the menu bar and then point to Options (Figure 1-48).**

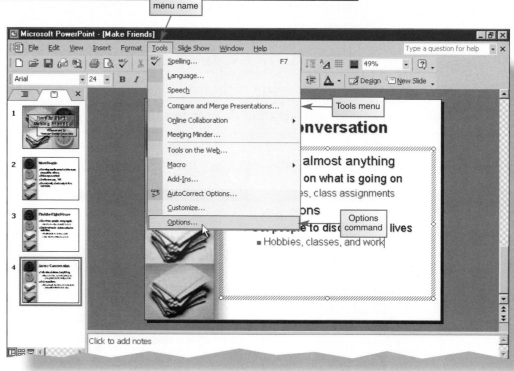

FIGURE 1-48

2 **Click Options. If necessary, click the View tab when the Options dialog box displays. Verify that the End with black slide check box is selected. If a check mark does not display, click End with black slide, and then point to the OK button.**

The Options dialog box displays (Figure 1-49). The View sheet contains settings for the overall PowerPoint display and for a particular slide show.

3 **Click the OK button.**

The End with black slide option will cause the slide show to end with a black slide until it is deselected.

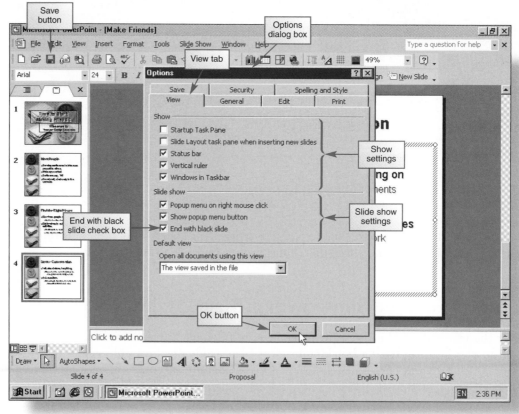

FIGURE 1-49

With all aspects of the presentation complete, it is important to save the additions and changes you have made to the Make Friends presentation.

Saving a Presentation with the Same File Name

Saving frequently cannot be overemphasized. When you first saved the presentation, you clicked the Save button on the Standard toolbar and the Save dialog box displayed. When you want to save the changes made to the presentation after your last save, you again click the Save button. This time, however, the Save dialog box does not display because PowerPoint updates the document called Make Friends.ppt on the floppy disk. Perform the following steps to save the presentation again.

TO SAVE A PRESENTATION WITH THE SAME FILE NAME

1 Be sure your floppy disk is in drive A.

2 Click the Save button on the Standard toolbar.

PowerPoint overwrites the old Make Friends.ppt document on the floppy disk in drive A with the revised presentation document. Slide 4 displays in the PowerPoint window.

Other Ways

1. In Voice Command mode, say "Save"

Moving to Another Slide in Normal View

When creating or editing a presentation in normal view, you often want to display a slide other than the current one. You can move to another slide using several methods. In the Outline tab, click any of the text in a particular slide to display that slide in the slide pane, or you can drag the scroll box on the vertical scroll bar up or down to move through the text in the presentation. In the slide pane, you can click the Previous Slide or Next Slide button on the vertical scroll bar. Clicking the **Next Slide button** advances to the next slide in the presentation. Clicking the **Previous Slide button** backs up to the slide preceding the current slide. You also can drag the scroll box on the vertical scroll bar. When you drag the scroll box, the **slide indicator** displays the number and title of the slide you are about to display. Releasing the mouse button displays the slide.

A slide's **Zoom setting** affects the portion of the slide displaying in the slide pane. PowerPoint defaults to a setting of approximately 50 percent so the entire slide displays. This percentage depends on the size and type of your monitor. If you want to display a small portion of the current slide, you would zoom in by clicking the **Zoom box arrow** and then clicking the desired magnification. You can display the entire slide in the slide pane by clicking **Fit** in the Zoom list. The Zoom setting affects the action of the vertical and horizontal scroll bars. If Zoom is set so the entire slide is not visible in the slide pane, clicking the up scroll arrow on the vertical scroll bar displays the next portion of the slide, not the previous slide.

More About

Zoom Settings

You can increase your Zoom setting as large as 400% when you want to see details on small objects. Likewise, you can decrease your Zoom setting as small as 10%. When you want to redisplay the entire slide, click Fit in the Zoom list.

Using the Scroll Box on the Slide Pane to Move to Another Slide

Before continuing with Project 1, you want to display the title slide. Perform the steps on the next page to move from Slide 4 to Slide 1 using the scroll box on the slide pane vertical scroll bar.

Steps **To Use the Scroll Box on the Slide Pane to Move to Another Slide**

1 **Position the mouse pointer on the scroll box. Press and hold down the mouse button.**

Slide: 4 of 4 Start a Conversation displays in the slide indicator (Figure 1-50). When you click the scroll box, the Slide 4 thumbnail is not shaded in the Slides tab.

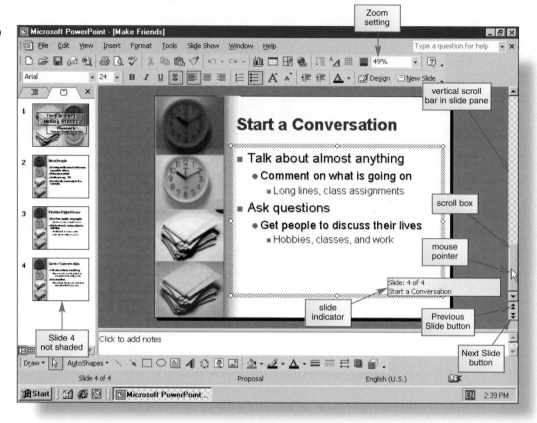

FIGURE 1-50

2 **Drag the scroll box up the vertical scroll bar until Slide: 1 of 4 Time to Start Making Friends displays in the slide indicator.**

Slide: 1 of 4 Time to Start Making Friends displays in the slide indicator (Figure 1-51). Slide 4 still displays in the PowerPoint window.

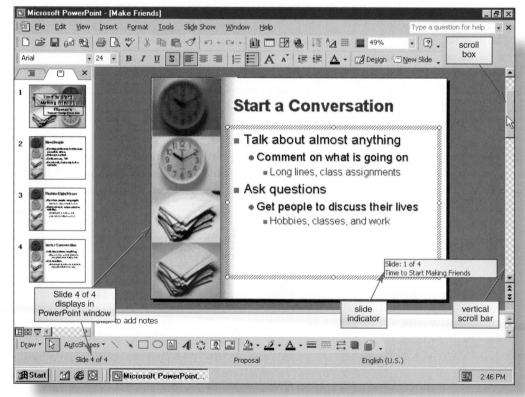

FIGURE 1-51

3 **Release the mouse button.**

Slide 1, titled Time to Start Making Friends, displays in the PowerPoint window (Figure 1-52). The Slide 1 thumbnail is shaded in the Slides tab indicating it is selected. **2000** *If using PowerPoint 2000, slide thumbnails will not display. Instead, the entered text will display to the right of each slide's icon in an outline pane.*

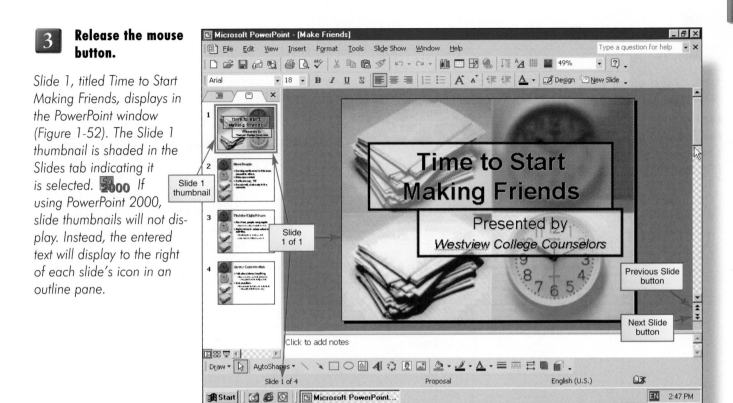

FIGURE 1-52

Viewing the Presentation in Slide Show View

The **Slide Show button**, located at the lower-left of the PowerPoint window above the status bar, allows you to display a presentation electronically using a computer. The computer acts like a slide projector, displaying each slide on a full screen. The full screen slide hides the toolbars, menus, and other PowerPoint window elements. When making a presentation, you use **slide show view**. You can start slide show view from normal view or slide sorter view.

Starting Slide Show View

Slide show view begins when you click the Slide Show button at the lower-left of the PowerPoint window above the status bar. PowerPoint then displays the current slide on the full screen without any of the PowerPoint window objects, such as the menu bar or toolbars. Perform the steps on the next page to start slide show view.

Other Ways

1. Click Next Slide button or Previous Slide button to move forward or back one slide
2. Press PAGE DOWN or PAGE UP to move forward or back one slide

Microsoft **PowerPoint**

To Start Slide Show View

1 **Point to the Slide Show button in the lower-left corner of the PowerPoint window above the status bar (Figure 1-53).**

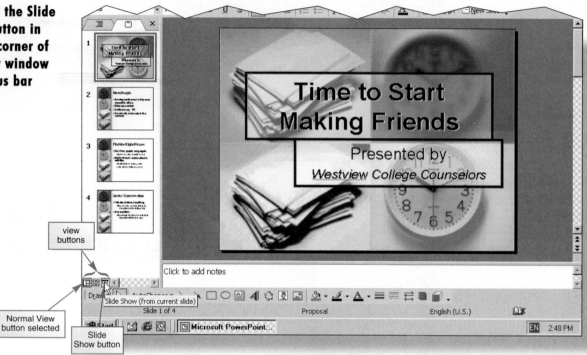

view buttons

Normal View button selected

Slide Show button

Slide Show (from current slide)

FIGURE 1-53

2 **Click the Slide Show button.**

A starting slide show message displays momentarily and then the title slide fills the screen (Figure 1-54). The PowerPoint window is hidden.

title slide in slide show view

FIGURE 1-54

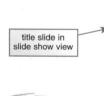

Other **Ways**

1. On View menu click Slide Show
2. Press F5
3. In Voice Command mode, say "View show"

Advancing Through a Slide Show Manually

After you begin slide show view, you can move forward or backward through the slides. PowerPoint allows you to advance through the slides manually or automatically. Perform the following steps to move manually through the slides.

 To Move Manually Through Slides in a Slide Show

1 **Click each slide until the Start a Conversation slide (Slide 4) displays.**

Slide 4 displays (Figure 1-55). Each slide in the presentation displays on the screen, one slide at a time. Each time you click the mouse button, the next slide displays.

Slide 4 displays in slide show view →

FIGURE 1-55

Start a Conversation

- ■ Talk about almost anything
  - ● Comment on what is going on
    - ▪ Long lines, class assignments
- ■ Ask questions
  - ● Get people to discuss their lives
    - ▪ Hobbies, classes, and work

2 **Click Slide 4.**

The black slide displays (Figure 1-56). The message at the top of the slide announces the end of the slide show. If you wanted to end the presentation at this point and return to normal view, you would click the black slide.

End of slide show, click to exit.

message

FIGURE 1-56

Using the Popup Menu to Go to a Specific Slide

Slide show view has a shortcut menu, called the **Popup menu**, that displays when you right-click a slide in slide show view. This menu contains commands to assist you during a slide show. For example, clicking the **Next command** moves to the next

Other Ways

1. Press PAGE DOWN to advance one slide at a time, or press PAGE UP to go backward one slide at a time

2. Press RIGHT or LEFT ARROW

slide. Clicking the **Previous command** moves to the previous slide. Pointing to the **Go command** and then clicking Slide Navigator allows you to move to any slide in the presentation. The **Slide Navigator dialog box** contains a list of the slides in the presentation. Go to the requested slide by double-clicking the name of that slide. Perform the following steps to go to the title slide (Slide 1) in the Make Friends presentation.

Steps **To Display the Popup Menu and Go to a Specific Slide**

1 **With the black slide displaying in slide show view, right-click the slide. Point to Go on the Popup menu, and then point to Slide Navigator on the Go submenu.**

The Popup menu displays on the black slide, and the Go submenu displays (Figure 1-57). Your screen may look different because the Popup menu displays near the location of the mouse pointer at the time you right-click.

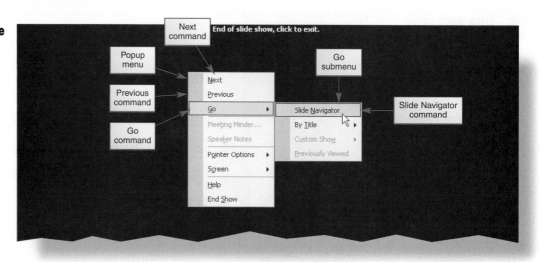

FIGURE 1-57

2 **Click Slide Navigator. When the Slide Navigator dialog box displays, point to 1. Time to Start Making Friends in the Slide titles list.**

The Slide Navigator dialog box contains a list of the slides in the presentation (Figure 1-58).

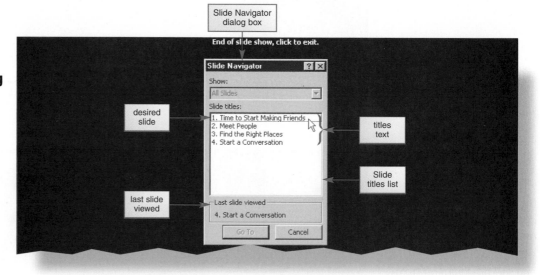

FIGURE 1-58

3 **Double-click 1. Time to Start Making Friends.**

The title slide, Time to Start Making Friends (shown in Figure 1-54 on page PP 1.48), displays.

Other **Ways**

1. Right-click slide, point to Go on Popup menu, click Slide Navigator, type slide number, press ENTER

Additional Popup menu commands allow you to write meeting minutes or to create a list of action items during a slide show, change the mouse pointer to a pen that draws in various colors, blacken the screen, and end the slide show. Popup menu commands are discussed as they are used.

Using the Popup Menu to End a Slide Show

The **End Show command** on the Popup menu ends slide show view and returns to the same view as when you clicked the Slide Show button. Perform the following steps to end slide show view and return to normal view.

 To Use the Popup Menu to End a Slide Show

1 **Right-click the title slide and then point to End Show on the Popup menu.**

The Popup menu displays on Slide 1 (Figure 1-59).

2 **Click End Show. If the Microsoft PowerPoint dialog box displays, click the Yes button.**

PowerPoint ends slide show view and returns to normal view (shown in Figure 1-60 on the next page). Slide 1 displays because it is the last slide displayed in slide show view.

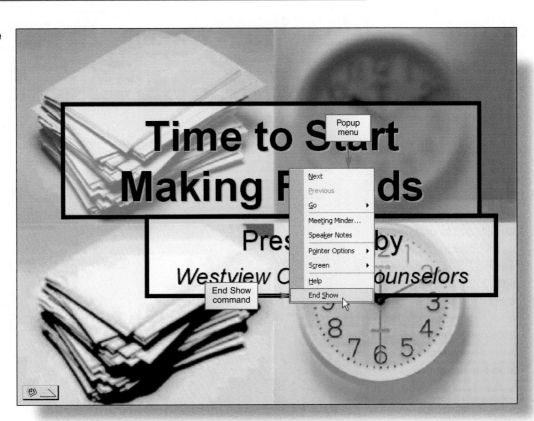

FIGURE 1-59

Quitting PowerPoint

The Make Friends presentation now is complete. When you quit PowerPoint, PowerPoint prompts you to save any changes made to the presentation since the last save, closes all PowerPoint windows, and then quits PowerPoint. Closing PowerPoint returns control to the desktop. Perform the steps on the next page to quit PowerPoint.

Steps **To Quit PowerPoint**

1 **Point to the Close button on the PowerPoint title bar (Figure 1-60).**

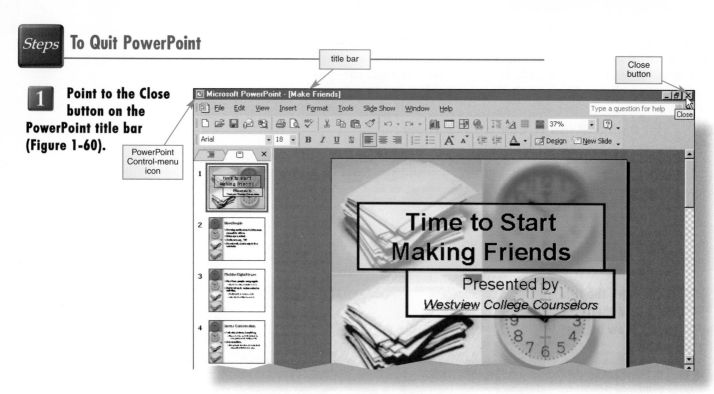

FIGURE 1-60

2 **Click the Close button.**

PowerPoint closes and the Windows desktop displays (Figure 1-61). If you made changes to the presentation since your last save, a Microsoft PowerPoint dialog box displays asking if you want to save changes. Clicking the Yes button saves the changes to the presentation before closing PowerPoint. Clicking the No button quits PowerPoint without saving the changes. Clicking the Cancel button returns to the presentation.

Other **Ways**

1. Double-click PowerPoint Control-menu icon; or click PowerPoint Control-menu icon, on Control menu click Close
2. On File menu click Exit
3. Press CTRL+Q or press ALT+F4

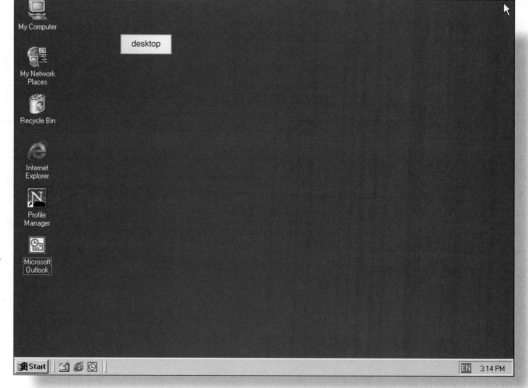

FIGURE 1-61

Opening a Presentation

Earlier, you saved the presentation on a floppy disk using the file name, Make Friends. Once you create and save a presentation, you may need to retrieve it from the floppy disk to make changes. For example, you may want to replace the design template or modify some text. Recall that a presentation is a PowerPoint document. Use the **Open Office Document command** to open an existing presentation.

Opening an Existing Presentation

Be sure that the floppy disk used to save the Make Friends presentation is in drive A. Then, perform the following steps to open the presentation using the Open Office Document command on the Start menu.

 To Open an Existing Presentation

1 **Click the Start button on the Windows taskbar and then point to Open Office Document.**

The Windows Start menu displays and Open Office Document is highlighted (Figure 1-62). The ScreenTip displays the function of the command.

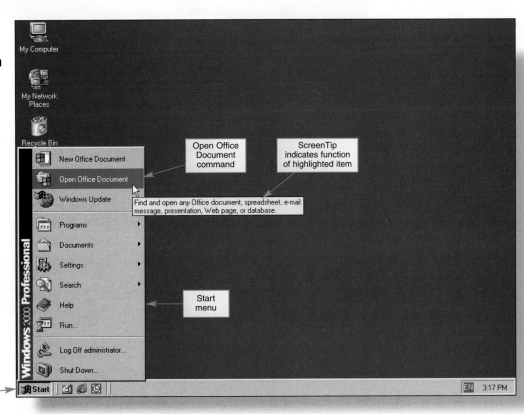

FIGURE 1-62

2 **Click Open Office Document. When the Open Office Document dialog box displays, if necessary, click the Look in box arrow and then click 3½ Floppy (A:) in the Look in list.**

The Open Office Document dialog box displays (Figure 1-63). A list of existing files displays on drive A. Notice that Office Files displays in the Files of type box. The file, Make Friends, is highlighted. Your list of existing files may be different depending on the files saved on your floppy disk.

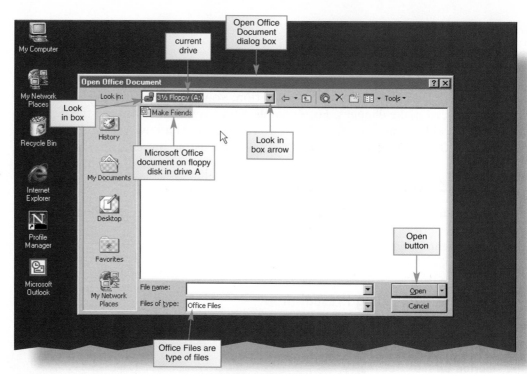

FIGURE 1-63

3 **Double-click the file name, Make Friends.**

PowerPoint starts, opens Make Friends on drive A, and displays the first slide in the PowerPoint window (Figure 1-64). The presentation displays in normal view because PowerPoint opens a presentation in the same view in which it was saved.

FIGURE 1-64

Other Ways

1. Click Open button on Standard toolbar, select file name, click Open button in Open Office Document dialog box

2. On File menu click Open, select file name, click Open button in Open dialog box

3. In Voice Command mode, say "Open file, [type file name], Open"

When you start PowerPoint and open Make Friends, the application name and file name display on a recessed button on the Windows taskbar. When more than one application is open, you can switch between applications by clicking the appropriate application button.

Checking a Presentation for Spelling and Consistency

After you create a presentation, you should check it visually for spelling errors and style consistency. In addition, you can use PowerPoint's Spelling and Style tools to identify possible misspellings and inconsistencies.

Checking a Presentation for Spelling Errors

PowerPoint checks the entire presentation for spelling mistakes using a standard dictionary contained in the Microsoft Office group. This dictionary is shared with the other Microsoft Office applications such as Word and Excel. A **custom dictionary** is available if you want to add special words such as proper names, cities, and acronyms. When checking a presentation for spelling errors, PowerPoint opens the standard dictionary and the custom dictionary file, if one exists. When a word displays in the Spelling dialog box, you perform one of the actions listed in Table 1-3.

More About

Spelling Checker

While PowerPoint's Spelling checker is a valuable tool, it is not infallible. You should proofread your presentation carefully by saying each word aloud and pointing to each word as you say it. Be mindful of commonly misused words such as its and it's, their and they're, and you're and your.

Table 1-3 Summary of Spelling Checker Actions	
FEATURE	*DESCRIPTION*
Ignore the word	Click the Ignore button when the word is spelled correctly but not found in the dictionaries. PowerPoint continues checking the rest of the presentation.
Ignore all occurrences of the word	Click the Ignore All button when the word is spelled correctly but not found in the dictionaries. PowerPoint ignores all occurrences of the word and continues checking the rest of the presentation.
Select a different spelling	Click the proper spelling of the word from the list in the Suggestions box. Click the Change button. PowerPoint corrects the word and continues checking the rest of the presentation.
Change all occurrences of the misspelling to a different spelling	Click the proper spelling of the word from the list in the Suggestions box. Click the Change All button. PowerPoint changes all occurrences of the misspelled word and continues checking the rest of the presentation.
Add a word to the custom dictionary	Click the Add button. PowerPoint opens the custom dictionary, adds the word, and continues checking the rest of the presentation.
View alternative spellings	Click the Suggest button. PowerPoint lists suggested spellings. Click the correct word from the Suggestions box or type the proper spelling. Then click the Change button. PowerPoint continues checking the rest of the presentation.
Add spelling error to AutoCorrect list	Click the AutoCorrect button. PowerPoint adds the spelling error and its correction to the AutoCorrect list. Any future misspelling of the word is corrected automatically as you type.
Close	Click the Close button to close the Spelling checker and return to the PowerPoint window.

The standard dictionary contains commonly used English words. It does not, however, contain proper names, abbreviations, technical terms, poetic contractions, or antiquated terms. PowerPoint treats words not found in the dictionaries as misspellings.

Starting the Spelling Checker

Perform the steps on the next page to start the Spelling checker and check the entire presentation.

Steps **To Start the Spelling Checker**

1 **Point to the Spelling button on the Standard toolbar (Figure 1-65).**

FIGURE 1-65

2 **Click the Spelling button. When the Spelling dialog box displays, point to the Ignore button.**

PowerPoint starts the Spelling checker and displays the Spelling dialog box (Figure 1-66). The word, Westview, displays in the Not in Dictionary box. Depending on the custom dictionary, Westview may not be recognized as a misspelled word.

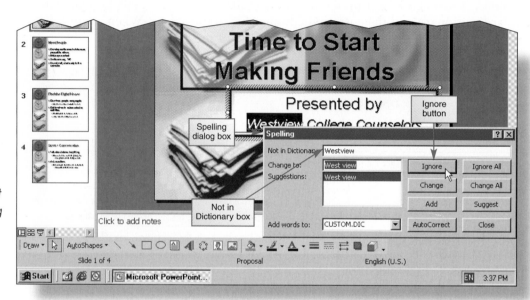

FIGURE 1-66

3 **Click the Ignore button. When the Microsoft PowerPoint dialog box displays, point to the OK button.**

PowerPoint ignores the word, Westview, and continues searching for additional misspelled words. PowerPoint may stop on additional words depending on your typing accuracy. When PowerPoint has checked all slides for misspellings, it displays the Microsoft PowerPoint dialog box informing you that the spelling check is complete (Figure 1-67).

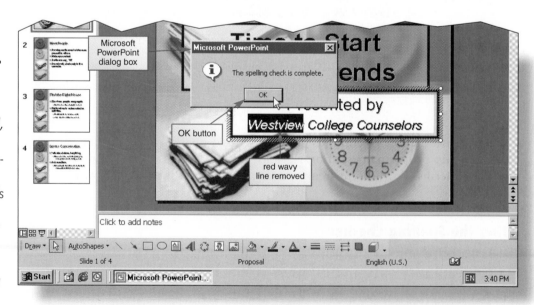

FIGURE 1-67

Click the OK button.

PowerPoint closes the Spelling checker and returns to the current slide, Slide 1 (Figure 1-68), or to the slide where a possible misspelled word displayed.

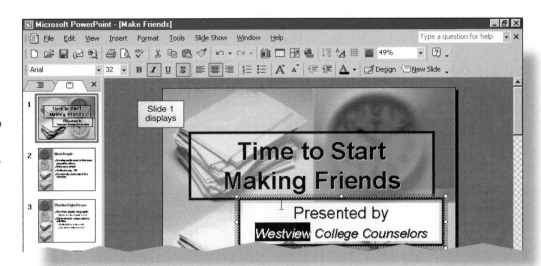

FIGURE 1-68

The red wavy line below the word, Westview, is gone because you instructed PowerPoint to ignore that word, which does not appear in the standard dictionary. You also could have added that word to the dictionary so it would not be flagged as a possible misspelled word in subsequent presentations you create using that word.

Correcting Errors

After creating a presentation and running the Spelling checker, you may find that you must make changes. Changes may be required because a slide contains an error, the scope of the presentation shifts, or the style is inconsistent. This section explains the types of errors that commonly occur when creating a presentation.

Types of Corrections Made to Presentations

You generally make three types of corrections to text in a presentation: additions, deletions, and replacements.

- **Additions** are necessary when you omit text from a slide and need to add it later. You may need to insert text in the form of a sentence, word, or single character. For example, you may want to add the rest of the presenter's first name on the title slide.
- **Deletions** are required when text on a slide is incorrect or no longer is relevant to the presentation. For example, a slide may look cluttered. Therefore, you may want to remove one of the bulleted paragraphs to add more space.
- **Replacements** are needed when you want to revise the text in a presentation. For example, you may want to substitute the word, their, for the word, there.

Editing text in PowerPoint basically is the same as editing text in a word processing package. The following sections illustrate the most common changes made to text in a presentation.

Deleting Text

You can delete text using one of four methods. One is to use the BACKSPACE key to remove text just typed. The second is to position the insertion point to the left of the text you wish to delete and then press the DELETE key. The third method is to double-click the word you wish to delete and then type the correct text. The fourth method is to drag through the text you wish to delete and then press the DELETE key. (Use the fourth method when deleting large sections of text.)

Replacing Text in an Existing Slide

When you need to correct a word or phrase, you can replace the text by selecting the text to be replaced and then typing the new text. As soon as you press any key on the keyboard, the highlighted text is deleted and the new text displays.

PowerPoint inserts text to the left of the insertion point. The text to the right of the insertion point moves to the right (and shifts downward, if necessary) to accommodate the added text.

Table 1-4	Appearance in Black and White View	
OBJECT	APPEARANCE IN BLACK AND WHITE VIEW	
Bitmaps	Grayscale	
Embossing	Hidden	
Fills	Grayscale	
Frame	Black	
Lines	Black	
Object shadows	Grayscale	
Pattern fills	Grayscale	
Slide backgrounds	White	
Text	Black	
Text shadows	Hidden	

Displaying a Presentation in Black and White

Printing handouts of a presentation allows you to use them to make overhead transparencies. The **Color/Grayscale button** on the Standard toolbar displays the presentation in black and white before you print. Table 1-4 identifies how PowerPoint objects display in black and white.

Perform the following steps to display the presentation in black and white.

Steps To Display a Presentation in Black and White

1 **Click the Color/ Grayscale button on the Standard toolbar and then point to Pure Black and White in the list.** **2000** **If using PowerPoint 2000, click the Grayscale Preview button on the Standard toolbar and then skip to Step 3 on the next page.**

The Color/Grayscale list displays (Figure 1-69). Pure Black and White alters the slides' appearance so that only black lines display on a white background. Grayscale displays varying degrees of gray.

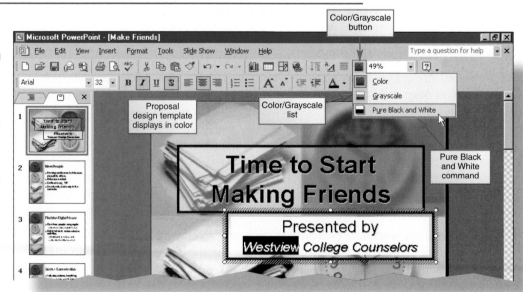

FIGURE 1-69

2 Click Pure Black and White.

Slide 1 displays in black and white in the slide pane (Figure 1-70). The four slide thumbnails display in color in the Slides tab. The Grayscale View toolbar displays. The Color/ Grayscale button on the Standard toolbar changes from color bars to black and white.

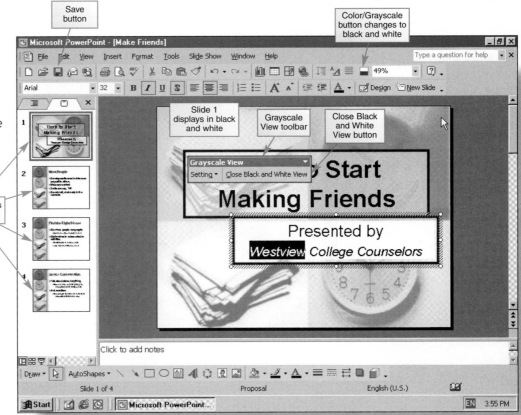

FIGURE 1-70

3 Click the Next Slide button three times to view all slides in the presentation in black and white. Point to the Close Black and White View button on the Grayscale View toolbar (Figure 1-71). If using PowerPoint 2000, click the Grayscale button on the Standard toolbar and then skip to the next page and the text that begins below the heading, Printing a Presentation.

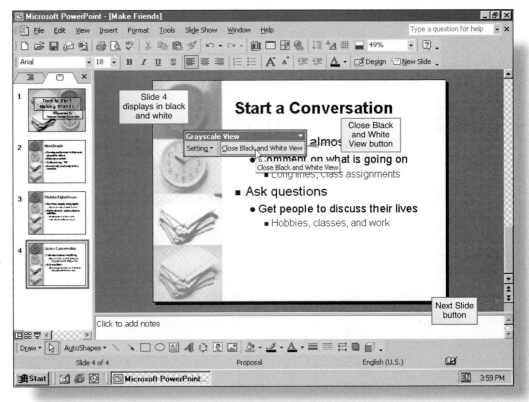

FIGURE 1-71

<table>
<tr><td>**4**</td><td>**Click the Close Black and White View button.**</td></tr>
</table>

Slide 4 displays with the default Proposal color scheme (Figure 1-72).

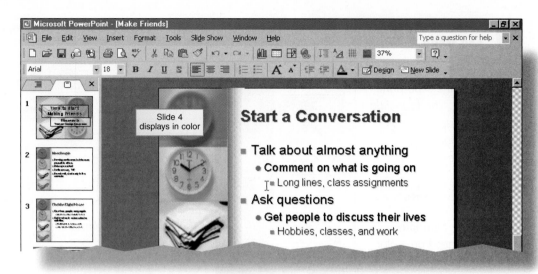

FIGURE 1-72

After you view the text objects in the presentation in black and white, you can make any changes that will enhance printouts produced from a black and white printer or photocopier.

Printing a Presentation

After you create a presentation, you often want to print it. A printed version of the presentation is called a **hard copy**, or **printout**. The first printing of the presentation is called a **rough draft**. The rough draft allows you to proofread the presentation to check for errors and readability. After correcting errors, you print the final copy of the presentation.

Saving Before Printing

Before printing a presentation, you should save your work in the event you experience difficulties with the printer. You occasionally may encounter system problems that can be resolved only by restarting the computer. In such an instance, you will need to reopen the presentation. As a precaution, always save the presentation before you print. Perform the following steps to save the presentation before printing.

TO SAVE A PRESENTATION BEFORE PRINTING

1   Verify that the floppy disk is in drive A.

2   Click the Save button on the Standard toolbar.

All changes made after your last save now are saved on a floppy disk.

Printing the Presentation

After saving the presentation, you are ready to print. Clicking the **Print button** on the Standard toolbar causes PowerPoint to print all slides in the presentation. Perform the following steps to print the presentation slides.

 **To Print a Presentation**

1 **Ready the printer according to the printer instructions. Then click the Print button on the Standard toolbar.**

The printer icon in the tray status area on the Windows taskbar indicates a print job is processing (Figure 1-73). After several moments, the slide show begins printing on the printer. When the presentation is finished printing, the printer icon in the tray status area on the Windows taskbar no longer displays.

2 **When the printer stops, retrieve the printouts of the slides.**

The presentation, Make Friends, prints on four pages (Figures 1-2a through 1-2d on page PP 1.09).

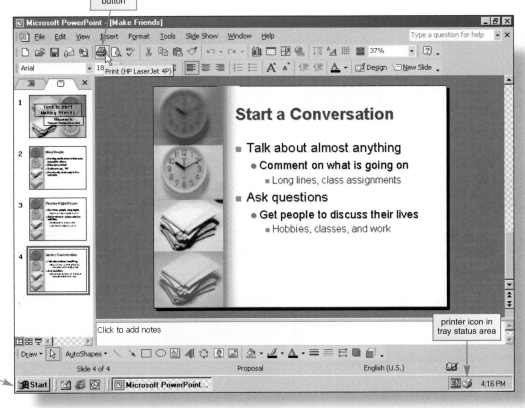

FIGURE 1-73

You can click the printer icon next to the clock in the tray status area on the Windows taskbar to obtain information about the presentations printing on your printer and to delete files in the print queue that are waiting to be printed.

Making a Transparency

With the handouts printed, you now can make overhead transparencies using one of several devices. One device is a printer attached to your computer, such as an ink-jet printer or a laser printer. Transparencies produced on a printer may be in black and white or color, depending on the printer. Another device is a photocopier. Because each of these devices requires a special transparency film, check the user's manual for the film requirement of your specific device, or ask your instructor.

PowerPoint Help System

You can get answers to PowerPoint questions at any time by using the **PowerPoint Help system**. Used properly, this form of assistance can increase your productivity and reduce your frustrations by minimizing the time you spend learning how to use PowerPoint.

Other Ways

1. On File menu click Print
2. Press CTRL+P or press CTRL+SHIFT+F12
3. In Voice Command mode, say "Print"

More About

The PowerPoint Help System

The best way to become familiar with the PowerPoint Help system is to use it. Appendix A includes detailed information on the PowerPoint Help system and exercises that will help you gain confidence in using it.

The following section shows how to get answers to your questions using the Ask a Question box on the menu bar. For additional information on using the PowerPoint Help system, see Appendix A and Table 1-5 on page PP 1.65.

Obtaining Help Using the Ask a Question Box on the Menu Bar

The **Ask a Question box** on the right side of the menu bar lets you type free-form questions such as, how do I save or how do I create a Web page, or you can type terms such as, copy, save, or format. PowerPoint responds by displaying a list of topics related to what you typed. The following steps show how to use the Ask a Question box to obtain information on formatting a presentation.

Steps **To Obtain Help Using the Ask a Question Box**

1 **Click the Ask a Question box on the right side of the menu bar and then type** bullet **(Figure 1-74).** **2000** **If using PowerPoint 2000, click the Microsoft PowerPoint Help button on the right side of the Standard toolbar. Type your question or short phrase in the What would you like to do? text box and then click the Search button.**

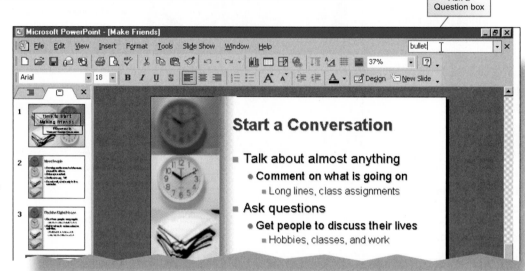

FIGURE 1-74

2 **Press the ENTER key. When the list of topics displays below the Ask a Question box, point to the topic, Change the bullet style in a list.**

A list of topics displays relating to the phrase, Change the bullet style in a list (Figure 1-75). The mouse pointer changes to a hand, which indicates it is pointing to a link.

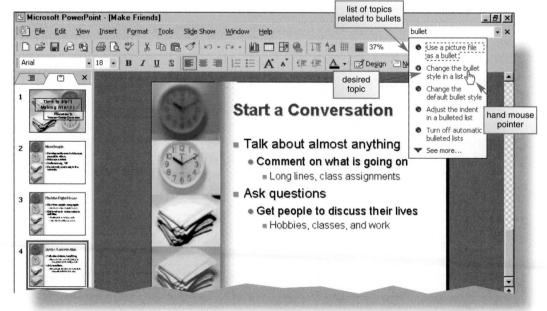

FIGURE 1-75

3 Click Change the bullet style in a list. When the Microsoft PowerPoint Help window displays, double-click its title bar to maximize it. Point to Change the bullet style for a single list.

A Microsoft PowerPoint Help window displays that provides Help information about changing the bullet style for a slide (Figure 1-76). The mouse pointer changes to a hand. The Index, Answer Wizard, or Contents sheet is active on the left side of the Microsoft PowerPoint Help window.

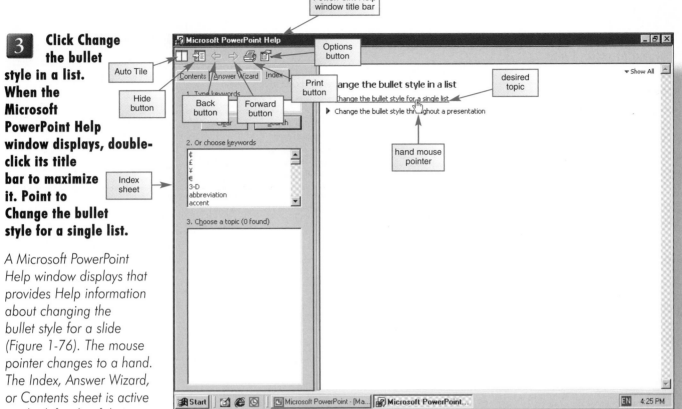

FIGURE 1-76

4 Click Change the bullet style for a single list. Point to Change the bullet color.

Directions for changing a bullet style on a single slide display. Options include changing a bullet character, changing a bullet size, and changing a bullet color (Figure 1-77).

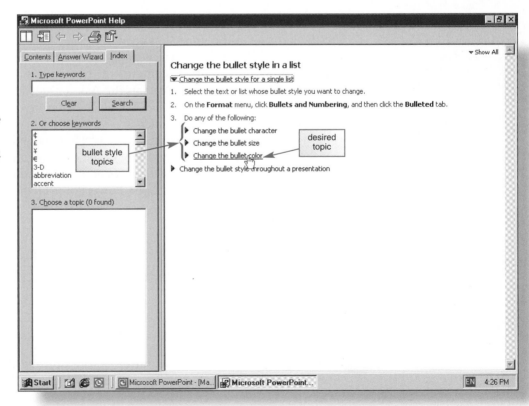

FIGURE 1-77

5 **Click Change the bullet color. Point to the Close button on the Microsoft PowerPoint Help window title bar.**

Specific details of changing the color of the bullets on a slide display (Figure 1-78).

6 **Click the Close button on the Microsoft PowerPoint Help window title bar.**

The PowerPoint Help window closes, and the PowerPoint presentation displays.

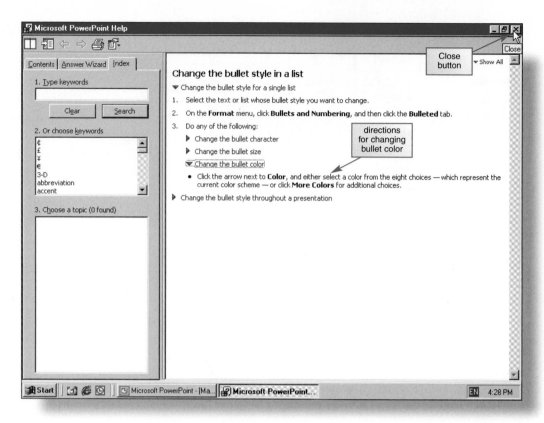

FIGURE 1-78

Other Ways

1. Click Microsoft PowerPoint Help button on Standard toolbar; or on Help menu click Microsoft PowerPoint Help
2. Press F1

Use the buttons in the upper-left corner of the Microsoft PowerPoint Help window (Figure 1-76 on the previous page) to navigate through the Help system, change the display, and print the contents of the window.

As you enter questions and terms in the Ask a Question box, PowerPoint adds them to its list. Thus, if you click the Ask a Question box arrow, a list of previously asked questions and terms will display.

Table 1-5 summarizes the 10 categories of Help available to you. Because of the way the PowerPoint Help system works, be certain to review the rightmost column of Table 1-5 if you have difficulties activating the desired category of help. For additional information on using the PowerPoint Help system, see Appendix A.

Quitting PowerPoint

Project 1 is complete. The final task is to close the presentation and quit PowerPoint. Perform the following steps to quit PowerPoint.

TO QUIT POWERPOINT

1 Click the Close button on the title bar.

2 If prompted to save the presentation before quitting PowerPoint, click the Yes button in the Microsoft PowerPoint dialog box.

Table 1-5 PowerPoint Help System

TYPE	DESCRIPTION	HOW TO ACTIVATE
Answer Wizard	Answers questions or searches for terms that you type in your own words.	Click the Microsoft PowerPoint Help button on the Standard toolbar. Click the Answer Wizard tab.
Ask a Question box	Answers questions or searches for terms that you type in your own words.	Type a question or term in the Ask a Question box on the menu bar and then press the ENTER key.
Contents sheet	Groups Help topics by general categories. Use when you know only the general category of the topic in question.	Click the Microsoft PowerPoint Help button on the Standard toolbar. Click the Contents tab.
Detect and Repair	Automatically finds and fixes errors in the application.	Click Detect and Repair on the Help menu.
Hardware and Software Information	Shows Product ID and allows access to system information and technical support information.	Click About Microsoft PowerPoint on the Help menu and then click the appropriate button.
Index sheet	Similar to an index in a book. Use when you know exactly what you want.	Click the Microsoft PowerPoint Help button on the Standard toolbar. If necessary, maximize the Help window by double-clicking its title bar. Click the Index tab.
Office Assistant	Similar to the Ask a Question box in that the Office Assistant answers questions that you type in your own words, offers tips, and provides help for a variety of PowerPoint features.	Click the Office Assistant icon if it is on the screen. If the Office Assistant does not display, click Show the Office Assistant on the Help menu.
Office on the Web	Used to access technical resources and download free product enhancements on the Web.	Click Office on the Web on the Help menu.
Question Mark button	Used to identify unfamiliar items in a dialog box.	Click the Question Mark button on the title bar of a dialog box and then click an item in the dialog box.
What's This? Command	Used to identify unfamiliar items on the screen.	Click What's This? on the Help menu, and then click an item on the screen.

C A S E   P E R S P E C T I V E   S U M M A R Y

Jennifer Williams is pleased with the Time to Start Making Friends PowerPoint slide show. The counseling staff will present methods of facing loneliness to incoming freshmen attending orientation sessions at your school. The four slides display a variety of ways students can make friends on campus. The title slide identifies the topic of the presentation, and the next three slides give key pointers regarding going to appropriate places to meet people and start a conversation. The counselors will use your slides to make overhead transparencies to organize their speeches, and the students will keep handouts of your slides for future reference.

Project Summary

Project 1 introduced you to starting PowerPoint and creating a presentation consisting of a title slide and single- and multi-level bulleted lists. You learned about PowerPoint design templates, objects, and attributes. This project illustrated how to create an interesting introduction to a presentation by changing the text font style to italic and increasing font size on the title slide. Completing these tasks, you saved the presentation. Then, you created three text slides with bulleted lists, two with multi-level bullets, to explain how to meet friends in college. Next, you learned how to view the presentation in slide show view. Then, you learned how to quit PowerPoint and how to open an existing presentation. You used the Spelling checker to search for spelling errors. You learned how to display the presentation in black and white. You learned how to print hard copies of the slides in order to make handouts and overhead transparencies. Finally, you learned how to use the PowerPoint Help system.

What You Should Know

Having completed this project, you now should be able to perform the following tasks:

▶ Add a New Slide and Enter a Slide Title *(PP 1.37)*

▶ Add a New Text Slide with a Bulleted List *(PP 1.32)*

▶ Change the Text Font Style to Italic *(PP 1.26)*

▶ Choose a Design Template *(PP 1.19)*

▶ Create a Third-Level Paragraph *(PP 1.41)*

▶ Create Slide 4 *(PP 1.41)*

▶ Customize the PowerPoint Window *(PP 1.12)*

▶ Display a Presentation in Black and White *(PP 1.58)*

▶ Display the Popup Menu and Go to a Specific Slide *(PP 1.50)*

▶ Display the Toolbars on Two Rows When Using PowerPoint 2000 *(PP 1.11)*

▶ End a Slide Show with a Black Slide *(PP 1.44)*

▶ Enter a Slide Title *(PP 1.34)*

▶ Enter the Presentation Subtitle *(PP 1.24)*

▶ Enter the Presentation Title *(PP 1.22)*

▶ Increase Font Size *(PP 1.27)*

▶ Move Manually Through Slides in a Slide Show *(PP 1.49)*

▶ Obtain Help Using the Ask a Question Box *(PP 1.62)*

▶ Open an Existing Presentation *(PP 1.53)*

▶ Print a Presentation *(PP 1.61)*

▶ Quit PowerPoint *(PP 1.52, 1.64)*

▶ Save a Presentation Before Printing *(PP 1.60)*

▶ Save a Presentation on a Floppy Disk *(PP 1.29)*

▶ Save a Presentation with the Same File Name *(PP 1.45)*

▶ Select a Text Placeholder *(PP 1.34)*

▶ Start PowerPoint *(PP 1.10)*

▶ Start Slide Show View *(PP 1.48)*

▶ Start the Spelling Checker *(PP 1.56)*

▶ Type a Multi-Level Bulleted List *(PP 1.38)*

▶ Type a Single-Level Bulleted List *(PP 1.35)*

▶ Type the Remaining Text for Slide 3 *(PP 1.40)*

▶ Type the Remaining Text for Slide 4 *(PP 1.43)*

▶ Use the Popup Menu to End a Slide Show *(PP 1.51)*

▶ Use the Scroll Box on the Slide Pane to Move to Another Slide *(PP 1.46)*

More About

Microsoft Certification

The Microsoft Office User Specialist (MOUS) Certification program provides an opportunity for you to obtain a valuable industry credential — proof that you have the PowerPoint 2002 skills required by employers. For more information, see Appendix E or visit the Shelly Cashman Series MOUS Web page at scsite.com/tdoff/cert.

In the Lab

Instructions: To complete the Learn It Online exercises, start your browser, click the Address bar, and then enter scsite.com/tdoff/exs. When the Teachers Discovering Office Learn It Online page displays, follow the instructions in the exercises below. To complete the Using the Office Training CD exercises, insert the Microsoft Office Training CD in your CD drive and access the appropriate section. Refer to the introduction chapter of this book to review step-by-step instructions for both installing and using the Microsoft Office CD.

Learn It online

1 Project Reinforcement – TF, MC, and SA

Below PowerPoint Project 1, click the Project Reinforcement link. Print the quiz by clicking Print on the File menu. Answer each question. Write your first and last name at the top of each page, and then hand in the printout to your instructor.

2 Flash Cards

Below PowerPoint Project 1, click the Flash Cards link. When Flash Cards displays, read the instructions. Type 20 (or a number specified by your instructor) in the Number of Playing Cards text box, type your name in the Name text box, and then click the Flip Card button. When the flash card displays, read the question and then click the Answer box arrow to select an answer. Flip through Flash Cards. Click Print on the File menu to print the last flash card if your score is 15 (75%) correct or greater and then hand it in to your instructor. If your score is less than 15 (75%) correct, then redo this exercise by clicking the Replay button.

3 Practice Test

Below PowerPoint Project 1, click the Practice Test link. Answer each question, enter your first and last name at the bottom of the page, and then click the Grade Test button. When the graded practice test displays on your screen, click Print on the File menu to print a hard copy. Continue to take practice tests until you score 80% or better. Hand in a printout of the final practice test to your instructor.

4 Who Wants to Be a Computer Genius?

Below PowerPoint Project 1, click the Computer Genius link. Read the instructions, enter your first and last name at the bottom of the page, and then click the Play button. Hand in your score to your instructor.

5 Wheel of Terms

Below PowerPoint Project 1, click the Wheel of Terms link. Read the instructions, and then enter your first and last name and your school name. Click the Play button. Hand in your score.

6 Crossword Puzzle Challenge

Below PowerPoint Project 1, click the Crossword Puzzle Challenge link. Read the instructions, and then enter your first and last name. Click the Play button. Work the crossword puzzle. When you are finished, click the Submit button. When the crossword puzzle redisplays, click the Print button. Hand in the printout.

Using the Microsoft Office Training CD

1 In and Out of the Classroom

With the Microsoft Office Training CD in your CD drive, click the In and Out of the Classroom tab. Review one of the PowerPoint tutorials that will help you learn how to use and integrate Microsoft PowerPoint in your classroom. The PowerPoint tutorials are available in the Office XP, Office 2000, or Office 2001 for the Mac links.

2 Tips and Tricks

With the Microsoft Office Training CD in your CD drive, click the Tips and Tricks tab. Review one of the PowerPoint tips and tricks that includes using PowerPoint to develop an interactive story, narrating a slide show, animating chart elements, using custom animation features, and more.

3 Tutorial Packs

With the Microsoft Office Training CD in your CD drive, click the Tutorial Packs tab. Review one of the step-by-step tutorials on using Microsoft PowerPoint to enhance your teaching and learning process.

*Productivity
in the Classroom*

Note: These labs require you to create presentations based on notes. When you design these slide shows, use the 7 × 7 rule, which states that each line should have a maximum of seven words, and each slide should have a maximum of seven lines.

1 Decades of Nutrition in the Twentieth Century

Problem: Your health class is studying nutrition and eating habits during the twentieth century. To present your lecture in an interesting manner, you prepare a presentation for your class discussing food and related health problems during 20-year periods. You first develop the notes shown in Figure 1-79, and then you create the presentation shown in Figures 1-80a through 1-80f on pages PP 1.69 and PP 1.70.

I) Decades of Nutrition
Eating in the Twentieth Century
  A) Presented by
  B) Ms. Melissa Ruiz
  C) 11th grade Health Class
II) 1900 - 1919
  A) Cold breakfast cereals introduced
  B) Ice cream sales soar
     1) First ice cream cone served
  C) Hershey introduces its chocolate bar
  D) Plump is preferred body type
     1) Slim is considered sickly
III) 1920 – 1939
  A) Kraft introduces Macaroni and Cheese
     1) Cooking from scratch begins to decline
  B) Red meat, vegetable intakes increase
  C) Heart disease on the rise
     1) Surpasses TB as leading cause of death
  D) Slim becomes preferred body type
IV) 1940 - 1959
  A) First McDonald's Hamburgers opens
     1) Home cooking begins to decline
  B) Research links heart disease with high saturated fats
  C) Fewer than 25 percent of Americans have healthy diets
V) 1960 - 1979
  A) Whole grains, Vitamin C gain popularity
  B) Soft drink consumption increases
     1) Exceeds milk consumption by 1980
  C) Federal committee finds unhealthy diets
     1) Too high in fats, sugar, salt, and meat
     2) Too low in grains, fruits, and vegetables
VI) 1980 - 1999
  A) Low-fat snacks flood grocery stores
     1) Americans still become more overweight
  B) Omega-3 fats found heart-healthy
     1) Found in fish, flaxseed
  C) Fish consumption increases
  D) Dairy and egg intakes decrease

FIGURE 1-79

Productivity in the Classroom

(a) Slide 1 (Title Slide)

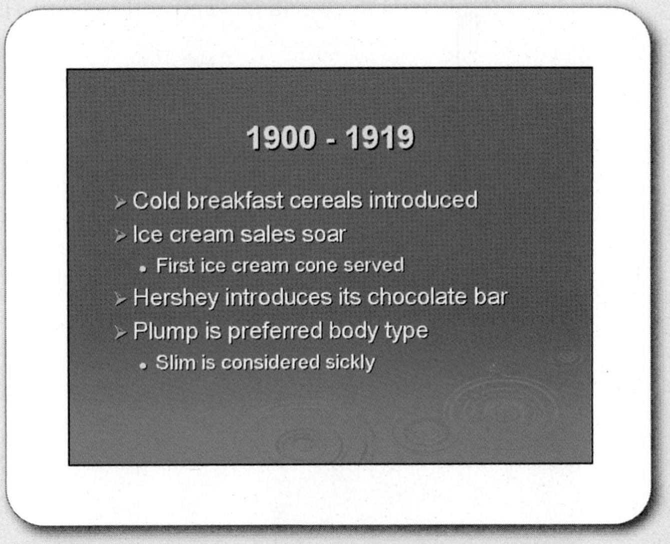

(b) Slide 2

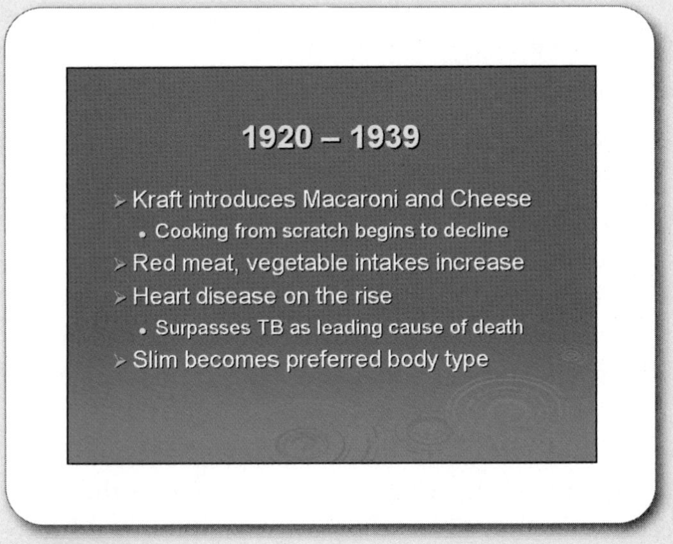

(c) Slide 3

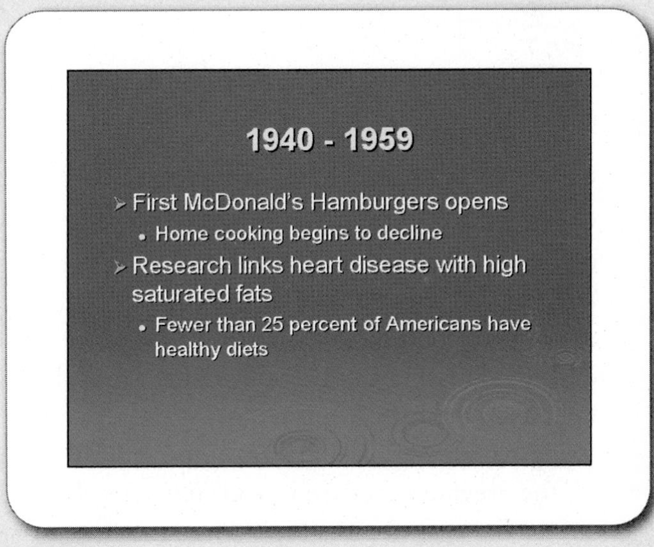

(d) Slide 4

FIGURE 1-80

(continued)

Productivity in the Classroom

Decades of Nutrition in the Twentieth Century *(continued)*

1960 - 1979

> Whole grains, Vitamin C gain popularity
> Soft drink consumption increases
  • Exceeds milk consumption by 1980
> Federal committee finds unhealthy diets
  • Too high in fats, sugar, salt, and meat
  • Too low in grains, fruits, and vegetables

(e) Slide 5

1980 - 1999

> Low-fat snacks flood grocery stores
  • Americans still become more overweight
> Omega-3 fats found heart-healthy
  • Found in fish, flaxseed
    › Fish consumption increases
> Dairy and egg intakes decrease

(f) Slide 6

FIGURE 1-80 *(continued)*

Instructions: Perform the following tasks.

1. Create a new presentation using the Microsoft PowerPoint 2002 Ripple design template, the Science Fair design template from the Microsoft Classroom Tools CD-ROM, or any appropriate template. To select an alternate design template that does not display in the PowerPoint 2002 Slide Design task pane, click Browse at the bottom of the Slide Design task pane. When the Apply Design Template dialog box displays, double-click the Presentation Designs folder. Scroll down and locate a template of your choice. Click the design and then click the Apply button.

2. Using the typed notes illustrated in Figure 1-79 on page PP 1.68, create the title slide shown in Figure 1-80a on the previous page using your name in place of Ms. Melissa Ruiz. Italicize your name. Decrease the font size of the second paragraph of the title text to 36. Decrease the font size of the paragraph, Presented by, to 28. Decrease the font size of the paragraph, 11th grade Health Class, to 24.

3. Using the typed notes in Figure 1-79, create the five text slides with bulleted lists shown in Figures 1-80b through 1-80f.

4. Click the Spelling button on the Standard toolbar. Correct any errors.

5. Save the presentation using the file name, Nutrition.

6. Display the presentation in black and white.

7. Print the black and white presentation. Quit PowerPoint.

Productivity in the Classroom

2 New Technologies Research Report

Problem: Your technology class is studying computer history and emerging technologies. Students are working in groups and each group is assigned different devices to research. Students create a PowerPoint presentation to help their classmates learn key features of the various devices. One group develops the list shown in Figure 1-81. Then the students select and modify a PowerPoint design template. Students create the presentation shown in Figures 1-82a through 1-82d on the next page.

I) Electronics Explosion
  A) Presented by
  B) Frank Snead
  C) Gissella Hermanez
II) High-Definition TV
  A) Screens from 34 to 61 inches
  B) Some models have two tuners
      1) Picture-in-picture
        a) Watch two shows at once
  C) Inputs maximize digital sources
      1) DVD and satellite
III) Digital Camcorders
  A) Razor-sharp recording
      1) Image stabilization
  B) Crystal-clear audio
  C) Digital still photos
      1) Store on removable memory card
        a) CompactFlash, Memory Stick
IV) Digital Cameras
  A) Megapixels increase clarity
      1) 4.3, 3.3, 2.1 megapixels
  B) Optical and digital zoom
  C) MPEG movie mode
      1) Up to 60 seconds
        a) 15 frames per second

FIGURE 1-81

(continued)

Productivity in the Classroom

New Technologies Research Report *(continued)*

Instructions: Perform the following tasks.

1. Create a new presentation using either the Fireworks design template, a template from the Microsoft Classroom Tools CD-ROM, or any appropriate template.
2. Using the list in Figure 1-81 on the previous page, create the title slide shown in Figure 1-82a using your name in place of Frank Snead and one of your student's names in place of Gissella Hermanez. Increase the font size of the paragraph, Electronics Explosion, to 48 and change the text font style to italic. Decrease the font size of the paragraph, Presented by, to 28.

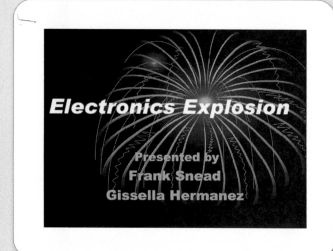

(a) Slide 1 (Title Slide)

(b) Slide 2

(c) Slide 3

(d) Slide 4

FIGURE 1-82

*Productivity
in the Classroom*

3. Using the notes in Figure 1-81 on page PP 1.71, create the three text slides with multi-level bulleted lists shown in Figures 1-82b through 1-82d.
4. Click the Spelling button on the Standard toolbar. Correct any errors.
5. Drag the scroll box to display Slide 1. Click the Slide Show button to start slide show view. Then click to display each slide.
6. Save the presentation using the file name, Electronics Explosion. Display and print the presentation in black and white. Quit PowerPoint.

3 West Shore High School Job Fair

Problem: You are planning a job fair for the seniors in your Internship class. Working with the Guidance Counselor, 50 companies and local businesses have been invited to promote their current and anticipated internship openings. The Guidance Counselor, Lou Birmingham, hands you the outline shown in Figure 1-83 on the next page and asks you to prepare a presentation and handouts to promote the event.

Instructions: Using the list in Figure 1-83 on the next page, design and create a presentation. The presentation must include a title slide and three text slides with bulleted lists. Perform the following tasks.

1. Create a new presentation using the Cliff design template, a template from the Microsoft Classroom Tools CD-ROM, or any appropriate template.
2. Create a title slide titled, West Shore High School Internship Fair. Include a subtitle, using your name in place of Lou Birmingham. Decrease the font size for paragraphs, Presented by, and, West Shore Guidance Office, to 28. Italicize your name.
3. Use Figure 1-83 to create three text slides with multi-level bulleted lists. On Slide 4, change the color of the diamond bullets from gold to white.
4. View the presentation in slide show view to look for errors. Correct any errors.
5. Check the presentation for spelling errors.
6. Save the presentation with the file name, Internship Fair. Print the presentation slides in black and white. Quit PowerPoint.

(continued)

Productivity in the Classroom

West Shore High School Job Fair *(continued)*

I) West Shore High School Internship Fair
   A) Presented by
   B) West Shore Guidance Office
   C) Lou Birmingham, Director
II) Who Is Coming?
   A) National corporations
      1) Progressive companies looking for high-quality candidates
   B) Local companies
      1) Full-time and part-time
         a) Numerous internships
III) When Is It?
   A) April 14 - 18
      1) Monday through Friday
   B) West Shore High School Media Center
   C) Convenient hours
      1) 9:00 a.m. to 3:30 p.m.
IV) How Should I Prepare?
   A) Bring plenty of resumes
      1) More than 50 companies expected
   B) Dress neatly
   C) View the Internship Class Web site
      1) Up-to-date information
      2) Company profiles

FIGURE 1-83

Integration in the Classroom

Introduction: Integration in the Classroom is designed for teachers and other educators who are looking for innovative ways to integrate technology into their content-specific curriculum. Educators can use Microsoft PowerPoint to spice up lectures, provide independent learning activities for students, and to create professional presentations for colleagues.

PowerPoint also can be integrated easily into the curriculum. Book reports, original stories, and research reports are just a few of the ways students can utilize PowerPoint to demonstrate their learning. Students are much more motivated to complete such tasks when allowed to use this medium. Students enjoy creating and presenting information using this multimedia application. When students design and create a presentation, they take greater pride in their work and more responsibility for their learning. PowerPoint is a great tool that can enhance learning in any classroom.

Explore the integration ideas below. Ideas are presented for elementary, middle, high school, and special education classrooms. These ideas are meant to be a springboard for creativity. Take an idea and expand, modify, and use it in your classroom. Furthermore, many of the ideas can be adapted to fit any level or learning situation.

Elementary

1. Your second grade class is studying the human body. You are introducing concepts about their skin. You are using print resources and the Internet to enhance your students' learning. To introduce this part of the unit, you decide to create a PowerPoint presentation to help the students understand the key points. You review the lesson you will present and develop the list shown in Figure 1-84 on the next page. You will develop a title slide and additional text slides that can be used again by your students to reinforce the unit. Use the concepts and techniques introduced in this project to create the presentation.

2. Your fourth grade students are investigating how animals stay warm in cold weather and exploring the science principles involved. The students also identify a human parallel for staying warm and create a PowerPoint presentation to demonstrate their learning. As an example, you prepare the notes shown in Figure 1-85 on page PP 1.77 and use them to develop a title slide and additional text slides. Your presentation will serve as an example for the students. Use the concepts and techniques introduced in this project to create the presentation. Add clip art to your presentation. *Hint:* Use Help to learn more about adding clip art to a presentation.

Middle School

3. As a part of your unit on the election process, your students will select and research their favorite president using the Internet and print resources. Then they will create a PowerPoint presentation to share their research with the class. Presentations must include a title slide with the name of their selected president and their name, additional text slides that identify their president's party affiliation, dates of presidency, offices held prior to being elected president, educational background, campaign platform, electoral votes received along with the states they won, and the president's most notable contribution. Select your favorite president and use the concepts and techniques presented in this project to create a PowerPoint presentation to use as an example for your students. If possible, include an image of your president. *Hint:* Use Help to learn more about adding a picture to a presentation.

(continued)

Integration in the Classroom

Integration in the Classroom *(continued)*

Our Skin
Learning About Ourselves
Mr. Jenkins' 2nd Grade Class

Our Bodies
Made up of
  Bones
  Muscles
  Organs
What protects all of these?
  Our Skin

Our Skin's Job
Protects us
  Bones
  Muscles
  Organs
Keeps us the right temperature
  Hot - sweat
  Cold - goose bumps

Our Skin's Job
Let's us feel things
  Hot
  Cold
  Soft
  Prickly
  Sticky

Just the Facts
Keeps Us From Getting Hurt
  Three layers: Epidermis, Dermis, Subcutaneous
Largest Organ
  Weighs 9 - 15 pounds
Let's Learn More!
  Internet resources

FIGURE 1-84

Integration
in the Classroom

I) Brrrrr, It's Cold!
  A) Presented by
  B) Ms. Honey
  C) 4th Grade Science
II) Staying Warm in Winter
  A) Let's brainstorm!
    1) Different ways animals stay warm
  B) Humans
    1) What do we do?
III) Let's Explore …
  A) Animals – Part 1
    1) Bundle up
        a) grow fur
        b) burrow in the snow or mud
    2) Snuggle up
        a) huddle together
IV) Animals – Part 2
  A) Seek shelter
    1) Trees
    2) Under rocks
    3) Underground
  B) Seek the heat
    1) Migrate south
    2) Locate heating source (i.e., hot springs)
V) Humans
  A) How do we compare?
    1) Bundle up
    2) Huddle together when outdoors
    3) Seek shelter indoors
    4) Seek warmer climates or heated shelter
VI) Let's Explore Further
  A) Print resources
  B) Internet resources
    1) http://www.nwf.org/rangerrick/warm1.html
    2) http://rabi.phys.virginia.edu/HTW/clothing_and_insulation.html

FIGURE 1-85

(continued)

Integration in the Classroom

Integration in the Classroom *(continued)*

Middle School

4. During Black History Month, you are having your eighth grade science class research notable African-American scientists. You provide your students with a list of African-American scientists and they select one person to research using the Internet and print resources. The students will create a PowerPoint presentation to share their research with the class. Their presentations must have a title slide with the name and life span (date of birth and death) of their scientist and their name. Presentations will include additional text slides that present bibliographical data including place of birth, education, etc., and contributions to the field of science. Students also will print their presentations and provide them as handouts. You will design an exam based on the information presented by the students. Using the techniques and concepts presented in this project, select an African-American scientist and create a PowerPoint presentation to use as an example with your students. Include an image of your selected scientist if possible.

High School

5. Your Driver's Education class is studying current safety issues and driving practices. Cellular telephones are very popular among high school students. Research states that more than 76 million Americans currently carry cellular telephones, and many use their telephones while driving. Although 87 percent of adults believe using a cellular telephone impairs their ability to drive, motorists continue to place and receive calls while driving. You prepare the notes shown in Figure 1-86 and use them to develop a title slide and additional text slides for a presentation and handouts. Use the concepts and techniques introduced in this project to create the slide show.

6. Every year people suffer from more than one billion colds. While no remedy cures the runny nose and sore throat that accompany the common cold, students can reduce their chances of catching a cold and feel better when they are sick. Your Health Occupations class is creating a presentation about how to thwart the common cold. Students should get plenty of rest, drink plenty of fluids, and consume chicken soup when they feel cold symptoms. If their throats are sore, they should gargle with warm salt water or let a lozenge with menthol and a mild anesthetic dissolve slowly in their mouths. Decongestants help relieve a stuffy nose by shrinking blood vessels, but these drugs should not be taken for more than three days. Antihistamines relieve a runny nose, itching, and sneezing by having a drying effect. To avoid a cold, students should stay away from other people with colds, wash their hands frequently and keep them away from their mouths and noses, and dispose of tissues promptly. Using the techniques presented in this project, prepare a title slide and several text slides for this presentation and for handouts.

Integration in the Classroom

Calling All Drivers
Using Your Cellular Telephone Safely in Your Car
Mr. Grudzinski
Driver's Education Class

Cellular telephones distract from driving

37 percent of drivers say they have had a near miss with someone using a cellular telephone

2 percent of drivers have had an accident with someone using a cellular telephone

Some communities have banned cellular telephone use behind the wheel

Your telephone can be a safety tool

More than 118,000 calls placed daily to 911 are from cellular telephones

Emergency response times have decreased as 911 calls have increased

Use your telephone responsibly

Place calls before pulling into traffic

Use your telephone's special features such as speed dial and redial

Do not call in hazardous weather or heavy traffic

Do not take notes or look up numbers while driving

Do not engage in emotional or stressful conversations

50 percent of drivers seldom or never use a telephone while driving

FIGURE 1-86

(continued)

Integration in the Classroom

Integration in the Classroom *(continued)*

Special Education

7. Your special education students struggle with writing and dislike writing tasks. To increase their motivation and enjoyment, you allow the students to create book reports using PowerPoint. The students must create a title slide with the book title, author, and their name. Students also must include additional text slides that outline the main characters, the problem or plot, the solution, and what they liked best about the story. If possible, the students also include an image from the story or that represents something from the story. Students can use a scanner, clip art, or digital camera. Students then present their book report to the class. Using the concepts and techniques presented in this project, create a presentation to use as an example with your students.

8. Completing a unit on fairy tales, you have your special education students write parallel stories. They select their favorite fairy tale and then write a story in their own words and with their own illustrations. In the past, you have done this activity with paper and pencil. You decide to allow the students to use PowerPoint to create their stories. Then, you will share their PowerPoint stories with other special education classrooms across the district. Students must include a title slide with the title of their story and their name as well as additional text slides that tell their story and use clip art for illustrations. They will finish their presentation with an About the Author slide. Using the concepts and techniques presented in this project, create a sample story to use as an example for your students consisting of a title slide and at least three additional text slides and an About the Author slide.

Microsoft
EXCEL

Microsoft Excel

PROJECT

1

Creating a Worksheet and Embedded Chart

You will have mastered the material in this project when you can:

OBJECTIVES

- Start Excel
- Describe the Excel worksheet
- Describe the speech recognition capabilities of Excel
- Select a cell or range of cells
- Enter text and numbers
- Use the AutoSum button to sum a range of cells
- Copy a cell to a range of cells using the fill handle
- Bold font, change font size, and change font color
- Center cell contents across a series of columns
- Apply the AutoFormat command to format a range
- Use the Name box to select a cell
- Create a Column chart using the Chart Wizard
- Save a workbook
- Print a worksheet
- Quit Excel
- Open a workbook
- Use the AutoCalculate area to determine totals
- Correct errors on a worksheet
- Use the Excel Help system to answer your questions

The Sky Is The Limit

It just takes the right tool

Astronomers have uncovered mysteries such as black holes, pulsars, planets, and quasars. But all these fade next to the discoveries Edwin Hubble made in a few remarkable years during the 1920s. At the time, it was believed the few hundred stars that comprised the Milky Way Galaxy made up the entire cosmos.

Fortunately, Hubble tracked and recorded events in the universe to prove different. From the chilly summit of Mount Wilson in Southern California, Hubble looked into space and discovered that the Milky Way is just one of millions of galaxies that dot the universe.

Hubble went on to show the star-dotted cosmos is expanding, inflating like a helium balloon. This idea led to the creation of the Big Bang theory, which describes the birth and evolution of the universe. He revealed the cosmos' existence, and in doing so, founded the science of cosmology.

Hubble's work continued. For years, astronomers had noted that light from the nebulae was redder than it should be. The most likely cause of red shifting was motion traveling away from the observer.

Hubble and his assistant, Milton Humason, began measuring the distance to these receding nebulae and found what is now known as Hubble's Law: the further away a galaxy is from earth, the faster it is racing away.

This key piece of research elated Albert Einstein because he knew the universe must either be expanding or contracting, yet astronomers had told him it was doing neither. With Hubble's finding, Einstein's general theory of relativity, discovered more than a decade earlier, had been confirmed. Einstein also discovered an antigravity force theory, which describes how the universe kept from collapsing in on itself.

Hubble crunched numbers to find exact coordinates, confirming the Milky Way is one among many star clusters in the galaxy. Individuals are seldom faced with documenting discoveries that have such universal impact. The ability to perform calculations in Excel may have helped Hubble discover the Big Bang theory sooner.

Today, students as young as eight and nine years old use Excel spreadsheets for many learning tasks in various curriculum-specific areas, including science, math, health, social studies, among others. For college students on a tight budget who need an efficient way to manage personal finances or record schedules, Excel with record keeping, financial planning and budget capabilities is perfect.

Of course, the potentials of spreadsheets extend beyond school into business, science, and many other fields. Business applications are numerous and familiar, from creating business plans to calculating actuarial tables, from forecasting sales to tracking and comparing airline traffic at airports. Going beyond these traditional uses, geographic data is being merged with statistics to create color-coded maps that track diverse factors such as global warming, health care needs, criminal justice, risk of damage by flood, even maps of what is selling where. For personal use, a number of sophisticated spreadsheet programs help to manage investment portfolios, balance checkbooks, and track household inventories for insurance purposes.

Spreadsheets also have become an important tool for improving productivity in law enforcement, an area that reaches everyone. In one application, the Los Angeles Police Department uses a system based on spreadsheets to save the equivalent of 368 additional police officers by speeding the paperwork. As many as 37 forms per incident is required from those on the force. For certain crimes, such as car theft or home burglaries, spreadsheet data is used to create maps showing crime frequencies. The maps are often distributed to communities in neighborhood watch newsletters.

Whether discovering the expanding universe, the theory of relativity or simply keeping your finances in order, Excel is a tool that is up to the task.

Microsoft Excel

Creating a Worksheet and Embedded Chart

PROJECT

1

CASE PERSPECTIVE

Three years ago while in school, Nadine Mitchell and four of her friends came up with the idea of starting a company that sold music to young adults through store outlets in malls. After graduation, they invested $5,000 each and started their dream company, Dynamite Music.

The friends opened their first music store in Boston. Initially, they sold compact discs, cassettes, and rare records (vintage vinyls). As sales grew, they opened additional outlets in Chicago, Denver, and Phoenix. Last year, they started selling their products on the Web. This year they began to sell music by allowing customers to download music to their personal computers.

As sales continue to grow, the management at Dynamite Music has realized it needs a better tracking system for sales by quarter. As a result, the company has asked you to prepare a fourth quarter sales worksheet that shows the sales for the fourth quarter.

In addition, Nadine has asked you to create a graphical representation of the fourth quarter sales because she finds it easier to work with than lists of numbers.

What Is Microsoft Excel?

Microsoft Excel is a powerful spreadsheet program that allows you to organize data, complete calculations, make decisions, graph data, develop professional looking reports, publish organized data to the Web, and access real-time data from Web sites. The four major parts of Excel are:

- **Worksheets** Worksheets allow you to enter, calculate, manipulate, and analyze data such as numbers and text. The term worksheet means the same as spreadsheet.
- **Charts** Charts pictorially represent data. Excel can draw a variety of two-dimensional and three-dimensional charts.
- **Databases** Databases manage data. For example, once you enter data onto a worksheet, Excel can sort the data, search for specific data, and select data that satisfy a criteria.
- **Web Support** Web support allows Excel to save workbooks or parts of a workbook in HTML format so they can be viewed and manipulated using a browser. You also can access real-time data using Web queries.

Project One — Dynamite Music Fourth Quarter Sales

From your meeting with Dynamite Music's management, you have determined the following: needs, source of data, calculations, and chart requirements.

Needs: An easy-to-read worksheet (Figure 1-1) that shows Dynamite Music's fourth quarter sales for each of the product groups (Cassettes, Compact Discs, Vintage Vinyls, and Web Downloads) by store (Boston, Chicago, Denver, and Phoenix). The worksheet also should include total sales for each product group, each store, and total company sales for the fourth quarter.

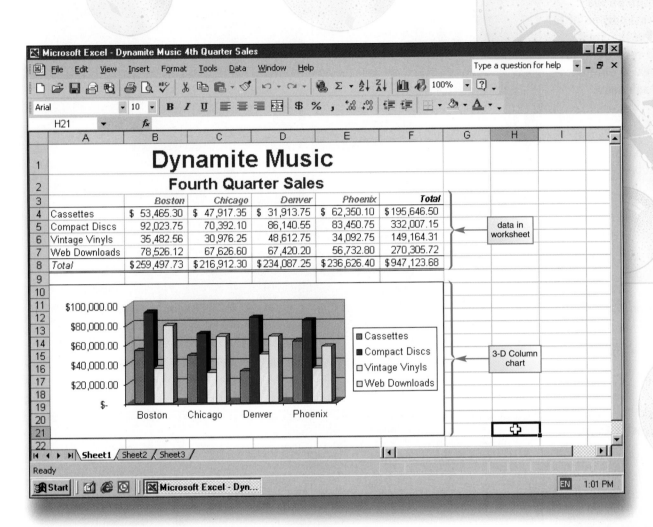

FIGURE 1-1

Source of Data: The data for the worksheet is available at the end of the fourth quarter from the chief financial officer (CFO) of Dynamite Music.

Calculations: You have determined that the following calculations must be made for the worksheet: (a) total fourth quarter sales for each of the four product groups; (b) total fourth quarter sales for each of the four stores; and (c) fourth quarter sales for the company.

Chart Requirements: Below the worksheet, construct a 3-D Column chart that compares the amount of sales for each product group within each store.

Starting and Customizing Excel

To start Excel, Windows must be running. Perform the steps on the next page to start Excel, or ask your instructor how to start Excel for your system.

Steps To Start Excel

1 **Click the Start button on the Windows taskbar, point to Programs on the Start menu, and then point to Microsoft Excel on the Programs submenu.**

The commands on the Start menu display above the Start button and the Programs submenu displays (Figure 1-2). If the Office Speech Recognition software is installed on your computer, then the Language bar may display somewhere on the desktop.

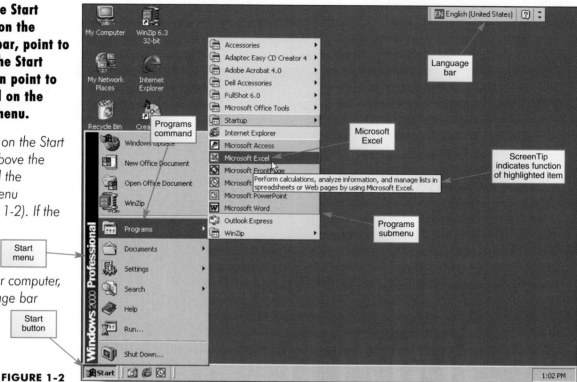

FIGURE 1-2

2 **Click Microsoft Excel.**

Excel starts. After several seconds, a blank workbook titled Book1 displays in the Excel window (Figure 1-3). If you are using Excel 2000, the Language bar and the New Workbook task pane will not display as these are features unique to Excel 2002.

3 **If the Excel window is not maximized, double-click its title bar to maximize it.**

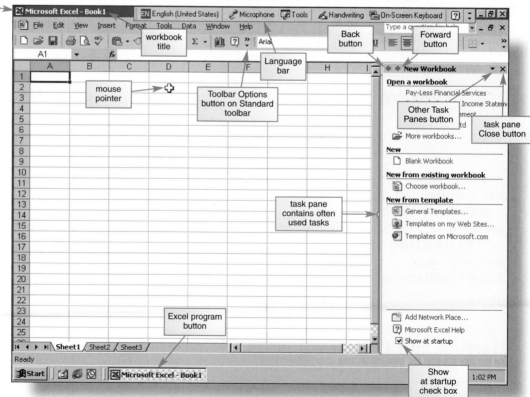

FIGURE 1-3

The screen in Figure 1-3 shows how the Excel 2002 window looks the first time you start Excel after installation on most computers. If the Office XP Speech Recognition software is installed on your system, then when you start Excel either the Language bar expands to include the functions available in Excel (shown at the top of Figure 1-3) or the language indicator displays on the right side of the Windows taskbar (Figure 1-7 on page E 1.11). In this project, the Language bar will be kept minimized. For additional information about the Language bar, see page E 1.16 and Appendix B.

Also, if you are using Excel 2002 a task pane displays on the screen and the buttons on the toolbar display on a single row. A **task pane** is a separate window that enables users to carry out some Excel tasks more efficiently. In this book, to allow the maximum number of columns to display in Excel, a task pane should not display. For more efficient use of the buttons, they should display on two separate rows instead of sharing a single row.

2000 If you are using Excel 2000, perform the following steps to display the toolbars on two rows, if necessary and then skip to the bottom of page E 1.10 and the text that begins under the heading, The Excel Worksheet.

TO DISPLAY THE TOOLBARS ON TWO ROWS WHEN USING EXCEL 2000

1 Click View on the menu bar, point to Toolbars, and then click Customize.

2 When the Customize dialog box displays, click the Options tab, click the Standard and Formatting toolbars share one row check box to remove the check mark, and then click the Close button.

If you are using Excel 2002, perform the following steps to close the New Workbook task pane, minimize the Language bar, and display the buttons on two separate rows.

Other **Ways**

1. Double-click Excel icon on desktop

2. Right-click Start button, click Open All Users, double-click New Office Document, click General tab, double-click Blank Workbook icon

3. Click Start button, click New Office Document, click General tab, double-click Blank Workbook icon

Steps **To Customize the Excel Window**

1 **If the New Workbook task pane displays in your Excel window, click the Show at startup check box to remove the check mark and then click the Close button in the upper-right corner of the task pane (Figure 1-3). If the Language bar displays, point to its Minimize button.**

Excel removes the check mark from the Show at startup check box. With the check mark removed,

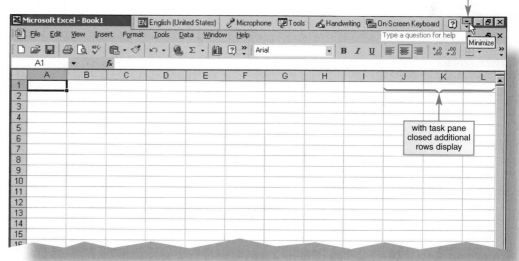

FIGURE 1-4

Excel will not display the New Workbook task pane the next time Excel starts. The New Workbook task pane closes resulting in additional columns displaying (Figure 1-4).

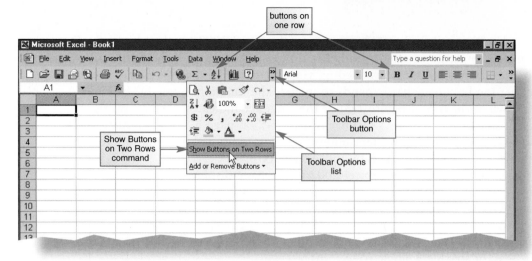

2 **Click the Minimize button on the Language bar. If the toolbars display positioned on the same row, click the Toolbar Options button and then point to Show Buttons on Two Rows.**

The Toolbar Options list displays showing the buttons that do not fit on the toolbars when buttons display on one row (Figure 1-5).

FIGURE 1-5

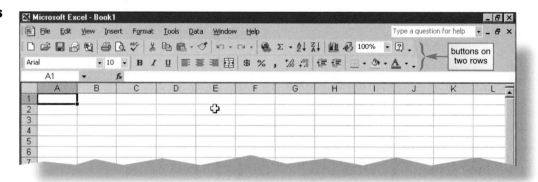

3 **Click Show Buttons on Two Rows.**

Excel displays the buttons on two separate rows (Figure 1-6). The Toolbar Options list shown in Figure 1-5 is empty because all of the buttons display on two rows.

FIGURE 1-6

As you work through creating a worksheet, you will find that certain Excel operations result in displaying a task pane. Besides the New Workbook task pane shown in Figure 1-3 on page E 1.08, Excel provides three additional task panes: the Clipboard task pane, the Search task pane, and the Insert Clip Art task pane. These task panes are discussed when they are used. You can display or hide a task pane by clicking the **Task Pane command** on the **View menu**. You can activate additional task panes by clicking the down arrow to the left of the Close button on the task pane title bar (Figure 1-3) and then selecting a task pane in the list. Using the Back and Forward buttons on the left side of the task pane title bar, you can switch between task panes.

The Excel Worksheet

When Excel starts, it creates a new blank workbook, called Book1. The **workbook** (Figure 1-7) is like a notebook. Inside the workbook are sheets, called **worksheets**. Each sheet name displays on a **sheet tab** at the bottom of the workbook. For example, Sheet1 is the name of the active worksheet displayed in the workbook called Book1. A new workbook opens with three worksheets. If necessary, you can add additional worksheets to a maximum of 255. If you click the tab labeled Sheet2, Excel displays the Sheet2 worksheet. This project uses only the Sheet1 worksheet.

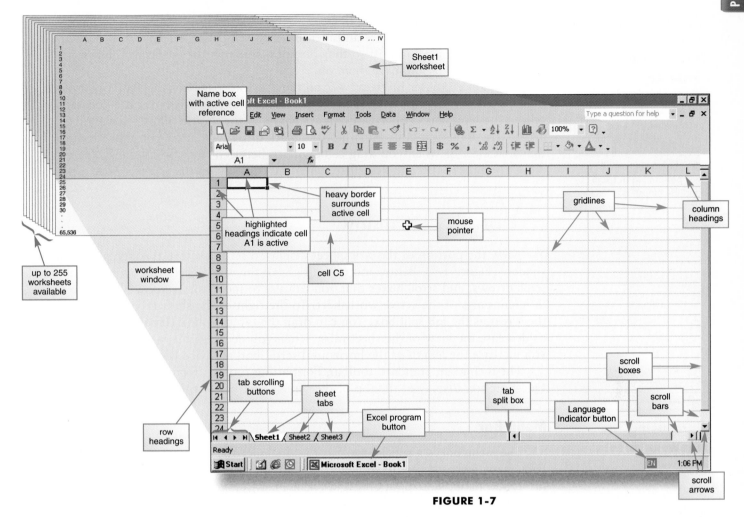

FIGURE 1-7

The Worksheet

The worksheet is organized into a rectangular grid containing columns (vertical) and rows (horizontal). A column letter above the grid, also called the **column heading**, identifies each column. A row number on the left side of the grid, also called the **row heading**, identifies each row. With the screen resolution set to 800 × 600, 12 columns (A through L) and 24 rows (1 through 24) of the worksheet display on the screen when the worksheet is maximized as shown in Figure 1-7.

The intersection of each column and row is a cell. A **cell** is the basic unit of a worksheet into which you enter data. Each worksheet in a workbook has 256 columns and 65,536 rows for a total of 16,777,216 cells. The column headings begin with A and end with IV. The row headings begin with 1 and end with 65,536. Only a small fraction of the active worksheet displays on the screen at one time.

A cell is referred to by its unique address, or **cell reference**, which is the coordinates of the intersection of a column and a row. To identify a cell, specify the column letter first, followed by the row number. For example, cell reference C5 refers to the cell located at the intersection of column C and row 5 (Figure 1-7).

One cell on the worksheet, designated the **active cell**, is the one into which you can enter data. The active cell in Figure 1-7 is A1. The active cell is identified in three ways. First, a heavy border surrounds the cell; second, the active cell reference displays immediately above column A in the **Name box**; and third, the column heading A and row heading 1 are highlighted so it is easy to see which cell is active (Figure 1-7).

More About

The Worksheet Size and Window

256 columns and 65,536 rows make for a huge worksheet that you might imagine takes up the entire wall of a large room. Your computer screen, by comparison, is a small window that allows you to view only a minute area of the worksheet at one time. While you cannot see the entire worksheet, you can move the window over the worksheet to view any part of it. To display the last row in a blank worksheet, press the END key and then press the DOWN ARROW key. Press CTRL+HOME to return to the top of the worksheet.

The Mouse Pointer

The mouse pointer can change to one of more than fifteen different shapes, such as an arrow, cross hair, or chart symbol, depending on the task you are performing in Excel and the mouse pointer's location on the screen.

The horizontal and vertical lines on the worksheet itself are called **gridlines**. Gridlines make it easier to see and identify each cell in the worksheet. If desired, you can turn the gridlines off so they do not display on the worksheet, but it is recommended that you leave them on.

The mouse pointer in Figure 1-7 on the previous page has the shape of a block plus sign. The mouse pointer displays as a **block plus sign** whenever it is located in a cell on the worksheet. Another common shape of the mouse pointer is the block arrow. The mouse pointer turns into the **block arrow** whenever you move it outside the worksheet or when you drag cell contents between rows or columns. The other mouse pointer shapes are described when they display on the screen.

Worksheet Window

You view the portion of the worksheet displayed on the screen through a **worksheet window** (Figure 1-7). Below and to the right of the worksheet window are **scroll bars**, **scroll arrows**, and **scroll boxes** that you can use to move the window around to view different parts of the active worksheet. To the right of the sheet tabs at the bottom of the screen is the **tab split box**. You can drag the tab split box (Figure 1-7) to increase or decrease the view of the sheet tabs. When you decrease the view of the sheet tabs, you increase the length of the horizontal scroll bar, and vice versa.

The menu bar, Standard toolbar, Formatting toolbar, formula bar, and Ask a Question box display at the top of the screen, just below the title bar (Figure 1-8a).

Menu Bar

The **menu bar** is a special toolbar that includes the menu names (Figure 1-8a). Each **menu name** represents a menu of commands that you can use to retrieve, store, print, and manipulate data on the worksheet. When you point to a menu name on the menu bar, the area of the menu bar containing the name changes to a button. To display a menu, such as the Edit menu, click the Edit menu name on the menu bar (Figures 1-8b and 1-8c). A **menu** is a list of commands. If you point to a command on the menu with an arrow to its right, a **submenu** displays from which you can choose a command.

When you click a menu name on the menu bar, a **short menu** displays listing the most recently used commands (Figure 1-8b). If you wait a few seconds or click the arrows at the bottom of the short menu, the full menu displays. The **full menu** lists all the commands associated with a menu (Figure 1-8c). You also can display a full menu immediately by double-clicking the menu name on the menu bar. In this book, when you display a menu, always display the full menu using one of the following techniques.

1. Click the menu name on the menu bar and then wait a few seconds.
2. Click the menu name and then click the arrows at the bottom of the short menu.
3. Click the menu name and then point to the arrows at the bottom of the short menu.
4. Double-click the menu name.

Both short and full menus display some **dimmed commands** that appear gray, or dimmed, instead of black, which indicates they are not available for the current selection. A command with a dark gray shading to the left of it on a full menu is called a **hidden command** because it does not display on a short menu. As you use Excel, it automatically personalizes the short menus for you based on how often you use commands. That is, as you use hidden commands, Excel *unhides* them and places them on the short menu.

Increasing the Viewing Area

If you want to increase the size of the viewing area to see more of the worksheet, click Full Screen on the View menu. You also can increase the viewing area by changing to a higher resolution. You change to a higher resolution by right-clicking the Windows desktop, clicking Properties, clicking the Settings tab, and increasing the Screen area.

(a) Menu Bar and Toolbars

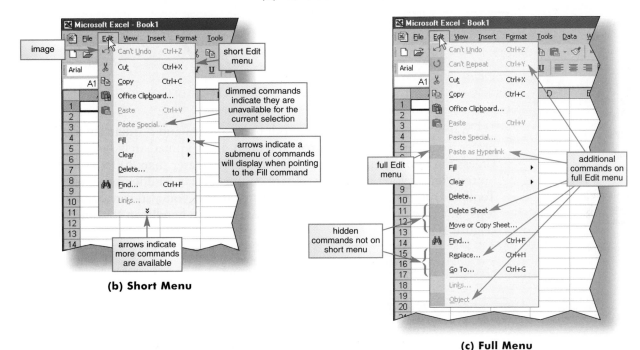

(b) Short Menu

(c) Full Menu

FIGURE 1-8

The menu bar can change to include other menu names depending on the type of work you are doing in Excel. For example, if you are working with a chart sheet rather than a worksheet, the Chart menu bar displays with menu names that reflect charting commands.

Standard Toolbar and Formatting Toolbar

The **Standard toolbar** and the **Formatting toolbar** (Figure 1-8a) contain buttons and list boxes that allow you to perform frequent tasks more quickly than when using the menu bar. For example, to print a worksheet, you click the Print button on the Standard toolbar. Each button has a picture on the button face that helps you remember the button's function. Also, when you move the mouse pointer over a button or box, the name of the button or box displays below it in a **ScreenTip**.

Figures 1-9a and 1-9b on the next page illustrate the Standard and Formatting toolbars and describe the functions of the buttons. Each of the buttons and boxes will be explained in detail when they are used.

Toolbars

You can move a toolbar to any location on the screen. Drag the move handle (Figure 1-10a on the next page) to the desired location. Once the toolbar is in the window area, drag the title bar to move it. Each side of the screen is called a dock. You can drag a toolbar to a dock so it does not clutter the window.

Microsoft **Excel**

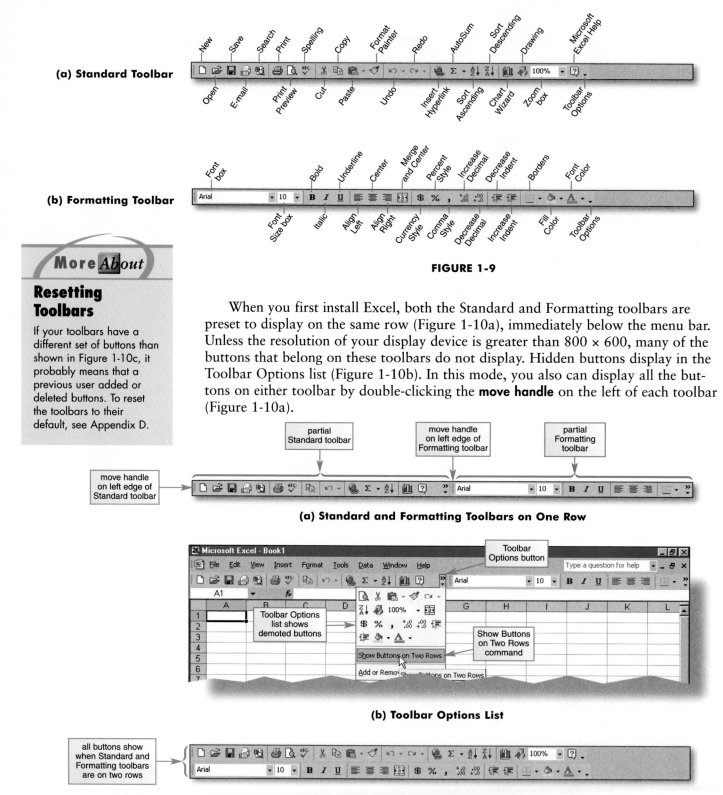

(a) Standard Toolbar

(b) Formatting Toolbar

FIGURE 1-9

When you first install Excel, both the Standard and Formatting toolbars are preset to display on the same row (Figure 1-10a), immediately below the menu bar. Unless the resolution of your display device is greater than 800 × 600, many of the buttons that belong on these toolbars do not display. Hidden buttons display in the Toolbar Options list (Figure 1-10b). In this mode, you also can display all the buttons on either toolbar by double-clicking the **move handle** on the left of each toolbar (Figure 1-10a).

(a) Standard and Formatting Toolbars on One Row

(b) Toolbar Options List

(c) Standard and Formatting Toolbars on Two Rows

FIGURE 1-10

In this book, the Standard and Formatting toolbars are shown on two rows, one under the other so that all buttons display (Figure 1-10c). You show the two toolbars on two rows by clicking the **Show Buttons on Two Rows command** in the Toolbar Options list (Figure 1-10b).

Formula Bar

Below the Standard and Formatting toolbars is the formula bar (Figure 1-11). As you type, the data displays in the **formula bar**. Excel also displays the active cell reference on the left side of the formula bar in the Name box.

Status Bar

Immediately above the Windows taskbar at the bottom of the screen is the status bar. The **status bar** displays a brief description of the command selected (highlighted) in a menu, the function of the button the mouse pointer is pointing to, or the mode of Excel. **Mode indicators,** such as Enter and Ready, display on the status bar and specify the current mode of Excel. When the mode is Ready, Excel is ready to accept the next command or data entry. When the mode indicator reads Enter, Excel is in the process of accepting data through the keyboard into the active cell.

In the middle of the status bar is the AutoCalculate area. The **AutoCalculate area** can be used in place of a calculator to view the sum, average, or other types of totals of a group of numbers on the worksheet. The AutoCalculate area is discussed in detail later in this project.

Keyboard indicators, such as CAPS (Caps Lock), NUM (Num Lock), and SCRL (Scroll) show which keys are engaged. Keyboard indicators display on the right side of the status bar within the small rectangular boxes (Figure 1-11).

Sizing Toolbar Buttons

If you have difficulty seeing the small buttons on the toolbars, you can increase their size by clicking View on the menu bar, pointing to Toolbars, clicking Customize on the Toolbars submenu, clicking the Options tab, clicking the Large icons check box, and clicking the Close button.

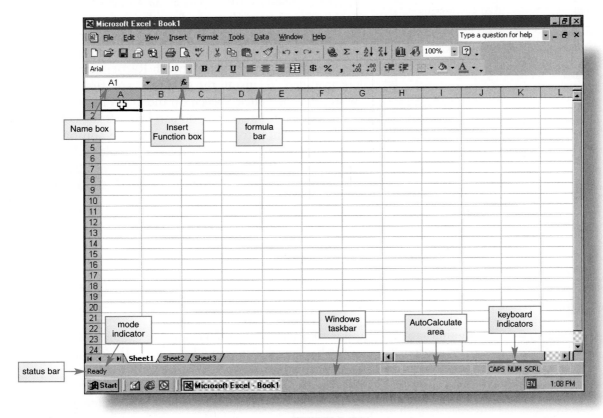

FIGURE 1-11

Speech Recognition and Speech Playback

With the **Office Speech Recognition software** installed and a microphone, you can speak the names of toolbar buttons, menus, menu commands, list items, alerts, and dialog box controls, such as OK and Cancel. You also can dictate cell entries, such as text and numbers. To indicate whether you want to speak commands or dictate cell entries, you use the **Language bar** (Figure 1-12a). You can display the Language bar in two ways: (1) click the Language Indicator button in the taskbar tray status area by the clock, and then click Show the Language bar on the menu (Figure 1-12b); or (2) point to the **Speech command** on the **Tools menu** and then click the **Speech Recognition command** on the **Speech submenu**.

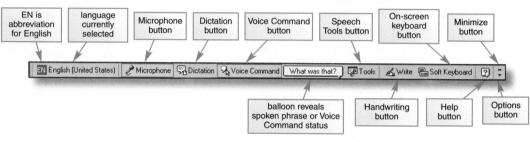

(a) **Language Bar**

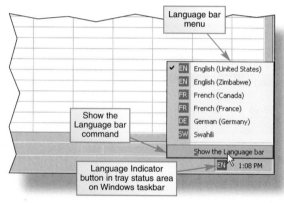

(b) **Language Bar Menu**

FIGURE 1-12

If the Language Indicator button does not display in the tray status area, and if the Speech command is dimmed on the Tools menu, the Office Speech Recognition software is not installed. To install the software, you first must start Word and then click Speech on the Tools menu.

If you have speakers, you can instruct the computer to read a worksheet to you. By selecting the appropriate option, you can have the worksheet read in a male or female voice.

Additional information on the speech recognition and speech playback capabilities in Excel is available in Appendix B.

Selecting a Cell

To enter data into a cell, you first must select it. The easiest way to **select a cell** (make it active) is to use the mouse to move the block plus sign to the cell and then click.

An alternative method is to use the **arrow keys** that are located just to the right of the typewriter keys on the keyboard. An arrow key selects the cell adjacent to the active cell in the direction of the arrow on the key.

You know a cell is selected (active) when a heavy border surrounds the cell (cell A1 in Figure 1-11 on the previous page) and the active cell reference displays in the Name box on the left side of the formula bar.

More About

Selecting a Cell

You can select any cell by entering the cell reference, such as b4, in the Name box on the left side of the formula bar.

Entering Text

In Excel, any set of characters containing a letter, hyphen (as in a telephone number), or space is considered **text**. Text is used to place titles on the worksheet, such as worksheet titles, column titles, and row titles. In Project 1 (Figure 1-13), the worksheet title, Dynamite Music, identifies the worksheet. The worksheet subtitle, Fourth Quarter Sales, identifies the type of report. The column titles in row 3 (Boston, Chicago, Denver, Phoenix, and Total) identify the numbers in each column. The row titles in column A (Cassettes, Compact Discs, Vintage Vinyls, Web Downloads, and Total) identify the numbers in each row.

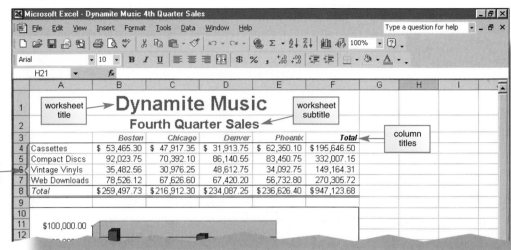

FIGURE 1-13

Entering the Worksheet Titles

The following steps show how to enter the worksheet titles in cells A1 and A2. Later in this project, the worksheet titles will be formatted so they display as shown in Figure 1-13. Perform the following steps to enter the worksheet titles.

 To Enter the Worksheet Titles

More About

Text

A text entry in a cell can contain from 1 to 32,767 characters. Although text entries are used primarily to identify parts of the worksheet, there are applications in which text entries are data.

1 **Click cell A1, if necessary.**

Cell A1 becomes the active cell and a heavy border surrounds it (Figure 1-14).

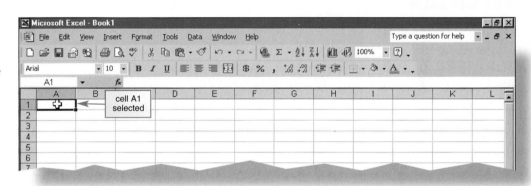

FIGURE 1-14

2 **Type** Dynamite Music **in cell A1.**

The title displays in the formula bar and in cell A1. The text in cell A1 is followed by the insertion point (Figure 1-15). The insertion point is a blinking vertical line that indicates where the next typed character will display.

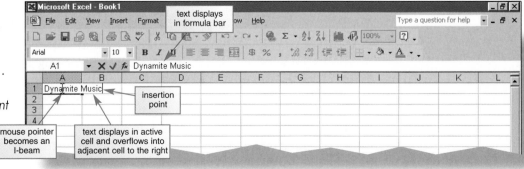

FIGURE 1-15

3 **Point to the Enter box (Figure 1-16).**

When you begin typing a cell entry, Excel displays two additional boxes in the formula bar: the Cancel box and the Enter box.

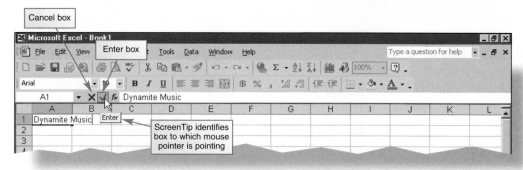

FIGURE 1-16

4 **Click the Enter box to complete the entry.**

Excel enters the worksheet title in cell A1 (Figure 1-17).

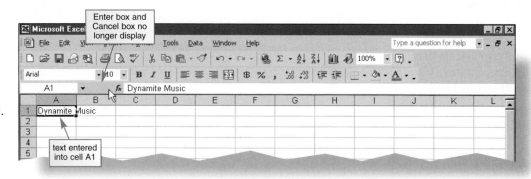

FIGURE 1-17

5 **Click cell A2 to select it. Type** Fourth Quarter Sales **as the cell entry. Click the Enter box to complete the entry.**

Excel enters the worksheet subtitle in cell A2 (Figure 1-18).

FIGURE 1-18

Other **Ways**

1. To complete entry, click any cell other than active cell
2. To complete entry, press ENTER key
3. To complete entry, press HOME, PAGE UP, PAGE DOWN, or END key
4. In Voice Command mode say, "Enter" to complete entry

In Steps 3 and 4, clicking the **Enter box** completes the entry. Clicking the **Cancel box** cancels the entry.

When you complete a text entry into a cell, a series of events occurs. First, Excel positions the text left-aligned in the cell. **Left-aligned** means the cell entry is positioned at the far left in the cell. Therefore, the D in the worksheet title, Dynamite Music, begins in the leftmost position of cell A1.

Second, when the text is longer than the width of a column, Excel displays the overflow characters in adjacent cells to the right as long as these adjacent cells contain no data. In Figure 1-17, the width of cell A1 is approximately nine characters. The text consists of 14 characters. Therefore, Excel displays the overflow characters from cell A1 in cell B1 because this cell is empty. If cell B1 contained data, only the first nine characters in cell A1 would display on the worksheet. Excel would hide the overflow characters, but they still would remain stored in cell A1 and display in the formula bar whenever cell A1 is the active cell.

Third, when you complete an entry by clicking the Enter box, the cell in which the text is entered remains the active cell.

Correcting a Mistake While Typing

If you type the wrong letter and notice the error before clicking the Enter box or pressing the ENTER key, use the BACKSPACE key to erase all the characters back to and including the one that is wrong. To cancel the entire entry before entering it into the cell, click the Cancel box in the formula bar or press the ESC key. If you see an error in a cell, select the cell and retype the entry. Later in this project, additional error-correction techniques are discussed.

AutoCorrect

The **AutoCorrect feature** of Excel works behind the scenes, correcting common mistakes when you complete a text entry in a cell. AutoCorrect makes three types of corrections for you:

1. Corrects two initial capital letters by changing the second letter to lowercase.
2. Capitalizes the first letter in the names of days.
3. Replaces commonly misspelled words with their correct spelling. For example, it will change the misspelled word *recieve* to *receive* when you complete the entry. AutoCorrect will correct the spelling automatically of more than 400 commonly misspelled words.

Entering Column Titles

To enter the column titles in row 3, select the appropriate cell and then enter the text, as described in the following steps.

 **To Enter Column Titles**

More *About*

The ENTER Key

When you first install Excel, the ENTER key not only completes the entry but moves the selection to an adjacent cell. You can instruct Excel not to move the selection after pressing the ENTER key by clicking Options on the Tools menu, clicking the Edit tab, removing the check mark from the Move Selection after Enter check box, and then clicking the OK button.

More *About*

The IntelliSense™ Technology

Office XP's IntelliSense™ Technology tries to understand what you are doing and helps you do it. The adoptive menus, Ask a Question box, Auto-Correct, AutoComplete, smart tags, and formula error checker are part of the IntelliSense™ Technology.

1 **Click cell B3.**

Cell B3 becomes the active cell. The active cell reference in the Name box changes from A2 to B3 (Figure 1-19).

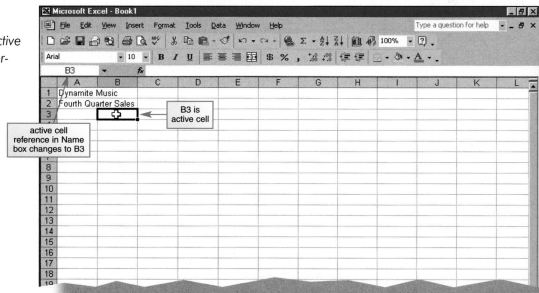

FIGURE 1-19

2   Type Boston in cell B3.

Excel displays Boston in the formula bar and in cell B3 (Figure 1-20).

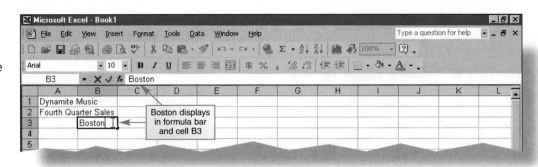

FIGURE 1-20

3   Press the RIGHT ARROW key.

Excel enters the column title, Boston, in cell B3 and makes cell C3 the active cell (Figure 1-21).

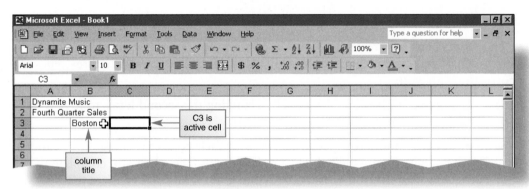

FIGURE 1-21

4   Repeat Steps 2 and 3 for the remaining column titles in row 2. That is, enter Chicago in cell C3, Denver in cell D3, Phoenix in cell E3, and Total in cell F3. Complete the last entry in cell F3 by clicking the Enter box in the formula bar.

The column titles display left-aligned as shown in Figure 1-22.

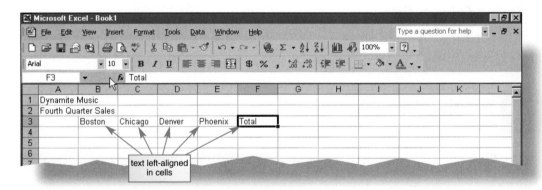

FIGURE 1-22

If the next entry is in an adjacent cell, use the arrow keys to complete the entry in a cell. When you press an arrow key to complete an entry, the adjacent cell in the direction of the arrow (up, down, left, or right) becomes the active cell. If the next entry is in a non-adjacent cell, click the next cell in which you plan to enter data, or click the Enter box or press the ENTER key and then click the appropriate cell for the next entry.

Entering Row Titles

The next step in developing the worksheet in Project 1 is to enter the row titles in column A. This process is similar to entering the column titles and is described in the following steps.

Steps **To Enter Row Titles**

1 **Click cell A4. Type** Cassettes **and then press the DOWN ARROW key.**

Excel enters the row title, Cassettes, in cell A4, and cell A5 becomes the active cell (Figure 1-23).

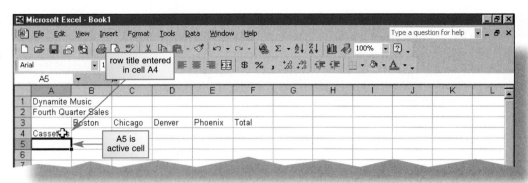

FIGURE 1-23

2 **Repeat Step 1 for the remaining row titles in column A. Enter** Compact Discs **in cell A5,** Vintage Vinyls **in cell A6,** Web Downloads **in cell A7, and** Total **in cell A8.**

The row titles display as shown in Figure 1-24.

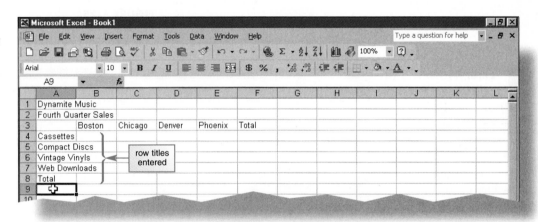

FIGURE 1-24

In Excel, text is left-aligned in a cell unless you change it by realigning it. Excel treats any combination of numbers, spaces, and nonnumeric characters as text. For example, the following entries are text:

401AX21, 921-231, 619 321, 883XTY

Table 1-1	Dynamite Music Fourth Quarter Data			
	BOSTON	**CHICAGO**	**DENVER**	**PHOENIX**
Cassettes	53465.30	47917.35	31913.75	62350.10
Compact Discs	92023.75	70392.10	86140.55	83450.75
Vintage Vinyls	35482.56	30976.25	48612.75	34092.75
Web Downloads	78526.12	67626.60	67420.20	56732.80

Entering Numbers

In Excel, you can enter numbers into cells to represent amounts. Numbers can contain only the following characters:

0 1 2 3 4 5 6 7 8 9 + - ( ) , / . $ % E e

If a cell entry contains any other keyboard character (including spaces), Excel interprets the entry as text and treats it accordingly. The use of the special characters is explained when they are used in the project.

In Project 1, the Dynamite Music Fourth Quarter numbers are summarized to the right in Table 1-1. These numbers, which represent fourth quarter sales for each of the stores and product groups, must be entered in rows 4, 5, 6, and 7. Perform the steps on the next page to enter these values one row at a time.

More About

Entering Numbers as Text

There are times when you will want Excel to treat numbers, such as zip codes and telephone numbers, as text. To enter a number as text, start the entry with an apostrophe (').

Steps **To Enter Numeric Data**

1 **Click cell B4. Type** 53465.30 **and then press the RIGHT ARROW key.**

Excel enters the number 53465.30 in cell B4 and changes the active cell to cell C4 (Figure 1-25). Excel does not display the insignificant zero. The zero will reappear when the numbers are formatted with dollar signs and commas later in this project.

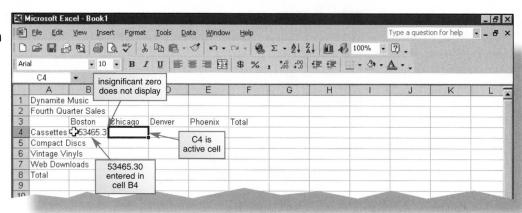

FIGURE 1-25

2 **Enter** 47917.35 **in cell C4,** 31913.75 **in cell D4, and** 62350.10 **in cell E4.**

Row 4 now contains the fourth quarter sales by store for the product group Cassettes (Figure 1-26). The numbers in row 4 are right-aligned, which means Excel displays the cell entry to the far right in the cell.

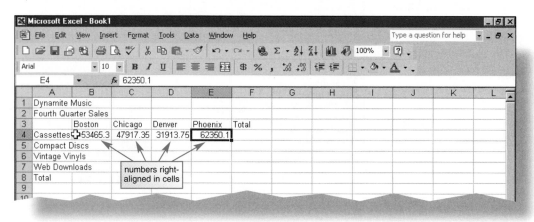

FIGURE 1-26

3 **Click cell B5. Enter the remaining fourth quarter sales provided in Table 1-1 on the previous page for each of the three remaining product groups in rows 5, 6, and 7.**

The fourth quarter sales display as shown in Figure 1-27.

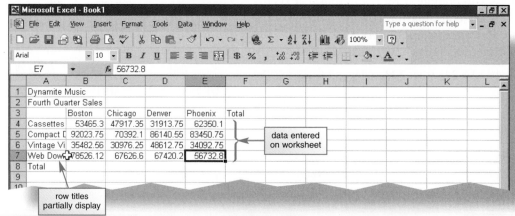

FIGURE 1-27

As you can see in Figure 1-27, when you enter data into the cell in column B, the row titles in column A partially display. Later when the worksheet is formatted, the row titles will display in their entirety.

Steps 1 through 3 complete the numeric entries. You are not required to type dollar signs, commas, or trailing zeros. As shown in Figure 1-27, trailing zeros do not display. When you enter a number that has cents, however, you must add the decimal point and the numbers representing the cents when you enter the number. Later in this project, dollar signs, commas, and trailing zeros will be added to improve the appearance and readability of the numbers.

Calculating a Sum

The next step in creating the worksheet is to determine the total fourth quarter sales for the Boston store in column B. To calculate this value in cell B8, Excel must add the numbers in cells B4, B5, B6, and B7. Excel's **SUM function** provides a convenient means to accomplish this task.

To use the SUM function, first you must identify the cell in which the sum will be stored after it is calculated. Then, you can use the **AutoSum button** on the Standard toolbar to enter the SUM function as shown in the following steps.

More About

Number Limits

In Excel, a number can be between approximately -1×10^{308} and 1×10^{308}. That is a negative 1 followed by 308 zeros or a positive 1 followed by 308 zeros. To enter a number such as 7,500,000,000,000 you can type it as shown or you can type 7.5E12, which stands for 7.5×10^{12}.

Steps **To Sum a Column of Numbers**

---

1 **Click cell B8 and then point to the AutoSum button on the Standard toolbar.**

Cell B8 becomes the active cell (Figure 1-28).

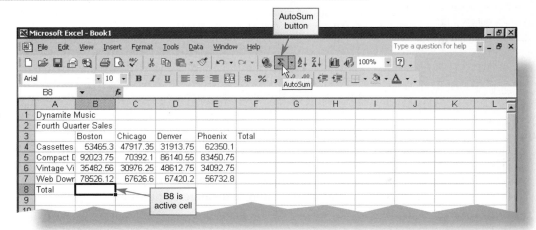

FIGURE 1-28

2 **Click the AutoSum button.**

*Excel responds by displaying =SUM(B4:B7) in the formula bar and in the active cell B8 (Figure 1-29). The B4:B7 within parentheses following the function name SUM is Excel's way of identifying the cells B4 through B7. Excel also surrounds the proposed cells to sum with a moving border, called a **marquee**. If using Excel 2002, a ScreenTip displays below the active cell.*

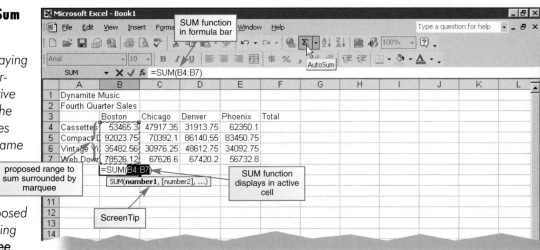

FIGURE 1-29

3 **Click the AutoSum button a second time.**

Excel enters the sum of the fourth quarter sales in cell B8 (Figure 1-30). The SUM function assigned to cell B8 displays in the formula bar when cell B8 is the active cell.

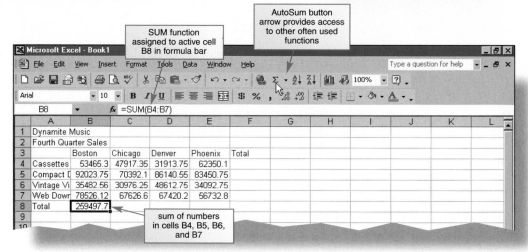

FIGURE 1-30

Other Ways

1. Click Insert Function button in formula bar, select SUM in Select a function list, click OK button, select range, click OK button

2. On Insert menu click Function, select SUM in Select a function list, click OK button, select range, click OK button

3. Press ALT+EQUAL SIGN (=) twice

4. In Voice Command mode say, "AutoSum, Sum, Enter"

When you enter the SUM function using the AutoSum button, Excel automatically selects what it considers to be your choice of the group of cells to sum. The group of adjacent cells B4, B5, B6, and B7 is called a **range**. A range is a series of two or more adjacent cells in a column or row or a rectangular group of cells. Many Excel operations, such as summing numbers, take place on a range of cells.

When proposing the range to sum, Excel first looks for a range of cells with numbers above the active cell and then to the left. If Excel proposes the wrong range, you can drag through the correct range anytime prior to clicking the AutoSum button a second time. You also can enter the correct range by typing the beginning cell reference, a colon (:), and the ending cell reference.

If you click the AutoSum button arrow on the right side of the AutoSum button, Excel displays a list of often used functions from which you can choose. The list includes functions that allow you to determine the average, the minimum value, and the maximum value of a range of numbers.

Using the Fill Handle to Copy a Cell to Adjacent Cells

Excel also must calculate the totals for Chicago in cell C8, Denver in cell D8, and for Phoenix in cell E8. Table 1-2 illustrates the similarities between the entry in cell B8 and the entries required for the totals in cells C8, D8, and E8.

To place the SUM functions in cells C8, D8, and E8, you can follow the same steps shown previously in Figures 1-28 through 1-30. A second, more efficient method is to copy the SUM function from cell B8 to the range C8:E8. The cell being copied is called the **source area** or **copy area**. The range of cells receiving the copy is called the **destination area** or **paste area**.

Although the SUM function entries are similar in Table 1-2, they are not exact copies. The range in each SUM function entry to the right of cell B8 uses cell references that are one column to the right of the previous column. When you copy cell references, Excel automatically adjusts them for each new position, resulting in the SUM function entries illustrated in Table 1-2. Each adjusted cell reference is called a **relative reference**.

Table 1-2	Function Entries in Row 8	
CELL	**SUM FUNCTION ENTRIES**	**REMARK**
B8	=SUM(B4:B7)	Sums cells B4, B5, B6, and B7
C8	=SUM(C4:C7)	Sums cells C4, C5, C6, and C7
D8	=SUM(D4:D7)	Sums cells D4, D5, D6, and D7
E8	=SUM(E4:E7)	Sums cells E4, E5, E6, and E7

The easiest way to copy the SUM formula from cell B8 to cells C8, D8, and E8 is to use the fill handle. The **fill handle** is the small black square located in the lower-right corner of the heavy border around the active cell. Perform the following steps to use the fill handle to copy cell B8 to the adjacent cells C8:E8.

 To Copy a Cell to Adjacent Cells in a Row

1 With cell B8 active, point to the fill handle.

The mouse pointer changes to a cross hair (Figure 1-31).

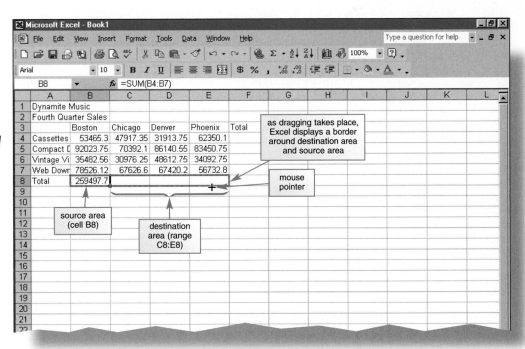

FIGURE 1-31

2 Drag the fill handle to select the destination area, range C8:E8.

Excel displays a shaded border around the destination area, range C8:E8, and the source area, cell B8 (Figure 1-32).

FIGURE 1-32

3 **Release the mouse button.**

Excel copies the SUM function in cell B8 to the range C8:E8 (Figure 1-33). In addition, Excel calculates the sums and enters the results in cells C8, D8, and E8. If using Excel 2002, the Auto Fill Options button displays to the right and below the destination area.

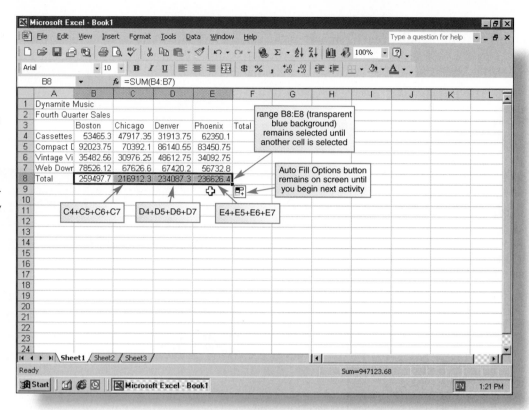

FIGURE 1-33

Once the copy is complete, Excel continues to display a heavy border and transparent (blue) background around cells B8:E8. The heavy border and transparent background indicate a selected range. Cell B8, the first cell in the range, does not display with the transparent background because it is the active cell. If you click any cell, Excel will remove the heavy border and transparent background. The heavy border and transparent (blue) background is called **see-through view**.

When you copy one range to another, Excel 2002 displays an Auto Fill Options button to the right and below the destination area (Figure 1-33). The **Auto Fill Options button** allows you choose whether you want to copy the value in the price area with formatting, without formatting, or only copy the format. To list the selections, click the Auto Fill Options button. The Auto Fill Options button disappears when you begin another activity.

Determining Row Totals

The next step in building the worksheet is to determine totals for each product group and total fourth quarter sales for the company in column F. Use the SUM function in the same manner as you did when the sales by store were totaled in row 8. In this example, however, all the rows will be totaled at the same time. The following steps illustrate this process.

Steps **To Determine Multiple Totals at the Same Time**

1   **Click cell F4.**

Cell F4 becomes the active cell (Figure 1-34).

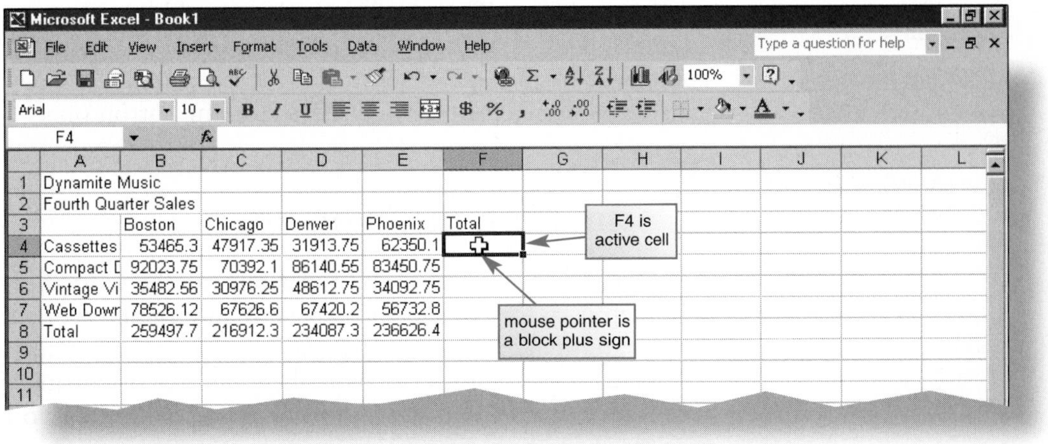

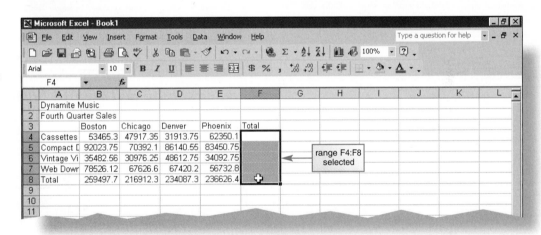

FIGURE 1-34

2   **With the mouse pointer in cell F4 and in the shape of a block plus sign, drag the mouse pointer down to cell F8.**

Excel highlights the range F4:F8 (Figure 1-35).

FIGURE 1-35

3   **Click the AutoSum button on the Standard toolbar.**

Excel assigns the appropriate SUM functions to cell F4, F5, F6, F7, and F8, and then calculates and displays the sums in the respective cells (Figure 1-36).

4   **Select cell A9 to deselect the range F4:F8.**

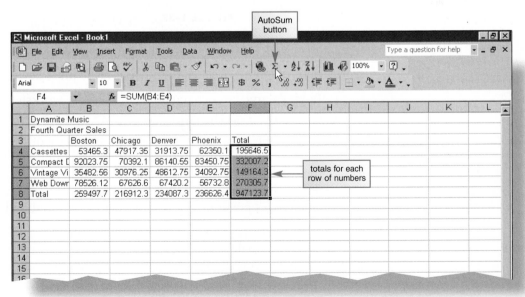

FIGURE 1-36

More *About*

Summing Columns and Rows

A more efficient way to determine the totals in row 8 and column F in Figure 1-36 is to select the range (B4:F8) and then click the AutoSum button. The range B4:F8 includes the numbers to sum plus an additional row (row 8) and an additional column (column F), in which the totals will display.

If each cell in the selected range is next to a row of numbers, Excel assigns the SUM function to each cell in the selected range when you click the AutoSum button. Thus, five SUM functions with different ranges were assigned to the selected range, one for each row. This same procedure could have been used earlier to sum the columns. That is, rather than selecting cell B8, clicking the AutoSum button twice, and then copying the SUM function to the range C8:E8, you could have selected the range B8:E8 and then clicked the AutoSum button once.

Formatting the Worksheet

The text, numeric entries, and functions for the worksheet now are complete. The next step is to format the worksheet. You **format** a worksheet to emphasize certain entries and make the worksheet easier to read and understand.

Figure 1-37a shows the worksheet before formatting. Figure 1-37b shows the worksheet after formatting. As you can see from the two figures, a worksheet that is formatted not only is easier to read, but also looks more professional.

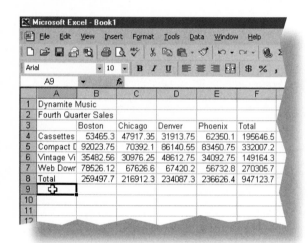

(a) Before Formatting   (b) After Formatting

FIGURE 1-37

To change the unformatted worksheet in Figure 1-37a to the formatted worksheet in Figure 1-37b, the following tasks must be completed:

1. Bold, enlarge, and change the color of the worksheet titles in cells A1 and A2.

2. Center the worksheet titles in cells A1 and A2 across columns A through F.

3. Format the body of the worksheet. The body of the worksheet, range A3:F8, includes the column titles, row titles, and numbers. Formatting the body of the worksheet results in numbers represented in a dollars-and-cents format, dollar signs in the first row of numbers and the total row, underlining that emphasizes portions of the worksheet, and modified column widths.

The process required to format the worksheet is explained in the remainder of this section. Although the format procedures will be carried out in the order described above, you should be aware that you can make these format changes in any order.

Fonts, Font Color, Font Size, and Font Style

Characters that display on the screen are a specific shape, size, color, and style. The **font type** defines the appearance and shape of the letters, numbers, and special characters. The **font size** specifies the size of the characters on the screen. Font size is gauged by a measurement system called points. A single point is about 1/72 of one inch in height. Thus, a character with a **point size** of 10 is about 10/72 of one inch in height.

Font style indicates how the characters are formatted. Common font styles include regular, bold, underlined, or italicized. The font also can display in a variety of colors.

When Excel begins, the preset font type for the entire workbook is Arial with a size and style of 10-point regular black. Excel allows you to change the font characteristics in a single cell, a range of cells, the entire worksheet, or the entire workbook.

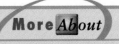

More *About*

Changing Fonts

In general, use no more than two font types and font styles in a worksheet.

Bolding a Cell

You **bold** an entry in a cell to emphasize it or make it stand out from the rest of the worksheet. Perform the following steps to bold the worksheet title in cell A1.

Steps **To Bold a Cell**

1 **Click cell A1 and then point to the Bold button on the Formatting toolbar.**

The ScreenTip displays immediately below the Bold button to identify the function of the button (Figure 1-38).

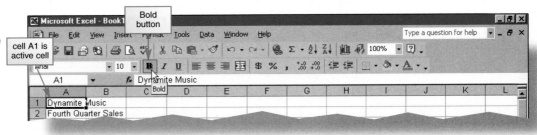

FIGURE 1-38

2 **Click the Bold button.**

Excel applies a bold format to the worksheet title, Dynamite Music (Figure 1-39).

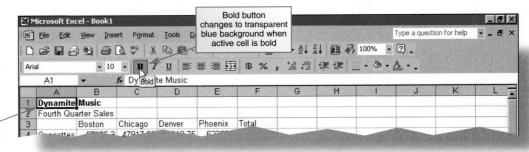

FIGURE 1-39

When the active cell is bold, the Bold button on the Formatting toolbar displays with a transparent blue background (Figure 1-39). Clicking the Bold button a second time removes the bold format.

Increasing the Font Size

Increasing the font size is the next step in formatting the worksheet title. You increase the font size of a cell so the entry stands out and is easier to read. Perform the steps on the next page to increase the font size of the worksheet title in cell A1.

Other **Ways**

1. On Format menu click Cells, click Font tab, click Bold, click OK button
2. Right-click cell, click Format Cells on shortcut menu, click Font tab, click Bold, click OK button
3. Press CTRL+B
4. In Voice Command mode say, "Bold"

Microsoft **Excel**

Steps To Increase the Font Size of a Cell Entry

1 **With cell A1 selected, click the Font Size box arrow on the Formatting toolbar and then point to 24 in the Font Size list.**

The Font Size list displays as shown in Figure 1-40.

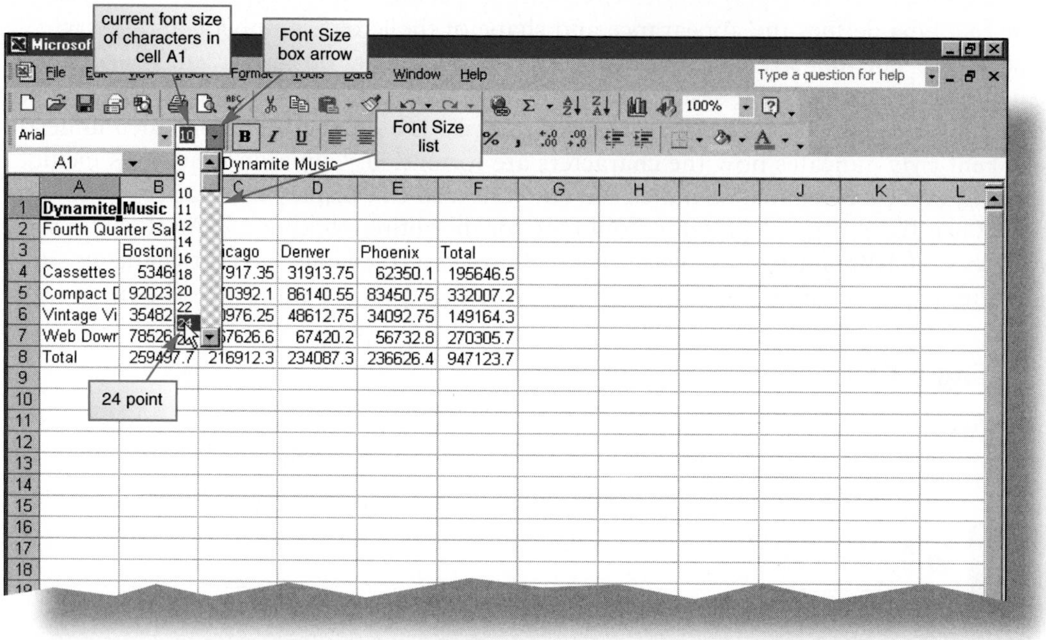

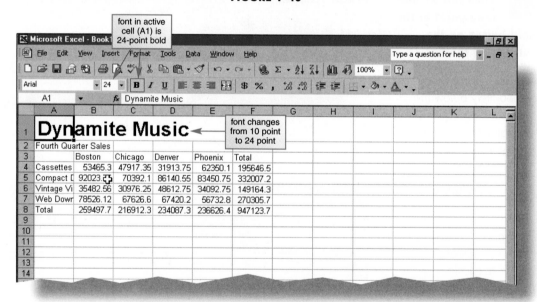

FIGURE 1-40

2 **Click 24.**

The font size of the characters in the worksheet title in cell A1 increase from 10 point to 24 point (Figure 1-41).

FIGURE 1-41

Other Ways

1. On Format menu click Cells, click Font tab, select font size in Size box, click OK button

2. Right-click cell, click Format Cells on shortcut menu, click Font tab, select font size in Size box, click OK button

3. In Voice Command mode say, "Font Size, [desired font size]"

An alternative to clicking a font size in the Font Size list is to click the Font Size box, type the font size, and then press the ENTER key. With cell A1 selected (Figure 1-41), the Font Size box shows the new font size 24 and the transparent blue Bold button shows the active cell is bold.

Changing the Font Color of a Cell

The next step is to change the color of the font in cell A1 from black to violet. Perform the following steps to change the color of the font.

Steps: To Change the Font Color of a Cell

1 **With cell A1 selected, click the Font Color button arrow on the Formatting toolbar. Point to the color Violet (column 7, row 3) on the Font Color palette.**

The Font Color palette displays (Figure 1-42).

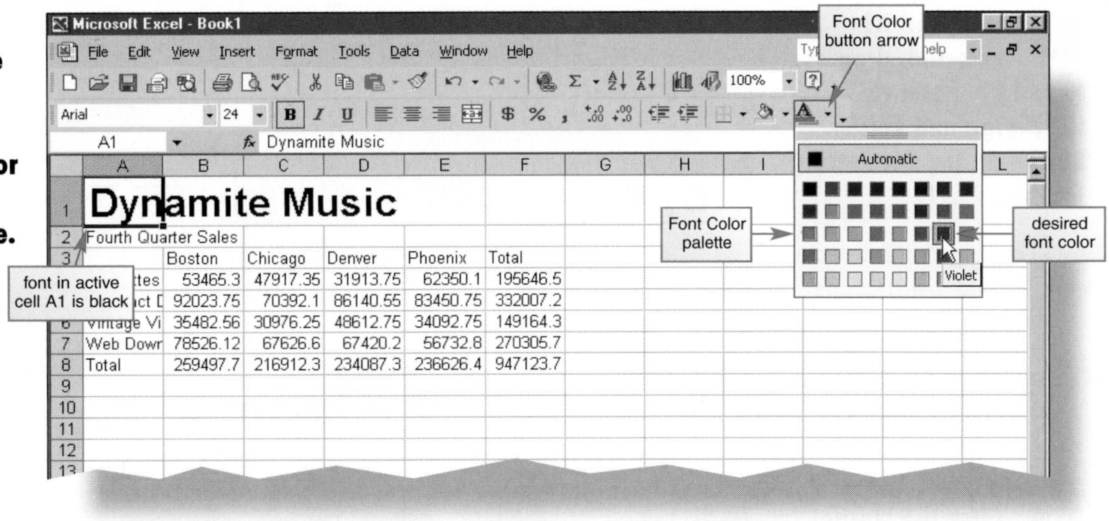

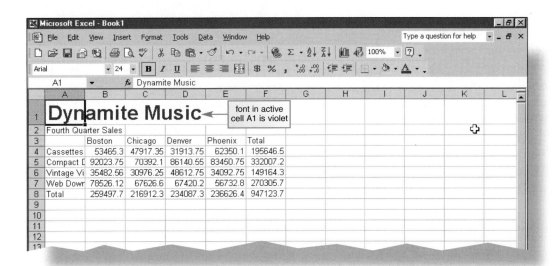

FIGURE 1-42

2 **Click Violet.**

The font in the worksheet title in cell A1 changes from black to violet (Figure 1-43).

FIGURE 1-43

You can choose from 40 different font colors in the Font Color palette in Figure 1-42. Your Font Color palette may have more or fewer colors, depending on color settings of your operating system. When you choose a color, Excel changes the Font Color button on the Formatting toolbar to the chosen color. Thus, to change the font color of the text in another cell to the same color, you need only select the cell and click the Font Color button.

Centering the Worksheet Title across Columns

The final step in formatting the worksheet title is to center it across columns A through F. Centering a worksheet title across the columns used in the body of the worksheet improves the worksheet's appearance. Perform the steps on the next page to center the worksheet title.

Other Ways

1. On Format menu, click Cells, click Font tab, click Color button, select color, click OK button

2. Right-click cell, click Format Cells on shortcut menu, click Font tab, click Color button, select color, click OK button

3. In Voice Command mode say, "Font Color, [desired color]"

Steps | To Center a Cell's Contents across Columns

1 **With cell A1 selected, drag to cell F1. Point to the Merge and Center button on the Formatting toolbar.**

Excel highlights the selected cells (Figure 1-44).

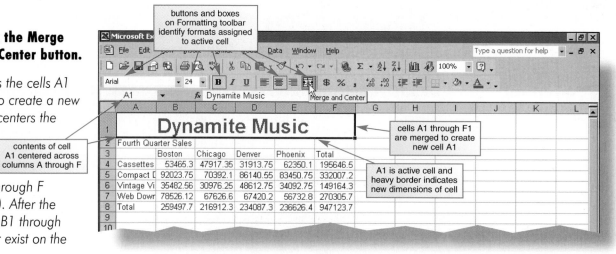

FIGURE 1-44

2 **Click the Merge and Center button.**

Excel merges the cells A1 through F1 to create a new cell A1 and centers the contents of cell A1 across columns A through F (Figure 1-45). After the merge, cells B1 through F1 no longer exist on the worksheet.

FIGURE 1-45

Other Ways

1. On Format menu click Cells, click Alignment tab, select Center Across Selection in Horizontal list, click OK button

2. Right-click cell, click Format Cells on shortcut menu, click Alignment tab, select Center Across Selection in Horizontal list, click OK button

3. In Voice Command mode say, "Merge and Center"

Excel not only centers the worksheet title across the range A1:F1, but it also merges cells A1 through F1 into one cell, cell A1. The alternative to merging cells is **splitting a cell**. You split a merged cell by selecting it and clicking the Merge and Center button. For example, if you click the Merge and Center button a second time in Step 2, it will change cell A1 to cells A1, B1, C1, D1, E1, and F1. For the Merge and Center button to work properly, all the cells except the leftmost cell in the range of cells must be empty.

Most formats assigned to a cell will display on the Formatting toolbar when the cell is selected. For example, with cell A1 selected in Figure 1-45 the font type and font size display in their appropriate boxes. Transparent blue buttons indicate an assigned format. To determine if less frequently used formats are assigned to a cell, point to the cell and right-click. Next, click Format Cells, and then click each of the tabs in the Format Cells dialog box.

Formatting the Worksheet Subtitle

The worksheet subtitle in cell A2 is to be formatted the same as the worksheet title in cell A1, except that the font size should be 16 rather than 24. Perform the following steps to format the worksheet subtitle in cell A2.

TO FORMAT THE WORKSHEET SUBTITLE

 Select cell A2.

 Click the Bold button on the Formatting toolbar.

 Click the Font Size arrow on the Formatting toolbar and click 16.

 Click the Font Color button.

 Select the range A2:F2 and then click the Merge and Center button on the Formatting toolbar.

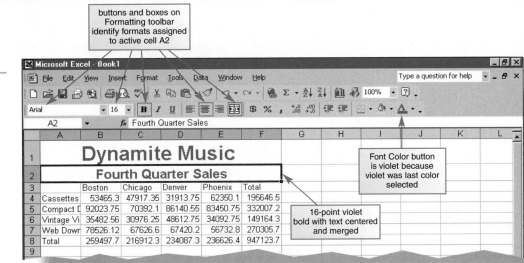

FIGURE 1-46

The worksheet subtitle in cell A2 displays as shown in Figure 1-46.

With cell A2 selected, the buttons and boxes on the Formatting toolbar describe the primary formats assigned to cell A2. The steps used to format the worksheet subtitle in cell A2 were the same as the steps used to assign the formats to the worksheet title in cell A1, except for assigning the font color. To color the worksheet title font in cell A1 violet, the Font Color arrow and Font Color palette were used. To color the worksheet subtitle in cell A2 violet, the Font Color button was used. Recall that the Font Color button is assigned the last font color used, which was violet.

Using AutoFormat to Format the Body of a Worksheet

Excel has several customized format styles called **table formats** that allow you to format the body of the worksheet. Using table formats can give your worksheet a professional appearance. Follow these steps to format the range A3:F8 automatically using the **AutoFormat command** on the **Format menu**.

Steps **To Use AutoFormat to Format the Body of a Worksheet**

 Select cell A3, the upper-left corner cell of the rectangular range to format. Drag the mouse pointer to cell F8, the lower-right corner cell of the range to format.

Excel highlights the range to format with a heavy border and transparent blue background (Figure 1-47).

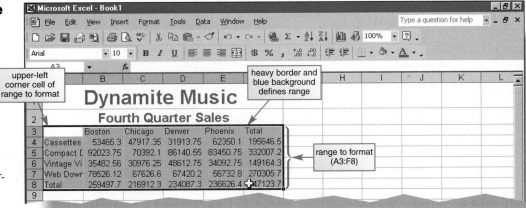

FIGURE 1-47

2 **Click Format on the menu bar and then point to AutoFormat.**

The Format menu displays (Figure 1-48).

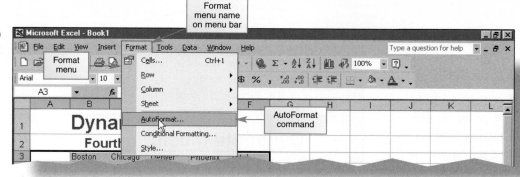

FIGURE 1-48

3 **Click AutoFormat. Click the Accounting 1 format in the AutoFormat dialog box. Point to the OK button.**

The AutoFormat dialog box displays with a list of customized formats (Figure 1-49). Each format illustrates how the body of the worksheet will display if it is chosen.

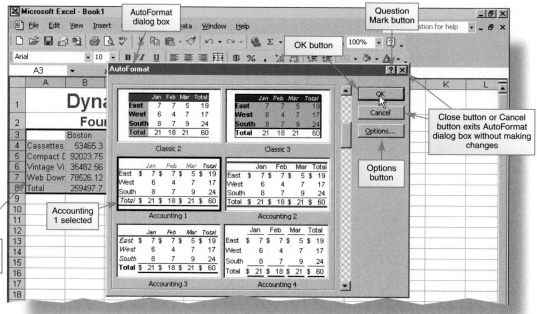

FIGURE 1-49

4 **Click the OK button. Select cell A10 to deselect the range A3:F8.**

Excel displays the worksheet with the range A3:F8 using the customized format, Accounting 1 (Figure 1-50).

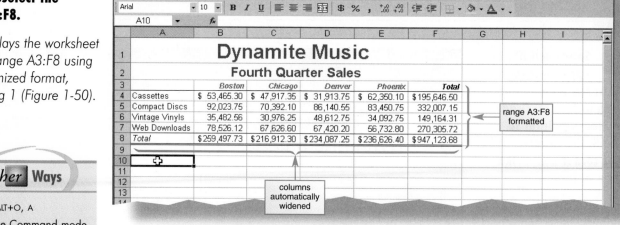

FIGURE 1-50

Other Ways

1. Press ALT+O, A
2. In Voice Command mode say, "Format, AutoFormat, [desired AutoFormat], OK"

The formats associated with Accounting 1 include bold, italic, right-aligned column titles; numbers displayed as dollars and cents with comma separators; numbers aligned on the decimal point; dollar signs in the first row of numbers and in the total row; and top and bottom rows display with borders. The width of column A also has been increased so the longest row title in cell A7, Web Downloads, just fits in the column. The widths of columns B through F have been increased so that the formatted numbers will fit in the cells.

The AutoFormat dialog box shown in Figure 1-49 includes 17 table formats and five buttons. Use the vertical scroll bar in the dialog box to view the 11 table formats that do not display. Each one of these table formats offers a different look. The one you choose depends on the worksheet you are creating. The last table format in the list, called None, removes all formats.

The five buttons in the dialog box allow you to cancel, complete the entries, get Help, and adjust a customized format. The **Close button** terminates current activity without making changes. You also can use the **Cancel button**, immediately below the **OK button**, for this purpose. Use the **Question Mark button**, to obtain Help on any box or button located in the dialog box. The **Options button** allows you to select additional formats to assign as part of the selected customized format.

The worksheet now is complete. The next step is to chart the fourth quarter sales for the four product groups by store. To create the chart, you must select the cell in the upper-left corner of the range to chart (cell A3). Rather than clicking cell A3 to select it, the next section describes how to use the Name box to select the cell.

More About

Merging Table Formats

It is not uncommon to apply two or more of the table formats in Figure 1-49 to the same range. If you assign two table formats to a range, Excel does not remove the original format from the range; it simply adds the second table format to the first. Thus, if you decide to change a table format to another, select the table format None from the bottom of the list to clear the first table format.

Using the Name Box to Select a Cell

The Name box is located on the left side of the formula bar. To select any cell, click the Name box and enter the cell reference of the cell you want to select. Perform the following steps to select cell A3.

Steps **To Use the Name Box to Select a Cell**

1 **Click the Name box in the formula bar. Type** a3 **in the Name box.**

Even though cell A10 is the active cell, the Name box displays the typed cell reference a3 (Figure 1-51).

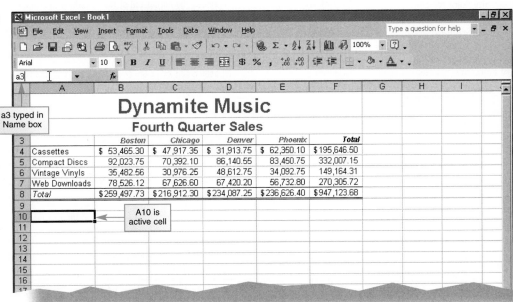

FIGURE 1-51

2 **Press the ENTER key.**

Excel changes the active cell from cell A10 to cell A3 (Figure 1-52).

A3 is active cell

	Dynamite Music					
	Fourth Quarter Sales					
	Boston	*Chicago*	*Denver*	*Phoenix*	*Total*	
Cassettes	$ 53,465.30	$ 47,917.35	$ 31,913.75	$ 62,350.10	$195,646.50	
Compact Discs	92,023.75	70,392.10	86,140.55	83,450.75	332,007.15	
Vintage Vinyls	35,482.56	30,976.25	48,612.75	34,092.75	149,164.31	
Web Downloads	78,526.12	67,626.60	67,420.20	56,732.80	270,305.72	
Total	$ 259,497.73	$ 216,912.30	$ 234,087.25	$ 236,626.40	$947,123.68	

FIGURE 1-52

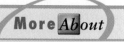

Naming Cells and Ranges

If you repeatedly select certain cells in a worksheet, consider naming the cells in the Name box. Select the cells one at a time and then type in a name in the Name box for each, such as Company Total for cell F8 in Figure 1-52. Then, when you want to select one of the named cells, click the Name box arrow and then click the cell name in the Name box list. You also can name ranges the same way.

As you will see in later projects, besides using the Name box to select any cell in a worksheet, you also can use it to assign names to a cell or range of cells.

Excel supports several additional ways to select a cell, as summarized in Table 1-3.

Table 1-3 Selecting Cells in Excel	
KEY, BOX, OR COMMAND	**FUNCTION**
ALT+PAGE DOWN	Selects the cell one window to the right and moves the window accordingly.
ALT+PAGE UP	Selects the cell one window to the left and moves the window accordingly.
ARROW	Selects the adjacent cell in the direction of the arrow on the key.
CTRL+ARROW	Selects the border cell of the worksheet in combination with the arrow keys and moves the window accordingly. For example, to select the rightmost cell in the row that contains the active cell, press CTRL+RIGHT ARROW. You also can press the END key, release it, and then press the arrow key to accomplish the same task.
CTRL+HOME	Selects cell A1 or the cell one column and one row below and to the right of frozen titles and moves the window accordingly.
Find command on Edit menu	Finds and selects a cell that contains specific contents that you enter in the Find dialog box. If necessary, Excel moves the window to display the cell. You can press SHIFT+F5 or CTRL+F to display the Find dialog box.
F5 or Go To command on Edit menu	Selects the cell that corresponds to the cell reference you enter in the Go To dialog box and moves the window accordingly. You can press CTRL+G to display the Go To dialog box.
HOME	Selects the cell at the beginning of the row that contains the active cell and moves the window accordingly.
Name box	Selects the cell in the workbook that corresponds to the cell reference you enter in the Name box.
PAGE DOWN	Selects the cell down one window from the active cell and moves the window accordingly.
PAGE UP	Selects the cell up one window from the active cell and moves the window accordingly.

Adding a 3-D Column Chart to the Worksheet

The 3-D Column chart in Figure 1-53 is called an **embedded chart** because it is drawn on the same worksheet as the data.

For the Boston store, the light blue column represents the fourth quarter sales for the Cassettes product group ($53,465.30); the purple column represents the fourth quarter sales for Compact Discs ($92,023.75); the light yellow column represents the fourth quarter sales for Vintage Vinyls ($35,482.56); and the turquoise column represents the fourth quarter sales for Web Downloads ($78,526.12). For the stores Chicago, Denver, and Phoenix, the columns follow the same color scheme to represent the comparable fourth quarter sales. The totals from the worksheet are not represented because the totals were not in the range specified for charting.

Excel derives the scale along the vertical axis (also called the **y-axis** or **value axis**) of the chart on the basis of the values in the worksheet. For example, no value in the range B4:E7 is less than zero or greater than $100,000.00. Excel also determines the $20,000.00 increments along the y-axis automatically. The format used by Excel for the numbers along the y-axis includes representing zero (0) with a dash (Figure 1-53).

With the range to chart selected, you click the **Chart Wizard button** on the Standard toolbar to initiate drawing the chart. The area on the worksheet where the chart displays is called the **chart location**. The chart location is the range A10:F20, immediately below the worksheet data.

Follow the steps below to draw a 3-D Column chart that compares the fourth quarter sales by product group for the four stores.

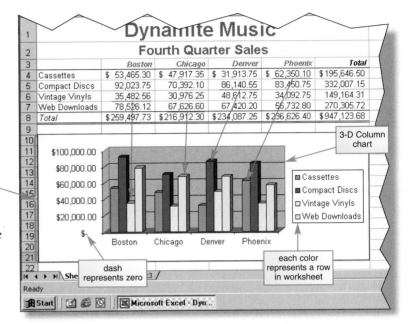

FIGURE 1-53

Steps | To Add a 3-D Column Chart to the Worksheet

1 With cell A3 selected, position the block plus sign mouse pointer within the cell's border and drag the mouse pointer to the lower-right corner cell (cell E7) of the range to chart (A3:E7). Point to the Chart Wizard button on the Standard toolbar.

Excel highlights the range to chart (Figure 1-54).

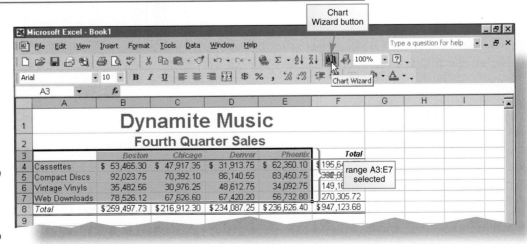

FIGURE 1-54

2 Click the Chart Wizard button.

The Chart Wizard - Step 1 of 4 - Chart Type dialog box displays.

3 With Column selected in the Chart type list, click the 3-D Column chart sub-type (column 1, row 2) in the Chart sub-type area. Point to the Finish button.

Column is highlighted in the Chart type list and Clustered column with a 3-D visual effect is highlighted in the Chart sub-type area (Figure 1-55).

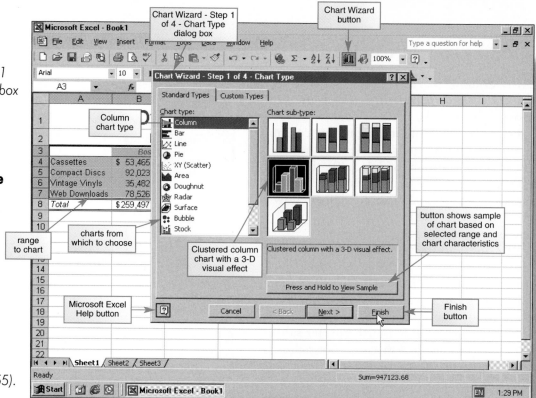

FIGURE 1-55

4 Click the Finish button. If the chart toolbar displays, click its Close button. When the chart displays, point to an open area in the lower-right section of the Chart Area so the ScreenTip, Chart Area, displays.

Excel draws the 3-D Clustered column chart (Figure 1-56). The chart displays in the middle of the window in a selection rectangle. The small sizing handles at the corners and along the sides of the selection rectangle indicate the chart is selected.

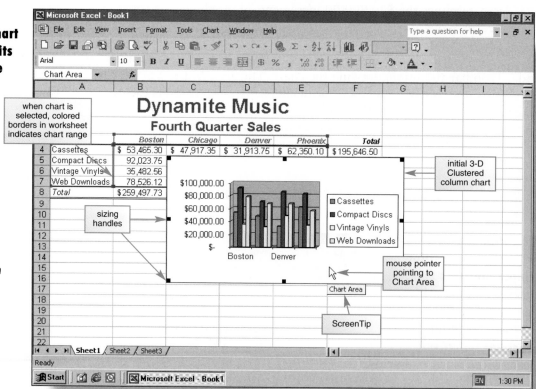

FIGURE 1-56

5 **Drag the chart down and to the left to position the upper-left corner of the dotted line rectangle over the upper-left corner of cell A10 (Figure 1-57).**

Excel displays a dotted line rectangle showing the new chart location. As you drag the selected chart, the mouse pointer changes to a cross hair with four arrowheads.

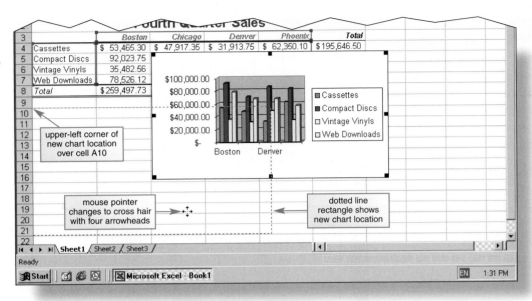

FIGURE 1-57

6 **Release the mouse button. Point to the middle sizing handle on the right edge of the selection rectangle.**

The chart displays in a new location (Figure 1-58). The mouse pointer changes to a horizontal line with two arrowheads when it points to a sizing handle.

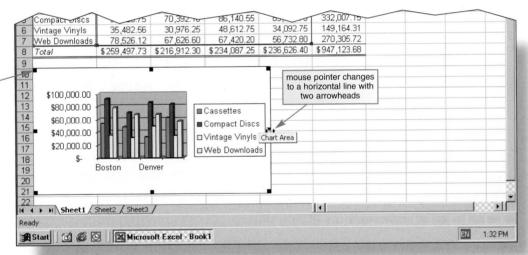

FIGURE 1-58

7 **While holding down the ALT key, drag the sizing handle to the right edge of column F. Release the mouse button.**

While you drag, the dotted line rectangle shows the new chart location (Figure 1-59). Holding down the ALT key while you drag a chart snaps (aligns) the new border to the worksheet gridlines.

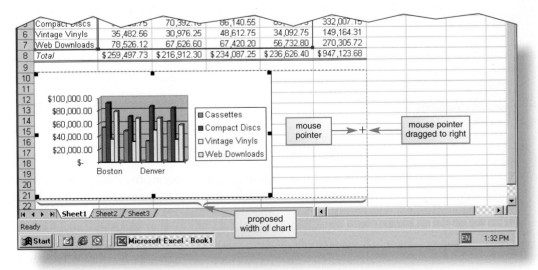

FIGURE 1-59

8 **If necessary, hold down the ALT key and drag the lower-middle sizing handle down to the bottom border of row 21. Click cell H21 to deselect the chart.**

The new chart location extends from the top of cell A10 to the bottom of cell F21 (Figure 1-60).

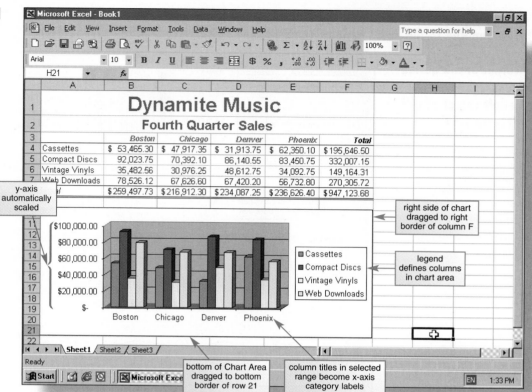

FIGURE 1-60

Other Ways

1. On Insert menu click Chart
2. Press F11
3. In Voice Command mode say, "Chart Wizard"

More About

Chart Types

You can change the embedded 3-D Column chart to another type by clicking the chart location and clicking the Chart Type button arrow on the Chart toolbar. You also can use the Chart toolbar to format the chart to make it look more professional. If the Chart toolbar does not display when you click the chart, right-click any toolbar and click Chart.

The embedded 3-D Column chart in Figure 1-60 compares the fourth quarter sales for the four product groups within each store. It also allows you to compare fourth quarter sales among the stores.

Excel automatically selects the entries in the topmost row of the range (row 3) as the titles for the horizontal axis (also called the **x-axis** or **category axis**) and draws a column for each of the 16 cells in the range containing numbers. The small box to the right of the column chart in Figure 1-55 on page E 1.38 contains the legend. The **legend** identifies each bar in the chart. Excel automatically selects the leftmost column of the range (column A) as titles within the legend. As indicated earlier, it also automatically scales the y-axis on the basis of the magnitude of the numbers in the chart range.

Excel offers 14 different chart types (Figure 1-55 on page E 1.38). The **default chart type** is the chart Excel draws if you click the Finish button in the first Chart Wizard dialog box. When you install Excel on a computer, the default chart type is the 2-D (two-dimensional) Column chart.

Saving a Workbook

While you are building a workbook, the computer stores it in memory. If the computer is turned off or if you lose electrical power, the workbook is lost. Hence, you must save on a floppy disk or hard disk any workbook that you will use later. A saved workbook is referred to as a **file**. The following steps illustrate how to save a workbook on a floppy disk in drive A using the Save button on the Standard toolbar.

Steps **To Save a Workbook**

1 **With a floppy disk in drive A, click the Save button on the Standard toolbar.**

The Save As dialog box displays (Figure 1-61). The preset Save in folder is Documents and Settings (your Save in folder may be different), the preset file name is Book1, and the file type is Microsoft Excel Workbook. The buttons on the top and on the side are used to select folders and change the display of file names and other information.

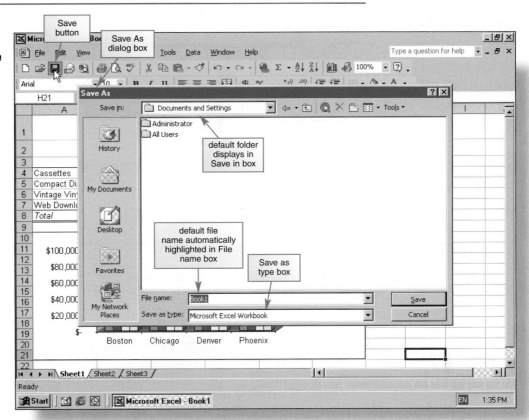

FIGURE 1-61

2 **Type** Dynamite Music 4th Quarter Sales **in the File name box. Point to the Save in box arrow.**

The new file name replaces Book1 in the File name text box (Figure 1-62). A file name can be up to 255 characters and can include spaces.

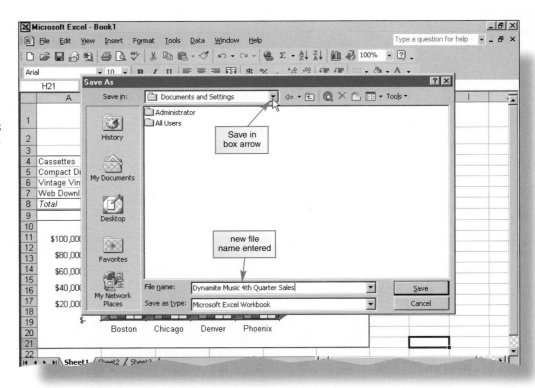

FIGURE 1-62

Microsoft **Excel**

3 **Click the Save in box arrow and then point to 3½ Floppy (A:).**

A list of available drives and folders displays (Figure 1-63).

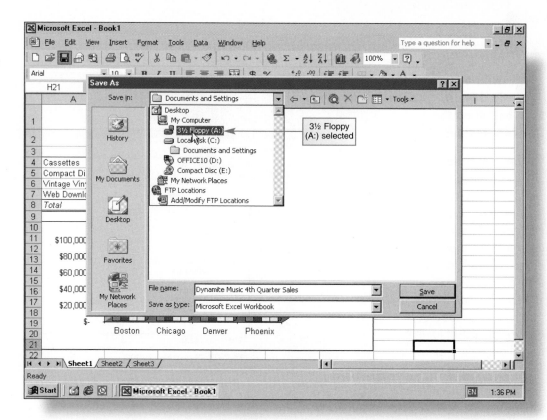

FIGURE 1-63

4 **Click 3½ Floppy (A:) and then point to the Save button in the Save As dialog box.**

Drive A becomes the selected drive (Figure 1-64).

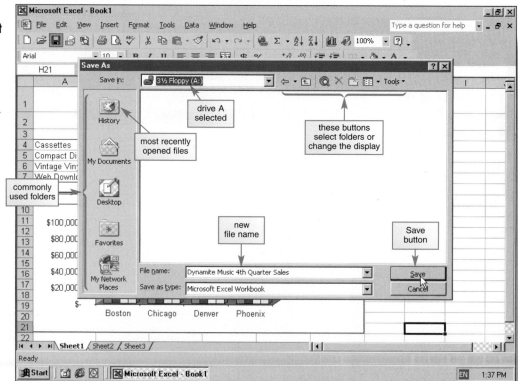

FIGURE 1-64

5 **Click the Save button.**

Excel saves the workbook on the floppy disk in drive A using the file name, Dynamite Music 4th Quarter Sales. Excel automatically appends the extension .xls to the file name you entered in Step 2, which stands for Excel workbook. Although the workbook is saved on a floppy disk, it also remains in memory and displays on the screen (Figure 1-65). The new file name displays on the title bar.

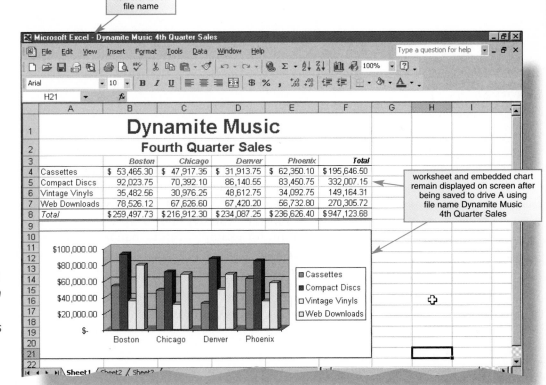

title bar displays new workbook file name

worksheet and embedded chart remain displayed on screen after being saved to drive A using file name Dynamite Music 4th Quarter Sales

FIGURE 1-65

Other Ways

1. On File menu click Save As, type file name, select drive or folder, click OK button
2. Press CTRL+S, type file name, select drive or folder, click OK button
3. In Voice Command mode say, "File, Save As, [type desired file name], Save"

While Excel is saving the workbook, it momentarily changes the word Ready on the status bar to Saving. It also displays a horizontal bar on the status bar indicating the amount of the workbook saved. After the save operation is complete, Excel changes the name of the workbook in the title bar from Book1 to Dynamite Music 4th Quarter Sales (Figure 1-65).

The seven buttons at the top and to the right in the Save As dialog box in Figure 1-64 and their functions are summarized in Table 1-4.

When you click the **Tools button** in the Save As dialog box, a list displays. The **General Options command** in the list allows you to save a backup copy of the workbook, create a password to limit access to the workbook, and carry out other functions that are discussed later. Saving a backup workbook means that each time you save a workbook, Excel copies the current version of the workbook on disk to a file with the same name, but with the words, Backup of, appended to the front of the file name. In the case of a power failure or some other problem, use the backup version to restore your work.

You also can use the General Options command on the Tools list to assign a password to a workbook so others cannot open it. A password is case-sensitive and can be up to 15 characters long. **Case-sensitive** means Excel can differentiate between uppercase and lowercase letters. If you assign a password and forget the password, you cannot access the workbook.

Table 1-4	Save As Dialog Box Toolbar Buttons	
BUTTON	**BUTTON NAME**	**FUNCTION**
	Default File Location	Displays contents of default file location
	Up One Level	Displays contents of next level up folder
	Search the Web	Starts browser and displays search engine
	Delete	Deletes selected file or folder
	Create New Folder	Creates new folder
	Views	Changes view of files and folders
	Tools	Lists commands to print or modify file names and folders

Saving Workbooks

Excel allows you to save a workbook in over 30 different file formats. You choose the file format by clicking the Save as type box arrow at the bottom of the Save As dialog box (Figure 1-64 on page E 1.42). Microsoft Excel Workbook is the default file format. But you can, for example, save a workbook in Web Page format so you can publish it to the World Wide Web.

The five buttons on the left of the Save As dialog box in Figure 1-64 on page E 1.42 allow you to select frequently used folders. The **History button** displays a list of shortcuts (pointers) to the most recently used files in a folder titled Recent. You cannot save workbooks to the Recent folder.

Printing a Worksheet

Once you have created the worksheet, you might want to print it. A printed version of the worksheet is called a **hard copy** or **printout**.

You might want a printout for several reasons. First, to present the worksheet and chart to someone who does not have access to a computer, it must be in printed form. A printout, for example, can be handed out in a management meeting about fourth quarter sales. In addition, worksheets and charts often are kept for reference by people other than those who prepare them. In many cases, worksheets and charts are printed and kept in binders for use by others. Perform the following steps to print the worksheet.

Steps **To Print a Worksheet**

1 Ready the printer according to the printer instructions. Point to the Print button on the Standard toolbar (Figure 1-66).

FIGURE 1-66

2 Click the Print button. When the printer stops printing the worksheet and the chart, retrieve the printout.

Excel sends the worksheet to the printer, which prints it (Figure 1-67).

Other Ways

1. On File menu click Print, click OK button
2. Right-click workbook Control-menu icon on menu bar, click Print on shortcut menu, click OK button
3. Press CTRL+P, click OK button
4. In Voice Command mode say, "Print"

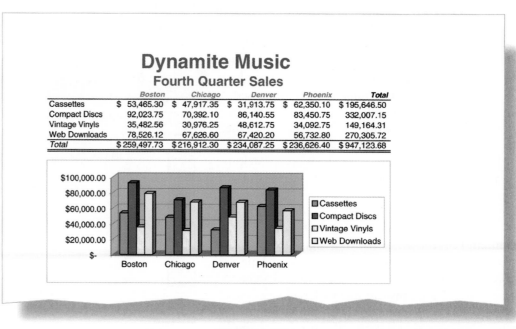

FIGURE 1-67

Prior to clicking the Print button, you can select which columns and rows in the worksheet to print. The range of cells you choose to print is called the **print area**. If you do not select a print area, as was the case in the previous set of steps, Excel automatically selects a print area on the basis of used cells. As you will see in future projects, Excel has many different print options, such as allowing you to preview the printout on the screen to see if the printout is satisfactory before sending it to the printer.

Quitting Excel

After you build, save, and print the worksheet and chart, Project 1 is complete. To quit Excel, complete the following steps.

More About

Saving Paper

If you are concerned with saving paper, you can preview the printout on your screen, make adjustments to the worksheet, and then print it only when it appears exactly as you want. The Print Preview button is immediately to the right of the Print button on the Standard toolbar.

Steps | To Quit Excel

1 Point to the Close button on the right side of the title bar (Figure 1-68).

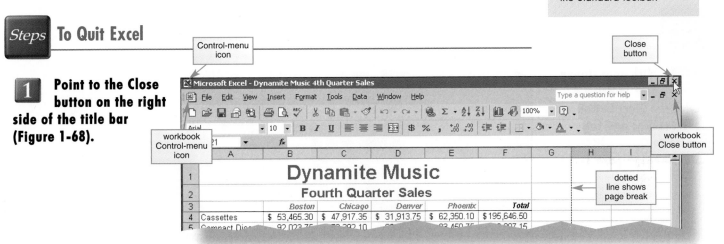

FIGURE 1-68

2 Click the Close button.

If you made changes to the workbook, the Microsoft Excel dialog box displays the question, Do you want to save the changes you made to 'Dynamite Music 4th Quarter Sales.xls'? (Figure 1-69). Clicking the Yes button saves the changes before quitting Excel. Clicking the No button quits Excel without saving the changes. Clicking the Cancel button cancels the exit and returns control to the worksheet.

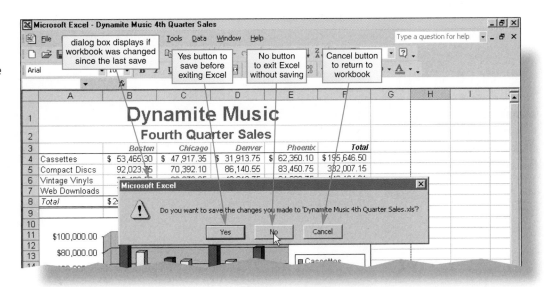

FIGURE 1-69

3 Click the No button.

Other Ways

1. On File menu click Exit
2. In Voice Command mode say, "File, Exit"

In Figure 1-68 on the previous page, you can see that two Close buttons and two Control-menu icons display. The Close button and Control-menu icon on the title bar close Excel. The Close button and Control-menu icon on the menu bar close the workbook, but not Excel.

Starting Excel and Opening a Workbook

Once you have created and saved a workbook, you often will have reason to retrieve it from a floppy disk. For example, you might want to review the calculations on the worksheet and enter additional or revised data on it. The following steps assume Excel is not running.

Steps **To Start Excel and Open a Workbook**

1 **With your floppy disk in drive A, click the Start button on the taskbar and then point to Open Office Document (Figure 1-70).**

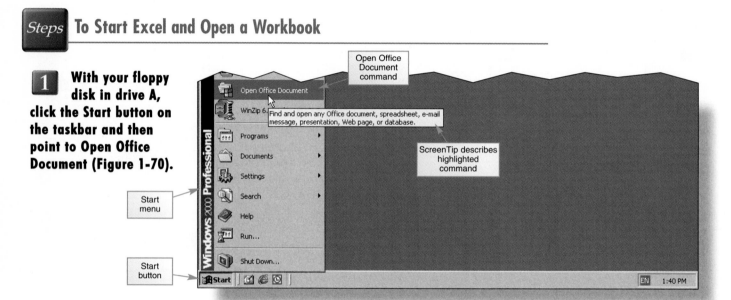

FIGURE 1-70

2 **Click Open Office Document. If necessary, click the Look in box arrow and then click 3½ Floppy (A:) in the Look in list.**

The Open Office Document dialog box displays (Figure 1-71).

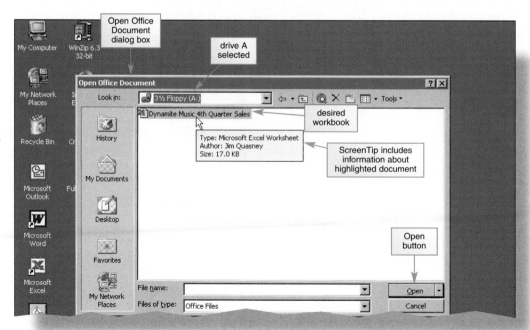

FIGURE 1-71

3 **Double-click the file name Dynamite Music 4th Quarter Sales.**

Excel starts, opens the workbook Dynamite Music 4th Quarter Sales.xls from drive A, and displays it on the screen (Figure 1-72). An alternative to double-clicking the file name is to click it and then click the Open button in the Open Office Document dialog box.

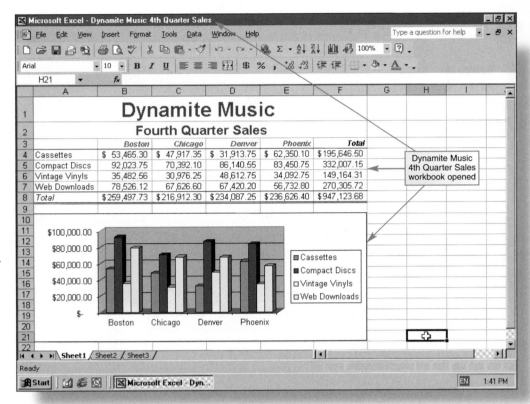

FIGURE 1-72

AutoCalculate

You easily can obtain a total, an average, or other information about the numbers in a range by using the AutoCalculate area on the status bar. All you need do is select the range of cells containing the numbers you want to check. Next, right-click the AutoCalculate area to display the shortcut menu (Figure 1-73 on the next page). The check mark to the left of the active function (Sum) indicates that the sum of the selected range displays. The function commands on the AutoCalculate shortcut menu are described in Table 1-5.

Other Ways

1. Right-click Start button, click Explore, display contents of drive A, double-click file name

2. In Microsoft Excel, in Voice Command mode say, "Open, [select file name], Open"

Table 1-5	AutoCalculate Shortcut Menu Commands
COMMAND	**FUNCTION**
None	No value displays in the AutoCalculate area
Average	Displays the average of the numbers in the selected range
Count	Displays the number of nonblank cells in the selected range
Count Nums	Displays the number of cells containing numbers in the selected range
Max	Displays the highest value in the selected range
Min	Displays the lowest value in the selected range
Sum	Displays the sum of the numbers in the selected range

The steps on the next page show how to display the average fourth quarter sales by store for the Cassettes product group.

Steps **To Use the AutoCalculate Area to Determine an Average**

1 **Select the range B4:E4. Right-click the AutoCalculate area on the status bar.**

The sum of the numbers in the range B4:E4 displays ($195,646.50) as shown in Figure 1-73 because Sum is active in the AutoCalculate area. You may see a total other than the sum in your AutoCalculate area. The shortcut menu listing the various types of functions displays above the AutoCalculate area.

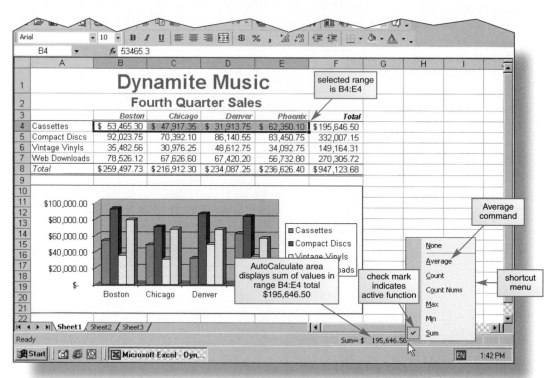

FIGURE 1-73

2 **Click Average on the shortcut menu.**

The average of the numbers in the range B4:E4 displays in the AutoCalculate area (Figure 1-74).

3 **Right-click the AutoCalculate area and then click Sum on the shortcut menu.**

The AutoCalculate area displays the sum as shown earlier in Figure 1-73.

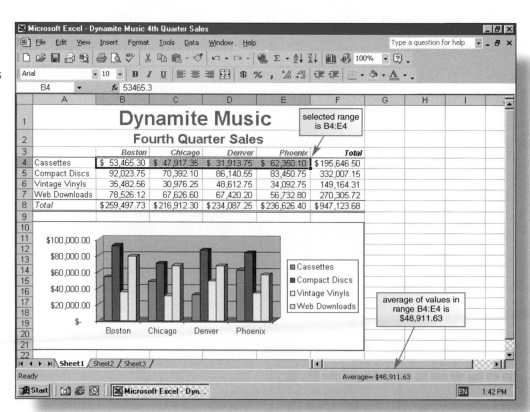

FIGURE 1-74

To change to any one of the other five functions for the range B4:E4, right-click the AutoCalculate area, then click the desired function.

The selection None at the top of the AutoCalculate shortcut menu in Figure 1-73 turns off the AutoCalculate area. Thus, if you select None, then no value will show in the AutoCalculate area when you select a range.

Correcting Errors

You can correct errors on a worksheet using one of several methods. The method you choose will depend on the extent of the error and whether you notice it while typing the data or after you have entered the incorrect data into the cell.

Correcting Errors While You Are Typing Data into a Cell

If you notice an error while you are typing data into a cell, press the BACKSPACE key to erase the portion in error and then type the correct characters. If the error is a major one, click the Cancel box in the formula bar or press the ESC key to erase the entire entry and then reenter the data from the beginning.

In-Cell Editing

If you find an error in the worksheet after entering the data, you can correct the error in one of two ways:

1. If the entry is short, select the cell, retype the entry correctly, and click the Enter box or press the ENTER key. The new entry will replace the old entry.
2. If the entry in the cell is long and the errors are minor, **Edit mode** may be a better choice. Use Edit mode as described below.
   a. Double-click the cell containing the error. Excel switches to Edit mode, the active cell contents display in the formula bar, and a flashing insertion point displays in the active cell (Figure 1-75). This editing procedure is called **in-cell editing** because you can edit the contents directly in the cell. The active cell contents also display in the formula bar.
   b. Make your changes, as indicated below.
      (1) To insert between two characters, place the insertion point between the two characters and begin typing. Excel inserts the new characters at the location of the insertion point.
      (2) To delete a character in the cell, move the insertion point to the left of the character you want to delete and then press the DELETE key, or place the insertion point to the right of the character you want to delete and then press the BACKSPACE key. You also can use the mouse to drag through the character or adjacent characters you want to delete and then press the DELETE key or click the **Cut button** on the Standard toolbar.
      (3) When you are finished editing an entry, click the Enter box or press the ENTER key.

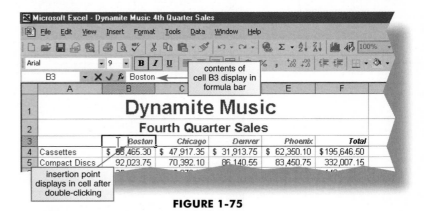

FIGURE 1-75

Editing the Contents of a Cell

Rather than using in-cell editing, you can select the cell and then click the formula bar to edit the contents.

When Excel enters Edit mode, the keyboard usually is in Insert mode. In **Insert mode**, as you type a character, Excel inserts the character and moves all characters one position to the right of the typed character. You can change to Overtype mode by pressing the INSERT key. In **Overtype mode**, Excel overtypes, or replaces, the character to the right of the insertion point. The INSERT key toggles the keyboard between Insert mode and Overtype mode.

While in Edit mode, you may have reason to move the insertion point to various points in the cell, select portions of the data in the cell, or switch from inserting characters to overtyping characters. Table 1-6 summarizes the more common tasks used during in-cell editing.

Table 1-6	Summary of In-Cell Editing Tasks	
TASK	**MOUSE**	**KEYBOARD**
Move the insertion point to the beginning of data in a cell	Point to the left of the first character and click	Press HOME
Move the insertion point to the end of data in a cell	Point to the right of the last character and click	Press END
Move the insertion point anywhere in a cell	Point to the appropriate position and click the character	Press RIGHT ARROW or LEFT ARROW
Highlight one or more adjacent characters	Drag the mouse pointer through adjacent characters	Press SHIFT+RIGHT ARROW or SHIFT+LEFT ARROW
Select all data in a cell	Double-click the cell with the insertion point in the cell	
Delete selected characters	Click the Cut button on the Standard toolbar	Press DELETE
Delete characters to the left of the insertion point		Press BACKSPACE
Toggle between Insert and Overtype modes		Press INSERT

Undoing the Last Entry

Excel provides the **Undo command** on the **Edit menu** and the **Undo button** on the Standard toolbar (Figure 1-76) that you can use to erase the most recent worksheet entries. Thus, if you enter incorrect data in a cell and notice it immediately, click the Undo command or Undo button and Excel changes the cell contents to what they were prior to entering the incorrect data.

Escaping an Activity

When it comes to canceling the current activity, the most important key on the keyboard is the ESC (Escape) key. Whether you are entering data into a cell or responding to a dialog box, pressing the ESC key cancels the current activity.

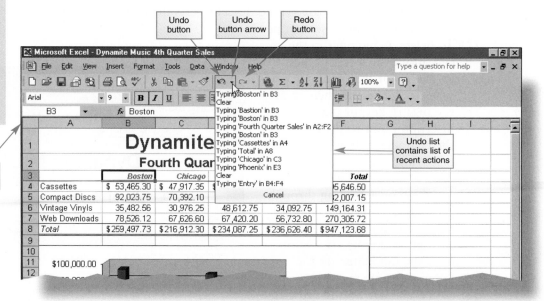

FIGURE 1-76

If Excel cannot undo an action, then the Undo button is inoperative. Excel remembers the last 16 actions you have completed. Thus, you can undo up to 16 previous actions by clicking the Undo button arrow to display the Undo list and clicking the action to be undone (Figure 1-76). You can drag through several actions in the Undo list to undo all of them at once.

Next to the Undo button on the Standard toolbar is the Redo button. The **Redo button** allows you to repeat previous actions. You also can click Redo on the Edit menu rather than using the Redo button.

Clearing a Cell or Range of Cells

If you enter data into the wrong cell or range of cells, you can erase, or clear, the data using one of several methods. *Never press the* SPACEBAR *to clear a cell.* Pressing the SPACEBAR enters a blank character. A blank character is text and is different from an empty cell, even though the cell may appear empty.

Excel provides four methods to clear the contents of a cell or a range of cells, which are discussed below.

TO CLEAR CELL CONTENTS USING THE FILL HANDLE

1 Select the cell or range of cells and point to the fill handle so the mouse pointer changes to a cross hair.

2 Drag the fill handle back into the selected cell or range until a shadow covers the cell or cells you want to erase. Release the mouse button.

TO CLEAR CELL CONTENTS USING THE SHORTCUT MENU

1 Select the cell or range of cells to be cleared.

2 Right-click the selection.

3 Click Clear Contents on the shortcut menu.

TO CLEAR CELL CONTENTS USING THE DELETE KEY

1 Select the cell or range of cells to be cleared.

2 Press the DELETE key.

TO CLEAR CELL CONTENTS USING THE CLEAR COMMAND

1 Select the cell or range of cells to be cleared.

2 Click Edit on the menu bar and then point to Clear.

3 Click All on the Clear submenu.

You also can select a range of cells and click the Cut button on the Standard toolbar or click Cut on the Edit menu. Be aware, however, that the Cut button or Cut command not only deletes the contents from the range, but also copies the contents of the range to the Office Clipboard.

Clearing the Entire Worksheet

Sometimes, everything goes wrong. If this happens, you may want to clear the worksheet entirely and start over. To clear the worksheet, follow the steps on the next page.

More About

The Undo Button

The Undo button can undo far more complicated worksheet activities than just removing the latest entry from a cell. In fact, most commands can be undone if you click the Undo button before you make another entry or issue another command. You cannot undo a save or print, but, as a general rule, the Undo button can restore the worksheet data and settings to what they were the last time Excel was in Ready mode. With Excel, you have multiple-level undo and redo capabilities.

More About

Getting Back to Normal

If you accidentally assign unwanted formats to a range of cells, you can use the Clear command on the Edit menu to delete the formats of a selected range. Doing so changes the format to Normal style. To view the characteristics of the Normal style, click Style on the Format menu or press ALT+APOSTROPHE (').

TO CLEAR THE ENTIRE WORKSHEET

1 Click the Select All button on the worksheet (Figure 1-76 on page E 1.50).

2 Press the DELETE key or click Edit on the menu bar, point to Clear and then click All on the Clear submenu.

The **Select All button** selects the entire worksheet. Instead of clicking the Select All button, you also can press CTRL+A. You also can clear an unsaved workbook by clicking the workbook's Close button or by clicking the **Close command** on the File menu. If you close the workbook, click the **New button** on the Standard toolbar or click the **New command** on the File menu to begin working on the next workbook.

To delete an embedded chart, complete the following steps.

TO DELETE AN EMBEDDED CHART

1 Click the chart to select it. Press the DELETE key.

Excel Help System

More About

The Excel 2002 Help System

The best way to become familiar with the Excel Help system is to use it. Appendix A includes detailed information on the Excel Help system and exercises that will help you gain confidence in using it.

At any time while you are using Excel, you can get answers to questions using the Excel Help system. You can activate the Excel Help system by using the Ask a Question box on the menu bar, the Microsoft Excel Help button on the Standard toolbar, or the Help menu (Figure 1-77). Used properly, this form of online assistance can increase your productivity and reduce your frustrations by minimizing the time you spend learning how to use Excel.

The following section shows how to get answers to your questions using the Ask a Question box. Additional information on using the Excel Help system is available in Appendix A and Table 1-7 on page E 1.54.

Obtaining Help Using the Ask a Question Box on the Menu Bar

The **Ask a Question box** on the right side of the menu bar lets you type free-form questions such as, *how do I save* or *how do I create a Web page*, or you can type in terms such as, *copy*, *save*, or *formatting*. Excel responds by displaying a list of topics related to what you entered. The following steps show how to use the Ask a Question box to obtain information on formatting a worksheet.

Steps **To Obtain Help Using the Ask a Question Box**

1 **Type** formatting **in the Ask a Question box on the right side of the menu bar (Figure 1-77).** 2000 **If you are using Excel 2000, click the Microsoft Excel Help button on the right side of the Standard toolbar. Type your question or short phrase in the What would you like to do? text box and then click the Search button.**

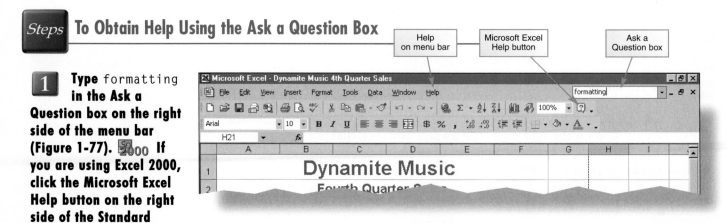

FIGURE 1-77

2 Press the ENTER key. When the list of topics displays below the Ask a Question box, point to the topic, About formatting worksheets and data.

A list of topics displays relating to the term, formatting. The mouse pointer changes to a hand indicating it is pointing to a link (Figure 1-78).

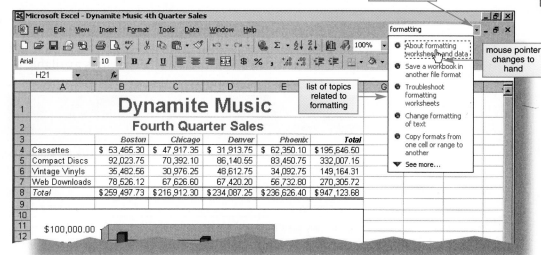

FIGURE 1-78

3 Click About formatting worksheets and data. When the Microsoft Excel Help window displays, double-click its title bar to maximize it.

Excel opens a Microsoft Excel Help window that provides Help information about worksheet formatting (Figure 1-79).

4 Click the Close button on the Microsoft Excel Help window title bar.

The Microsoft Excel Help window closes and the worksheet is active.

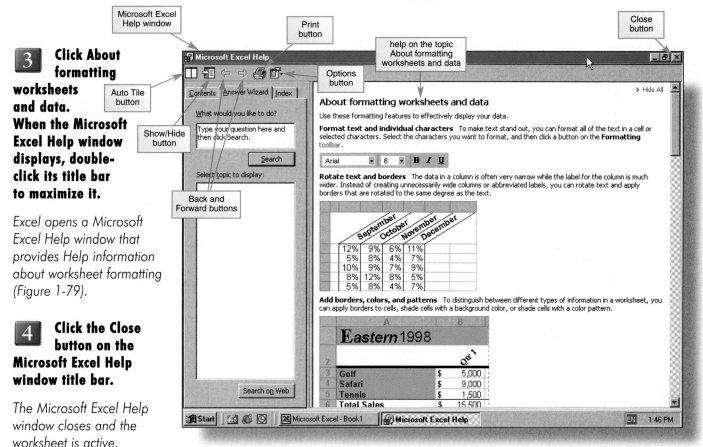

FIGURE 1-79

Use the buttons in the upper-left corner of the Microsoft Excel Help window (Figure 1-79) to navigate through the Help system, change the display, and print the contents of the window.

As you enter questions and terms in the Ask a Question box, Excel adds them to its list. Thus, if you click the Ask a Question box arrow (Figure 1-78), a list of previously asked questions and terms will display.

Table 1-7 summarizes the 11 categories of Help available to you. Because of the way the Excel Help system works, be sure to review the rightmost column of Table 1-7 if you have difficulties activating the desired category of Help. Additional information on using the Excel Help system is available in Appendix A.

Table 1-7 Excel Help System		
TYPE	**DESCRIPTION**	**HOW TO ACTIVATE**
Answer Wizard	Answers questions or searches for terms that you type in your own words.	Click the Microsoft Excel Help button on the Standard toolbar. Click the Answer Wizard tab.
Ask a Question box	Answers questions or searches for terms that you type in your own words.	Type a question or term in the Ask a Question box on the menu bar and then press the ENTER key.
Contents sheet	Groups Help topics by general categories. Use when you know only the general category of the topic in question.	Click the Microsoft Excel Help button on the Standard toolbar. Click the Contents tab.
Detect and Repair	Automatically finds and fixes errors in the application.	Click Detect and Repair on the Help menu.
Hardware and Software Information	Shows Product ID and allows access to system information and technical support information.	Click About Microsoft Excel on the Help menu and then click the appropriate button.
Help for Lotus 1-2-3 Users	Used to assist Lotus 1-2-3 users who are learning Microsoft Excel.	Click Lotus 1-2-3 Help on the Help menu.
Index sheet	Similar to an index in a book. Use when you know exactly what you want.	Click the Microsoft Excel Help button on the Standard toolbar. If necessary, maximize the Help window by double-clicking its title bar. Click the Index tab.
Office Assistant	Similar to the Ask a Question box in that the Office Assistant answers questions that you type in your own words, offers tips, and provides help for a variety of Excel features.	Click the Office Assistant icon. If the Office Assistant does not display, click Show the Office Assistant on the Help menu.
Office on the Web	Used to access technical resources and download free product enhancements on the Web.	Click Office on the Web on the Help menu.
Question Mark button	Used to identify unfamiliar items in a dialog box.	Click the Question Mark button on the title bar of a dialog box and then click an item in the dialog box.
What's This? command	Used to identify unfamiliar items on the screen.	Click What's This? on the Help menu, and then click an item on the screen.

Quitting Excel

To quit Excel, complete the following steps.

More About

Quitting Excel

Do not forget to remove your floppy disk from drive A after quitting Excel, especially if you are working in a laboratory environment. Nothing can be more frustrating than leaving all of your hard work behind on a floppy disk for the next user.

TO QUIT EXCEL

1 Click the Close button on the right side of the title bar (see Figure 1-68 on page E 1.45).

2 If the Microsoft Excel dialog box displays, click the No button.

CASE PERSPECTIVE SUMMARY

The worksheet created in this project allows the management of Dynamite Music to examine fourth quarter sales for the four key product groups. Furthermore, the 3-D Column chart should meet the needs of Nadine Mitchell, who as you recall, would rather view the numbers graphically.

Project Summary

In creating the Dynamite Music Fourth Quarter Sales worksheet and chart in this project, you gained a broad knowledge of Excel. First, you were introduced to starting Excel. You learned about the Excel window and how to enter text and numbers to create a worksheet. You learned how to select a range and how to use the AutoSum button to sum numbers in a column or row. Using the fill handle, you learned how to copy a cell to adjacent cells.

Once the worksheet was built, you learned how to change the font size of the title, bold the title, and center the title across a range using buttons on the Formatting toolbar. Using the steps and techniques presented in the project, you formatted the body of the worksheet using the AutoFormat command, and you used the Chart Wizard to add a 3-D Column chart. After completing the worksheet, you saved the workbook on disk, printed the worksheet and chart, and then quit Excel. You learned how to start Excel by opening an Excel document, use the AutoCalculate area, and edit data in cells. Finally, you learned how to use the Excel Help system to answer your questions.

What You Should Know

Having completed this project, you now should be able to perform the following tasks:

- Add a 3-D Column Chart to the Worksheet (E 1.37)
- Bold a Cell (E 1.29)
- Center a Cell's Contents across Columns (E 1.32)
- Change the Font Color of a Cell (E 1.31)
- Clear Cell Contents Using the Clear Command (E 1.51)
- Clear Cell Contents Using the DELETE Key (E 1.51)
- Clear Cell Contents Using the Fill Handle (E 1.51)
- Clear Cell Contents Using the Shortcut Menu (E 1.51)
- Clear the Entire Worksheet (E 1.52)
- Copy a Cell to Adjacent Cells in a Row (E 1.25)
- Customize the Excel Window (E 1.09)
- Delete an Embedded Chart (E 1.52)
- Determine Multiple Totals at the Same Time (E 1.27)
- Display the Toolbars on the Two Rows When Using Excel 2000 (E 1.09)
- Enter Column Titles (E 1.19)
- Enter Numeric Data (E 1.22)
- Enter Row Titles (E 1.21)
- Enter the Worksheet Titles (E 1.17)
- Format the Worksheet Subtitle (E 1.33)
- Increase the Font Size of a Cell Entry (E 1.30)
- Obtain Help Using the Ask a Question Box (E 1.52)
- Print a Worksheet (E 1.44)
- Quit Excel (E 1.45, E 1.54)
- Save a Workbook (E 1.41)
- Start Excel (E 1.08)
- Start Excel and Open a Workbook (E 1.46)
- Sum a Column of Numbers (E 1.23)
- Use AutoFormat to Format the Body of a Worksheet (E 1.33)
- Use the AutoCalculate Area to Determine an Average (E 1.48)
- Use the Name Box to Select a Cell (E 1.35)

More About

Microsoft Certification

The Microsoft Office User Specialist (MOUS) Certification program provides an opportunity for you to obtain a valuable industry credential — proof that you have the Excel 2002 skills required by employers. For more information, see Appendix E or visit the Shelly Cashman Series MOUS Web page at scsite.com/tdoff/cert.

In the Lab

Instructions: To complete the Learn It Online exercises, start your browser, click the Address bar, and then enter scsite.com/tdoff/exs. When the Teachers Discovering Office Learn It Online page displays, follow the instructions in the exercises below. To complete the Using the Office Training CD exercises, insert the Microsoft Office Training CD in your CD drive and access the appropriate section. Refer to the introduction chapter of this book to review step-by-step instructions for both installing and using the Microsoft Office Training CD.

Learn It online

1 Project Reinforcement – TF, MC, and SA

Below Excel Project 1, click the Project Reinforcement link. Print the quiz by clicking Print on the File menu. Answer each question. Write your first and last name at the top of each page, and then hand in the printout to your instructor.

2 Flash Cards

Below Excel Project 1, click the Flash Cards link. When Flash Cards displays, read the instructions. Type 20 (or a number specified by your instructor) in the Number of Playing Cards text box, type your name in the Name text box, and then click the Flip Card button. When the flash card displays, read the question and then click the Answer box arrow to select an answer. Flip through Flash Cards. Click Print on the File menu to print the last flash card if your score is 15 (75%) correct or greater and then hand it in to your instructor. If your score is less than 15 (75%) correct, then redo this exercise by clicking the Replay button.

3 Practice Test

Below Excel Project 1, click the Practice Test link. Answer each question, enter your first and last name

at the bottom of the page, and then click the Grade Test button. When the graded practice test displays on your screen, click Print on the File menu to print a hard copy. Continue to take practice tests until you score 80% or better. Hand in a printout of the final practice test to your instructor.

4 Who Wants to Be a Computer Genius?

Below Excel Project 1, click the Computer Genius link. Read the instructions, enter your first and last name at the bottom of the page, and then click the Play button. Hand in your score to your instructor.

5 Wheel of Terms

Below Excel Project 1, click the Wheel of Terms link. Read the instructions, and then enter your first and last name and your school name. Click the Play button. Hand in your score to your instructor.

6 Crossword Puzzle Challenge

Below Excel Project 1, click the Crossword Puzzle Challenge link. Read the instructions, and then enter your first and last name. Click the Play button. Work the crossword puzzle. When you are finished, click the Submit button. When the crossword puzzle redisplays, click the Print button. Hand in the printout.

Using the Microsoft Office Training CD

1 In and Out of the Classroom

With the Microsoft Office Training CD in your CD drive, click the In and Out of the Classroom tab. Review one of the Excel tutorials that will help you learn how to use and integrate Microsoft Excel in your classroom. The Excel tutorials are available in the Office XP, Office 2000, or Office 2001 for the Mac links.

2 Tips and Tricks

With the Microsoft Office Training CD in your CD drive, click the Tips and Tricks tab. Review one of the Excel tips and tricks that includes drawing borders around cells, saving an Excel spreadsheet as a Web page, exporting Excel data into other Office applications, calculating daily fat calories, creating a timeline in Excel, and more.

3 Tutorial Packs

With the Microsoft Office Training CD in your CD drive, click the Tutorial Packs tab. Review one of the step-by-step tutorials on using Microsoft Excel to enhance your teaching and learning process.

Productivity in the Classroom

1 Parent Teacher Student Association Annual Sales Analysis Worksheet

Problem: The president of the Magellan High School PTSA needs a sales analysis worksheet to summarize the annual fund-raising activities similar to the one shown in Figure 1-80. Your task is to develop the worksheet.

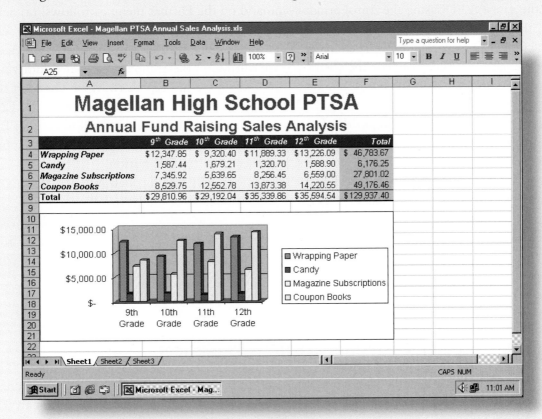

FIGURE 1-80

Instructions: Perform the following tasks.

1. Create the worksheet shown in Figure 1-80 using the sales amounts and categories in Table 1-8.

Table 1-8	PTSA Annual Sales Data			
	9TH GRADE	**10TH GRADE**	**11TH GRADE**	**12TH GRADE**
Wrapping Paper	12347.85	9320.40	11889.33	13226.09
Candy	1587.44	1679.21	1320.70	1588.90
Magazine Subscriptions	7345.92	5639.65	8256.45	6559.00
Coupon Books	8529.75	12552.78	13873.38	14220.55

2. Determine the totals for the types of products, grade levels, and total sales.
3. Format the worksheet title, Magellan High School PTSA, to 26-point Arial, bold brown font, centered across columns A through F. Do not be concerned if the edges of the worksheet title do not display.

(continued)

Productivity in the Classroom

Parent Teacher Student Association Annual Sales Analysis Worksheet *(continued)*

4. Format the worksheet subtitle, Annual Fund Raising Sales Analysis, to 18-point Arial, bold brown font, centered across columns A through F.

5. Format the range A3:F8 using the AutoFormat command on the Format menu as follows: (a) Select the range A3:F8 and then apply the table format Accounting 1; and (b) with the range A3:F8 still selected, apply the table format Colorful 2. Excel appends the formats of Colorful 2 to the formats of Accounting 1.

6. Select the range A3:E7 and then use the Chart Wizard button on the Standard toolbar to draw a Clustered column with a 3-D visual effect chart (column 1, row 2 in Chart sub-type list). Move the chart to the upper-left corner of cell A10 and then drag the lower-right corner of the chart location to cell F21. If all the labels along the horizontal axis do not display as shown in Figure 1-80, select a cell in column F, click Format on the menu bar, point to Column on the Format menu, click Width on the Column submenu, increase the column width by two or more units, and then click the OK button.

7. Enter your name, course, current date, and instructor name in cells A24 through A28.

8. Save the workbook using the file name Magellan PTSA Annual Sales Analysis.

9. Print the worksheet.

10. Make the following two corrections to the sales amounts: $7,477.82 for 10th grade Magazine Subscriptions sales (cell C6), $10,998.45 for 12th Grade Wrapping Paper sales (cell E4). After you enter the corrections, the PTSA totals should equal $129,547.93 in cell F8.

11. Print the revised worksheet. Close the workbook without saving the changes.

2 Razor Sharp Scooter 3rd Quarter Expenses Worksheet

Problem: Your economics students are studying profit and loss. The students selected a product, created mock companies, and now are learning about corporate expenses. Next, they create a worksheet to analyze expenses for their company by department and expense category (Figure 1-81). One group's expenses for the 3rd quarter are shown in Figure 1-81.

Table 1-9 Razor Sharp Scooter 3rd Quarter Expenses					
	FINANCE	HELP DESK	MARKETING	SALES	SYSTEMS
Benefits	12378.23	11934.21	15823.10	10301.60	4123.89
Travel	23761.45	15300.89	6710.35	18430.15	6510.25
Wages	18001.27	13235.50	17730.58	12000.45	20931.53
Other	6145.20	3897.21	4910.45	8914.34	1201.56

Instructions: Perform the following tasks.

1. Create the worksheet shown in Figure 1-81 using the data in Table 1-9.

2. Direct Excel to determine total expenses for the five departments, the totals for each expense category, and the company total.

3. Format the worksheet title, Razor Sharp Scooter, in 24-point Arial bold violet font, and center it across columns A through G.

Productivity
in the Classroom

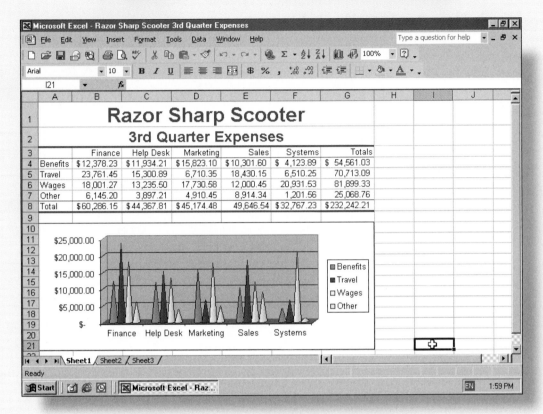

FIGURE 1-81

4. Format the worksheet subtitle, 3rd Quarter Expenses, in 18-point Arial bold violet font, and center it across columns A through G.

5. Use the AutoFormat command on the Format menu to format the range A3:G8. Use the table format Accounting 2.

6. Use the Chart Wizard button on the Standard toolbar to draw the 3-D Cone chart (column 1, row 1 in the Chart sub-type list), as shown in Figure 1-81. Chart the range A3:F7 and use the chart location A10:G21. If all the labels along the horizontal axis do not display as shown in Figure 1-81, select a cell in column G, click Format on the menu bar, point to Column on the Format menu, click Width on the Column submenu, increase the column width by two or more units, and then click the OK button.

7. Enter your name, course, current date, and instructor name in cells A24 through A28.

8. Save the workbook using the file name, Razor Sharp Scooter 3rd Quarter Expenses. Print the worksheet.

9. Make the following two corrections: $22,537.43 for wages in the Finance department and $21,962.75 for travel in the Sales department. After you enter the two corrections, the company total should equal $240,310.97 in cell G8. Print the revised worksheet.

10. Use the Undo button to change the worksheet back to the original numbers in Table 1-9. Use the Redo button to change the worksheet back to the revised state.

11. Hand in all printouts to your instructor. Close the workbook without saving the changes.

Productivity in the Classroom

3 College Cash Flow Analysis Worksheet

Problem: Your students are studying budgeting. Each student has selected a college, researched the associated costs, and is allocated a specific amount of funds. Then, they organize their resources and expenses in a worksheet. The data one student used to prepare the worksheet is shown in Table 1-10.

Table 1-10 College Cash Flow Analysis				
RESOURCES	**FRESHMAN**	**SOPHOMORE**	**JUNIOR**	**SENIOR**
Financial Aid	5,025.00	5326.50	5646.09	5984.86
Job	1,525.00	1616.50	1713.49	1816.30
Parents	2,600.00	2756.00	2921.36	3096.64
Savings	1,100.00	1166.00	1235.96	1310.12
EXPENSES	**FRESHMAN**	**SOPHOMORE**	**JUNIOR**	**SENIOR**
Clothes	540.00	572.40	606.74	643.15
Entertainment	725.00	768.50	814.61	863.49
Miscellaneous	355.00	376.30	398.88	422.81
Room & Board	3480.00	3688.80	3910.13	4144.74
Tuition & Books	5150.00	5459.00	5786.54	6133.73

Part 1 Instructions: Using the numbers in Table 1-10, follow the steps below to create the worksheet shown in columns A through F in Figure 1-82.

1. Enter the worksheet title in cell A1 and the section titles, Resources and Expenses, in cells A2 and A9, respectively.
2. Use the AutoSum button to calculate the totals in rows 8 and 16 and column F.
3. Increase the font in the worksheet title to 24 and change its color to red. Center the worksheet title in cell A1 across columns A through F. Increase the font size in the table titles in cells A2 and A9 to 18 and change their color to green.
4. Format the range A3:F8 using the AutoFormat command on the Format menu as follows: (a) Select the range A3:F8 and then apply the table format Accounting 1; and (b) with the range A3:F8 still selected, apply the table format List 1. Format the range A10:F16 using the AutoFormat command on the Format menu as follows: (a) Select the range A10:F16 and then apply the table format Accounting 1; and (b) with the range A10:F16 still selected, apply the table format List 1.
5. Enter your name in cell A19 and your course, current date, and instructor name in cells A20 through A23. Save the workbook using the file name, College Resources and Expenses.
6. Print the worksheet in landscape orientation. You print in landscape orientation by clicking Landscape on the Page tab in the Page Setup dialog box. Click Page Setup on the File menu to display the Page Setup dialog box. Click the Save button on the Standard toolbar to save the workbook with the new print settings.
7. All Junior-year expenses in column D increased by $500. Re-enter the new Junior-year expenses. Change the financial aid for the Junior year by the amount required to cover the increase in expenses. The totals in cells F8 and F16 should equal $47,339.82. Print the worksheet. Close the workbook without saving changes. Hand in the two printouts to your instructor.

Productivity in the Classroom

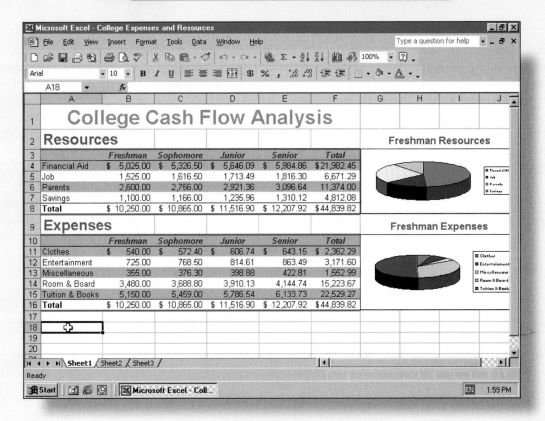

FIGURE 1-82

Part 2 Instructions: Open the workbook College Resources and Expenses created in Part 1. Draw a 3-D Pie chart in the range G3:J8 that shows the contribution of each category of resource for the freshman year. Chart the range A4:B7. Add the Pie chart title shown in cell G2 in Figure 1-82. Change the Pie chart title's font to 12-point, bold green. Center the Pie chart title over the range G2:J2. Draw a 3-D Pie chart in the range G10:J16 that shows the contribution of each category of expense for the Freshman year. Chart the range A11:B15. Add the Pie chart title shown in cell G9 in Figure 1-82. Change the Pie chart title's font to 12-point, bold green. Center the Pie chart title over the range G9:J9. Save the workbook using the file name, College Resources and Expenses 2. Print the worksheet. Hand in the printout to your instructor.

Part 3 Instructions: Open the workbook College Resources and Expenses 2 created in Part 2. A close inspection of Table 1-10 shows a 6% increase each year over the previous year. Use the Ask a Question box on the menu bar to learn how to enter the data for the last three years using a formula and the Copy command. For example, the formula to enter in cell C4 is =B4 * 1.06. Enter formulas to replace all the numbers in the range C4:E7 and C11:E15. If necessary, reformat the tables as described in Part 1. The worksheet should appear as shown in Figure 1-82, except that some of the totals will be off by 0.01 due to round-off errors. Save the worksheet using the file name, College Resources and Expenses 3. Print the worksheet. Press CTRL+ACCENT (`) to display the formulas. Print the formulas version. Hand in both printouts to your instructor.

Integration
in the Classroom

Introduction: Integration in the Classroom is designed for teachers and other educators who are looking for innovative ways to integrate technology into their content-specific curriculum. Educators can use Microsoft Excel to simplify numerous daily tasks and can integrate Excel easily into their curriculum as well. Excel is not just for the math and science curriculum. Spreadsheets and charts can be used in a variety of creative ways and can assist students in developing higher-order thinking skills. Charts provide visual representation of information, which also appeals to different learning styles. Many effective ways are available to use spreadsheets and charts in any curriculum area.

Explore the integration ideas below. Ideas are presented for elementary, middle, high school, and special education classrooms. These ideas are meant to be a springboard for creativity. Take an idea and expand, modify, and use it in your classroom. Furthermore, many of the ideas can be adapted to fit any level or learning situation.

1. You are working on categorizing with your first grade students. Students group themselves according to eye color and record the results in a worksheet. Then, your students survey the other first grade classes to gather the same information. Together with the students, you prepare a worksheet and chart to help your students compare and analyze the information (Table 1-11). Use the concepts and techniques presented in this project to create the worksheet and chart.

Table 1-11	First Grade Students' Eye Color				
	MRS. WOODS	*MR. ROGERS*	*MS. COLEMAN*	*MRS. WILKOWSKI*	*MS. YIN-SHEN*
Blue	10	15	13	5	11
Brown	12	9	11	7	10
Hazel	5	2	4	3	6

2. Working cooperatively with the technology teacher, your fifth grade students design a survey for determining the favorite authors of fourth and fifth grade students. To expand the project, the technology teacher connects your class with other fifth grade classes in different states via the Internet. Your students post their survey on the Internet to gather information from these other classes and include this information in their data analysis. Each participating class also surveys all of the fourth and fifth grade classes at their respective schools. Your students collect the data (Table 1-12) from all of the participating schools and create a worksheet and 3-D Column chart that illustrates the findings of the project. Use the concepts and techniques presented in this project to create the worksheet and chart.

Table 1-12	Favorite Authors of Fourth & Fifth Grade Students				
	BIRCH GROVE ELEMENTARY, UTAH	*NH JONES ELEMENTARY, MAINE*	*SANDLAKE ELEMENTARY, TEXAS*	*MT. VIEW ELEMENTARY, NORTH CAROLINA*	*SUNRISE ELEMENTARY, OHIO*
J.K. Rowling	97	133	107	114	88
Madeline L'Engle	49	56	34	66	67
R.L. Stine	78	99	110	87	95
Roald Dahl	56	34	43	62	68

Elementary

Integration in the Classroom

3. As a part of your unit on the election process, your students are studying the Electoral College. Working with the language arts teacher, the students are preparing an article on the coming election based on research conducted in your class using the Internet, print materials, and a recent survey of the electorate, arranged by age of those polled (Table 1-13). You have the students produce a worksheet to accompany the article. Use the concepts and techniques presented in this project to create the worksheet and an embedded Column chart.

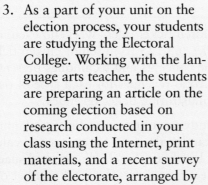

Table 1-13	Valley Heights Mayoral Race Election Poll Results				
	18-29	30-41	42-53	54-65	66+
Groen	625	301	512	440	205
Sabol	235	279	357	213	410
Walker	462	732	433	176	399
Webb	724	521	321	835	276

4. Your business education class is studying the rapid increase in computer technology and the increase in accessibility. Part of the unit examines the dramatic increase in computer sales. Specifically, students research and compare the number of servers, desktop computers, notebook computers, and handheld computers sold each year from 1999 through 2003, as indicated in Table 1-14. Create a worksheet and 3-D Column chart that illustrates these increases. Use the concepts and techniques presented in this project to create the worksheet and chart.

Table 1-14	Computer Discount Sales 1999-2003			
	SERVERS	DESKTOPS	NOTEBOOKS	HANDHELDS
1999	7323	22231	6125	225
2000	7498	32356	26315	1257
2001	7615	38489	36727	13313
2002	7734	42501	46501	24407
2003	7944	52578	56623	26761

Middle School

High School

5. Your video production class is studying the popularity of virtual reality movies. Your students work in groups to research the current market trends for this type of entertainment. As an extension of this project, a local virtual reality movie house is re-evaluating its ticket structure and your class will prepare a worksheet and Bar chart to illustrate ticket revenues based on a typical week. The movie house shows movies at weekday evenings, weekend matinees, and weekend evening screenings. Three types of tickets are sold at each presentation: general admission, senior citizen, and children. During an average week, weekday evening shows generate $9,835 from general admission ticket sales, $5,630 from senior citizen ticket sales, and $1,675 from children ticket sales. Weekend matinee shows make $7,250 from general admission ticket sales, $2,345 from senior

(continued)

Integration in the Classroom

Integration in the Classroom *(continued)*

High School

citizen ticket sales, and $3,300 from children ticket sales. Weekend evening shows earn $9,230 from general admission ticket sales, $8,125 from senior citizen ticket sales, and $1,600 from children ticket sales. Use the concepts and techniques presented in this project to prepare a worksheet that includes total revenues for each type of ticket and for each presentation time, and a Bar chart illustrating ticket revenues.

6. Your high school culinary arts class is studying nutrition and menu planning. One of the projects for the unit is for students to examine the total fat grams and calories in meals they prepare. They will plan a menu for breakfast, lunch, dinner, and snacks for one week. The students will create a worksheet that shows the total number of fat grams and calories for each day of the week, the total number of fat and calories for each meal for the week, and the total fat grams and calories for the week to determine which meals are the healthiest. The students will include an embedded chart to illustrate their data. Using the concepts and techniques presented in this project, prepare a sample worksheet and a Bar chart to demonstrate the project for your students.

7. You teach math, reading, and life skills to special education students through a printing business. You have received donations from local organizations and businesses of equipment and paper. Your students design and create small notepads, medium notepads, note cards, and greeting cards. Students manage all aspects of the business. The students create flyers advertising their products using Microsoft Word, take orders for their products, produce, and distribute their products. As a part of the business, they create a quarterly report and annual report. Using the information in Table 1-15 and the concepts and techniques presented in this project, create a worksheet and a 3-D Column chart that illustrates the profits from the business.

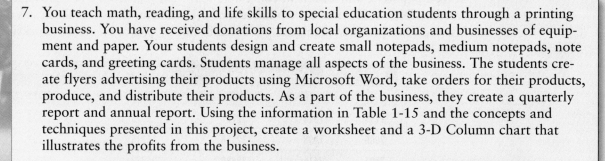

Table 1-15 Printing Business Profits	QUARTER 1	QUARTER 2	QUARTER 3	QUARTER 4
Small Notepads	433	566	245	365
Medium Notepads	522	685	326	398
Note Cards	389	450	125	250
Greeting Cards	197	344	164	225

Special Education

8. Your special education class is studying a unit on the weather. The students use the Internet and local newspapers to track the weather for one week. Students create a worksheet entering the daily highs and lows and they also calculate the mean. The students illustrate their information by creating an embedded chart. To extend the project, your students will give the daily weather report on your school news program and write up a weather report for the school newspaper. Using the concepts and techniques presented in this project, track the weather for one week and create a sample worksheet and embedded chart as a sample for your students.

Microsoft

ACCESS

Microsoft Access

Creating a Database Using Design and Datasheet Views

You will have mastered the material in this project when you can:

OBJECTIVES

- Describe databases and database management systems
- Describe the speech recognition capabilities of Access
- Start Access
- Describe the features of the Access desktop
- Create a database
- Create a table and define the fields in a table
- Open a table
- Add records to a table
- Close a table
- Close a database and quit Access
- Open a database
- Print the contents of a table
- Use a form to view data
- Create a custom report
- Use the Access Help system to answer your questions
- Design a database to eliminate redundancy

Education and Mentoring

Enriching the Learning Experience

Advocates of educational reform are making a difference in the learning experience. They work in partnership with educators, students, community members, and financial supporters. Their goal is to enhance student learning, deliver a common message to the education system, align priorities, encourage collaboration at every level, document successful outcomes from a variety of programs, and work toward long-term systemic change. They strive to improve the quality of education, reduce classroom sizes, integrate technology, and strengthen relationships among the partners.

One effective way of enriching the learning process is to involve various groups in education. College students, for example, who qualify for the Federal Work-Study Community Service Program work off campus helping students in kindergarten through ninth grade in the America Reads Program, whose goal is to ensure that every child can read well and independently by the end of the third grade and the America Counts Program, whose purpose is to help students through the ninth grade in developing and building strong mathematical skills.

More than 6,600 schools serving 1,600 communities have received grants and participate in the 21st Century Community Learning Centers program, which is a key component in the U.S. Department of Education Administration's efforts to keep children safe and provide academic development and other recreational and enrichment opportunities.

The International Telementor Center, hosted by the Center for Science, Mathematics & Technology

Education (CSMATE) at Colorado State University, assists telementoring relationships between professional adults and students worldwide. The goal of telementoring, which combines mentoring with electronic communication, is to help students in the important subject areas of math, science, engineering, communications, and career and education planning.

In mythology, Mentor advised Odysseus, who led the Greeks in the Trojan War. Today, mentors instruct and lead others in need of guidance and direction. Common partnerships in the computer field bring together network experts with culturally diverse school districts to network classrooms within the region; technology buffs to develop distance education programs for students in remote areas; and software experts to install programs in computer labs and then train teachers.

Building these partnerships requires superb technological and organizational skills, strong marketing, and dedicated staff members. The nation's largest nonprofit computerization assistance center, CompuMentor, is one of these successful partnering organizations. CompuMentor has linked its staff with more than 23,000 schools and other nonprofit organizations since 1987.

The heart of its success is matching computer experts with the appropriate school or organization. Some mentors volunteer long term, while others agree to work intensively for a few days, particularly in telecommunications areas. Potential mentors complete an application at CompuMentor's Web site (www.compumentor.org) by entering specific information in boxes, called fields, pertaining to their knowledge of

operating systems, networking, and hardware repair. They give additional information about their available working hours, training experience, and special skills in office and accounting applications, databases, and desktop publishing.

This information structures records in the CompuMentor database. The staff then can search these records to find a volunteer whose skills match the school's or organization's needs. This project, you will use the Access database management system to enter records in the Alisa Vending Services database so the staff can match drivers with vendors whose machines require replenishing, maintenance, and repairs.

Uniting schools with appropriate experts increases awareness of educational issues and ultimately improves the learning process. For more information on building mentoring relationships, visit the U.S. Department of Education Web site (www.ed.gov) or call 1-800-USA-LEARN.

Microsoft Access

Creating a Database Using Design and Datasheet Views

C A S E   P E R S P E C T I V E

Alisa Vending Services is a company that places vending machines in its customers' facilities. In return for the privilege of placing the vending machine, Alisa pays each customer a share of the profits from the machine. Payments are made quarterly. Alisa must track the amount already paid to each customer this year. It also must track the amount due to each customer for the current quarter.

Alisa employs drivers to service its customers. Each customer has a specific driver who replenishes the food and beverage items in the machine, collects the money, and performs routine maintenance and simple repairs.

To ensure operations run smoothly, Alisa Vending Services needs to maintain data on its drivers and their assigned customers. Rather than using a manual system, Alisa wants to organize the data in a database, managed by a database management system such as Access. In this way, Alisa can keep its data current and accurate while management can analyze the data for trends and produce a variety of useful reports. Your task is to help Alisa Vending Services in creating and using their database.

What Is Microsoft Access?

Microsoft Access is a powerful database management system (DBMS) that functions in the Windows environment and allows you to create and process data in a database. Some of the key features are:

▸ **Data entry and update**   Access provides easy mechanisms for adding, changing, and deleting data, including the ability to make mass changes in a single operation.

▸ **Queries (questions)**   Using Access, it is easy to ask complex questions concerning the data in the database and receive instant answers.

▸ **Forms**   In Access, you can produce attractive and useful forms for viewing and updating data.

▸ **Reports**   Access contains a feature to create sophisticated reports easily for presenting your data.

▸ **Web Support**   Access allows you to save objects, reports, and tables in HTML format so they can be viewed using a browser. You also can create data access pages to allow real-time access to data in the database via the Internet.

Project One — Alisa Vending Services

Creating, storing, sorting, and retrieving data are important tasks. In their personal lives, many people keep a variety of records such as names, addresses, and telephone numbers of friends and business associates, records of investments, records of expenses for tax purposes, and so on. These records must be arranged for quick access. Businesses also must be able to store and access information quickly and easily. Personnel and inventory records, payroll information, client records, order data, and accounts receivable information all are crucial and must be available readily.

The term **database** describes a collection of data organized in a manner that allows access, retrieval, and use of that data. A database management system, such as Access, allows you to use a computer to create a database; add, change, and delete data in the database; sort the data in the database; retrieve data in the database; and create forms and reports using the data in the database.

In Access, a database consists of a collection of tables. Figure 1-1 shows a sample database for Alisa Vending Services, which consists of two tables. The Customer table contains information about the customers to whom Alisa Vending Services provides services. Each customer is assigned to a specific driver. The Driver table contains information about the drivers to whom these customers are assigned.

The rows in the tables are called **records**. A record contains information about a given person, product, or event. A row in the Customer table, for example, contains information about a specific customer.

The columns in the tables are called fields. A **field** contains a specific piece of information within a record. In the Customer table, for example, the fourth field, City, contains the city where the customer is located.

> **More About**
>
> **Databases in Access**
>
> In some DBMSs, every table, query, form, or report is stored in a separate file. This is not the case in Access, in which a database is stored in a single file on disk. The file contains all the tables, queries, forms, reports, and programs that you create for this database.

fields

customers of driver Larissa Tuttle

records

Customer table

CUSTOMER NUMBER	NAME	ADDRESS	CITY	STATE	ZIP CODE	AMOUNT PAID	CURRENT DUE	DRIVER NUMBER
BA95	Bayside Hotel	287 Riley	Hansen	FL	38513	$21,876.00	$892.50	30
BR46	Baldwin-Reed	267 Howard	Fernwood	FL	37023	$26,512.00	$2,672.00	60
CN21	Century North	1562 Butler	Hansen	FL	38513	$8,725.00	$0.00	60
FR28	Friend's Movies	871 Adams	Westport	FL	37070	$4,256.00	$1,202.00	75
GN62	Grand Nelson	7821 Oak	Wood Key	FL	36828	$8,287.50	$925.50	30
GS29	Great Screens	572 Lee	Hansen	FL	38513	$21,625.00	$0.00	60
LM22	Lenger Mason	274 Johnson	Westport	FL	37070	$0.00	$0.00	60
ME93	Merks College	561 Fairhill	Bayville	FL	38734	$24,761.00	$1,572.00	30
RI78	Riter University	26 Grove	Fernwood	FL	37023	$11,682.25	$2,827.50	75
TU20	Turner Hotel	8672 Quincy	Palmview	FL	36114	$8,521.50	$0.00	60

driver Larissa Tuttle

Driver table

DRIVER NUMBER	LAST NAME	FIRST NAME	ADDRESS	CITY	STATE	ZIP CODE	HOURLY RATE	YTD EARNINGS
30	Tuttle	Larissa	7562 Hickory	Laton Springs	FL	37891	$16.00	$21,145.25
60	Powers	Frank	57 Ravenwood	Gillmore	FL	37572	$15.00	$19,893.50
75	Ortiz	Jose	341 Pierce	Douglas	FL	37613	$17.00	$23,417.00

FIGURE 1-1

The first field in the Customer table is the Customer Number. This is a code assigned by Alisa Vending Services to each customer. Similar to many organizations, Alisa Vending Services calls it a *number* although it actually contains letters. The customer numbers have a special format. They consist of two uppercase letters followed by a two-digit number.

These numbers are unique; that is, no two customers will be assigned the same number. Such a field can be used as a **unique identifier**. This simply means that a given customer number will display only in a single record in the table. Only one record exists, for example, in which the customer number is CN21. A unique identifier also is called a **primary key**. Thus, the Customer Number field is the primary key for the Customer table.

The next seven fields in the Customer table are Name, Address, City, State, Zip Code, Amount Paid, and Current Due. The Amount Paid field contains the amount that Alisa has paid already to the customer this year. The Current Due field contains the amount due from Alisa to the customer for the current period, but not yet paid.

For example, customer BA95 is Bayside Hotel. It is located at 287 Riley in Hansen, Florida. The zip code is 38513. The customer has been paid $21,876.00 so far this year and is due to be paid $892.50 for the current period.

Each customer is assigned to a single driver. The last field in the Customer table, Driver Number, gives the number of the customer's driver.

The first field in the Driver table, Driver Number, is the number assigned by Alisa Vending Services to the driver. These numbers are unique, so Driver Number is the primary key of the Driver table.

The other fields in the Driver table are Last Name, First Name, Address, City, State, Zip Code, Hourly Rate, and YTD Earnings. The Hourly Rate field gives the driver's hourly billing rate, and the YTD Earnings field contains the total amount that has been paid to the driver for services so far this year.

For example, driver 30 is Larissa Tuttle. She lives at 7562 Hickory in Laton Springs, Florida. Her zip code is 37891. Her hourly billing rate is $16.00 and her YTD earnings are $21,145.25.

The driver number displays in both the Customer table and the Driver table. It is used to relate customers and drivers. For example, in the Customer table, you see that the driver number for customer BA95 is 30. To find the name of this driver, look for the row in the Driver table that contains 30 in the Driver Number field. Once you have found it, you know the customer is assigned to Larissa Tuttle. To find all the customers assigned to Larissa Tuttle, on the other hand, look through the Customer table for all the customers that contain 30 in the Driver Number field. Her customers are BA95 (Bayside Hotel), GN62 (Grand Nelson), and ME93 (Merks College).

Together with the management of Alisa Vending Services, you have determined the data that must be maintained in the database is that shown in Figure 1-1 on the previous page. You first must create the database and the tables it contains. In the process, you must define the fields included in the two tables, as well as the type of data each field will contain. You then must add the appropriate records to the tables. You also must print the contents of the tables. Finally, you must create a report with the Customer Number, Name, Amount Paid, and Current Due fields for each customer served by Alisa Vending Services. Other reports and requirements for the database at Alisa Vending Services will be addressed with the Alisa Vending Services management in the future.

More*About*

The Access 2002 Help System

Need Help? It is no further than the Ask a Question box in the upper-right corner of the window. Click the box that contains the text Type a question for help (Figure 1-3), type help and then press the ENTER key. Access will respond with a list of items you can click to learn about obtaining help on any Access-related topic. To find out what is new in Access 2002, type what's new in Access in the Ask a Question box.

Starting Access

To start Access, Windows must be running. Perform the following steps to start Access.

Steps To Start Access

1 **Click the Start button on the Windows taskbar, point to Programs on the Start menu, and then point to Microsoft Access on the Programs submenu.**

The commands on the Start menu display above the Start button and the Programs submenu displays (Figure 1-2). If the Office Voice Recognition software is installed on your computer, then the Language bar may display somewhere on the desktop.

2 **Click Microsoft Access.**

If using Access 2002, Access starts and the Microsoft Access window displays (Figure 1-3). 🔲2000 *If using Access 2000, Access starts and a Microsoft Access dialog box displays that allows you to create a new database using a Blank Access database or Access database wizards, pages, and projects.*

3 🔲2000 **If using Access 2000, select the Blank Access database option button, click the OK button, and then skip to page A 1.11 and the heading, Creating a New Database.**

🔲2000 *Access 2000 displays the File New Database dialog box (see Figure 1-5 on page A 1.11).*

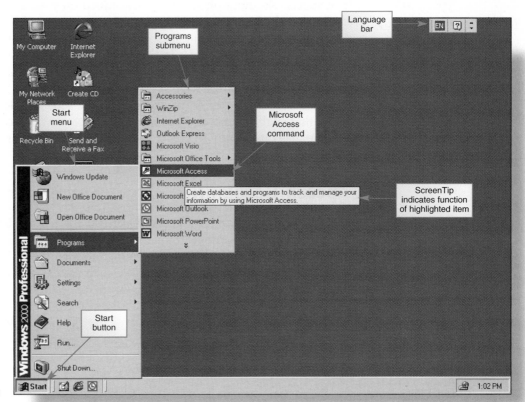

FIGURE 1-2

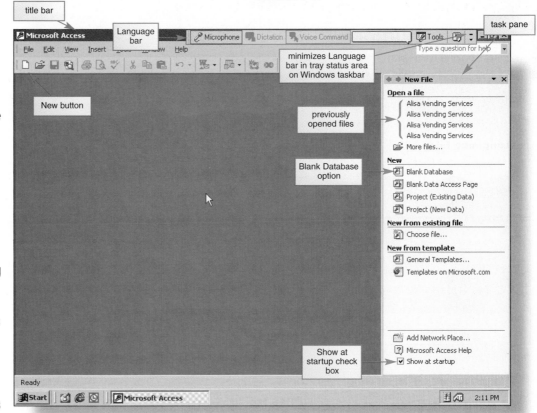

FIGURE 1-3

Microsoft **Access**

More About

Task Panes

When you first start Access, a small window called a task pane may display docked on the right side of the screen. You can drag a task pane title bar to float the pane in your work area or dock it on either the left or right side of a screen, depending on your personal preference.

The screen in Figure 1-3 on the previous page shows how the Access window looks the first time you start Access after installation on most computers. If the Office Speech Recognition software is installed on your system, then when you start Access either the Language bar displays somewhere on the desktop (shown at the top of Figure 1-3) or the Language Indicator button displays on the right side of the Windows taskbar (Figure 1-5). In this book, the Language bar will be kept minimized until it is used. For additional information about the Language bar, see Appendix B on page A B.01.

Notice also that a task pane displays on the screen. A **task pane** is a separate window that enables users to carry out some Access tasks more efficiently. In this book, the task pane is used only to create a new database and then it should not display.

Speech Recognition (Not Available in Access 2000)

When you begin working in Access, if you have the **Office Speech Recognition software** installed and a microphone, you can speak the names of toolbar buttons, menus, menu commands, list items, alerts, and dialog box controls, such as OK and Cancel. You also can dictate field entries, such as text and numbers. To indicate whether you want to speak commands or dictate field entries, you use the **Language bar** (Figure 1-4a).

You can display the Language bar in two ways: (1) click the Language Indicator button in the tray status area on the Windows taskbar by the clock, and then click Show the Language bar on the menu (Figure 1-4b), or (2) point to the **Speech command** on the **Tools menu** and then click the **Speech Recognition command** on the **Speech submenu**.

If the Language Indicator button does not display in the tray status area, and if the Speech command is unavailable (dimmed) on the Tools menu, the Office Speech Recognition software is not installed. To install the software, you first must start Word and then click Speech on the Tools menu.

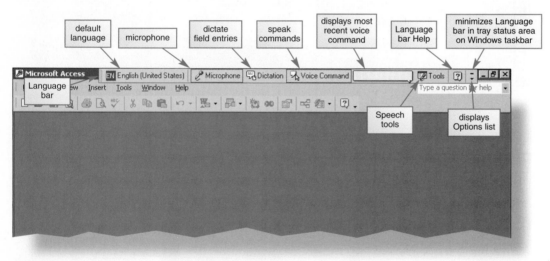

(a) Language Bar

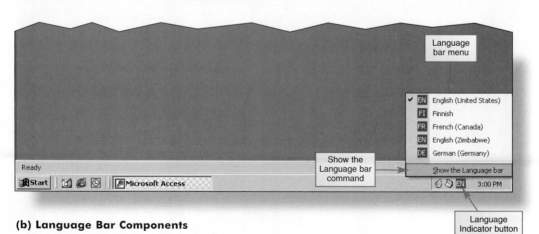

(b) Language Bar Components

FIGURE 1-4

If you have speakers, you can instruct the computer to read a document to you. By selecting the appropriate option, you can have the document read in a male or female voice.

Additional information on the Office speech and handwriting recognition capabilities is available in Appendix B.

Creating a New Database

In Access, all the tables, reports, forms, and queries that you create are stored in a single file called a database. Thus, before creating any of these objects, you first must create the database that will hold them. You use the Blank Database option in the task pane to create a new database. To allow the full Access window to display when you work with a database, you should close the task pane after creating a new database. Perform the following steps to create a new database and save the database on a floppy disk in drive A.

More *About*

Creating a Database: The Database Wizard

Access includes a Database Wizard that can guide you by suggesting some commonly used databases. To use the Database Wizard, click New on the Database toolbar, and then click General Templates in the New File task pane. When the Templates dialog box displays, click the Databases tab, and then click the database that is most appropriate for your needs. Follow the instructions in the Database Wizard dialog boxes to create the database.

Steps **To Create a New Database**

1 **If using Access 2002 and if the Language bar displays, click its Minimize button. If a dialog box displays, click the OK button. If necessary, click the New button on the Database toolbar to display the task pane. Click the Blank Database option in the task pane (see Figure 1-3 on page A 1.09), and then click the Save in box arrow. Point to 3½ Floppy (A:). 2000 If using Access 2000, click the Save in box arrow and then point to 3½ Floppy (A:).**

The Save in list displays in the File New Database dialog box (Figure 1-5). Your file name text box may display db1.mdb.

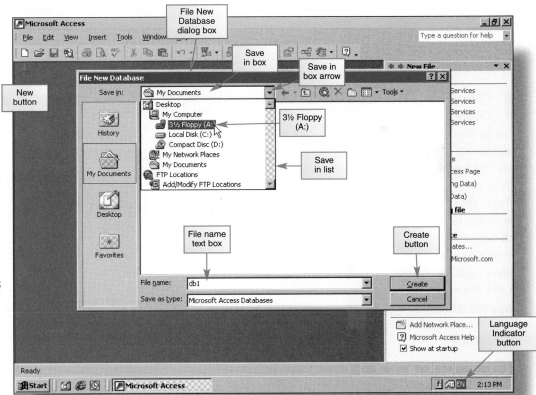

FIGURE 1-5

1 **Click 3½ Floppy (A:). Click the File name text box. Repeatedly press the BACKSPACE key to delete db1 and then type** Alisa Vending Services **as the file name. Point to the Create button.**

The file name is changed to Alisa Vending Services (Figure 1-6).

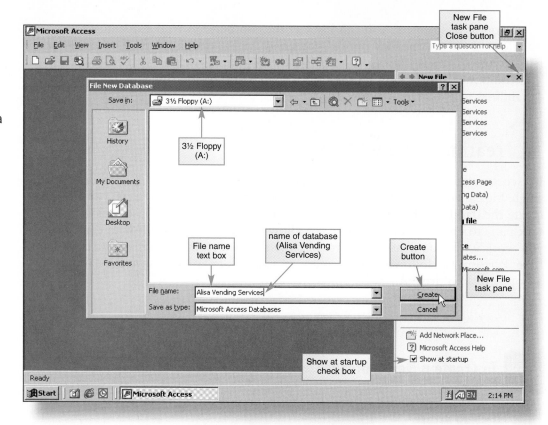

FIGURE 1-6

3 **Click the Create button to create the database. If using Access 2002 and if the task pane displays, click the Show at startup check box at the bottom of the task pane to remove the check mark and then click the Close button in the upper-right corner to close the task pane.**

The Alisa Vending Services database is created. The Alisa Vending Services : Database window displays on the desktop (Figure 1-7). The New File task pane does not display.

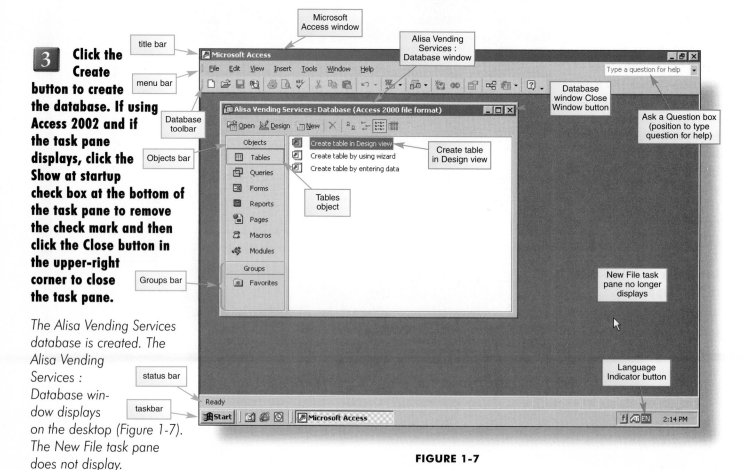

FIGURE 1-7

The Access Desktop and the Database Window

The first bar on the desktop (Figure 1-7) is the **title bar**. It displays the title of the product, Microsoft Access. The button on the right is the **Close button**. Clicking the Close button closes the window.

The second bar is the **menu bar**. It contains a list of menu names. To open a menu from the menu bar, click the menu name. Initially a personalized version of the menu, a short menu that consists of commands you have selected most recently, displays. After a few seconds, the full menu displays. If the command you wish to select is on the short menu, you can select it immediately. If not, wait a few seconds to view the full menu. (The menus shown throughout this book are the full menus, the ones that display after a few seconds.)

The third bar is the **Database toolbar**. The Database toolbar contains buttons that allow you to perform certain tasks more quickly than using the menu bar. Each button contains a picture, or **icon**, depicting its function. The specific toolbar or toolbars that display will vary, depending on the task on which you are working.

The **taskbar** at the bottom of the screen displays the Start button, any active windows, and the current time.

Immediately above the Windows taskbar is the **status bar** (Figure 1-7). It contains special information that is appropriate for the task on which you are working. Currently, it contains the word, Ready, which means Access is ready to accept commands.

The **Database window**, referred to in Figure 1-7 as the Alisa Vending Services : Database window, is a special window that allows you to access easily and rapidly a variety of objects such as tables, queries, forms, and reports. To do so, you will use the various components of the window.

Creating a Table

An Access database consists of a collection of tables. Once you have created the database, you must create each of the tables within it. In this project, for example, you must create both the Customer and Driver tables shown in Figure 1-1 on page A 1.07.

To create a table, you describe the **structure** of the table to Access by describing the fields within the table. For each field, you indicate the following:

1. **Field name** — Each field in the table must have a unique name. In the Customer table (Figure 1-8 on the next page), for example, the field names are Customer Number, Name, Address, City, State, Zip Code, Amount Paid, Current Due, and Driver Number.

2. **Data type** — Data type indicates to Access the type of data the field will contain. Some fields can contain only numbers. Others, such as Amount Paid and Current Due, can contain numbers and dollar signs. Still others, such as Name and Address, can contain letters.

3. **Description** — Access allows you to enter a detailed description of the field.

You also can assign field widths to text fields (fields whose data type is Text). This indicates the maximum number of characters that can be stored in the field. If you do not assign a width to such a field, Access assumes the width is 50.

More About

Toolbars

Normally, the correct Access toolbar automatically will display. If it does not, click View on the menu bar, and then click Toolbars. Click the toolbar for the activity in which you are engaged and then click the Close button. See Appendix D for additional details.

More About

Creating a Table: The Table Wizard

Access includes a Table Wizard that guides you by suggesting some commonly used tables and fields. To use the Table Wizard, click the Tables object in the Database window. Right-click Create table by using wizard and then click Open on the shortcut menu. Follow the directions in the Table Wizard dialog boxes. After you create the table, you can modify it at any time by opening the table in Design view.

Structure of Customer table

FIELD NAME	DATA TYPE	FIELD SIZE	PRIMARY KEY?	DESCRIPTION
Customer Number	Text	4	Yes	Customer Number (Primary Key)
Name	Text	20		Customer Name
Address	Text	15		Street Address
City	Text	15		City
State	Text	2		State (Two-Character Abbreviation)
Zip Code	Text	5		Zip Code (Five-Character Version)
Amount Paid	Currency			Amount Paid to Customer this Year
Current Due	Currency			Amount Due to Customer this Period
Driver Number	Text	2		Number of Customer's Driver

Data for Customer table

CUSTOMER NUMBER	NAME	ADDRESS	CITY	STATE	ZIP CODE	AMOUNT PAID	CURRENT DUE	DRIVER NUMBER
BA95	Bayside Hotel	287 Riley	Hansen	FL	38513	$21,876.00	$892.50	30
BR46	Baldwin-Reed	267 Howard	Fernwood	FL	37023	$26,512.00	$2,672.00	60
CN21	Century North	1562 Butler	Hansen	FL	38513	$8,725.00	$0.00	60
FR28	Friend's Movies	871 Adams	Westport	FL	37070	$4,256.00	$1,202.00	75
GN62	Grand Nelson	7821 Oak	Wood Key	FL	36828	$8,287.50	$925.50	30
GS29	Great Screens	572 Lee	Hansen	FL	38513	$21,625.00	$0.00	60
LM22	Lenger Mason	274 Johnson	Westport	FL	37070	$0.00	$0.00	60
ME93	Merks College	561 Fairhill	Bayville	FL	38734	$24,761.00	$1,572.00	30
RI78	Riter University	26 Grove	Fernwood	FL	37023	$11,682.25	$2,827.50	75
TU20	Turner Hotel	8672 Quincy	Palmview	FL	36114	$8,521.50	$0.00	60

FIGURE 1-8

Data Types (General)

Different database management systems have different available data types. Even data types that are essentially the same can have different names. The Access Text data type, for example, is referred to as Character in some systems and Alpha in others.

You also must indicate which field or fields make up the **primary key**; that is, the unique identifier, for the table. In the sample database, the Customer Number field is the primary key of the Customer table and the Driver Number field is the primary key of the Driver table.

The rules for field names are:

1. Names can be up to 64 characters in length.
2. Names can contain letters, digits, and spaces, as well as most of the punctuation symbols.
3. Names cannot contain periods, exclamation points (!), accent graves (`), or square brackets ([ ]).
4. The same name cannot be used for two different fields in the same table.

Each field has a **data type**. This indicates the type of data that can be stored in the field. The data types you will use in this project are:

1. **Text** — The field can contain any characters.
2. **Number** — The field can contain only numbers. The numbers either can be positive or negative. Fields are assigned this type so they can be used in arithmetic operations. Fields that contain numbers but will not be used for arithmetic operations usually are assigned a data type of Text. The Driver Number field, for example, is a text field because the driver numbers will not be involved in any arithmetic.
3. **Currency** — The field can contain only dollar amounts. The values will be displayed with dollar signs, commas, decimal points, and with two digits following the decimal point. Like numeric fields, you can use currency fields in arithmetic operations. Access assigns a size to currency fields automatically.

The field names, data types, field widths, primary key information, and descriptions for the Customer table are shown in Figure 1-8. With this information, you are ready to begin creating the table. To create the table, use the following steps.

Steps To Create a Table

1 **Right-click Create table in Design view and then point to Open on the shortcut menu.**

The shortcut menu for creating a table in Design view displays (Figure 1-9).

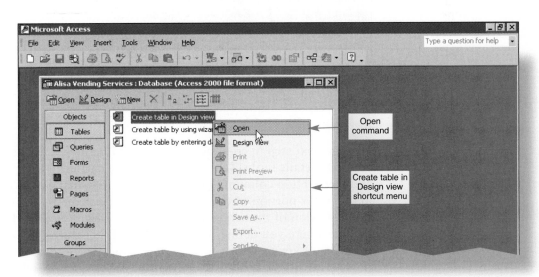

FIGURE 1-9

2 **Click Open and then point to the Maximize button for the Table1 : Table window.**

The Table1 : Table window displays (Figure 1-10).

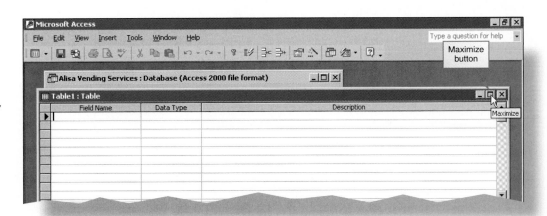

FIGURE 1-10

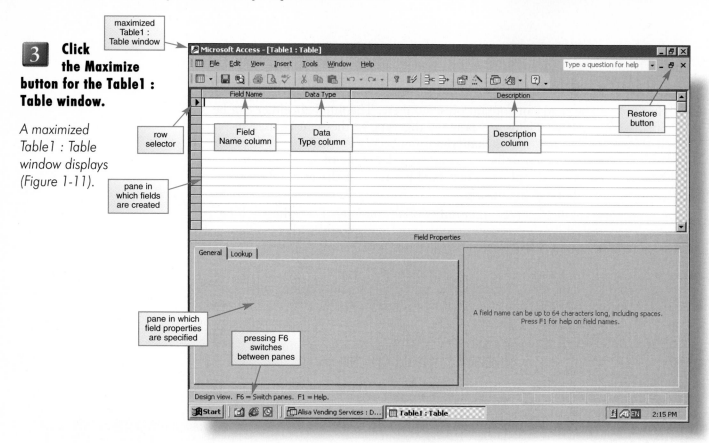

FIGURE 1-11

3 **Click the Maximize button for the Table1 : Table window.**

A maximized Table1 : Table window displays (Figure 1-11).

Other Ways

1. Click New button on Database window toolbar
2. On Insert menu click Table
3. Press ALT+N
4. In Voice Command mode, say "Insert, Table"

Defining the Fields

The next step in creating the table is to define the fields by specifying the required details in the Table window. Make entries in the Field Name, Data Type, and Description columns. Enter additional information in the Field Properties box in the lower portion of the Table window. Press the F6 key to move from the upper **pane** (portion of the screen), the one where you define the fields, to the lower pane, the one where you define field properties. Enter the appropriate field size and then press the F6 key to return to the upper pane. As you define the fields, the **row selector** (Figure 1-11), the small box or bar that, when clicked, selects the entire row, indicates the field you currently are describing. It is positioned on the first field, indicating Access is ready for you to enter the name of the first field in the Field Name column.

Perform the following steps to define the fields in the table.

Steps To Define the Fields in a Table

1 **Type** Customer Number **(the name of the first field) in the Field Name column and then press the TAB key.**

The words, Customer Number, display in the Field Name column and the insertion point advances to the Data Type column, indicating you can enter the data type (Figure 1-12). The word, Text, one of the possible data types, currently displays. The arrow indicates a list of data types is available by clicking the arrow. The field properties for the Customer Number field display in the lower pane.

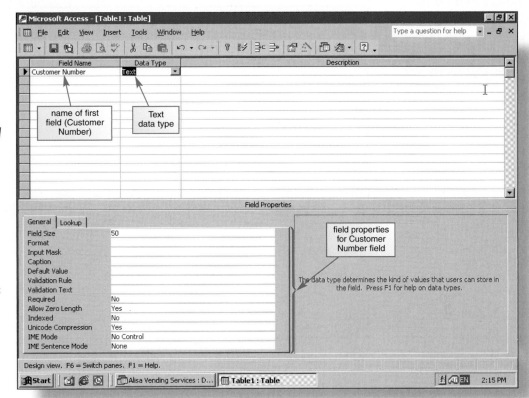

FIGURE 1-12

2 **Because Text is the correct data type, press the TAB key to move the insertion point to the Description column, type** Customer Number (Primary Key) **as the description and then point to the Primary Key button on the Table Design toolbar.**

A ScreenTip, which is a description of the button, displays partially obscuring the description of the first field (Figure 1-13).

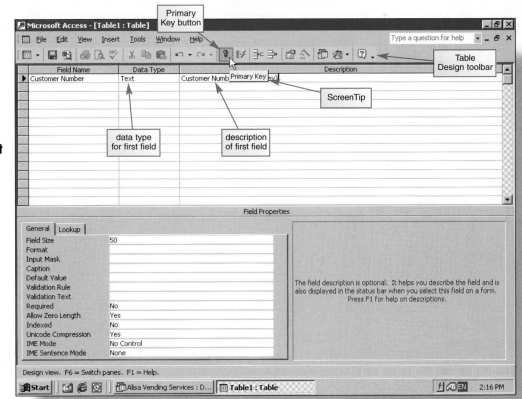

FIGURE 1-13

3 **Click the Primary Key button to make Customer Number the primary key and then press the F6 key to move the insertion point to the Field Size property box.**

The Customer Number field is the primary key as indicated by the key symbol that displays in the row selector (Figure 1-14). The current entry in the Field Size property box (50) is selected.

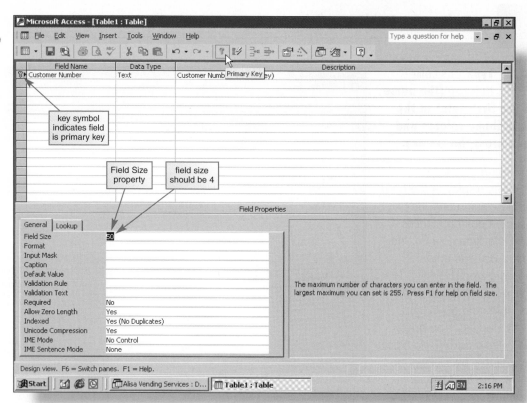

FIGURE 1-14

4 **Type 4 as the size of the Customer Number field. Press the F6 key to return to the Description column for the Customer Number field and then press the TAB key to move to the Field Name column in the second row.**

The insertion point moves to the second row just below the field name Customer Number (Figure 1-15).

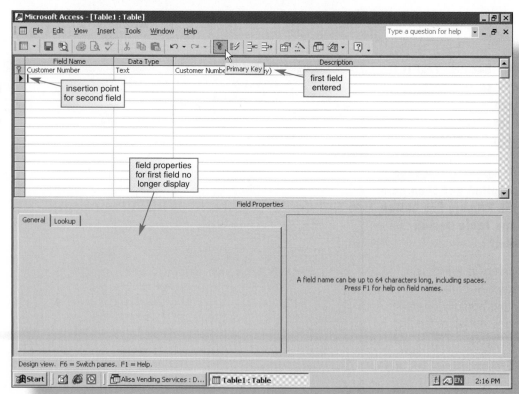

FIGURE 1-15

5 Use the techniques illustrated in Steps 1 through 4 to make the entries from the Customer table structure shown in Figure 1-8 on page A 1.14 up through and including the name of the Amount Paid field. Click the Data Type box arrow and then point to Currency.

The additional fields are entered (Figure 1-16). A list of available data types displays in the Data Type column for the Amount Paid field.

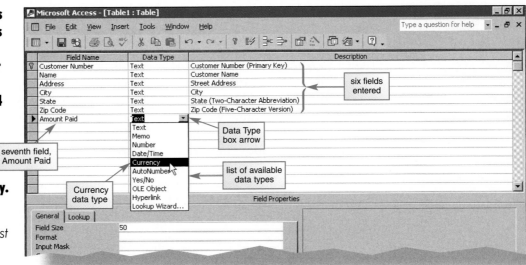

FIGURE 1-16

6 Click Currency and then press the TAB key. Make the remaining entries from the Customer table structure shown in Figure 1-8.

The fields are all entered (Figure 1-17).

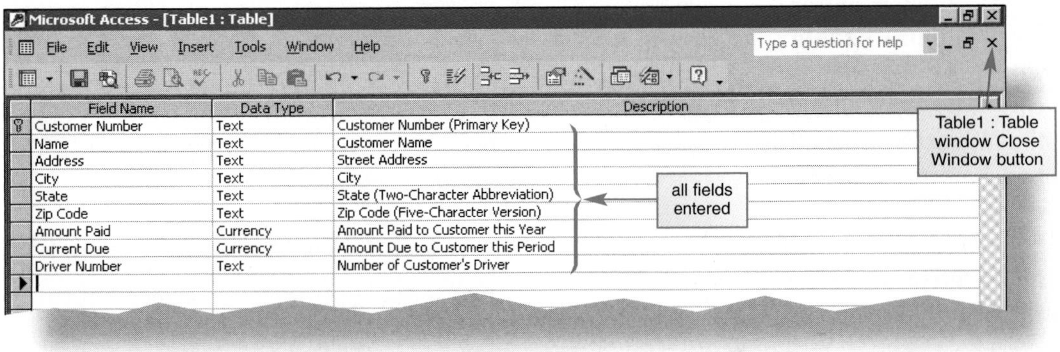

FIGURE 1-17

Correcting Errors in the Structure

When creating a table, check the entries carefully to ensure they are correct. If you make a mistake and discover it before you press the TAB key, you can correct the error by repeatedly pressing the BACKSPACE key until the incorrect characters are removed. Then, type the correct characters. If you do not discover a mistake until later, you can click the entry, type the correct value, and then press the ENTER key.

If you accidentally add an extra field to the structure, select the field by clicking the row selector (the leftmost column on the row that contains the field to be deleted). Once you have selected the field, press the DELETE key. This will remove the field from the structure.

If you forget a field, select the field that will follow the field you wish to add by clicking the row selector, and then press the INSERT key. The remaining fields move down one row, making room for the missing field. Make the entries for the new field in the usual manner.

If you made the wrong field a primary key field, click the correct primary key entry for the field and then click the Primary Key button on the Table Design toolbar.

As an alternative to these steps, you may want to start over. To do so, click the Close Window button for the Table1 : Table window and then click No. The original desktop displays and you can repeat the process you used earlier.

More About

Correcting Errors

Even after you have entered data, it still is possible to correct errors in the structure. Access will make all the necessary adjustments to the structure of the table as well as to the data within it. (It is simplest to make the correction, however, before any data is entered.)

Adding Records

As soon as you have entered or modified a record and moved to another record, the original record is saved. This is different from other tools. The rows entered in a spreadsheet, for example, are not saved until the entire spreadsheet is saved.

Saving and Closing a Table

The Customer table structure now is complete. The final step is to save the table within the database. At this time, you should give the table a name. Once you save the table structure, you can continue working in the Table window or you can close the window. To continue working in the Table Design window, click the Save button on the Table Design toolbar. To save the table and close the Table Design window, click the Close Window button. If you close the Table window without saving first, Access provides an opportunity to do so.

Table names are from 1 to 64 characters in length and can contain letters, numbers, and spaces. The two table names in this project are Customer and Driver.

To save and close the table, complete the following steps.

Steps To Save and Close a Table

1 **Click the Close Window button for the Table1 : Table window. (Be sure not to click the Close button on the Microsoft Access title bar, because this would close Microsoft Access.) Point to the Yes button in the Microsoft Access dialog box.**

The Microsoft Access dialog box displays (Figure 1-18).

2 **Click the Yes button in the Microsoft Access dialog box and then type** Customer **as the name of the table. Point to the OK button.**

The Save As dialog box displays (Figure 1-19). The table name is entered.

3 **Click the OK button in the Save As dialog box.**

The table is saved. The window containing the table design no longer displays.

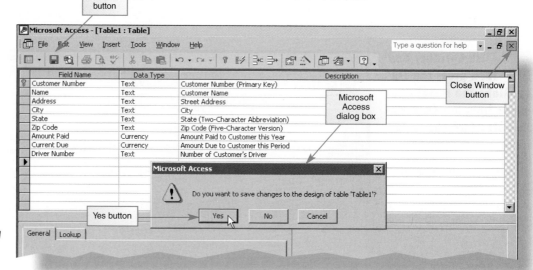

FIGURE 1-18

FIGURE 1-19

Adding Records to a Table

Creating a table by building the structure and saving the table is the first step in a two-step process. The second step is to add records to the table. To add records to a table, the table must be open. To open a table, right-click the table in the Database window and then click Open on the shortcut menu. The table displays in Datasheet view. In **Datasheet view**, the table is represented as a collection of rows and columns called a **datasheet**. It looks very much like the tables shown in Figure 1-1 on page A 1.07.

You often add records in phases. You may, for example, not have enough time to add all the records in one session. To illustrate this process, this project begins by adding the first two records in the Customer table (Figure 1-20). The remaining records are added later.

Customer table (first 2 records)								
CUSTOMER NUMBER	*NAME*	*ADDRESS*	*CITY*	*STATE*	*ZIP CODE*	*AMOUNT PAID*	*CURRENT DUE*	*DRIVER NUMBER*
BA95	Bayside Hotel	287 Riley	Hansen	FL	38513	$21,876.00	$892.50	30
BR46	Baldwin-Reed	267 Howard	Fernwood	FL	37023	$26,512.00	$2,672.00	60

FIGURE 1-20

To open the Customer table and then add records, perform the following steps.

Steps **To Add Records to a Table**

1 **Right-click the Customer table in the Alisa Vending Services : Database window and then point to Open on the shortcut menu.**

The shortcut menu for the Customer table displays (Figure 1-21). The Alisa Vending Services : Database window is maximized because the previous window, the Customer : Table window, was maximized. (If you wanted to restore the Database window to its original size, you would click the Restore Window button.)

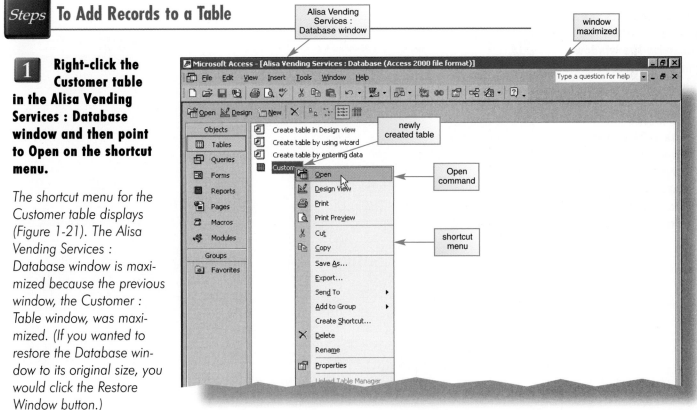

FIGURE 1-21

2 **Click Open on the shortcut menu.**

The Customer : Table window displays (Figure 1-22). The window contains the Datasheet view for the Customer table. The *record selector*, the small box or bar that, when clicked, selects the entire record, is positioned on the first record. The status bar at the bottom of the window also indicates that the record selector is positioned on record 1.

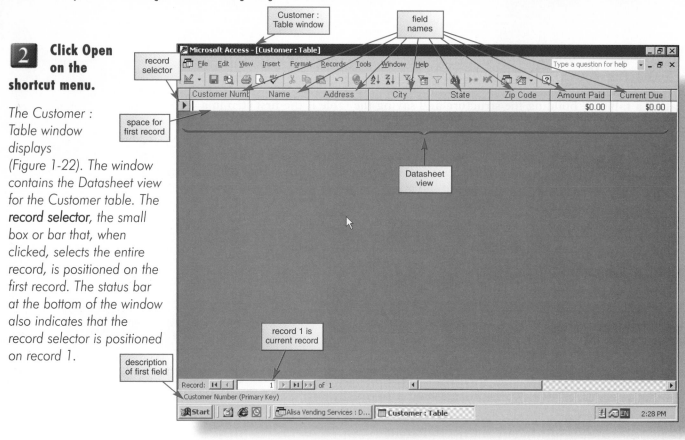

FIGURE 1-22

3 **If your window is not already maximized, click the Maximize button to maximize the window containing the table. Type** BA95 **as the first customer number (see Figure 1-20 on the previous page). Be sure you type the letters in uppercase, because that is the way they are to be entered in the database.**

The customer number is entered, but the insertion point is still in the Customer Number field (Figure 1-23).

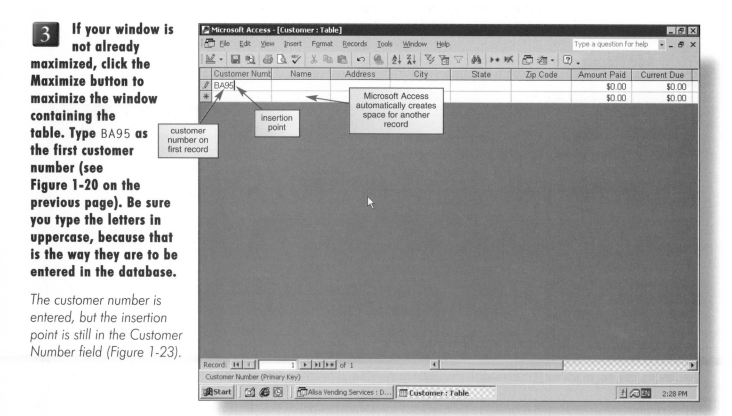

FIGURE 1-23

4 Press the TAB key to complete the entry for the Customer Number field. Type the following entries, pressing the TAB key after each one: Bayside Hotel **as the name,** 287 Riley **as the address,** Hansen **as the city,** FL **as the state, and** 38513 **as the zip code.**

The Name, Address, City, State, and Zip Code fields are entered (Figure 1-24).

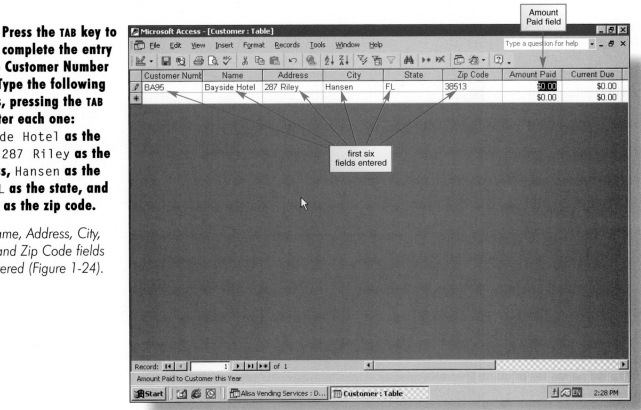

FIGURE 1-24

5 Type 21876 **as the amount paid amount and then press the TAB key. (You do not need to type dollar signs or commas. In addition, because the digits to the right of the decimal point were both zeros, you did not need to type either the decimal point or the zeros.) Type** 892.50 **as the current due amount and then press the TAB key. Type** 30 **as the driver number to complete the record.**

The fields have shifted to the left (Figure 1-25). The amount paid and current due values display with dollar signs and decimal points. The insertion point is positioned in the Driver Number field.

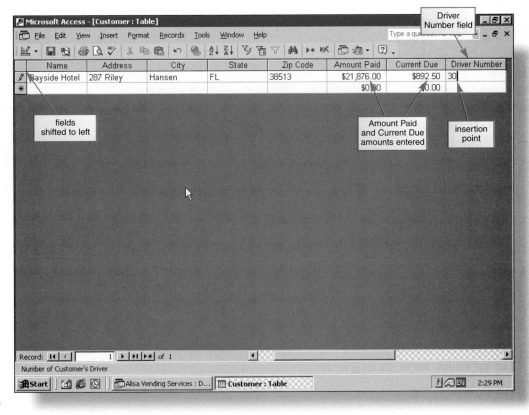

FIGURE 1-25

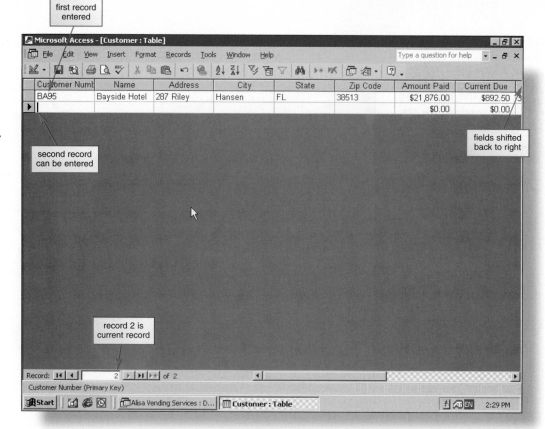

6 **Press the TAB key.**

The fields shift back to the right, the record is saved, and the insertion point moves to the customer number on the second row (Figure 1-26).

FIGURE 1-26

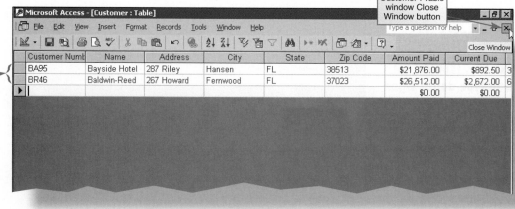

7 **Use the techniques shown in Steps 3 through 6 to add the data for the second record in Figure 1-20 on page A 1.21. Point to the Close Window button.**

The second record is added and the insertion point moves to the customer number on the third row (Figure 1-27).

FIGURE 1-27

Closing a Table and Database

It is a good idea to close a table as soon as you have finished working with it. It keeps the screen from getting cluttered and prevents you from making accidental changes to the data in the table. Assuming that these two records are the only records you plan to add during this session, perform the following steps to close the table and the database. If you no longer will work with the database, you should close the database as well.

Steps **To Close a Table and Database**

1 **Click the Close Window button for the Customer : Table window (see Figure 1-27). Point to the Close Window button for the Alisa Vending Services : Database window.**

The datasheet for the Customer table no longer displays (Figure 1-28).

2 **Click the Close Window button for the Alisa Vending Services : Database window.**

The Alisa Vending Services : Database window no longer displays.

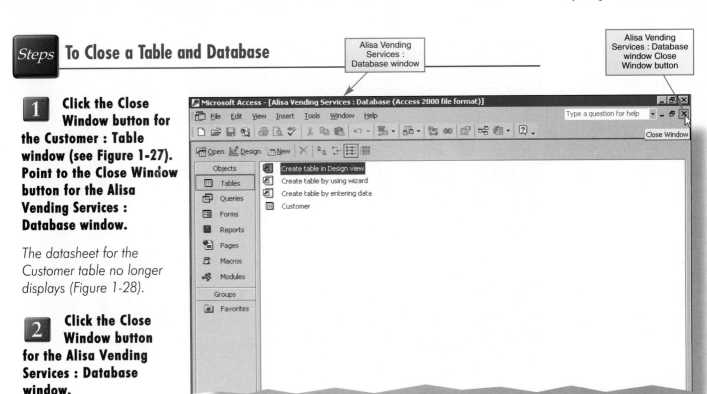

FIGURE 1-28

Opening a Database

To work with any of the tables, reports, or forms in a database, the database must be open. To open a database from within Access, click Open on the Database tool-bar. To resume adding records to the Customer table, open the database by performing the following steps.

Steps **To Open a Database**

1 **Point to the Open button on the Database toolbar (Figure 1-29).**

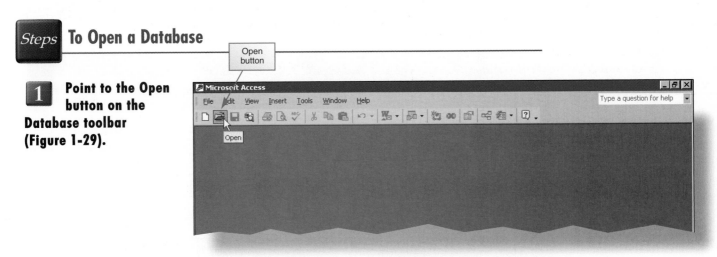

FIGURE 1-29

2 **Click the Open button. If necessary, click the Look in box arrow and then click 3½ Floppy (A:) in the Look in box. If it is not selected already, click the Alisa Vending Services database name. Point to the Open button.**

The Open dialog box displays (Figure 1-30). The 3½ Floppy (A:) folder displays in the Look in box and the files on the floppy disk in drive A display. (Your list may be different.)

3 **Click the Open button.**

The database opens and the Alisa Vending Services : Database window displays.

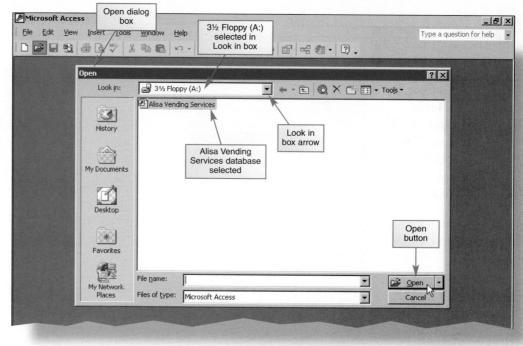

FIGURE 1-30

Table 1-1	Navigation Buttons in Datasheet View
BUTTON	**PURPOSE**
First Record	Moves to the first record in the table
Previous Record	Moves to the previous record
Next Record	Moves to the next record
Last Record	Moves to the last record in the table
New Record	Moves to the end of the table to a position for entering a new record

Adding Additional Records

You can add records to a table that already contains data using a process almost identical to that used to add records to an empty table. The only difference is that you place the insertion point after the last data record before you enter the additional data. To do so, use the **Navigation buttons** found near the lower-left corner of the screen. The purpose of each of the Navigation buttons is described in Table 1-1.

Complete the following steps to add the remaining records (Figure 1-31) to the Customer table.

Customer table (last 8 records)								
CUSTOMER NUMBER	**NAME**	**ADDRESS**	**CITY**	**STATE**	**ZIP CODE**	**AMOUNT PAID**	**CURRENT DUE**	**DRIVER NUMBER**
CN21	Century North	1562 Butler	Hansen	FL	38513	$8,725.00	$0.00	60
FR28	Friend's Movies	871 Adams	Westport	FL	37070	$4,256.00	$1,202.00	75
GN62	Grand Nelson	7821 Oak	Wood Key	FL	36828	$8,287.50	$925.50	30
GS29	Great Screens	572 Lee	Hansen	FL	38513	$21,625.00	$0.00	60
LM22	Lenger Mason	274 Johnson	Westport	FL	37070	$0.00	$0.00	60
ME93	Merks College	561 Fairhill	Bayville	FL	38734	$24,761.00	$1,572.00	30
RI78	Riter University	26 Grove	Fernwood	FL	37023	$11,682.25	$2,827.50	75
TU20	Turner Hotel	8672 Quincy	Palmview	FL	36114	$8,521.50	$0.00	60

FIGURE 1-31

Steps **To Add Additional Records to a Table**

1 Right-click the Customer table in the Alisa Vending Services : Database window and then click Open on the shortcut menu. When the Customer table displays, maximize the window by clicking the Maximize button. Point to the New Record button.

The datasheet displays (Figure 1-32).

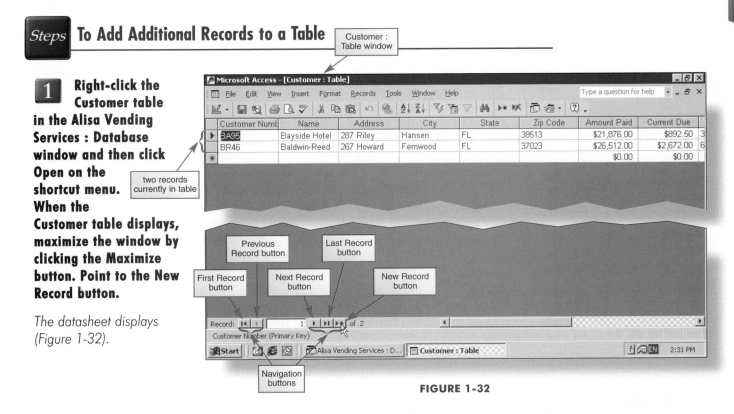

Customer : Table window

two records currently in table

Previous Record button
Last Record button
First Record button
Next Record button
New Record button

Navigation buttons

FIGURE 1-32

2 Click the New Record button.

Access places the insertion point in position to enter a new record (Figure 1-33).

Customer Numb	Name	Address	City	State	Zip Code	Amount Paid	Current Due	
BA95	Bayside Hotel	287 Riley	Hansen	FL	38513	$21,876.00	$892.50	3
BR46	Baldwin-Reed	267 Howard	Fernwood	FL	37023	$26,512.00	$2,672.00	6
						$0.00	$0.00	

insertion point positioned on new record

FIGURE 1-33

3 Add the remaining records from Figure 1-31 using the same techniques you used to add the first two records. Point to the Close Window button.

The additional records are added (Figure 1-34).

4 Click the Close Window button.

The window containing the table closes and the Alisa Vending Services : Database window displays.

Close Window button

Close Window

Customer Numb	Name	Address	City	State	Zip Code	Amount Paid	Current Due	
BA95	Bayside Hotel	287 Riley	Hansen	FL	38513	$21,876.00	$892.50	3
BR46	Baldwin-Reed	267 Howard	Fernwood	FL	37023	$26,512.00	$2,672.00	6
CN21	Century North	1562 Butler	Hansen	FL	38513	$8,725.00	$0.00	6
FR28	Friend's Movies	871 Adams	Westport	FL	37070	$4,256.00	$1,202.00	7
GN62	Grand Nelson	7821 Oak	Wood Key	FL	36828	$8,287.50	$925.50	3
GS29	Great Screens	572 Lee	Hansen	FL	38513	$21,625.00	$0.00	6
LM22	Lenger Mason	274 Johnson	Westport	FL	37070	$0.00	$0.00	6
ME93	Merks College	561 Fairhill	Bayville	FL	38734	$24,761.00	$1,572.00	3
RI78	Riter University	26 Grove	Fernwood	FL	37023	$11,682.25	$2,827.50	7
TU20	Turner Hotel	8672 Quincy	Palmview	FL	36114	$8,521.50	$0.00	6
						$0.00	$0.00	

all 10 records entered

FIGURE 1-34

Correcting Errors in the Data

Check your entries carefully to ensure they are correct. If you make a mistake and discover it before you press the TAB key, correct it by pressing the BACKSPACE key until the incorrect characters are removed and then typing the correct characters.

If you discover an incorrect entry later, correct the error by clicking the incorrect entry and then making the appropriate correction. If the record you must correct is not on the screen, use the Navigation buttons (Next Record, Previous Record, and so on) to move to it. If the field you want to correct is not visible on the screen, use the horizontal scroll bar along the bottom of the screen to shift all the fields until the one you want displays. Then make the correction.

If you add an extra record accidentally, select the record by clicking the record selector that immediately precedes the record. Then, press the DELETE key. This will remove the record from the table. If you forget a record, add it using the same procedure as for all the other records. Access will place it in the correct location in the table automatically.

If you cannot determine how to correct the data, you are, in effect, stuck on the record. Access neither allows you to move to any other record until you have made the correction, nor allows you to close the table. If you encounter this situation, simply press the ESC key. Pressing the ESC key will remove from the screen the record you are trying to add. You then can move to any other record, close the table, or take any other action you desire.

Previewing and Printing the Contents of a Table

When working with a database, you often will need to print a copy of the table contents. Figure 1-35 shows a printed copy of the contents of the Customer table. (Yours may look slightly different, depending on your printer.) Because the Customer table is wider substantially than the screen, it also will be wider than the normal printed page in portrait orientation. **Portrait orientation** means the printout is across the width of the page. **Landscape orientation** means the printout is across the length of the page. Thus, to print the wide database table, use landscape orientation. If you are printing the contents of a table that fits on the screen, you will not need landscape orientation. A convenient way to change to landscape orientation is to **preview** what the printed copy will look like by using Print Preview. This allows you to determine whether landscape orientation is necessary and, if it is, to change easily the orientation to landscape. In addition, you also can use Print Preview to determine whether any adjustments are necessary to the page margins.

Customer   9/8/2003

Customer Num	Name	Address	City	State	Zip Code	Amount Paid	Current Due	Driver Number
BA95	Bayside Hotel	287 Riley	Hansen	FL	38513	$21,876.00	$892.50	30
BR46	Baldwin-Reed	267 Howard	Fernwood	FL	37023	$26,512.00	$2,672.00	60
CN21	Century North	1562 Butler	Hansen	FL	38513	$8,725.00	$0.00	60
FR28	Friend's Movies	871 Adams	Westport	FL	37070	$4,256.00	$1,202.00	75
GN62	Grand Nelson	7821 Oak	Wood Key	FL	36828	$8,287.50	$925.50	30
GS29	Great Screens	572 Lee	Hansen	FL	38513	$21,625.00	$0.00	60
LM22	Lenger Mason	274 Johnson	Westport	FL	37070	$0.00	$0.00	60
ME93	Merks College	561 Fairhill	Bayville	FL	38734	$24,761.00	$1,572.00	30
RI78	Riter University	26 Grove	Fernwood	FL	37023	$11,682.25	$2,827.50	75
TU20	Turner Hotel	8672 Quincy	Palmview	FL	36114	$8,521.50	$0.00	60

FIGURE 1-35

Perform the following steps to use Print Preview to preview and then print the Customer table.

 To Preview and Print the Contents of a Table

1 **Right-click the Customer table and then point to Print Preview on the shortcut menu.**

The shortcut menu for the Customer table displays (Figure 1-36).

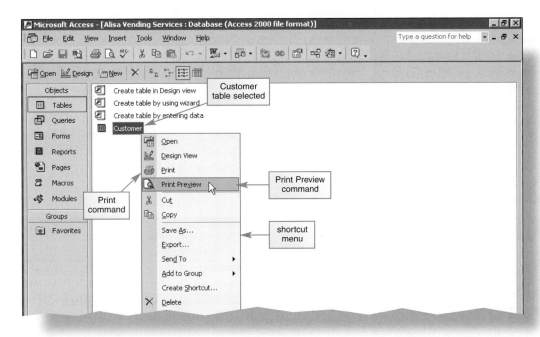

FIGURE 1-36

2 **Click Print Preview on the shortcut menu. Point to the approximate position shown in Figure 1-37.**

The preview of the report displays. The mouse pointer shape changes to a magnifying glass, indicating you can magnify a portion of the report.

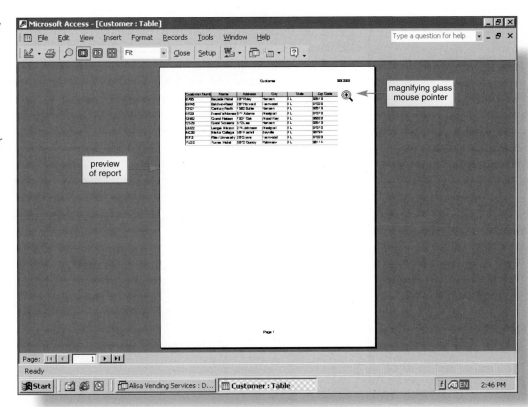

FIGURE 1-37

3 **Click the magnifying glass mouse pointer in the approximate position shown in Figure 1-37 on the previous page.**

The portion surrounding the mouse-pointer is magnified (Figure 1-38). The last field that displays is the Zip Code field. The Amount Paid, Current Due, and Driver Number fields do not display. To display the additional fields, you will need to switch to landscape orientation.

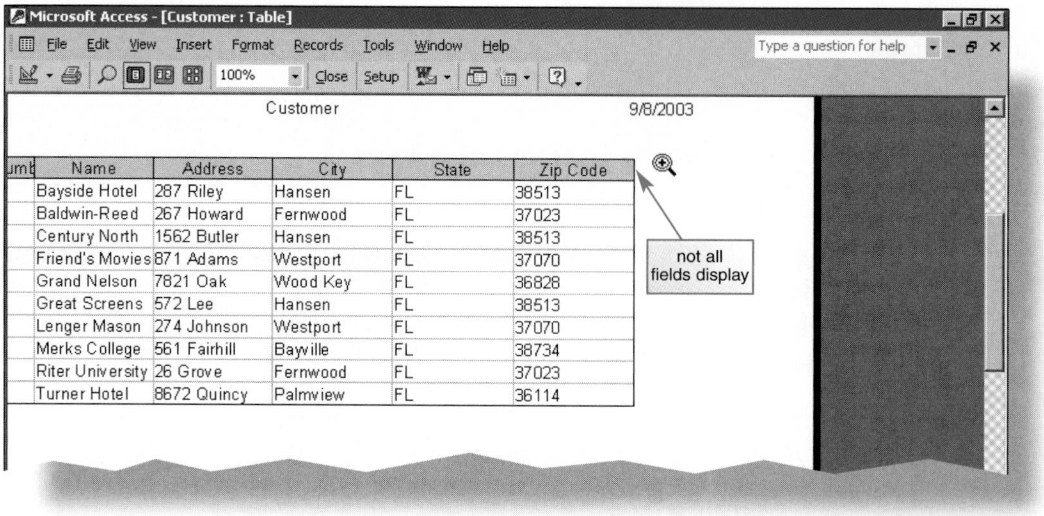

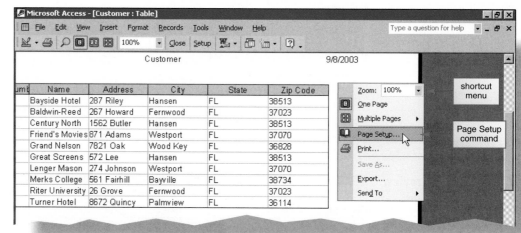

FIGURE 1-38

4 **With the mouse pointer in the approximate position shown in Figure 1-38, right-click the report and then point to Page Setup.**

The shortcut menu displays (Figure 1-39).

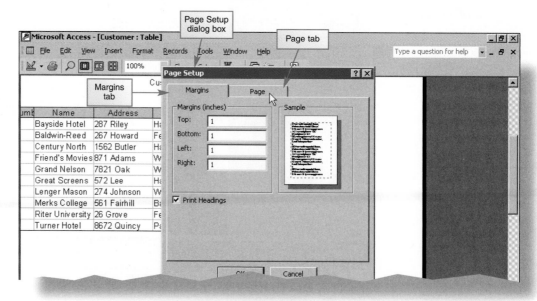

FIGURE 1-39

5 **Click Page Setup and then point to the Page tab.**

The Page Setup dialog box displays (Figure 1-40).

FIGURE 1-40

6 **Click the Page tab and then point to the Landscape option button.**

The Page sheet displays (Figure 1-41). The Portrait option button currently is selected. (Option button refers to the round button that indicates choice in a dialog box. When the corresponding option is selected, the button contains within it a solid circle. Clicking an option button selects it, and deselects all others.)

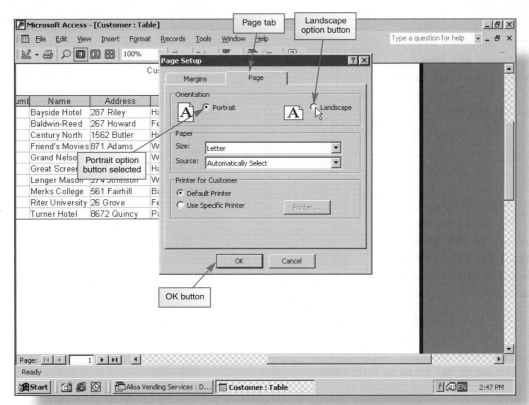

FIGURE 1-41

7 **Click Landscape and then click the OK button. Point to the Print button on the Print Preview toolbar.**

The orientation is changed to landscape as shown by the report that displays on the screen (Figure 1-42). The last field that displays is the Driver Number field, so all fields currently display. If they did not, you could decrease the left and right margins; that is, the amount of space left by Access on the left and right edges of the report.

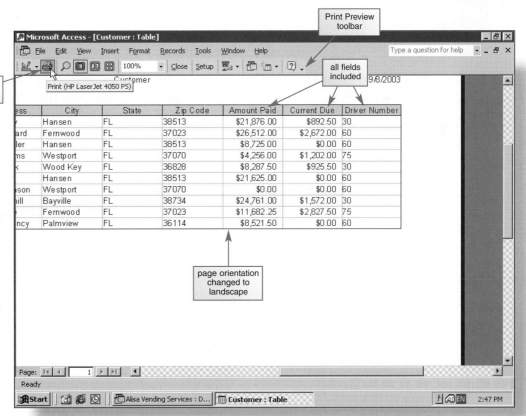

FIGURE 1-42

8 **Click the Print button to print the report and then point to the Close button on the Print Preview toolbar (Figure 1-43).**

The report prints. It looks like the report shown in Figure 1-35 on page A 1.28.

9 **Click the Close button on the Print Preview toolbar when the report has been printed to close the Print Preview window.**

The Print Preview window closes and the Alisa Vending Services : Database window displays.

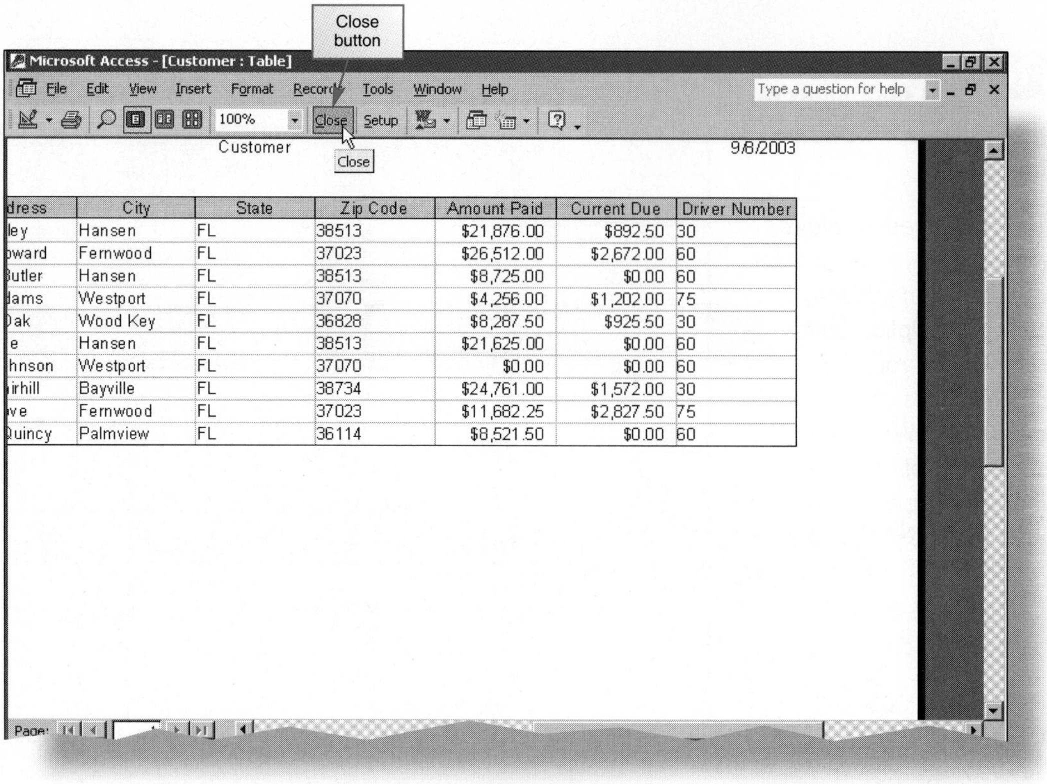

FIGURE 1-43

Other Ways

1. On File menu click Print Preview to preview
2. On File menu click Print to print
3. Press CTRL+P to print
4. In Voice Command mode, say "Print Preview" to preview; say "Print" to print

Creating Additional Tables

A database typically consists of more than one table. The sample database contains two, the Customer table and the Driver table. You need to repeat the process of creating a table and adding records for each table in the database. In the sample database, you need to create and add records to the Driver table. The structure for the table is given in Figure 1-44a and the data for the table is given in Figure 1-44b. The steps to create the table follow.

Structure of Driver table

FIELD NAME	DATA TYPE	FIELD SIZE	PRIMARY KEY?	DESCRIPTION
Driver Number	Text	2	Yes	Driver Number (Primary Key)
Last Name	Text	10		Last Name of Driver
First Name	Text	8		First Name of Driver
Address	Text	15		Street Address
City	Text	15		City
State	Text	2		State (Two-Character Abbreviation)
Zip Code	Text	5		Zip Code (Five-Character Version)
Hourly Rate	Currency			Hourly Rate of Driver
YTD Earnings	Currency			YTD Earnings of Driver

FIGURE 1-44a

Data for Driver table

DRIVER NUMBER	LAST NAME	FIRST NAME	ADDRESS	CITY	STATE	ZIP CODE	HOURLY RATE	YTD EARNINGS
30	Tuttle	Larissa	7562 Hickory	Laton Springs	FL	37891	$16.00	$21,145.25
60	Powers	Frank	57 Ravenwood	Gillmore	FL	37572	$15.00	$19,893.50
75	Ortiz	Jose	341 Pierce	Douglas	FL	37613	$17.00	$23,417.00

FIGURE 1-44b

Steps To Create an Additional Table

1 Make sure the Alisa Vending Services database is open. Right-click Create table in Design view and then click Open on the shortcut menu. Enter the data for the fields for the Driver table from Figure 1-44a. Be sure to click the Primary Key button when you enter the Driver Number field. Point to the Close Window button for the Table1 : Table window after you have entered all the fields.

The entries display (Figure 1-45).

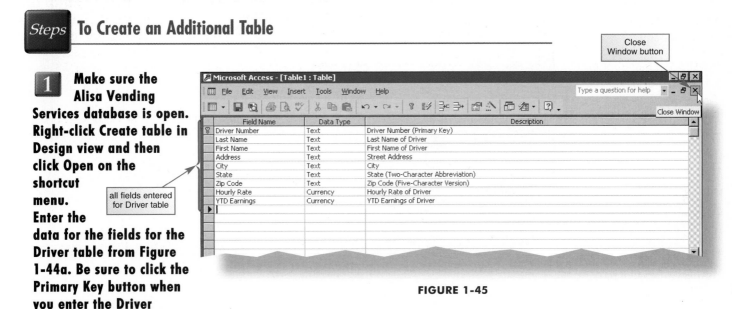

all fields entered for Driver table

Close Window button

FIGURE 1-45

2 Click the Close Window button, click the Yes button in the Microsoft Access dialog box when asked if you want to save the changes, type Driver as the name of the table, and then point to the OK button in the Save As dialog box.

The Save As dialog box displays (Figure 1-46). The table name is entered.

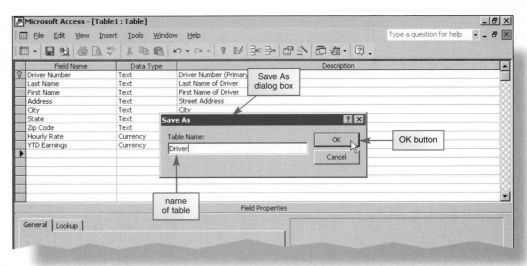

Save As dialog box

OK button

name of table

FIGURE 1-46

3 Click the OK button.

The table is saved in the Alisa Vending Services database. The window containing the table structure no longer displays.

Adding Records to the Additional Table

Now that you have created the Driver table, use the following steps to add records to it.

1 **Right-click the Driver table and point to Open on the shortcut menu.**

The shortcut menu for the Driver table displays (Figure 1-47).

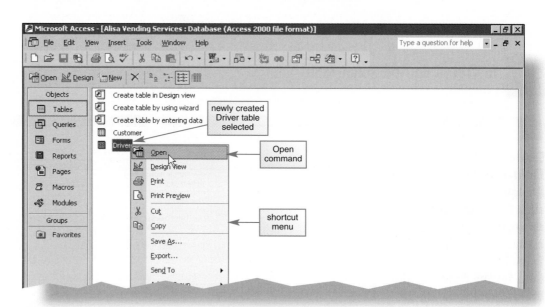

FIGURE 1-47

2 **Click Open on the shortcut menu and then enter the Driver data from Figure 1-44b on the previous page into the Driver table. Point to the Close Window button.**

The datasheet displays with three records entered (Figure 1-48).

FIGURE 1-48

3 **Click the Close Window button for the Driver : Table window.**

Access closes the table and removes the datasheet from the screen.

Using a Form to View Data

In creating tables, you have used Datasheet view; that is, the data on the screen displayed as a table. You also can use **Form view**, in which you see a single record at a time.

The advantage with Datasheet view is you can see multiple records at once. It has the disadvantage that, unless you have few fields in the table, you cannot see all the fields at the same time. With Form view, you see only a single record, but you can see all the fields in the record. The view you choose is a matter of personal preference.

Creating a Form

To use Form view, you first must create a form. The simplest way to create a form is to use the New Object: AutoForm button on the Database toolbar. To do so, first select the table for which the form is to be created in the Database window and then click the New Object: AutoForm button. A list of available objects displays. Click AutoForm in the list to select it.

Perform the following steps using the New Object: AutoForm button to create a form for the Customer table.

More About

Forms

Attractive and functional forms can improve greatly the data entry process. Forms are not restricted to data from a single table, but can incorporate data from multiple tables as well as special types of data like pictures and sounds. A good DBMS like Access furnishes an easy way to create sophisticated forms.

Steps To Use the New Object: AutoForm Button to Create a Form

---

1 Make sure the Alisa Vending Services database is open, the Database window displays, and the Customer table is selected. Point to the New Object: AutoForm button arrow on the Database toolbar (Figure 1-49).

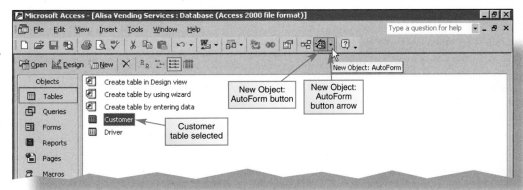

FIGURE 1-49

2 Click the New Object: AutoForm button arrow and then point to AutoForm.

A list of objects that can be created displays (Figure 1-50).

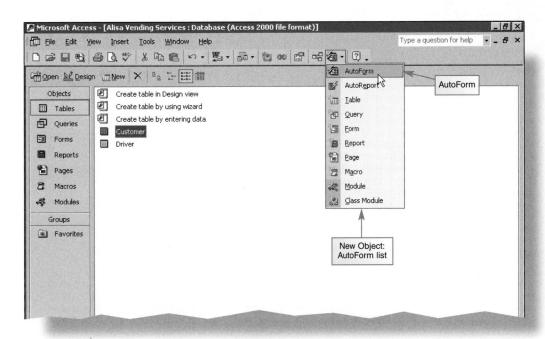

FIGURE 1-50

3 **Click AutoForm in the New Object: AutoForm list.**

After a brief delay, the form displays (Figure 1-51). If you do not move the mouse pointer after clicking AutoForm, the ScreenTip for the Database Window button may display when the form opens. An additional toolbar, the Formatting toolbar, also displays. (When you close the form, this toolbar no longer displays.)

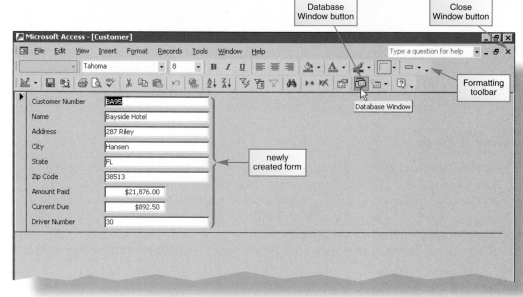

FIGURE 1-51

Other **Ways**

1. On Insert menu click AutoForm
2. In Voice Command mode, say "New Object, AutoForm"
3. In Voice Command mode, say "Insert, AutoForm"

Closing and Saving the Form

Closing a form is similar to closing a table. The only difference is that you will be asked if you want to save the form unless you previously have saved it. Perform the following steps to close the form and save it as Customer.

Steps **To Close and Save a Form**

1 **Click the Close Window button for the Customer window (see Figure 1-51). Point to the Yes button in the Microsoft Access dialog box.**

The Microsoft Access dialog box displays (Figure 1-52).

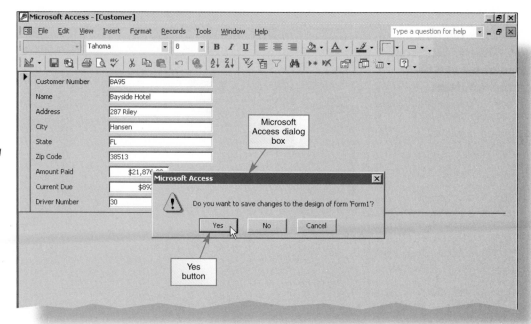

FIGURE 1-52

2 **Click the Yes button and then point to the OK button in the Save As dialog box.**

The Save As dialog box displays (Figure 1-53). The name of the table (Customer) becomes the name of the form automatically. This name could be changed, if desired.

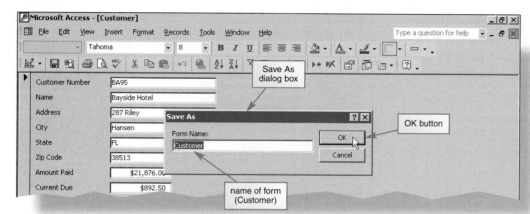

FIGURE 1-53

3 **Click the OK button.**

The form is saved as part of the database and the form closes. The Alisa Vending Services : Database window again displays.

Opening the Saved Form

Once you have saved a form, you can use it at any time in the future by opening it. Opening a form is similar to opening a table; that is, make sure the form to be opened is selected, right-click, and then click Open on the shortcut menu. Before opening the form, however, the Forms object, rather than the Tables object, must be selected.

Perform the following steps to open the Customer form.

Other **Ways**

1. Double-click Control-menu icon on title bar for window
2. On File menu click Close
3. In Voice Command mode, say "File, Close"

Steps **To Open a Form**

1 **With the Alisa Vending Services database open and the Database window on the screen, click Forms on the Objects bar.**

The Forms object is selected and the list of available forms displays (Figure 1-54). Currently, the Customer form is the only form.

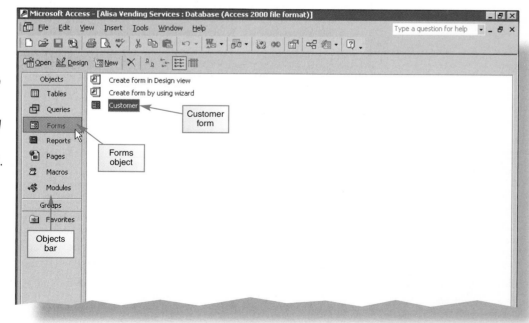

FIGURE 1-54

2 Right-click the Customer form, and then point to Open on the shortcut menu.

The shortcut menu for the Customer form displays (Figure 1-55).

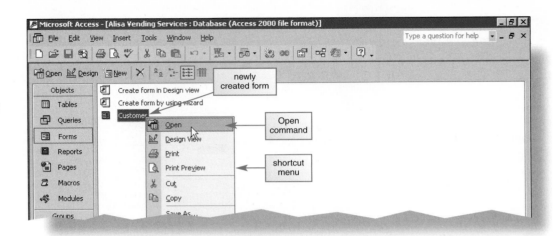

FIGURE 1-55

3 Click Open on the shortcut menu and then point to the Next Record button in preparation for the next task.

The Customer form displays (Figure 1-56).

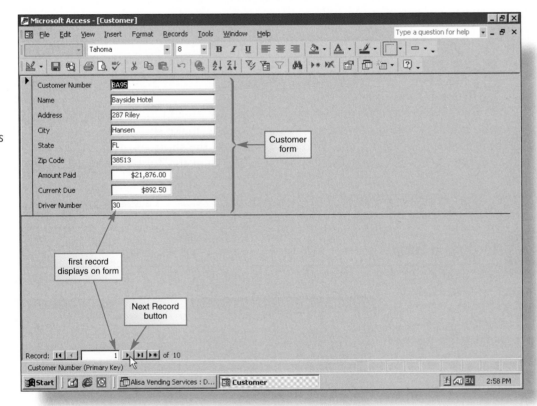

FIGURE 1-56

Other Ways

1. Click Forms object, double-click desired form
2. Click Forms object, click desired form, click Open button
3. Click Forms object, click desired form, press ALT+O
4. In Voice Command mode, say "Forms, [click desired form], Open"

Using the Form

You can use the form just as you used Datasheet view. You use the Navigation buttons to move between records. You can add new records or change existing ones. To delete the record displayed on the screen, after selecting the record by clicking its record selector, press the DELETE key. Thus, you can perform database operations using either Form view or Datasheet view.

Because you can see only one record at a time in Form view, to see a different record, such as the fifth record, use the Navigation buttons to move to it. To move from record to record in Form view, perform the following step.

PROJECT 1

 **To Use a Form**

1 **Click the Next Record button four times.**

The fifth record displays on the form (Figure 1-57).

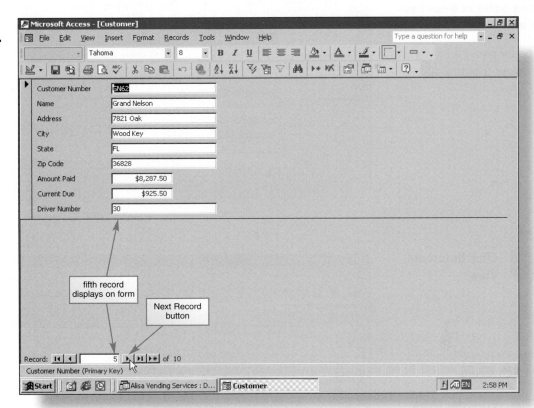

fifth record displays on form

Next Record button

FIGURE 1-57

Switching Between Form View and Datasheet View

In some cases, once you have seen a record in Form view, you will want to move to Datasheet view to again see a collection of records. To do so, click the View button arrow on the Form View toolbar and then click Datasheet View in the list that displays.

Perform the following steps to switch from Form view to Datasheet view.

Steps **To Switch from Form View to Datasheet View**

1 **Point to the View button arrow on the Form View toolbar (Figure 1-58).**

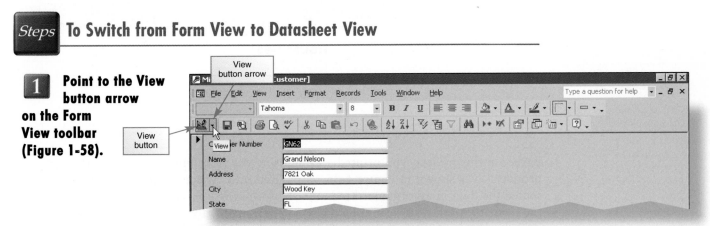

View button arrow

View button

FIGURE 1-58

2 **Click the View button arrow and then point to Datasheet View.**

The list of available views displays (Figure 1-59).

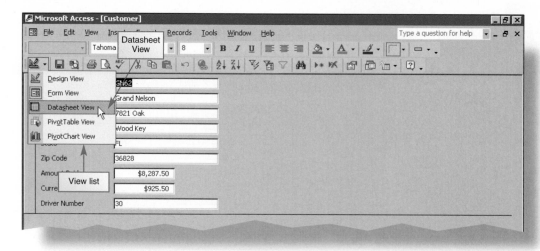

FIGURE 1-59

3 **Click Datasheet View.**

The table displays in Datasheet view (Figure 1-60). The record selector is positioned on the fifth record.

4 **Click the Close Window button.**

The Customer window closes and the datasheet no longer displays.

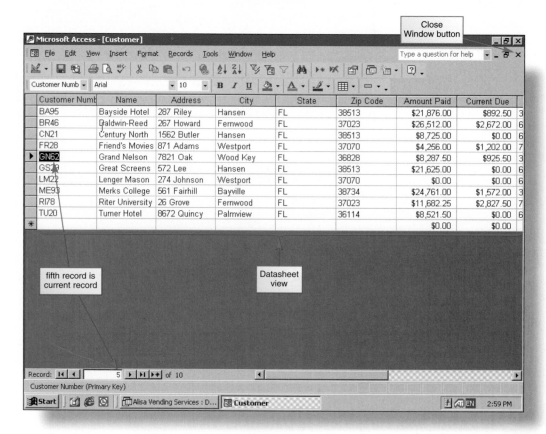

FIGURE 1-60

Other Ways

1. On View menu click Datasheet View

Creating a Report

Earlier in this project, you printed a table using the Print button. The report you produced was shown in Figure 1-35 on page A 1.28. While this type of report presented the data in an organized manner, the format is very rigid. You cannot select the fields to display, for example; the report automatically includes all the fields and they display in precisely the same order as in the table. There is no way to change the title, which will automatically be the same as the name of the table.

In this section, you will create the report shown in Figure 1-61. This report features significant differences from the one in Figure 1-35. The portion at the top of the report in Figure 1-61, called a **page header**, contains a custom title. The contents of this page header display at the top of each page. The **detail lines**, which are the lines that are printed for each record, contain only those fields you specify and in the order you specify.

Customer Amount Report

Customer Number	Name	Amount Paid	Current Due
BA95	Bayside Hotel	$21,876.00	$892.50
BR46	Baldwin-Reed	$26,512.00	$2,672.00
CN21	Century North	$8,725.00	$0.00
FR28	Friend's Movies	$4,256.00	$1,202.00
GN62	Grand Nelson	$8,287.50	$925.50
GS29	Great Screens	$21,625.00	$0.00
LM22	Lenger Mason	$0.00	$0.00
ME93	Merks College	$24,761.00	$1,572.00
RI78	Riter University	$11,682.25	$2,827.50
TU20	Turner Hotel	$8,521.50	$0.00

FIGURE 1-61

Perform the following steps to create the report in Figure 1-61.

Steps **To Create a Report**

1 **Click Tables on the Objects bar. Make sure the Customer table is selected. Click the New Object: AutoForm button arrow on the Database toolbar and then point to Report.**

The list of available objects displays (Figure 1-62).

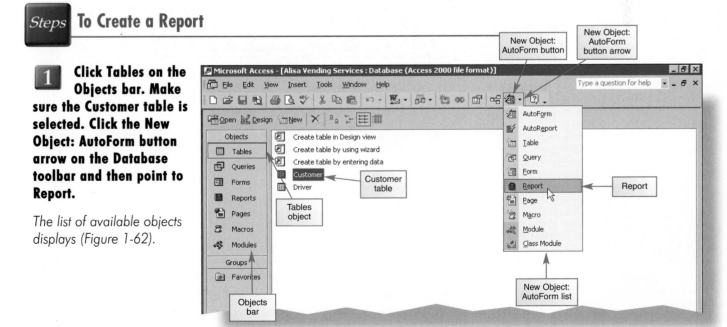

FIGURE 1-62

2 Click Report and then point to Report Wizard.

The New Report dialog box displays (Figure 1-63).

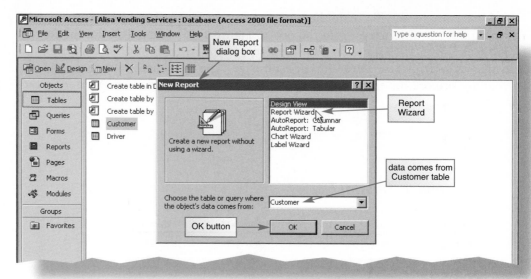

FIGURE 1-63

3 Click Report Wizard and then click the OK button. Point to the Add Field button.

The Report Wizard dialog box displays (Figure 1-64).

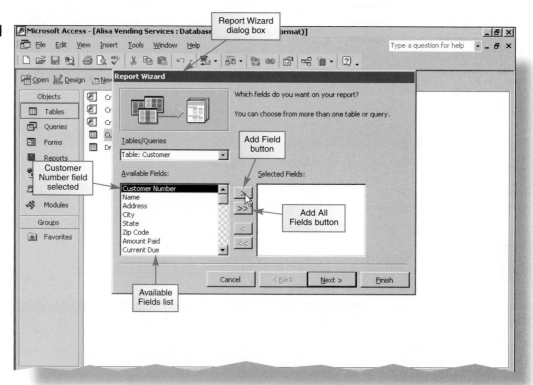

FIGURE 1-64

Selecting the Fields for the Report

To select a field for the report, that is, to indicate the field is to be included in the report, click the field in the Available Fields list. Next, click the Add Field button. This will move the field from the Available Fields box to the Selected Fields box, thus including the field in the report. If you wanted to select all fields, a shortcut is available simply by clicking the Add All Fields button.

To select the Customer Number, Name, Amount Paid, and Current Due fields for the report, perform the following steps.

Steps **To Select the Fields for a Report**

1 **Click the Add Field button to add the Customer Number field. Add the Name field by clicking it and then clicking the Add Field button. Add the Amount Paid and Current Due fields just as you added the Customer Number and Name fields. Point to the Next button.**

The fields for the report display in the Selected Fields box (Figure 1-65).

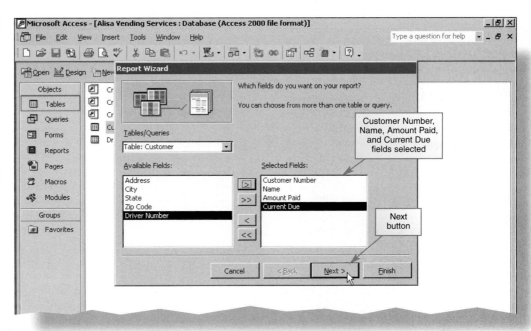

FIGURE 1-65

2 **Click the Next button.**

The Report Wizard dialog box displays (Figure 1-66).

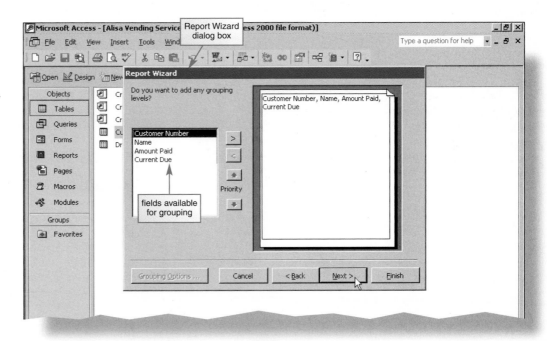

FIGURE 1-66

Completing the Report

Several additional steps are involved in completing the report. With the exception of changing the title, the Access selections are acceptable, so you simply will click the Next button.

Perform the steps on the next page to complete the report.

Steps **To Complete a Report**

1 **Because you will not specify any grouping, click the Next button in the Report Wizard dialog box (see Figure 1-66 on the previous page). Click the Next button a second time because you will not need to change the sort order for the records.**

The Report Wizard dialog box displays (Figure 1-67). In this dialog box, you can change the layout or orientation of the report.

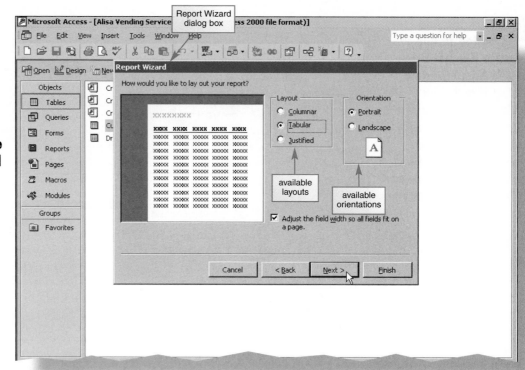

FIGURE 1-67

2 **Make sure that Tabular is selected as the layout and Portrait is selected as the orientation and then click the Next button.**

The Report Wizard dialog box displays (Figure 1-68). In this dialog box, you can select a style for the report.

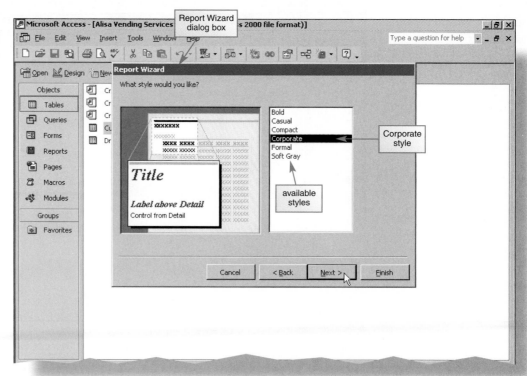

FIGURE 1-68

3 Be sure that the Corporate style is selected, click the Next button, type Customer Amount Report as the new title, and then point to the Finish button.

The Report Wizard dialog box displays (Figure 1-69). The title is typed.

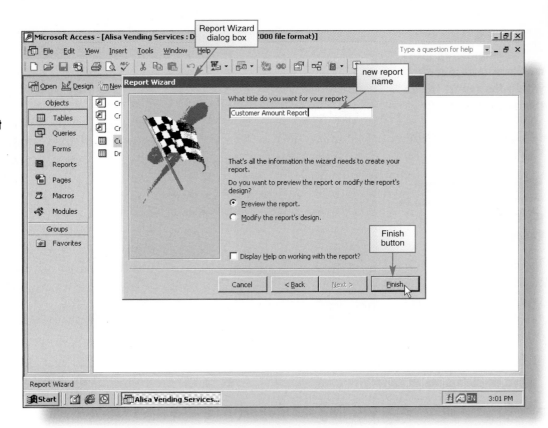

FIGURE 1-69

4 Click the Finish button.

A preview of the report displays (Figure 1-70). Yours may look slightly different, depending on your printer.

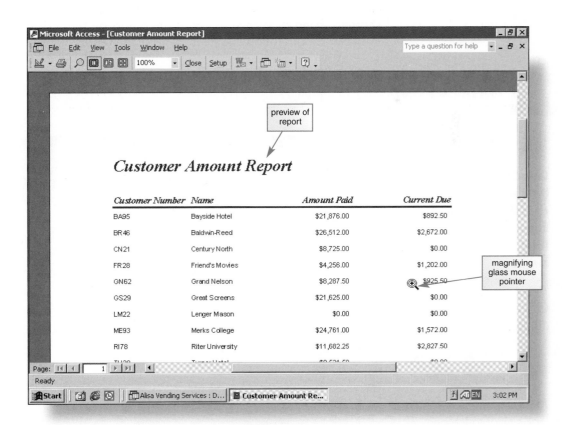

FIGURE 1-70

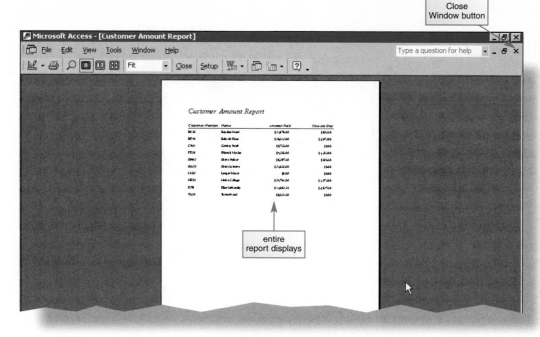

5 **Click the magnifying glass mouse pointer anywhere within the report to see the entire report.**

The entire report displays (Figure 1-71).

6 **Click the Close Window button in the Customer Amount Report window.**

The report no longer displays. It has been saved automatically using the name Customer Amount Report.

FIGURE 1-71

Printing the Report

To print a report from the Database window, first right-click the report. Then click Print on the shortcut menu to print the report or click Print Preview on the shortcut menu to see a preview of the report on the screen.

Perform the following steps to print the report.

 To Print a Report

1 **If necessary, click Reports on the Objects bar in the Database window, right-click the Customer Amount Report, and then point to Print on the shortcut menu.**

The shortcut menu for the Customer Amount Report displays (Figure 1-72).

2 **Click Print on the shortcut menu.**

The report prints. It should look similar to the one shown in Figure 1-61 on page A 1.41.

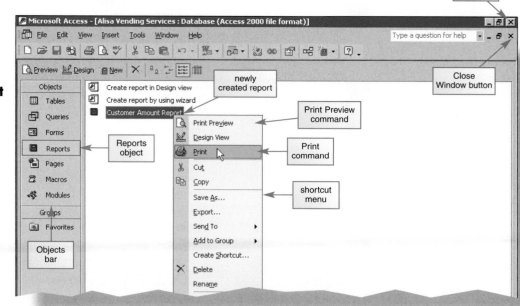

FIGURE 1-72

Closing the Database

Once you have finished working with a database, you should close it. The following step closes the database by closing its Database window.

TO CLOSE A DATABASE

1 Click the Close Window button for the Alisa Vending Services : Database window.

Access Help System

At any time while you are using Access, you can get answers to questions by using the Access Help system. Used properly, this form of online assistance can increase your productivity and reduce your frustrations by minimizing the time you spend learning how to use Access.

The following section shows how to get answers to your questions using the Ask a Question box. For additional information on using the Access Help system, see Appendix A on page A A.01 and Table 1-2 on page A 1.49.

Obtaining Help Using the Ask a Question Box on the Menu Bar

The **Ask a Question box** on the right side of the menu bar lets you type in free-form questions, such as *how do I save* or *how do I create a Web page*, or you can type in terms, such as *copy*, *save*, or *formatting*. Access responds by displaying a list of topics related to what you entered. The following steps show how to use the Ask a Question box to obtain information on removing a primary key.

More *About*

The Access 2002 Help System

The best way to become familiar with the Access Help system is to use it. Appendix A includes detailed information on the Access Help system and exercises that will help you gain confidence in using it.

Steps To Obtain Help Using the Ask a Question Box

1 **Click the Ask a Question box on the right side of the menu bar. Type** how do I remove a primary key **in the box (Figure 1-73).** **If using Access 2000, click the Microsoft Access Help button on the right side of the Standard toolbar. Type your question or short phrase in the What would you like to do? text box and then click the Search button.**

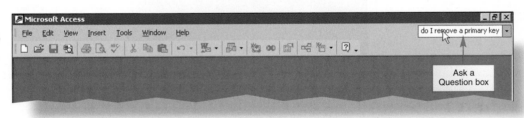

FIGURE 1-73

2 **Press the ENTER key.**

A list of topics displays relating to the question, "how do I remove a primary key" (Figure 1-74).

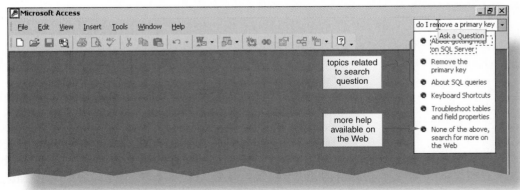

FIGURE 1-74

3 **Point to the Remove the primary key topic.**

The mouse pointer changes to a hand indicating it is pointing to a link (Figure 1-75).

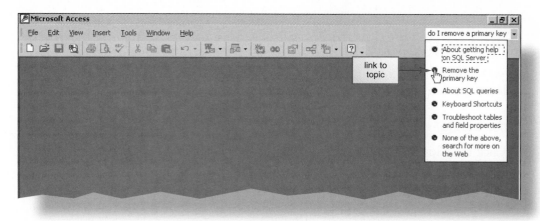

FIGURE 1-75

4 **Click Remove the primary key.**

Access displays a Microsoft Access Help window that provides Help information about removing the primary key (Figure 1-76).

5 **Click the Close button on the Microsoft Access Help window title bar.**

The Microsoft Access Help window closes.

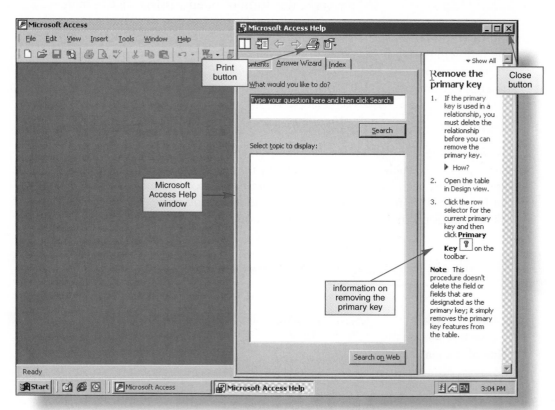

FIGURE 1-76

Use the buttons in the upper-left corner of the Microsoft Access Help window (Figure 1-76) to navigate through the Help system, change the display, and print the contents of the window.

As you enter questions and terms in the Ask a Question box, Access adds them to its list. Thus, if you click the Ask a Question box arrow, a list of previously asked questions and terms will display.

Table 1-2 summarizes the 10 categories of Help available to you. Because of the way the Access Help system works, be sure to review the rightmost column of Table 1-2 if you have difficulties activating the desired category of Help. Additional information on using the Access Help system is available in Appendix A.

Table 1-2 Access Help System

TYPE	DESCRIPTION	HOW TO ACTIVATE
Answer Wizard	Answers questions or searches for terms that you type in your own words.	Click the Microsoft Access Help button on the Database window toolbar. Click the Answer Wizard tab.
Ask a Question box	Answers questions or searches for terms that you type in your own words.	Type a question or term in the Ask a Question box on the menu bar and then press the ENTER key.
Contents sheet	Groups Help topics by general categories. Use when you know only the general category of the topic in question.	Click the Microsoft Access Help button on the Database window toolbar. Click the Contents tab.
Detect and Repair	Automatically finds and fixes errors in the application.	Click Detect and Repair on the Help menu.
Hardware and Software Information	Shows Product ID and allows access to system information and technical support information.	Click About Microsoft Access on the Help menu and then click the appropriate button.
Index sheet	Similar to an index in a book. Use when you know exactly what you want.	Click the Microsoft Access Help button on the Database window toolbar. If necessary, maximize the Help window by double-clicking its title bar. Click the Index tab.
Office Assistant	Similar to the Ask a Question box in that the Office Assistant answers questions that you type in your own words, offers tips, and provides help for a variety of Access features.	Click the Office Assistant icon. If the Office Assistant does not display, click Show the Office Assistant on the Help menu.
Office on the Web	Used to access technical resources and download free product enhancements on the Web.	Click Office on the Web on the Help menu.
Question Mark button	Used to identify unfamiliar items in a dialog box.	Click the Question Mark button on the title bar in a dialog box and then click an item in the dialog box.
What's This? command	Used to identify unfamiliar items on the screen.	Click What's This? on the Help menu and then click an item on the screen.

You can use the Office Assistant to search for Help on any topic concerning Access. For additional information on using the Access Help system, see Appendix A.

Quitting Access

After you close a database, you can open another database, create a new database, or simply quit Access and return to the Windows desktop. The following step quits Access.

TO QUIT ACCESS

1 Click the Close button in the Microsoft Access window (see Figure 1-72 on page A 1.46).

Designing a Database

Database design refers to the arrangement of data into tables and fields. In the example in this project, the design is specified, but in many cases, you will have to determine the design based on what you want the system to accomplish.

With large, complex databases, the database design process can be extensive. Major sections of advanced database textbooks are devoted to this topic. Often, however, you should be able to design a database effectively by keeping one simple principle in mind: Design to remove redundancy. **Redundancy** means storing the same fact in more than one place.

To illustrate, you need to maintain the following information shown in Figure 1-77. In the figure, all the data is contained in a single table. Notice that the data for a given driver (number, name, address, and so on) occurs on more than one record.

Customer table

CUSTOMER NUMBER	NAME	ADDRESS	CITY	STATE	ZIP CODE	AMOUNT PAID	CURRENT DUE	DRIVER NUMBER	LAST NAME	FIRST NAME	ADDRESS
BA95	Bayside Hotel	287 Riley	Hansen	FL	38513	$21,876.00	$892.50	30	Tuttle	Larissa	7562 Hickory
BR46	Baldwin-Reed	267 Howard	Fernwood	FL	37023	$26,512.00	$2,672.00	60	Powers	Frank	57 Ravenwood
CN21	Century North	1562 Butler	Hansen	FL	38513	$8,725.00	$0.00	60	Powers	Frank	57 Ravenwood
FR28	Friend's Movies	871 Adams	Westport	FL	37070	$4,256.00	$1,202.00	75	Ortiz	Jose	341 Pierce
GN62	Grand Nelson	7821 Oak	Wood Key	FL	36828	$8,287.50	$925.50	30	Tuttle	Larissa	7562 Hickory
GS29	Great Screens	572 Lee	Hansen	FL	38513	$21,625.00	$0.00	60	Powers	Frank	57 Ravenwood
LM22	Lenger Mason	274 Johnson	Westport	FL	37070	$0.00	$0.00	60	Powers	Frank	57 Ravenwood
ME93	Merks College	561 Fairhill	Bayville	FL	38734	$24,761.00	$1,572.00	30	Tuttle	Larissa	7562 Hickory
RI78	Riter University	26 Grove	Fernwood	FL	37023	$11,682.25	$2,827.50	75	Ortiz	Jose	341 Pierce
TU20	Turner Hotel	8672 Quincy	Palmview	FL	36114	$8,521.50	$0.00	60	Powers	Frank	57 Ravenwood

FIGURE 1-77

duplicate driver names

Storing this data on multiple records is an example of redundancy, which causes several problems, including:

1. Redundancy wastes space on the disk. The address of driver 30 (Larissa Tuttle), for example, should be stored only once. Storing this fact several times is wasteful.
2. Redundancy makes updating the database more difficult. If, for example, Larissa Tuttle moves, her address would need to be changed in several different places.
3. A possibility of inconsistent data exists. Suppose, for example, that you change the address of Larissa Tuttle on customer GN62's record to 146 Valley, but do not change it on customer BA95's record. In both cases, the driver number is 30, but the addresses are different. In other words, the data is inconsistent.

The solution to the problem is to place the redundant data in a separate table, one in which the data will no longer be redundant. If, for example, you place the data for drivers in a separate table (Figure 1-78), the data for each driver will display only once.

Notice that you need to have the driver number in both tables. Without it, no way exists to tell which driver is associated with which customer. All the other driver data, however, was removed from the Customer table and placed in the Driver table. This new arrangement corrects the problems of redundancy in the following ways:

1. Because the data for each driver is stored only once, space is not wasted.
2. Changing the address of a driver is easy. You have only to change one row in the Driver table.
3. Because the data for a driver is stored only once, inconsistent data cannot occur.

driver data is in separate table

Driver table

DRIVER NUMBER	LAST NAME	FIRST NAME	ADDRESS	CITY	STATE	ZIP CODE	HOURLY RATE	YTD EARNINGS
30	Tuttle	Larissa	7562 Hickory	Laton Springs	FL	37891	$16.00	$21,145.25
60	Powers	Frank	57 Ravenwood	Gillmore	FL	37572	$15.00	$19,893.50
75	Ortiz	Jose	341 Pierce	Douglas	FL	37613	$17.00	$23,417.00

Customer table

CUSTOMER NUMBER	NAME	ADDRESS	CITY	STATE	ZIP CODE	AMOUNT PAID	CURRENT DUE	DRIVER NUMBER
BA95	Bayside Hotel	287 Riley	Hansen	FL	38513	$21,876.00	$892.50	30
BR46	Baldwin-Reed	267 Howard	Fernwood	FL	37023	$26,512.00	$2,672.00	60
CN21	Century North	1562 Butler	Hansen	FL	38513	$8,725.00	$0.00	60
FR28	Friend's Movies	871 Adams	Westport	FL	37070	$4,256.00	$1,202.00	75
GN62	Grand Nelson	7821 Oak	Wood Key	FL	36828	$8,287.50	$925.50	30
GS29	Great Screens	572 Lee	Hansen	FL	38513	$21,625.00	$0.00	60
LM22	Lenger Mason	274 Johnson	Westport	FL	37070	$0.00	$0.00	60
ME93	Merks College	561 Fairhill	Bayville	FL	38734	$24,761.00	$1,572.00	30
RI78	Riter University	26 Grove	Fernwood	FL	37023	$11,682.25	$2,827.50	75
TU20	Turner Hotel	8672 Quincy	Palmview	FL	36114	$8,521.50	$0.00	60

FIGURE 1-78

Designing to omit redundancy will help you to produce good and valid database designs.

CASE PERSPECTIVE SUMMARY

In Project 1, you assisted Alisa Vending Services in their efforts to place their data in a database. You created the database that Alisa will use. Within the Alisa Vending Services database, you created the Customer and Driver tables by defining the fields within them. You then added records to these tables. Once you created the tables, you printed the contents of the tables. You also used a form to view the data in the table. Finally, you used the Report Wizard to create a report containing the Customer Number, Name, Amount Paid, and Current Due fields for each customer served by Alisa Vending Services.

Project Summary

In Project 1, you learned about databases and database management systems. You learned how to create a database and how to create the tables within a database. You saw how to define the fields in a table by specifying the characteristics of the fields. You learned how to open a table, how to add records to it, and how to close it. You also printed the contents of a table. You created a form to view data on the screen and also created a custom report. You learned how to use Microsoft Access Help. Finally, you learned how to design a database to eliminate redundancy.

What You Should Know

Having completed this project, you now should be able to perform the following tasks:

▶ Add Additional Records to a Table (*A 1.27*)

▶ Add Records to a Table (*A 1.21*)

▶ Add Records to an Additional Table (*A 1.34*)

▶ Close a Database (*A 1.47*)

▶ Close a Table and Database (*A 1.25*)

▶ Close and Save a Form (*A 1.36*)

▶ Complete a Report (*A 1.44*)

▶ Create a New Database (A 1.11)

▶ Create a Report (*A 1.41*)

▶ Create a Table (*A 1.15*)

▶ Create an Additional Table (*A 1.33*)

▶ Define the Fields in a Table (*A 1.17*)

▶ Obtain Help Using the Ask a Question Box (*A 1.47*)

▶ Open a Database (*A 1.25*)

▶ Open a Form (*A 1.37*)

▶ Preview and Print the Contents of a Table (*A 1.29*)

▶ Print a Report (*A 1.46*)

▶ Quit Access (A 1.49)

▶ Save and Close a Table (A 1.20)

▶ Select the Fields for a Report (*A 1.43*)

▶ Start Access (*A 1.09*)

▶ Switch from Form View to Datasheet View (*A 1.39*)

▶ Use a Form (*A 1.39*)

▶ Use the New Object: AutoForm Button to Create a Form (*A 1.35*)

More About

Microsoft Certification

The Microsoft Office User Specialist (MOUS) Certification program provides an opportunity for you to obtain a valuable industry credential — proof that you have the Access 2002 skills required by employers. For more information, see Appendix E or visit the Shelly Cashman Series MOUS Web page at scsite.com/tdoff/cert.

In the Lab

Instructions: To complete the Learn It Online exercises, start your browser, click the Address bar, and then enter scsite.com/tdoff/exs. When the Teachers Discovering Office Learn It Online page displays, follow the instructions in the exercises below. To complete the Using the Office Training CD exercises, insert the Microsoft Office Training CD in your CD drive and access the appropriate section. Refer to the introduction chapter of this book to review step-by-step instructions for both installing and using the Microsoft Office Training CD.

Learn It online

1 Project Reinforcement – TF, MC, and SA

Below Access Project 1, click the Project Reinforcement link. Print the quiz by clicking Print on the File menu. Answer each question. Write your first and last name at the top of each page, and then hand in the printout to your instructor.

2 Flash Cards

Below Access Project 1, click the Flash Cards link. When Flash Cards displays, read the instructions. Type 20 (or a number specified by your instructor) in the Number of Playing Cards text box, type your name in the Name text box, and then click the Flip Card button. When the flash card displays, read the question and then click the Answer box arrow to select an answer. Flip through Flash Cards. Click Print on the File menu to print the last flash card if your score is 15 (75%) correct or greater and then hand it in to your instructor. If your score is less than 15 (75%) correct, then redo this exercise by clicking the Replay button.

3 Practice Test

Below Access Project 1, click the Practice Test link. Answer each question, enter your first and last name at the bottom of the page, and then click the Grade Test button. When the graded practice test displays on your screen, click Print on the File menu to print a hard copy. Continue to take practice tests until you score 80% or better. Hand in a printout of the final practice test to your instructor.

4 Who Wants to Be a Computer Genius?

Below Access Project 1, click the Computer Genius link. Read the instructions, enter your first and last name at the bottom of the page, and then click the Play button. Hand in your score to your instructor.

5 Wheel of Terms

Below Access Project 1, click the Wheel of Terms link. Read the instructions, and then enter your first and last name and your school name. Click the Play button. Hand in your score to your instructor.

6 Crossword Puzzle Challenge

Below Access Project 1, click the Crossword Puzzle Challenge link. Read the instructions, and then enter your first and last name. Click the Play button. Work the crossword puzzle. When you are finished, click the Submit button. When the crossword puzzle redisplays, click the Print button. Hand in the printout.

Using the Microsoft Office Training CD

1 In and Out of the Classroom

With the Microsoft Office Training CD in your CD drive, click the In and Out of the Classroom tab. Review one of the Access tutorials that will help you learn how to use and integrate Microsoft Access in your classroom. The Access tutorials are available in the Office XP, Office 2000, or Office 2001 for the Mac links.

2 Tips and Tricks

With the Microsoft Office Training CD in your CD drive, click the Tips and Tricks tab. Review one of the Access tips and tricks that includes building relationships between tables when using Access, evaluating student survey data, sorting dinosaur information, and more.

3 Tutorial Packs

With the Microsoft Office Training CD in your CD drive, click the Tutorial Packs tab. Review one of the step-by-step tutorials on using Microsoft Access to enhance your teaching and learning process.

Productivity in the Classroom

1 Creating the Wooden Crafts Database

Problem: Your advanced woodshop class has a business that sells handcrafted wooden items for children, such as trains, tractors, and puzzles. You purchase the designs for these items from individuals. Your students calculate the cost of producing each item and determine a selling price. To track all of this information, you create a database that your students maintain. The database consists of two tables. The Product table contains information on products available for sale. The Supplier table contains information on the individuals that supply the designs.

Instructions: Perform the following tasks.

1. Create a new database in which to store all the objects related to the merchandise data. Call the database Wooden Crafts.

2. Create the Product table using the structure shown in Figure 1-79. Use the name Product for the table.

3. Add the data shown in Figure 1-79 to the Product table.

4. Print the Product table.

5. Create the Supplier table using the structure shown in Figure 1-80. Use the name Supplier for the table.

6. Add the data shown in Figure 1-80 to the Supplier table.

7. Print the Supplier table.

8. Create a form for the Product table. Use the name Product for the form.

9. Create and print the report shown in Figure 1-81 for the Product table.

Structure of Product table

FIELD NAME	DATA TYPE	FIELD SIZE	PRIMARY KEY?	DESCRIPTION
Product Id	Text	4	Yes	Product Id Number (Primary Key)
Description	Text	20		Description of Product
On Hand	Number			Number of Units On Hand
Cost	Currency			Cost of Product
Selling Price	Currency			Selling Price of Product
Supplier Code	Text	2		Code of Product Supplier

Data for Product table

PRODUCT ID	DESCRIPTION	ON HAND	COST	SELLING PRICE	SUPPLIER CODE
BF01	Barnyard Friends	3	$54.00	$60.00	PL
BL23	Blocks in Box	5	$29.00	$32.00	AP
CC14	Coal Car	8	$14.00	$18.00	BH
FT05	Fire Truck	7	$9.00	$12.00	AP
LB34	Lacing Bear	4	$12.00	$16.00	AP
MR06	Midget Railroad	3	$31.00	$34.00	BH
PJ12	Pets Jigsaw	10	$8.00	$12.00	PL
RB02	Railway Bridge	1	$17.00	$20.00	BH
SK10	Skyscraper	6	$25.00	$30.00	PL
UM09	USA Map	12	$14.00	$18.00	AP

FIGURE 1-79

Productivity in the Classroom

Structure for Supplier table

FIELD NAME	DATA TYPE	FIELD SIZE	PRIMARY KEY?	DESCRIPTION
Supplier Code	Text	2	Yes	Supplier Code (Primary Key)
First Name	Text	10		First Name of Supplier
Last Name	Text	15		Last Name of Supplier
Address	Text	20		Street Address
City	Text	20		City
State	Text	2		State (Two-Character Abbreviation)
Zip Code	Text	5		Zip Code (Five-Character Version)
Telephone Number	Text	12		Telephone Number (999-999-9999 Version)

Data for Supplier table

SUPPLIER CODE	FIRST NAME	LAST NAME	ADDRESS	CITY	STATE	ZIP CODE	TELEPHONE NUMBER
AP	Antonio	Patino	34 Fourth	Bastrop	NM	75123	505-555-1111
BH	Bert	Huntington	67 Beafort	Richford	CA	95418	707-555-3334
PL	Ping	Luang	12 Crestview	Mockington	AZ	85165	602-555-9990

FIGURE 1-80

2 Creating the Restaurant Supply Database

Problem: To provide your math students with an authentic learning experience, a local distributor of restaurant supplies has agreed to let your students create a supply database. The distributor sells non-food supplies such as napkins, paper towels, and cleaning supplies. The distributor employs sales representatives who receive a base salary as well as a commission on sales. The database consists of two tables. The Customer table contains information on the restaurants that buy supplies from the distributor. The Sales Rep table contains information on the sales representative assigned to the restaurant account.

Inventory Report

Product Id	Description	On Hand	Cost
BF01	Barnyard Friends	3	$54.00
BL23	Blocks in Box	5	$29.00
CC14	Coal Car	8	$14.00
FT05	Fire Truck	7	$9.00
LB34	Lacing Bear	4	$12.00
MR06	Midget Railroad	3	$31.00
PJ12	Pets Jigsaw	10	$8.00
RB02	Railway Bridge	1	$17.00
SK10	Skyscraper	6	$25.00
UM09	USA Map	12	$14.00

FIGURE 1-81

(continued)

Productivity in the Classroom

Creating the Restaurant Supply Database *(continued)*

Instructions: Perform the following tasks.

1. Create a new database in which to store all the objects related to the restaurant data. Call the database Restaurant Supply.
2. Create the Customer table using the structure shown in Figure 1-82. Use the name Customer for the table.
3. Add the data shown in Figure 1-82 to the Customer table.
4. Print the Customer table.
5. Create the Sales Rep table using the structure shown in Figure 1-83. To change the field size for the Comm Rate field, click the row selector for the field, and then click the Field Size property box. Click the Field Size property box arrow, and then click Double in the list. Use the name Sales Rep for the table.

Structure of Customer table

DATA FIELD NAME	DATA TYPE	FIELD SIZE	PRIMARY KEY?	DESCRIPTION
Customer Number	Text	4	Yes	Customer Number (Primary Key)
Name	Text	20		Name of Customer
Address	Text	15		Street Address
Telephone	Text	8		Telephone (999-9999 Version)
Balance	Currency			Amount Currently Due
Amount Paid	Currency			Amount Paid Year-to-Date
Sales Rep Number	Text	2		Number of Sales Representative

Data for Customer table

CUSTOMER NUMBER	NAME	ADDRESS	TELEPHONE	BALANCE	AMOUNT PAID	SALES REP NUMBER
AM23	American Pie	223 Johnson	555-2150	$95.00	$1,595.00	44
BB34	Bob's Café	1939 Jackson	555-1939	$50.00	$0.00	51
BI15	Bavarian Inn	3294 Devon	555-7510	$445.00	$1,250.00	49
CB12	China Buffet	1632 Clark	555-0804	$45.00	$610.00	49
CM09	Curry and More	3140 Halsted	555-0604	$195.00	$980.00	51
EG07	El Gallo	1805 Broadway	555-1404	$0.00	$1,600.00	44
JS34	Joe's Seafood	2200 Lawrence	555-0313	$260.00	$600.00	49
LV20	Little Venice	13 Devon	555-5161	$100.00	$1,150.00	49
NC25	New Crete	1027 Wells	555-4210	$140.00	$450.00	44
RD03	Reuben's Deli	787 Monroe	555-7657	$0.00	$875.00	51
VG21	Veggie Gourmet	1939 Congress	555-6554	$60.00	$625.00	44

FIGURE 1-82

6. Add the data shown in Figure 1-83 to the Sales Rep table.
7. Print the Sales Rep table.
8. Create a form for the Customer table. Use the name Customer for the form.

Productivity in the Classroom

Structure of Sales Rep table

FIELD NAME	DATA TYPE	FIELD SIZE	PRIMARY KEY?	DESCRIPTION
Sales Rep Number	Text	2	Yes	Sales Rep Number (Primary Key)
Last Name	Text	15		Last Name of Sales Rep
First Name	Text	10		First Name of Sales Rep
Address	Text	15		Street Address
City	Text	15		City
State	Text	2		State (Two-Character Abbreviation)
Zip Code	Text	5		Zip Code (Five-Character Version)
Salary	Currency			Annual Base Salary
Comm Rate	Number	Double		Commission Rate
Commission	Currency			Year-to-Date Total Commissions

Data for Sales Rep table

SALES REP NUMBER	LAST NAME	FIRST NAME	ADDRESS	CITY	STATE	ZIP CODE	SALARY	COMM RATE	COMMISSION
44	Charles	Pat	43 Fourth	Lawncrest	WA	67845	$19,000.00	0.05	$213.50
49	Gupta	Pinn	678 Hillcrest	Manton	OR	68923	$20,000.00	0.06	$216.60
51	Ortiz	Jose	982 Victoria	Lawncrest	WA	67845	$18,500.00	0.05	$92.75

FIGURE 1-83

9. Open the form you created and change the address for customer number EG07 to 185 Broad.
10. Change to Datasheet view and delete the record for customer number BB34.
11. Print the Customer table.
12. Create and print the report shown in Figure 1-84 for the Customer table.

Customer Status Report

Customer Number	Name	Balance	Amount Paid
AM23	American Pie	$95.00	$1,595.00
BI15	Bavarian Inn	$445.00	$1,250.00
CB12	China Buffet	$45.00	$610.00
CM09	Curry and More	$195.00	$980.00
EG07	El Gallo	$0.00	$1,600.00
JS34	Joe's Seafood	$260.00	$600.00
LV20	Little Venice	$100.00	$1,150.00
NC25	New Crete	$140.00	$450.00
RD03	Reuben's Deli	$0.00	$875.00
VG21	Veggie Gourmet	$60.00	$625.00

FIGURE 1-84

Productivity in the Classroom

3 Creating the Condo Management Database

Problem: Your Entrepreneurship class has selected property investment and rental as their business enterprise for this semester. Working with a local condo management company in a ski resort community, your students create and maintain the database. The company rents the condos by the week to ski vacationers. The database consists of two tables. The Condo table contains information on the units available for rent. The Owner table contains information on the owners of the rental units.

Instructions: Perform the following tasks.

1. Create a new database in which to store all the objects related to the rental data. Call the database Condo Management.
2. Create the Condo table using the structure shown in Figure 1-85. Use the name Condo for the table. Note that the table uses a new data type, Yes/No for the Powder Room and Linens fields. The Yes/No data type stores data that has one of two values. A Powder Room is a half-bathroom; that is, there is a sink and a toilet but no shower or tub.
3. Add the data shown in Figure 1-85 to the Condo table. To add a Yes value to the Powder Room and Linens fields, click the check box that displays in each field.

Structure of Condo table

FIELD NAME	DATA TYPE	FIELD SIZE	PRIMARY KEY?	DESCRIPTION
Unit Number	Text	3	Yes	Condo Unit Number (Primary Key)
Bedrooms	Number			Number of Bedrooms
Bathrooms	Number			Number of Bathrooms
Sleeps	Number			Maximum Number that can sleep in rental unit
Powder Room	Yes/No			Does the condo have a powder room?
Linens	Yes/No			Are linens (sheets and towels) furnished?
Weekly Rate	Currency			Weekly Rental Rate
Owner Id	Text	4		Id of Condo Unit's Owner

Data for Condo table

UNIT NUMBER	BEDROOMS	BATHROOMS	SLEEPS	POWDER ROOM	LINENS	WEEKLY RATE	OWNER ID
101	1	1	2			$675.00	HJ05
108	2	1	3		Y	$1,050.00	AB10
202	3	2	8	Y	Y	$1,400.00	BR18
204	2	2	6	Y		$1,100.00	BR18
206	2	2	5		Y	$950.00	GM50
308	2	2	6	Y	Y	$950.00	GM50
403	1	1	2			$700.00	HJ05
405	1	1	3			$750.00	AB10
500	3	3	8	Y	Y	$1,100.00	AB10
510	2	1	4	Y	Y	$825.00	BR18

FIGURE 1-85

Productivity
in the Classroom

Structure of Owner table

FIELD NAME	DATA TYPE	FIELD SIZE	PRIMARY KEY?	DESCRIPTION
Owner Id	Text	4	Yes	Owner Id (Primary Key)
Last Name	Text	15		Last Name of Owner
First Name	Text	10		First Name of Owner
Address	Text	15		Street Address
City	Text	15		City
State	Text	2		State (Two-Character Abbreviation)
Zip Code	Text	5		Zip Code (Five-Character Version)
Telephone	Text	12		Telephone Number (999-999-9999 Version)

4. Use Microsoft Access Help to learn how to resize column widths in Datasheet view and then reduce the size of the Unit Number, Bedrooms, Bathrooms, Sleeps, Powder Room, and Linens columns. Be sure to save the changes to the layout of the table.

Data for Owner table

OWNER ID	LAST NAME	FIRST NAME	ADDRESS	CITY	STATE	ZIP CODE	TELEPHONE
AB10	Alonso	Bonita	281 Robin	Whitehall	OK	45241	405-555-6543
BR18	Beerne	Renee	39 Oak	Pearton	WI	48326	715-555-7373
GM50	Graty	Mark	21 West 8th	Greenview	KS	31904	913-555-2225
HJ05	Heulbert	John	314 Central	Munkton	MI	49611	616-555-3333

FIGURE 1-86

5. Print the Condo table.
6. Create the Owner table using the structure shown in Figure 1-86. Use the name Owner for the table.
7. Add the data shown in Figure 1-86 to the Owner table.
8. Print the Owner table.
9. Create a form for the Condo table. Use the name Condo for the form.
10. Open the form you created and change the weekly rate for Unit Number 206 to $925.00.
11. Print the Condo table.
12. Create and print the report shown in Figure 1-87 for the Condo table.

Available Condo Rentals Report

Unit Number	Bedrooms	Bathrooms	Weekly Rate	Owner Id
101	1	1	$675.00	HJ05
108	2	1	$1,050.00	AB10
202	3	2	$1,400.00	BR18
204	2	2	$1,100.00	BR18
206	2	2	$925.00	GM50
308	2	2	$950.00	GM50
403	1	1	$700.00	HJ05
405	1	1	$750.00	AB10
500	3	3	$1,100.00	AB10
510	2	1	$825.00	BR18

FIGURE 1-87

Integration in the Classroom

Introduction: Integration in the Classroom is designed for teachers and other educators who are looking for innovative ways to integrate technology into their content-specific curriculum. Educators can use Microsoft Access to create, store, sort, retrieve, and maintain a variety of classroom data such as textbook inventories or student information. Access can make the process of maintaining such information easier and less time consuming.

Access also can be integrated easily into the curriculum. Any curriculum area can utilize databases in a variety of creative and motivating ways. Using databases can help students develop higher order thinking skills. Students learn to organize data, compare data by conducting queries and creating reports, and to evaluate and analyze data. Access is a very powerful database program that assists students in developing excellent thinking and information processing skills; skills that will serve them today and in the job market tomorrow.

Explore the integration ideas below. Ideas are presented for elementary, middle, high school, and special education classrooms. These ideas are meant to be a springboard for creativity. Take an idea and expand, modify, and use it in your classroom. Furthermore, many of the ideas can be adapted to fit any level or learning situation.

1. As an extension of your unit, "Ourselves and Our Families," you create a database where students enter their information with the assistance of a parent volunteer and they keep it updated throughout the year. In addition, you want to keep track of which students your parent volunteers work with. You and your students will use this information for a variety of purposes: assigning field trip groups, tutoring, creating thank you cards, tracking birthdays, learning about their community, their classmates, etc. You create the Student Information table using the structure shown in Figure 1-88 and the Parent Volunteer table using the structure shown in Figure 1-89.

Structure of Student Information table

FIELD NAME	DATA TYPE	FIELD SIZE	PRIMARY KEY?	DESCRIPTION
First Name	Text	10		First Name of Student
Middle Initial	Text	3		Middle Initial of Student
Last Name	Text	15		Last Name of Student
Date of Birth	Date/Time	12		Month/Day/Year
Address	Text	15		Street Address
City	Text	15		City
State	Text	2		State (Two-Character Abbreviation)
Zip Code	Text	5		Zip Code (Five-Character Version)
Telephone	Text	12		Telephone Number (999-999-9999) Version
Emergency Contact	Text	25		First and Last Name
Emergency Telephone Number	Text	12		Telephone Number (999-999-9999) Version
Parent Volunteer	Text	5		Initials of Parent Volunteer

FIGURE 1-88

Elementary

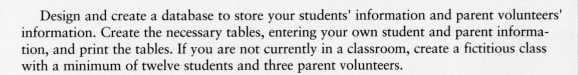

Integration in the Classroom

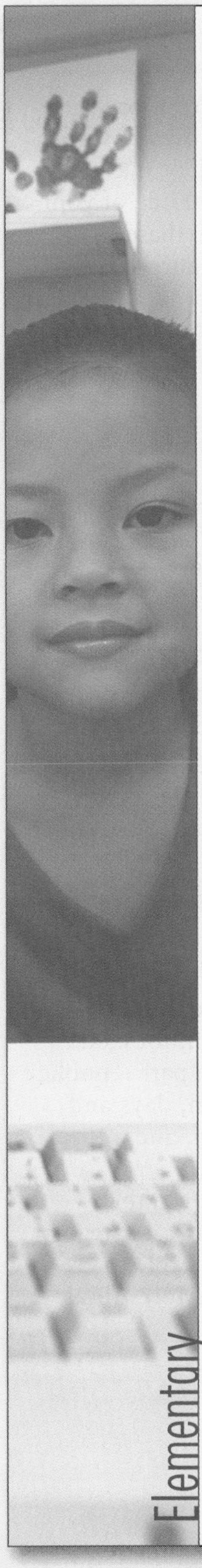

Design and create a database to store your students' information and parent volunteers' information. Create the necessary tables, entering your own student and parent information, and print the tables. If you are not currently in a classroom, create a fictitious class with a minimum of twelve students and three parent volunteers.

Structure of Parent Volunteer table				
FIELD NAME	DATA TYPE	FIELD SIZE	PRIMARY KEY?	DESCRIPTION
First Name	Text	10		First Name of Volunteer
Last Name	Text	15		Last Name of Volunteer
Initials	Text	3		First Initial of First Name, First Initial of Last Name
Telephone	Text	12		Telephone Number (999-999-9999) Version

FIGURE 1-89

2. As an extension of your fifth grade students' favorite author project, you have the students create a database. Students will include all of the titles of books written by the four authors used in the survey (J.K. Rowling, Madeline L'Engle, R.L. Stine, and Roald Dahl). In addition, the students will include other authors of books they are reading, both at home and at school, and the works of those authors as well. You also want the students to learn about creating a bibliography. Use the structure shown in Figure 1-90 for the Author table and the structure shown in Figure 1-91 for the Bibliography table.

Design and create a database to store the data related to your author project. Create the necessary tables. Include at least three titles for each author and at least four different publishing companies.

Structure of Author table				
FIELD NAME	DATA TYPE	FIELD SIZE	PRIMARY KEY?	DESCRIPTION
Last Name	Text	15		Last Name of Author
First Name	Text	10		First Name of Author
Title	Text	50		Title of Book
Number of Pages	Number			Number of Pages in the Book
Year Published	Text	5		Year Published
Publisher	Text	25		Name of Publisher

FIGURE 1-90

Structure of Bibliography table				
FIELD NAME	DATA TYPE	FIELD SIZE	PRIMARY KEY?	DESCRIPTION
Publisher	Text	25		Name of Publisher
City	Text	15		City
State	Text	2		State (Two-Character Abbreviation)

Elementary

FIGURE 1-91

(continued)

Integration
in the Classroom

Integration in the Classroom (*continued*)

3. You are teaching a unit on math in sports to your middle school students. Your town has recently obtained a minor league baseball team. The team owners and the town government are vigorously promoting the benefits of the new team. As a part of their marketing strategy, they are selling items with the new team logo. The team owners are one of your school's business partners. As a part of your unit, your students create a database to keep track of inventory and suppliers. The current inventory is shown in Figure 1-92. Your students will maintain the database throughout the school year.

Design and create a database to store the team's inventory. Then create the necessary tables, enter the data from Figure 1-92, and print the tables.

ITEM ID	DESCRIPTION	UNITS ON HAND	COST	SELLING PRICE	SUPPLIER CODE	SUPPLIER NAME	SUPPLIER TELEPHONE
3663	Baseball Cap	30	$10.15	$18.95	LG	Logo Goods	517-555-3853
3683	Coasters (4)	12	$7.45	$9.00	BH	Beverage Holders	317-555-4747
4563	Coffee Mug	20	$1.85	$4.75	BH	Beverage Holders	317-555-4747
4593	Glasses (4)	8	$8.20	$10.75	BH	Beverage Holders	317-555-4747
5923	Jacket	12	$44.75	$54.95	LG	Logo Goods	517-555-3853
5953	Shorts	10	$14.95	$19.95	AC	Al's Clothes	616-555-9228
6189	Sports Towel	24	$3.25	$6.75	LG	Logo Goods	517-555-3853
6343	Sweatshirt	9	$27.45	$34.95	AC	Al's Clothes	616-555-9228
7810	Tee Shirt	32	$9.50	$14.95	AC	Al's Clothes	616-555-9228
7930	Travel Mug	11	$2.90	$3.25	BH	Beverage Holders	317-555-4747

FIGURE 1-92

4. As a group project, students in your geography class select a state and research all of the attractions. The students organize their information by type of attraction, for example, museums, historic sites, zoos, botanical gardens, nature trails, hike/bike paths, public parks, or other attractions. Students need to list the address of the attraction, days and times it is open, whether or not there is a cost associated with the attraction, and a telephone number for more information.

Design and create a database for your students to use. Create the necessary tables, enter some sample data, and print the tables. **Note:** Type of attraction is really a category into which the attraction fits. Use the Table Wizard and select the Category table to create this table. If you want, you can rename the files in the table. (**Hint:** See More About Creating a Table: The Table Wizard on page A 1.13.)

Middle School

Integration
in the Classroom

5. You assist seniors in your advanced technology class to raise money for college. Your students form a small business that helps local organizations in need of computer expertise. You have established a small clientele and have the students manage the business using a database. The students have gathered the information shown in Figure 1-93.

   Design and create a database to store the data related to the students' business. Then create the necessary tables, enter the data from Figure 1-93, and print the tables. To personalize this database, replace Jan Smith's name with your own name and the helpers' names with names of your students.

CUSTOMER NUMBER	NAME	ADDRESS	TELEPHONE NUMBER	BALANCE	HELPER ID	HELPER LAST NAME	HELPER FIRST NAME	HOURLY RATE
AL35	Alores Gifts	12 Thistle	555-1222	$145.00	89	Smith	Jan	$12.50
AR43	Arsan Co.	34 Green	555-3434	$180.00	82	Ortega	Javier	$12.45
BK18	Byrd's Kites	56 Pampas	555-5678	$0.00	82	Ortega	Javier	$12.45
CJ78	Cee J's	24 Thistle	555-4242	$170.00	78	Chang	Pinn	$12.35
CL45	Class Act	89 Lime	555-9876	$129.00	89	Smith	Jan	$12.50
LB42	Le Boutique	12 Lemon	555-9012	$160.00	82	Ortega	Javier	$12.45
LK23	Learn n Kids	44 Apple	555-4004	$0.00	78	Chang	Pinn	$12.35
ME30	Meeker Co.	789 Poppy	555-0987	$195.00	89	Smith	Jan	$12.50
RE20	Ready Eats	90 Orange	555-9123	$0.00	78	Chang	Pinn	$12.35
SR34	Shoe Repair	62 Lime	555-4378	$140.00	89	Smith	Jan	$12.50

FIGURE 1-93

6. The high school Math club has started a tutoring program. Math club members are tutoring elementary students in basic math concepts. Each math club member is assigned one or more students to tutor. The elementary students who participate can earn points that can be redeemed for prizes donated by local merchants. Club members who participate keep track of the hours they spend tutoring. The state has promised to reward the high school club with the most number of tutoring hours. The club must keep track of the elementary students including each student's name, school the student attends, year in school, identity of the high school student tutor, and hours tutored. The club also must keep track of the high school students recording such information as name, year in school, and total number of hours spent tutoring.

   Design and create a database to meet the Math club's needs.

High School

(continued)

Integration in the Classroom

Integration in the Classroom *(continued)*

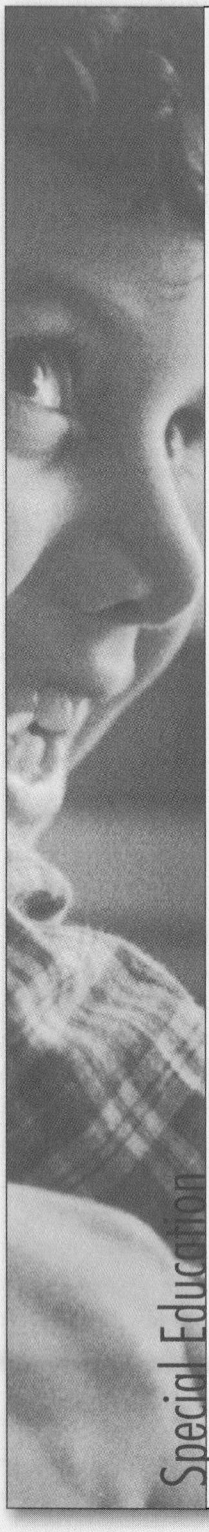

7. As a cross-curricular project, your ESE second grade class will study zoo animals and the countries they come from. As a culminating activity you are taking a field trip to the zoo. You want the students to have the opportunity to learn about animals in a creative way. Students will gather information about zoo animals from books, the Internet, and multi-media CD-ROMs. With the help of a parent volunteer, the students will enter information into a database. In addition, the students will enter information about the countries the animals come from. Use the structure shown in Figure 1-94 on the next page for the Animal table and the structure shown in Figure 1-95 on the next page for the Country of Origin table.

   Design and create a database for this project. Create the necessary tables. Include at least three animals and at least three different countries.

Structure of Animal table				
FIELD NAME	*DATA TYPE*	*FIELD SIZE*	*PRIMARY KEY?*	*DESCRIPTION*
Animal Name	Text	15	Yes	Animal Name
Habitat	Text	25		Habitat of Animal
Food	Text	40		What the Animal Eats
Weight/Size	Number	5		Weight or Size of the Animal
Number of Offspring	Number	2		Number of Offspring
Country of Origin	Text	5		Country (Abbreviation)

FIGURE 1-94

Structure of Country of Origin table				
FIELD NAME	*DATA TYPE*	*FIELD SIZE*	*PRIMARY KEY?*	*DESCRIPTION*
Country Code	Text	5		Country Abbreviation
Region	Text	15		Region of Country
Climate	Text	15		Climate

FIGURE 1-95

8. As a part of your special education students' printing business, you have the students create a database to track their business information. The database consists of two tables. The Product table contains information on the products available for sale (small notepads, medium notepads, note cards, and greeting cards). The Supplier table contains information on the individuals that supply the products.

   Determine the type of data you will include in the database, then design and create a database for this project. Create the necessary tables, enter some sample data, and print the tables.

Special Education

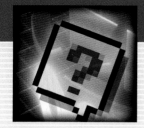

APPENDIX A
Microsoft Office XP Help System

Using the Microsoft Office Help System

This appendix demonstrates how you can use the Microsoft Office XP Help system to answer your questions. At anytime while you are using one of the Microsoft Office XP applications, you can interact with the Help system to display information on any topic associated with the application. To illustrate the use of the Microsoft Office XP Help system, you will use the Microsoft Word 2002 application in this appendix. The Help systems in other Microsoft Office XP applications respond in a similar fashion.

As shown in Figure A-1, you can access Word's Help system in four primary ways:

1. Ask a Question box on the menu bar
2. Function key F1 on the keyboard
3. Microsoft Word Help command on the Help menu
4. Microsoft Word Help button on the Standard toolbar

If you use the Ask a Question box on the menu bar, Word responds by opening the Microsoft Word Help window, which gives you direct access to its Help system. If you use one of the other three ways to access Word's Help system, Word responds in one of two ways:

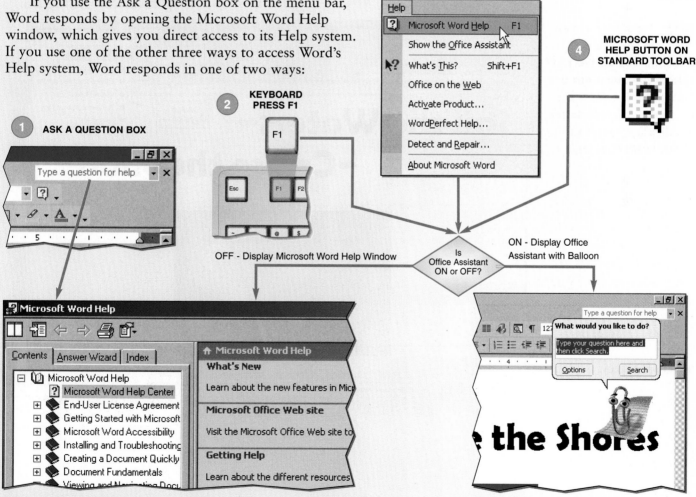

FIGURE A-1

1. If the Office Assistant is turned on, then the Office Assistant displays with a balloon (lower-right side in Figure A-1 on the previous page).
2. If the Office Assistant is turned off, then the Microsoft Word Help window displays (lower-left side in Figure A-1 on the previous page).

The best way to familiarize yourself with the Word Help system is to use it. The next several pages show examples of how to use the Help system. Following the examples are a set of exercises titled Use Help that will sharpen your Word Help system skills.

Ask a Question Box

The **Ask a Question box** on the right side of the menu bar lets you type questions in your own words, or you can type terms, such as template, smart tags, or speech. Word responds by displaying a list of topics related to the term(s) you entered. The following steps show how to use the Ask a Question box to obtain information about how smart tags work.

Steps **To Obtain Help Using the Ask a Question Box**

1 **Type** smart tags **in the Ask a Question box on the right side of the menu bar and then press the ENTER key. When the Ask a Question list displays, point to the About smart tags link.**

The Ask a Question list displays (Figure A-2). Clicking the See more link displays a new list of topics in the Ask a Question list. As you enter questions and terms in the Ask a Question box, Word adds them to its list. If you click the Ask a Question box arrow, a list of previously asked questions and terms will display.

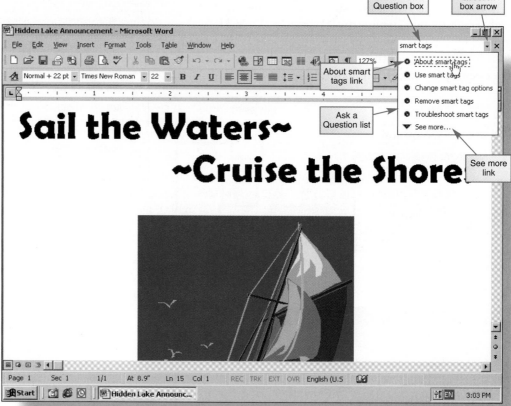

FIGURE A-2

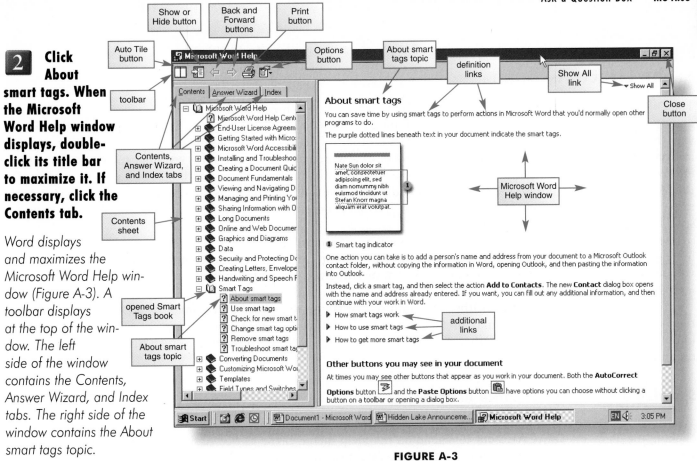

FIGURE A-3

2 **Click About smart tags. When the Microsoft Word Help window displays, double-click its title bar to maximize it. If necessary, click the Contents tab.**

Word displays and maximizes the Microsoft Word Help window (Figure A-3). A toolbar displays at the top of the window. The left side of the window contains the Contents, Answer Wizard, and Index tabs. The right side of the window contains the About smart tags topic.

3 **Click the Close button on the Microsoft Word Help window title bar.**

The Microsoft Word Help window closes and the document window is active.

The right side of the Microsoft Word Help window shown in Figure A-3 contains the About smart tags topic. The two links at the top of the window, smart tags and actions, display in blue font. Clicking either of these links displays a definition in green font following the link. Clicking again removes the definition. The How smart tags work link, How to use smart tags link, and How to get more smart tags link also display on the right side of the window. Clicking one of these links displays additional information about the link. Clicking again removes the information. Clicking the Show All link in the upper-right corner of the window causes the text associated with each link to display. In addition, the Hide All link replaces the Show All link.

If the Contents sheet is active on the left side of the Microsoft Word Help window, then Word opens the book that pertains to the topic for which you are requesting help. In this case, Word opens the Smart Tags book, which includes a list of topics related to smart tags. If you need additional information about the topic, you can click one of the topics listed below the Smart Tags book name.

The six buttons on the toolbar in the Microsoft Word Help window (Figure A-3) allow you to navigate through the Help system, change the display, and print the contents of the window. Table A-1 lists the function of each button on the toolbar.

Table A-1	Microsoft Word Help Toolbar Buttons	
BUTTON	**NAME**	**FUNCTION**
	Auto Tile	Tiles the Microsoft Word Help window and Microsoft Word window when the Microsoft Word Help window is maximized
or	Show or Hide	Displays or hides the Contents, Answer Wizard, and Index tabs
	Back	Displays the previous Help topic
	Forward	Displays the next Help topic
	Print	Prints the current Help topic
	Options	Displays a list of commands

The Office Assistant

The **Office Assistant** is an icon that displays in the Word window (shown in the lower-right side of Figure A-1 on page MO A.01) when it is turned on and not hidden. It has dual functions. First, it will respond in the same way the Ask a Question box does with a list of topics that relate to an entry you make in the text box at the bottom of the balloon. The entry can be in the form of a word, phrase, or question written as if you were talking. For example, if you want to learn more about saving a file, in the balloon text box, you can type any of the following terms or phrases: save, save a file, how do I save a file, or anything similar. The Office Assistant responds by displaying a list of topics from which you can choose. Once you choose a topic, it displays the corresponding information.

Second, the Office Assistant monitors your work and accumulates tips during a session on how you might increase your productivity and efficiency. You can view the tips at anytime. The accumulated tips display when you activate the Office Assistant balloon. Also, if at anytime you see a lightbulb above the Office Assistant, click it to display the most recent tip.

You may or may not want the Office Assistant to display on the screen at all times. You can hide it, and then show it at a later time. You may prefer not to use the Office Assistant at all. Thus, not only do you need to know how to show and hide the Office Assistant, but you also need to know how to turn the Office Assistant on and off.

Showing and Hiding the Office Assistant

When Word initially is installed, the Office Assistant may be off. You turn on the Office Assistant by clicking the **Show the Office Assistant command** on the Help menu. If the Office Assistant is on the screen and you want to hide it, you click the **Hide the Office Assistant command** on the Help menu. You also can right-click the Office Assistant to display its shortcut menu and then click the **Hide command** to hide it. You can move it to any location on the screen. You can click it to display the Office Assistant balloon, which allows you to request Help.

Turning the Office Assistant On and Off

The fact that the Office Assistant is hidden, does not mean it is turned off. To turn the Office Assistant off, it must be displaying in the Word window. You right-click it to display its shortcut menu (right side of Figure A-4). Next, click Options on the shortcut menu. When you click the **Options command**, the **Office Assistant dialog box** displays (left side of Figure A-4).

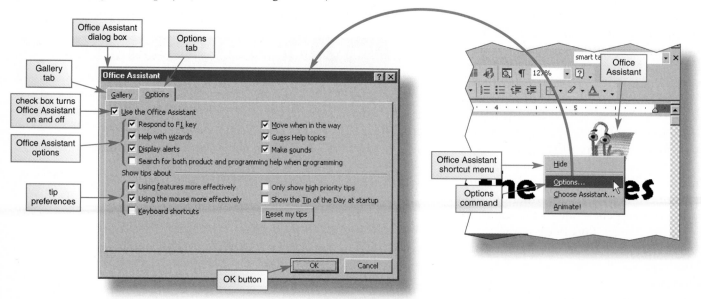

FIGURE A-4

In the **Options sheet** in the Office Assistant dialog box, the **Use the Office Assistant check box** at the top of the sheet determines whether the Office Assistant is on or off. To turn the Office Assistant off, remove the check mark from the Use the Office Assistant check box and then click the OK button. As shown in Figure A-1 on page MO A.01, if the Office Assistant is off when you invoke Help, then Word displays the Microsoft Word Help window instead of displaying the Office Assistant. To turn the Office Assistant on later, click the **Show the Office Assistant command** on the Help menu.

Through the Options command on the Office Assistant shortcut menu, you can change the look and feel of the Office Assistant. For example, you can hide the Office Assistant, turn the Office Assistant off, change the way it works, choose a different Office Assistant icon, or view an animation of the current one. These options also are available by clicking the **Options button** that displays in the Office Assistant balloon (Figure A-5).

The **Gallery sheet** (Figure A-4) in the Office Assistant dialog box allows you to change the appearance of the Office Assistant. The default is the paper clip (Clippit). You can change it to a bouncing red happy face (The Dot), a robot (F1), the Microsoft Office logo (Office Logo), a wizard (Merlin), the earth (Mother Nature), a cat (Links), or a dog (Rocky).

Using the Office Assistant

As indicated earlier, the Office Assistant allows you to enter a word, phrase, or question and then responds by displaying a list of topics from which you can choose to display Help. The following steps show how to use the Office Assistant to obtain Help on speech recognition.

Steps To Use the Office Assistant

1 **If the Office Assistant is not turned on, click Help on the menu bar and then click Show the Office Assistant. Click the Office Assistant. When the Office Assistant balloon displays, type** what is speech recognition **in the text box immediately above the Options button. Point to the Search button.**

The Office Assistant balloon displays and the question, what is speech recognition, displays in the text box (Figure A-5).

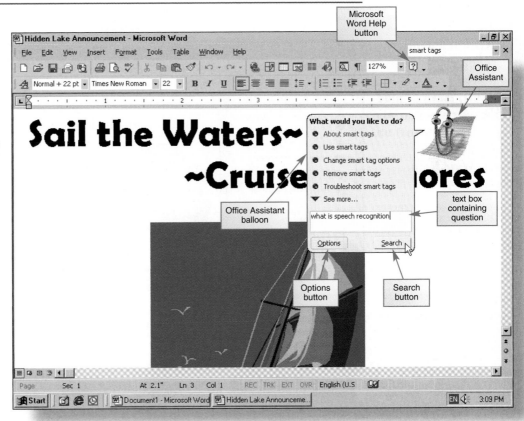

FIGURE A-5

2 **Click the Search button. When the Office Assistant balloon redisplays, point to the topic, About speech recognition.**

A list of links displays in the Office Assistant balloon (Figure A-6).

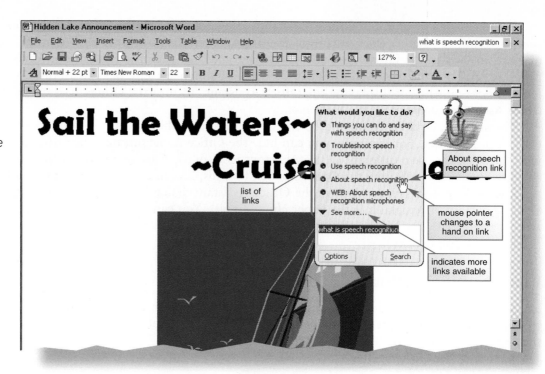

FIGURE A-6

3 **Click the topic, About speech recognition (Figure A-7). If necessary, move or hide the Office Assistant so you can view all of the text on the right side of the Microsoft Word Help window.**

The About speech recognition topic displays on the right side of the Microsoft Word Help window (Figure A-7). Clicking the Show All link in the upper-right corner of the window expands all links.

4 **Click the Close button on the Microsoft Word Help window title bar to close Help.**

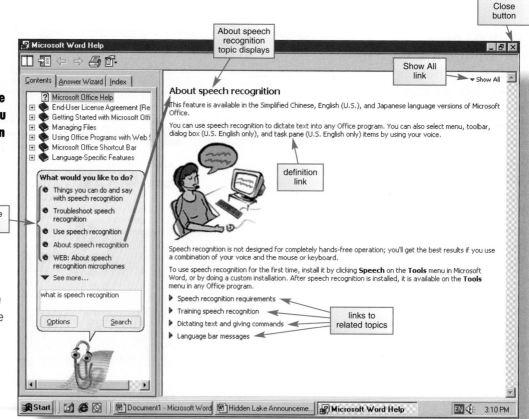

FIGURE A-7

The Microsoft Word Help Window

If the Office Assistant is turned off and you click the Microsoft Word Help button on the Standard toolbar, the Microsoft Word Help window displays (Figure A-8). The left side of this window contains three tabs: Contents, Answer Wizard, and Index. Each tab displays a sheet with powerful look-up capabilities.

Use the Contents sheet as you would a table of contents at the front of a book to look up Help. The Answer Wizard sheet answers your queries the same as the Office Assistant. You use the Index sheet in the same fashion as an index in a book to look up Help. Click the tabs to move from sheet to sheet.

Besides clicking the Microsoft Word Help button on the Standard toolbar, you also can click the Microsoft Word Help command on the Help menu, or press the F1 key to display the Microsoft Word Help window to gain access to the three sheets. To close the Microsoft Word Help window, click the Close button in the upper-right corner on the title bar.

Using the Contents Sheet

The **Contents sheet** is useful for displaying Help when you know the general category of the topic in question, but not the specifics. The following steps show how to use the Contents sheet to obtain information about handwriting recognition.

TO OBTAIN HELP USING THE CONTENTS SHEET

1 Click the Microsoft Word Help button on the Standard toolbar (shown in Figure A-5 on page MO A.05).

2 When the Microsoft Word Help window displays, double-click the title bar to maximize the window. If necessary, click the Show button to display the tabs.

3 Click the Contents tab. Double-click the Handwriting and Speech Recognition book in the Contents sheet. Double-click the Handwriting Recognition book.

4 Click the subtopic, About handwriting recognition, below the Handwriting Recognition book (Figure A-8).

5 Close the Microsoft Help window.

Word displays Help on the subtopic, About handwriting recognition (Figure A-8).

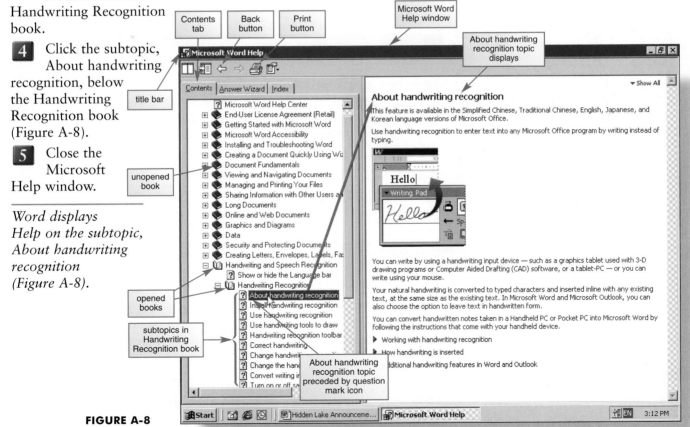

FIGURE A-8

Once the information on the subtopic displays, you can read it or you can click the Print button to obtain a printed copy. If you decide to click another subtopic on the left or a link on the right, you can get back to the Help page shown in Figure A-8 on the previous page by clicking the Back button.

Each topic in the Contents list is preceded by a book icon or question mark icon. A **book icon** indicates subtopics are available. A **question mark icon** means information on the topic will display if you double-click the title. The book icon opens when you double-click the book (or its title) or click the plus sign (+) to the left of the book icon.

Using the Answer Wizard Sheet

The **Answer Wizard sheet** works like the Office Assistant in that you enter a word, phrase, or question and it responds by listing topics from which you can choose to display Help. The following steps show how to use the Answer Wizard sheet to obtain Help on translating or looking up text in the dictionary of another language.

TO OBTAIN HELP USING THE ANSWER WIZARD SHEET

1 With the Office Assistant turned off, click the Microsoft Word Help button on the Standard toolbar (shown in Figure A-5 on page MO A.05).

2 When the Microsoft Word Help window displays, double-click the title bar to maximize the window. If necessary, click the Show button to display the tabs.

3 Click the Answer Wizard tab. Type translation in the What would you like to do? text box on the left side of the window. Click the Search button.

4 When a list of topics displays in the Select topic to display list, click Translate or look up text in the dictionary of another language (Figure A-9).

5 Close the Microsoft Help window.

Word displays Help on how to translate or look up text in the dictionary of a different language on the right side of the Microsoft Word Help window (Figure A-9).

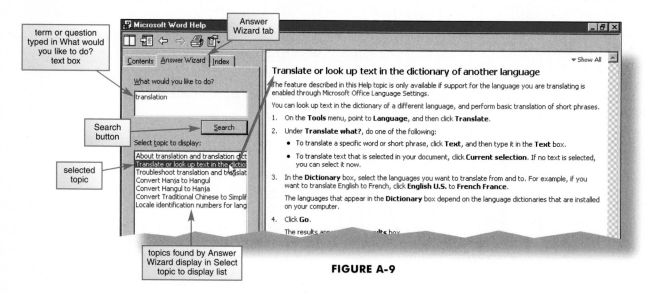

FIGURE A-9

If the topic, Translate or look up text in the dictionary of another language, does not include the information you are seeking, click another topic in the list. Continue to click topics until you find the desired information.

Using the Index Sheet

The third sheet in the Microsoft Word Help window is the Index sheet. Use the **Index sheet** to display Help when you know the keyword or the first few letters of the keyword you want to look up. The following steps show how to use the Index sheet to obtain Help on understanding the readability scores available to evaluate the reading level of a document.

What's This? Command and Question Mark Button • MO A.09

APPENDIX A

TO OBTAIN HELP USING THE INDEX SHEET

1 With the Office Assistant turned off, click the Microsoft Word Help button on the Standard toolbar (shown in Figure A-5 on page MO A.05).

2 When the Microsoft Word Help window displays, double-click the title bar to maximize the window. If necessary, click the Show button to display the tabs.

3 Click the Index tab. Type `readability` in the Type keywords text box on the left side of the window. Click the Search button.

4 When a list of topics displays in the Choose a topic list, click Readability scores.

5 When the Readability scores topic displays on the right side of the window (Figure A-10), click the Show All link in the upper-right corner of the right side of the window.

Word displays information about readability scores and two links on the right side of the window (Figure A-10). Clicking the Show All link expands the two links and displays the Hide All link. As you type readability into the Type keywords box, Word recognizes and completes the word and automatically appends a semicolon to the keyword.

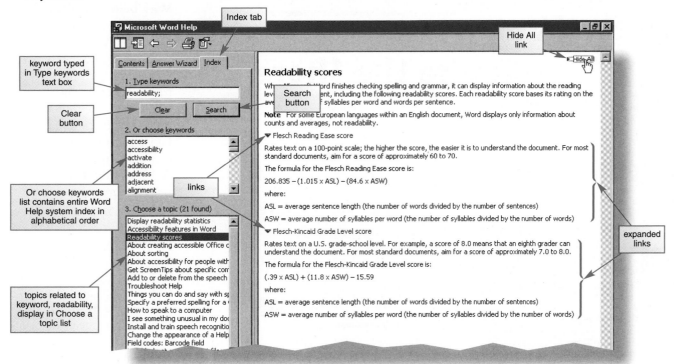

FIGURE A-10

An alternative to typing a keyword in the Type keywords text box is to scroll through the Or choose keywords list (the middle list on the left side of the window). When you locate the keyword you are searching for, double-click it to display Help on the topic. Also in the Or choose keywords list, the Word Help system displays other topics that relate to the new keyword. As you begin typing a new keyword in the Type keywords text box, Word jumps to that point in the middle list box. To begin a new search, click the Clear button.

What's This? Command and Question Mark Button

Use the What's This? command on the Help menu or the Question Mark button in a dialog box when you are not sure what an object on the screen is or what it does.

Microsoft **Office**

What's This? Command

You use the **What's This? command** on the Help menu to display a detailed ScreenTip. When you click this command, the mouse pointer changes to an arrow with a question mark. You then click any object on the screen, such as a button, to display the ScreenTip. For example, after you click the What's This? command on the Help menu and then click the Zoom box on the Standard toolbar, a description of the Zoom box displays (Figure A-11). You can print the ScreenTip by right-clicking it and then clicking Print Topic on the shortcut menu.

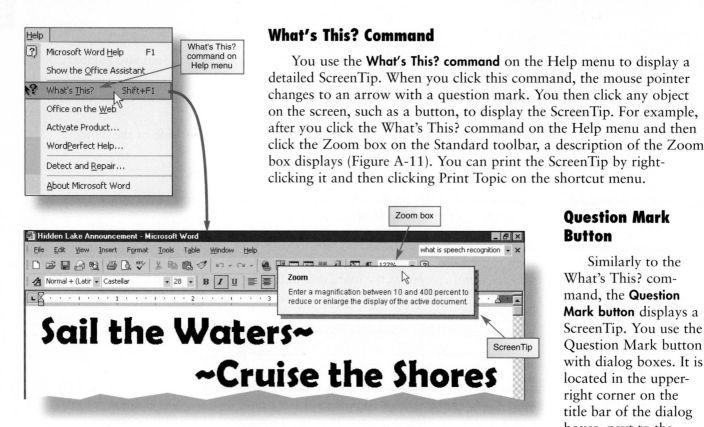

FIGURE A-11

Question Mark Button

Similarly to the What's This? command, the **Question Mark button** displays a ScreenTip. You use the Question Mark button with dialog boxes. It is located in the upper-right corner on the title bar of the dialog boxes, next to the Close button. For example, in Figure A-12, the Print dialog box displays on the screen. If you click the Question Mark button in the upper-right corner of the dialog box and then click the Print to file check box, an explanation of the Print to file check box displays in a ScreenTip. You can print the ScreenTip by right-clicking it and clicking Print Topic on the shortcut menu.

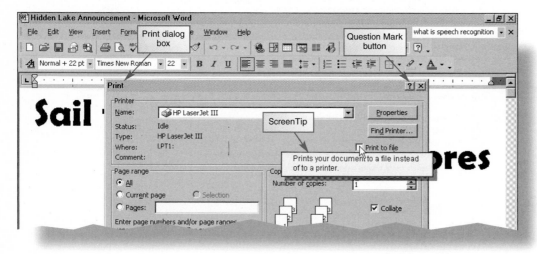

FIGURE A-12

If a dialog box does not include a Question Mark button, press SHIFT+F1. This combination of keys will change the mouse pointer to an arrow with a question mark. You then can click any object in the dialog box to display the ScreenTip.

Office on the Web Command

The **Office on the Web command** on the Help menu displays a Microsoft Web page containing up-to-date information on a variety of Office-related topics. To use this command, you must be connected to the Internet. When you invoke the Office on the Web command, the Assistance Center Home page displays. Read through the links that in general pertain to topics that relate to all Office XP topics. Scroll down and click the Word link in the Help By Product area to display the Assistance Center Word Help Articles Web page (Figure A-13). This Web page contains numerous helpful links related to Word.

Other Help Commands

Four additional commands available on the Help menu are Activate Product, WordPerfect Help, Detect and Repair, and About Microsoft Word. The WordPerfect Help command is available only if it was included as part of a custom installation of Word 2002.

Activate Product Command

The **Activate Product command** on the Help menu lets you activate your Microsoft Office subscription if you selected the Microsoft Office Subscription mode.

WordPerfect Help Command

The **WordPerfect Help command** on the Help menu offers assistance to WordPerfect users

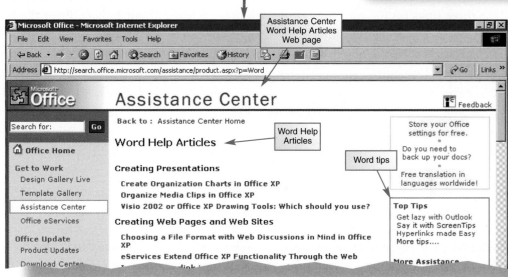

FIGURE A-13

switching to Word. When you choose this command, Word displays the Help for WordPerfect Users dialog box. The instructions in the dialog box step the user through the appropriate selections.

Detect and Repair Command

Use the **Detect and Repair command** on the Help menu if Word is not running properly or if it is generating errors. When you invoke this command, the Detect and Repair dialog box displays. Click the Start button in the dialog box to initiate the detect and repair process.

About Microsoft Word Command

The **About Microsoft Word command** on the Help menu displays the About Microsoft Word dialog box. The dialog box lists the owner of the software and the product identification. You need to know the product identification if you call Microsoft for assistance. The three buttons below the OK button are the System Info button, Tech Support button, and Disabled Items button. The **System Info button** displays system information, including hardware resources, components, software environment, Internet Explorer 5, and Office XP applications. The **Tech Support button** displays technical assistance information. The **Disabled Items button** displays a list of items that were disabled because they prevented Word from functioning correctly.

Use Help

1 Using the Ask a Question Box

Instructions: Perform the following tasks using the Word Help system.

1. Click the Ask a Question box on the menu bar, and then type how do I add a bullet. Press the ENTER key.
2. Click Add bullets or numbering in the Ask a Question list. If the Word window is not maximized, double-click the Microsoft Word Help window title bar. Read and print the information. One at a time, click the three links on the right side of the window to learn about bullets. Print the information. Hand in the printouts to your instructor.
3. If necessary, click the Show button to display the tabs. Click the Contents tab to prepare for the next step. Click the Close button in the Microsoft Word Help window.
4. Click the Ask a Question box and then press the ENTER key. Click About bulleted lists in the Ask a Question box. When the Microsoft Word Help window displays, maximize the window. Read and print the information. Click the two links on the right side of the window. Print the information. Hand in the printouts to your instructor.

2 Expanding on the Word Help System Basics

Instructions: Use the Word Help system to understand the topics better and answer the questions listed below. Answer the questions on your own paper, or hand in the printed Help information to your instructor.

1. If the Office Assistant is on, right-click the Office Assistant. When the shortcut menu displays, click Options. Click Use the Office Assistant to remove the check mark, and then click the OK button.
2. Click the Microsoft Word Help button on the Standard toolbar. Maximize the Microsoft Word Help window. Click Getting Help on the right side of the window. Click the five links in the About getting help while you work topic. Print the information and hand in the printouts to your instructor. Close the Microsoft Word Help window.
3. Press the F1 key. Maximize the Microsoft Word Help window. Click the Answer Wizard tab. Type help in the What would you like to do? text box, and then click the Search button. Click Guidelines for searching Help. Click the four links on the right side of the window. Print the information and hand in the printouts to your instructor.
4. Click the Contents tab. Click the plus sign (+) to the left of the Document Fundamentals book. Click the plus sign (+) to the left of the Selecting Text and Graphics book. One at a time, click the three topics below the Selecting Text and Graphics book. Read and print each one. Close the Microsoft Word Help window. Hand in the printouts to your instructor.
5. Click Help on the menu bar and then click What's This? Click the E-mail button on the Standard toolbar. Right-click the ScreenTip, click Print Topic on the shortcut menu, and click the Print button. Click Format on the menu bar and then click Paragraph. When the Paragraph dialog box displays, click the Question Mark button on the title bar. Click the Special box. Right-click the ScreenTip, click Print Topic, and then click the Print button. Close the Paragraph dialog box and Microsoft Word window.

APPENDIX B
Speech and Handwriting Recognition and Speech Playback

Introduction

This appendix discusses how you can create and modify documents using Office XP's new input technologies. Office XP provides a variety of **text services**, which enable you to speak commands and enter text in an application. The most common text service is the keyboard. Two new text services included with Office XP are speech recognition and handwriting recognition. The following pages use Word to illustrate the speech and hand-writing recognition capabilities of Office XP. Depending on the application you are using, some special features within speech or handwriting recognition may not be available.

When Windows was installed on your computer, you specified a default language. For example, most users in the United States select English (United States) as the default language. Through text services, you can add more than 90 additional languages and varying dialects such as Basque, English (Zimbabwe), French (France), French (Canada), German (Germany), German (Austria), and Swahili. With multiple languages available, you can switch from one language to another while working in an Office XP application. If you change the language or dialect, then text services may change the functions of the keys on the keyboard, adjust speech recognition, and alter handwriting recognition.

The Language Bar

You know that text services are installed properly when the Language Indicator button displays by the clock in the tray status area on the Windows taskbar (Figure B-1a) or the Language bar displays on the screen (Figure B-1b or B-1c). If the Language Indicator button displays in the tray status area, click it, and then click the **Show the Language bar command** (Figure B-1a). The Language bar displays on the screen in the same location it displayed last time.

You can drag the Language bar to any location in the window by pointing to its move handle, which is the vertical line on its left side (Figure B-1b). When the mouse pointer changes to a four-headed arrow, drag the Language bar to the desired location.

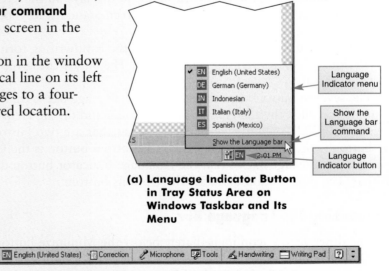

(a) Language Indicator Button in Tray Status Area on Windows Taskbar and Its Menu

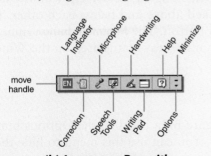

(b) Language Bar with Text Labels Disabled

(c) Language Bar with Text Labels Enabled

FIGURE B-1

If you are sure that one of the services was installed and neither the Language Indicator button nor the Language bar displays, then do the following:

1. Click Start on the Windows taskbar, point to Settings, click Control Panel, and then double-click the Text Services icon in the Control Panel window.
2. When the Text Services dialog box displays, click the Language Bar button, click the Show the Language bar on the desktop check box to select it, and then click the OK button in the Language Bar Settings dialog box.
3. Click the OK button in the Text Services dialog box.
4. Close the Control Panel window.

You can perform tasks related to text services by using the **Language bar**. The Language bar may display with just the icon on each button (Figure B-1b on the previous page) or it may display with text labels to the right of the icon on each button (Figure B-1c on the previous page). Changing the appearance of the Language bar will be discussed shortly.

Buttons on the Language Bar

The Language bar shown in Figure B-2a contains nine buttons. The number of buttons on your Language bar may be different. These buttons are used to select the language, customize the Language bar, control the microphone, control handwriting, and obtain help.

When you click the **Language Indicator button** on the far left side of the Language bar, the Language Indicator menu displays a list of the active languages (Figure B-2b) from which you can choose. When you select text and then click the **Correction button** (the second button from the left), a list of correction alternatives displays in the Word window (Figure B-2c). You can use the Correction button to correct both speech recognition and handwriting recognition errors. The **Microphone button**, the third button from the left, enables and disables the microphone. When the microphone is enabled, text services adds two buttons and a balloon to the Language toolbar (Figure B-2d). These additional buttons and the balloon will be discussed shortly.

The fourth button from the left on the Language bar is the Speech Tools button. The **Speech Tools button** displays a menu of commands (Figure B-2e) that allows you to hide or show the balloon on the Language bar; train the Speech Recognition service so that it can better interpret your voice; add and delete words from its dictionary, such as names and other words not understood easily; and change the user profile so more than one person can use the microphone on the same computer.

The fifth button from the left on the Language bar is the Handwriting button. The **Handwriting button** displays the **Handwriting menu** (Figure B-2f), which lets you choose the Writing Pad (Figure B-2g), Write Anywhere (Figure B-2h), the Drawing Pad (Figure B-2i), or the on-screen keyboard (Figure B-2j). The **On-Screen Symbol Keyboard command** on the Handwriting menu displays an on-screen keyboard that allows you to enter special symbols that are not available on the On-Screen Standard Keyboard. You can choose only one form of handwriting at a time.

The sixth button indicates which one of the handwriting forms is active. For example, in Figure B-1a on the previous page, the Writing Pad is active. The handwriting recognition capabilities of text services will be discussed shortly.

The seventh button from the left on the Language bar is the Help button. The **Help button** displays the Help menu. If you click the Language Bar Help command on the Help menu, the Language Bar Help window displays (Figure B-2k). On the far right of the Language bar are two buttons stacked above and below each other. The top button is the Minimize button and the bottom button is the Options button. The **Minimize button** minimizes (hides) the Language bar so that the Language Indicator button displays in the tray status area on the Windows taskbar. The next section discusses the Options button.

Customizing the Language Bar

The down arrow icon immediately below the Minimize button in Figure B-2a is called the Options button. The **Options button** displays a menu of text services options (Figure B-2l). You can use this menu to hide the Correction, Speech Tools, Handwriting, and Help buttons on the Language bar by clicking their names to remove the check mark to the left of each button. The Settings command on the Options menu displays a dialog box that lets you customize the Language bar. This command will be discussed shortly. The Restore Defaults command redisplays hidden buttons on the Language bar.

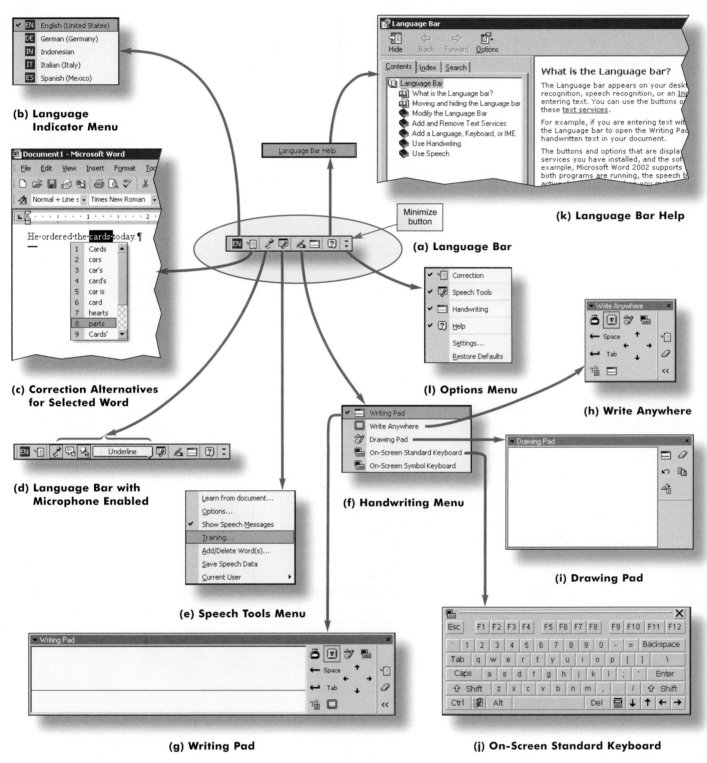

FIGURE B-2

If you right-click the Language bar, a shortcut menu displays (Figure B-3a on the next page). This shortcut menu lets you further customize the Language bar. The **Minimize command** on the shortcut menu minimizes the Language bar the same as the Minimize button on the Language bar. The **Transparency command** toggles the Language bar between being solid and transparent. You can see through a transparent Language bar (Figure B-3b). The **Text Labels command** toggles text labels on the Language bar on (Figure B-3c) and off (Figure B-3a). The **Additional icons in taskbar command** toggles between only showing the Language Indicator button in the tray status area and showing icons that represent the text services that are active (Figure B-3d).

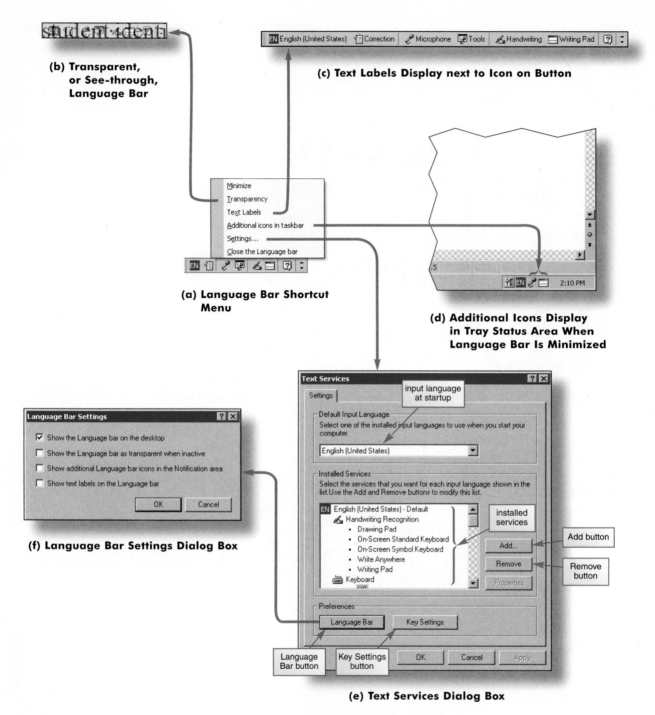

(b) Transparent, or See-through, Language Bar

(c) Text Labels Display next to Icon on Button

(a) Language Bar Shortcut Menu

(d) Additional Icons Display in Tray Status Area When Language Bar Is Minimized

(f) Language Bar Settings Dialog Box

(e) Text Services Dialog Box

FIGURE B-3

The **Settings command** displays the Text Services dialog box (Figure B-3e). The **Text Services dialog box** allows you to select the language at startup; add and remove text services; modify keys on the keyboard; and modify the Language bar. If you want to remove any one of the entries in the Installed Services list, select the entry, and then click the Remove button. If you want to add a service, click the Add button. The Key Settings button allows you to modify the keyboard. If you click the **Language Bar button** in the Text Services dialog box, the **Language Bar Settings dialog box** displays (Figure B-3f). This dialog box contains Language bar options, some of which are the same as the commands on the Language bar shortcut menu described earlier.

The **Close the Language bar command** on the shortcut menu shown in Figure B-3a closes the Language bar and hides the Language Indicator button in the tray status area on the Windows taskbar. If you close the Language bar and want to redisplay it, follow the instructions at the top of page MO B.02.

Speech Recognition

The **Speech Recognition service** available with all Office XP applications enables your computer to recognize human speech through a microphone. The microphone has two modes: dictation and voice command. The example in Figure B-4 uses Word to illustrate the speech recognition modes of Office XP. You switch between the two modes by clicking the Dictation button and the Voice Command button on the Language bar. These buttons display only when you turn on Speech Recognition by clicking the **Microphone button** on the Language bar (Figure B-5 on the next page). If you are using the Microphone button for the very first time in Word, it will require that you check your microphone settings and step through voice training before activating the Speech Recognition service.

The **Dictation button** places the microphone in Dictation mode. In **Dictation mode**, whatever you speak is entered as text at the location of the insertion point. The **Voice Command button** places the microphone in Voice Command mode. In **Voice Command mode**, whatever you speak is interpreted as a command. If you want to turn off the microphone, click the Microphone button on the Language bar or in Voice Command mode say, "Mic off" (pronounced mike off). It is important to remember that minimizing the Language bar does not turn off the microphone.

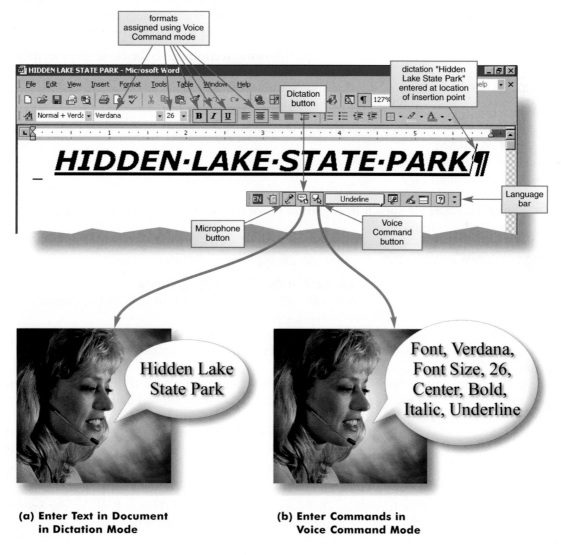

**(a) Enter Text in Document
in Dictation Mode**

**(b) Enter Commands in
Voice Command Mode**

FIGURE B-4

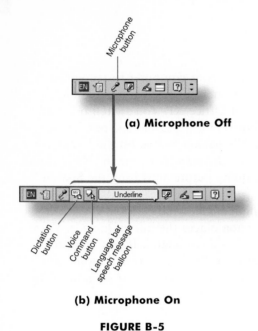

(a) Microphone Off

(b) Microphone On

FIGURE B-5

The **Language bar speech message balloon** shown in Figure B-5b displays messages that may offer help or hints. In Voice Command mode, the name of the last recognized command you said displays. If you use the mouse or keyboard instead of the microphone, a message will appear in the Language bar speech message balloon indicating the word you could say. In Dictation mode, the message, Dictating, usually displays. The Speech Recognition service, however, will display messages to inform you that you are talking too soft, too loud, too fast, or to ask you to repeat what you said by displaying, What was that?

Getting Started with Speech Recognition

For the microphone to function properly, you should follow these steps:

1. Make sure your computer meets the minimum requirements.
2. Install Speech Recognition.
3. Set up and position your microphone, preferably a close-talk headset with gain adjustment support.
4. Train the Speech Recognition service.

The following sections describe these steps in more detail.

SPEECH RECOGNITION SYSTEM REQUIREMENTS   For Speech Recognition to work on your computer, it needs the following:

1. Microsoft Windows 98 or later or Microsoft Windows NT 4.0 or later
2. At least 128 MB RAM
3. 400 MHz or faster processor
4. Microphone and sound card

INSTALLING SPEECH RECOGNITION   If Speech Recognition is not installed on your computer, start Microsoft Word and then click Speech on the Tools menu.

SET UP AND POSITION YOUR MICROPHONE   Set up your microphone as follows:

1. Connect your microphone to the sound card in the back of the computer.
2. Position the microphone approximately one inch out from and to the side of your mouth. Position it so you are not breathing into it.
3. On the Language bar, click the Speech Tools button, and then click Options (Figure B-6a).
4. When the Speech Properties dialog box displays (Figure B-6b), if necessary, click the Speech Recognition tab.
5. Click the Configure Microphone button. Follow the Microphone Wizard directions as shown in Figures B-6c, B-6d, and B-6e. The Next button will remain dimmed in Figure B-6d until the volume meter consistently stays in the green area.
6. If someone else installed Speech Recognition, click the New button in the Speech Properties dialog box and enter your name and then click the Finish button. Click the Train Profile button and step through the Voice Training Wizard. The Voice Training Wizard will require that you enter your gender and age group. It then will step you through voice training.

You can adjust the microphone further by clicking the **Settings button** (Figure B-6b) in the Speech Properties dialog box. The Settings button displays the **Recognition Profile Settings dialog box** that allows you to adjust the pronunciation sensitivity and accuracy versus recognition response time.

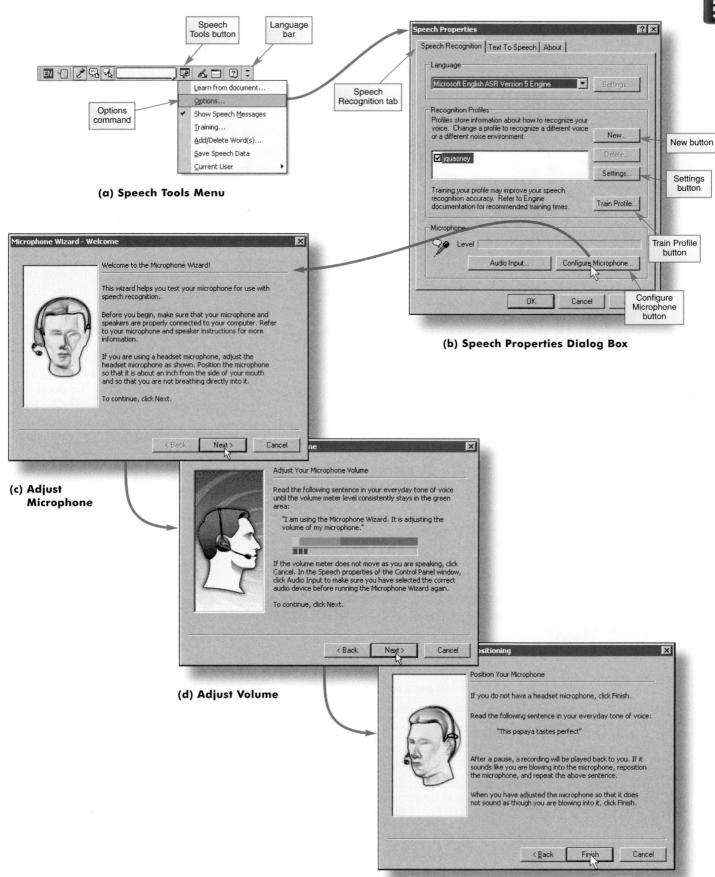

(a) **Speech Tools Menu**

(b) **Speech Properties Dialog Box**

(c) **Adjust Microphone**

(d) **Adjust Volume**

(e) **Test Microphone**

FIGURE B-6

TRAIN THE SPEECH RECOGNITION SERVICE   The Speech Recognition service will understand most commands and some dictation without any training at all. It will recognize much more of what you speak, however, if you take the time to train it. After one training session, it will recognize 85 to 90 percent of your words. As you do more training, accuracy will rise to 95 percent. If you feel that too many mistakes are being made, then continue to train the service. The more training you do, the more accurately it will work for you. Follow these steps to train the Speech Recognition service:

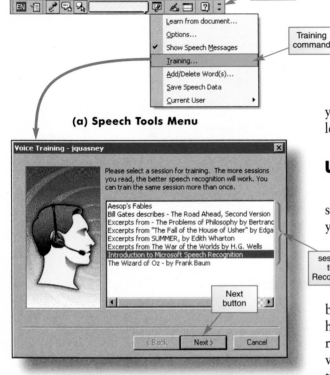

(a) Speech Tools Menu

(b) Voice Training Dialog Box

FIGURE B-7

1. Click the Speech Tools button on the Language bar and then click Training (Figure B-7a).
2. When the **Voice Training dialog box** displays (Figure B-7b), click one of the sessions and then click the Next button.
3. Complete the training session, which should take less than 15 minutes.

If you are serious about using a microphone to speak to your computer, you need to take the time to go through at least three of the eight training sessions listed in Figure B-7b.

Using Speech Recognition

Speech recognition lets you enter text into a document similarly to speaking into a tape recorder. Instead of typing, you can dictate text that you want to display in the document, and you can issue voice commands. In **Voice Command mode**, you can speak menu names, commands on menus, toolbar button names, and dialog box option buttons, check boxes, list boxes, and button names. Speech Recognition, however, is not a completely hands-free form of input. Speech recognition works best if you use a combination of your voice, the keyboard, and the mouse. You soon will discover that Dictation mode is far less accurate than Voice Command mode. Table B-1 lists some tips that will improve the Speech Recognition service's accuracy considerably.

Table B-1	Tips to Improve Speech Recognition
NUMBER	**TIP**
1	The microphone hears everything. Though the Speech Recognition service filters out background noise, it is recommended that you work in a quiet environment.
2	Try not to move the microphone around once it is adjusted.
3	Speak in a steady tone and speak clearly.
4	In Dictation mode, do not pause between words. A phrase is easier to interpret than a word. Sounding out syllables in a word will make it more difficult for the Speech Recognition service to interpret what you are saying.
5	If you speak too loudly or too softly, it makes it difficult for the Speech Recognition service to interpret what you said. Check the Language bar speech message balloon for an indication that you may be speaking too loudly or too softly.
6	If you experience problems after training, adjust the recognition options that control accuracy and rejection by clicking the Settings button shown in Figure B-6b on the previous page.
7	When you are finished using the microphone, turn it off by clicking the Microphone button on the Language bar or in Voice Command mode say, "Mic off." Leaving the microphone on is the same as leaning on the keyboard.
8	If the Speech Recognition service is having difficulty with unusual words, then add the words to its dictionary by using the Learn from document command or Add/Delete Word(s) command on the Speech Tools menu (Figure B-8a). The last names of individuals and the names of companies are good examples of the types of words you should add to the dictionary.
9	Training will improve accuracy; practice will improve confidence.

The last command on the Speech Tools menu is the Current User command (Figure B-8a). The **Current User command** is useful for multiple users who share a computer. It allows them to configure their own individual profiles, and then switch between users as they use the computer.

For additional information on the Speech Recognition service, click the Help button on the Standard toolbar, click the Answer Wizard tab, and search for the phrase, Speech Recognition.

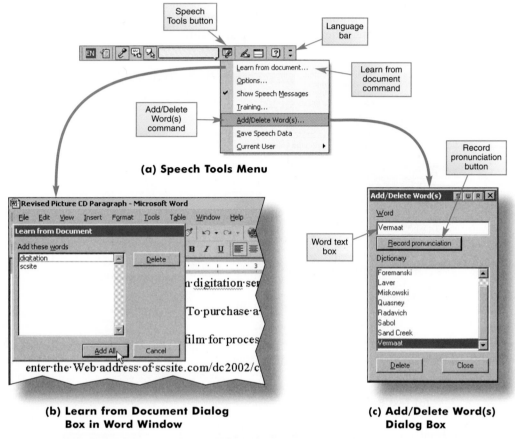

FIGURE B-8

Handwriting Recognition

Using the Office XP handwriting recognition capabilities, you can enter text and numbers into all Office XP applications by writing instead of typing. You can write using a special handwriting device that connects to your computer or you can write on the screen using your mouse. Four basic methods of handwriting are available by clicking the **Handwriting button** on the Language bar: Writing Pad, Write Anywhere, Drawing Pad, and On-Screen Keyboard. Although the on-screen keyboard does not involve handwriting recognition, it is part of the Handwriting menu and, therefore, will be discussed in this section. The following pages use Word to illustrate the handwriting recognition capabilities available in most Office XP applications.

If your Language bar does not include the Handwriting button (Figures B-1b or B-1c on page MO B.01), then for installation instructions click the Help button on the Standard toolbar, click the Answer Wizard tab, and search for the phrase Install Handwriting Recognition.

Writing Pad

To display the Writing Pad, click the Handwriting button on the Language bar and then click Writing Pad. The **Writing Pad** resembles a note pad with one or more lines on which you can use freehand to print or write in cursive. You can form letters on the line by moving the mouse while holding down the mouse button. With the **Text button** selected, the handwritten text is converted to typed characters and inserted into the document (Figure B-9a on the next page).

Consider the example in Figure B-9a. With the insertion point at the top of the document, the name, Millie, is written in cursive on the **Pen line** in the Writing Pad. As soon as the name is complete, the Handwriting Recognition service automatically converts the handwriting to typed characters and inserts the name into the document at the location of the insertion point.

With the **Ink button** selected, the text is inserted in handwritten form into the document. Once inserted, you can change the font size and color of the handwritten text (Figure B-9b).

To the right of the note pad is a rectangular toolbar. Use the buttons on this toolbar to adjust the Writing Pad, move the insertion point, and activate other handwriting applications.

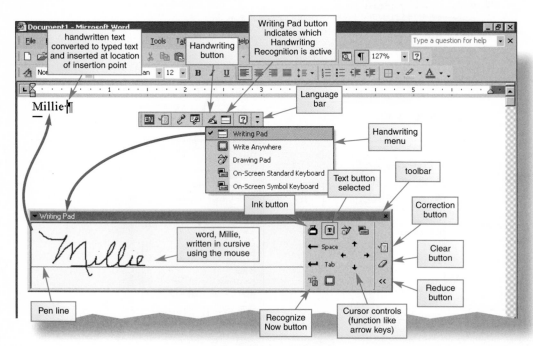

(a) Text Button Selected

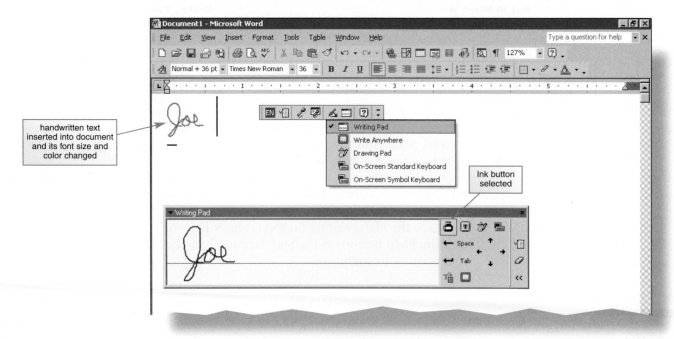

(b) Ink Button Selected

FIGURE B-9

You can customize the Writing Pad by clicking the **Options button** on the left side of the title bar and then clicking the Options command (Figure B-10a). Invoking the **Options command** causes the Handwriting Options dialog box to display. The **Handwriting Options dialog box** contains two sheets: Common and Writing Pad. The **Common sheet** lets you change the pen color and pen width, adjust recognition, and customize the toolbar area of the Writing Pad. The **Writing Pad sheet** allows you to change the background color and the number of lines that display in the Writing Pad. Both sheets contain a **Restore Default button** to restore the settings to what they were when the software was installed initially.

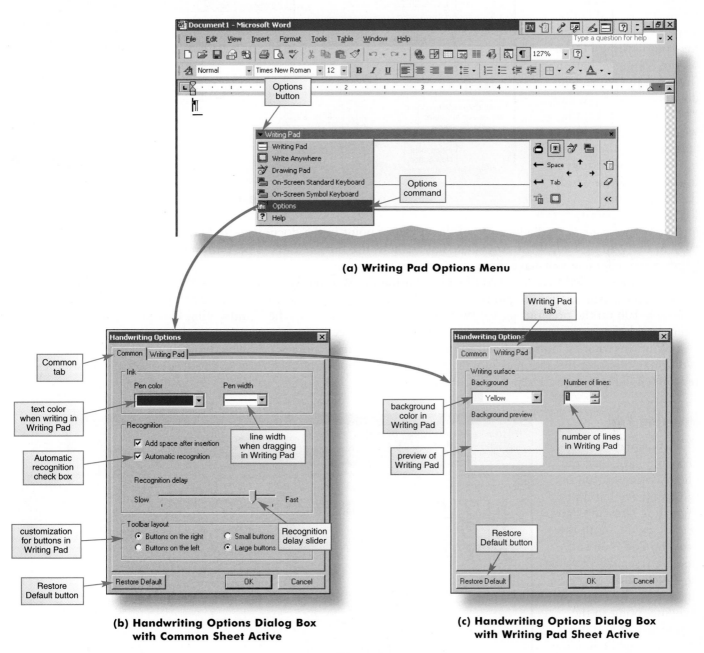

(a) Writing Pad Options Menu

**(b) Handwriting Options Dialog Box
with Common Sheet Active**

**(c) Handwriting Options Dialog Box
with Writing Pad Sheet Active**

FIGURE B-10

When you first start using the Writing Pad, you may want to remove the check mark from the **Automatic recognition check box** in the Common sheet in the Handwriting Options dialog box (Figure B-10b). With the check mark removed, the Handwriting Recognition service will not interpret what you write in the Writing Pad until you click the **Recognize Now button** on the toolbar (Figure B-9a). This allows you to pause and adjust your writing.

The best way to learn how to use the Writing Pad is to practice with it. Also, for more information, click the Help button on the Standard toolbar, click the Answer Wizard tab, and search for the phrase, Handwriting Recognition.

Write Anywhere

Rather than use a Writing Pad, you can write anywhere on the screen by invoking the **Write Anywhere command** on the Handwriting menu (Figure B-11) that displays when you click the Handwriting button on the Language bar. In this case, the entire window is your writing pad.

In Figure B-11, the word, Chip, is written in cursive using the mouse button. Shortly after you finish writing the word, the Handwriting Recognition service

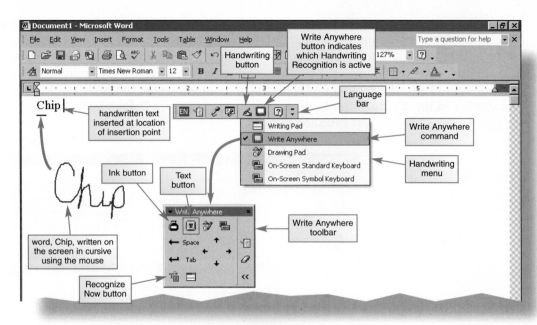

FIGURE B-11

interprets it, assigns it to the location of the insertion point in the document, and erases what you wrote. Similarly to the Writing Pad, Write Anywhere has both an Ink button and a Text button so you can insert either handwritten characters or have them converted to typed text.

It is recommended that when you first start using the Writing Anywhere service that you remove the check mark from the Automatic recognition check box in the Common sheet in the Handwriting Options dialog box (Figure B-10b on the previous page). With the check mark removed, the Handwriting Recognition service will not interpret what you write on the screen until you click the Recognize Now button on the toolbar (Figure B-11).

Write Anywhere is more difficult to use than the Writing Pad, because when you click the mouse button, Word may interpret the action as moving the insertion point rather than starting to write. For this reason, it is recommended that you use the Writing Pad.

Drawing Pad

To display the Drawing Pad, click the Handwriting button on the Language bar and then click Drawing Pad (Figure B-12). With the **Drawing Pad**, you can insert a freehand drawing or sketch into a Word document. To create the drawing, point in the Drawing Pad and move the mouse while holding down the mouse button.

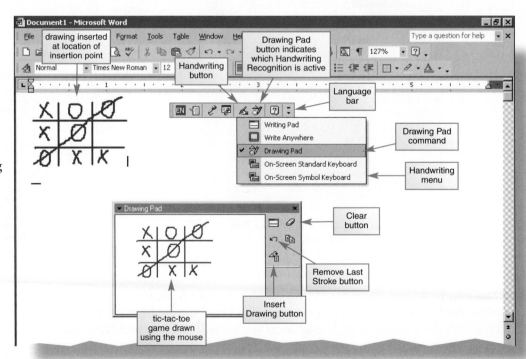

FIGURE B-12

In Figure B-12, the mouse button was used to draw a tic-tac-toe game in the Drawing Pad. To insert the drawing into the Word document at the location of the insertion point, click the Insert Drawing button on the rectangular toolbar to the right of the Drawing Pad. Other buttons on the toolbar allow you to erase a drawing, erase your last drawing stroke, copy the drawing to the Office Clipboard, or activate the Writing Pad.

You can customize the Drawing Pad by clicking the Options button on the left side of the title bar and then clicking the Options command (Figure B-13a). Invoking the **Options command** causes the Draw Options dialog box to display (Figure B-13b). The **Draw Options dialog box** lets you change the pen color and pen width and customize the toolbar area of the Drawing Pad. The dialog box also contains a Restore Default button that restores the settings to what they were when the software was installed initially.

The best way to learn how to use the Drawing Pad is to practice with it. Also, for more information, click the Help button on the Standard toolbar, click the Answer Wizard tab, and search for the phrase, Drawing Pad.

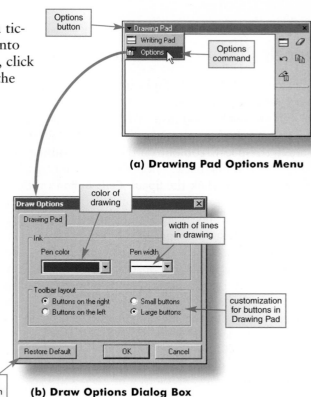

(a) Drawing Pad Options Menu

(b) Draw Options Dialog Box

FIGURE B-13

On-Screen Keyboard

The **On-Screen Standard Keyboard command** on the Handwriting menu (Figure B-14) displays an on-screen keyboard. The **on-screen keyboard** lets you enter characters into a document by using your mouse to click the keys. The on-screen keyboard is similar to the type found on handheld computers.

The **On-Screen Symbol Keyboard command** on the Handwriting menu (Figure B-14) displays a special on-screen keyboard that allows you to enter symbols that are not on your keyboard, as well as Unicode characters. **Unicode characters** use a coding scheme capable of representing all the world's current languages.

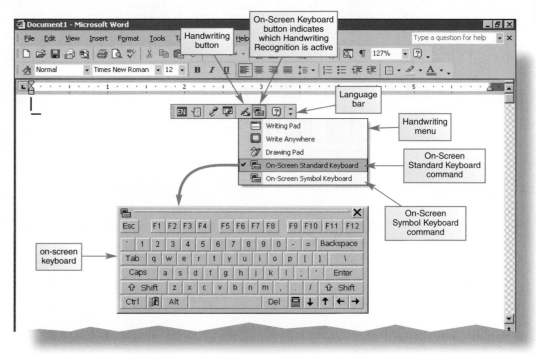

FIGURE B-14

Speech Playback in Excel

Excel is the only Office XP application that supports speech playback. With Excel, you can use **speech playback** to have your computer read back the data in a worksheet. To enable speech playback, you use the **Text To Speech toolbar** (Figure B-15). You display the toolbar by right-clicking a toolbar and then clicking Text To Speech on the shortcut menu. You also can display the toolbar by pointing to Speech on the Tools menu and then clicking Show Text To Speech Toolbar on the Speech submenu.

To use speech playback, select the cell where you want the computer to start reading back the data in the worksheet and then click the **Speak Cells button** on the Text To Speech toolbar (Figure B-15). The computer stops reading after it reads the last cell with an entry in the worksheet. An alternative is to select a range before you turn on speech playback. When you select a range, the computer reads from the upper-left corner of the range to the lower-right corner of the range. It reads the data in the worksheet by rows or by columns. You choose the direction you want it to read by clicking the **By Rows button** or **By Columns button** on the Text To Speech toolbar. Click the **Stop Speaking button** or hide the Text To Speech toolbar to stop speech playback.

The rightmost button on the Text To Speech toolbar is the Speak On Enter button. When you click the **Speak On Enter button** to enable it, the computer reads data in a cell immediately after you complete the entry by pressing the ENTER key or clicking another cell. It does not read the data if you click the Enter box on the formula bar to complete the entry. You disable this feature by clicking the Speak On Enter button while the feature is enabled. If you do not turn the Speak On Enter feature off, the computer will continue to read new cell entries even if the toolbar is hidden.

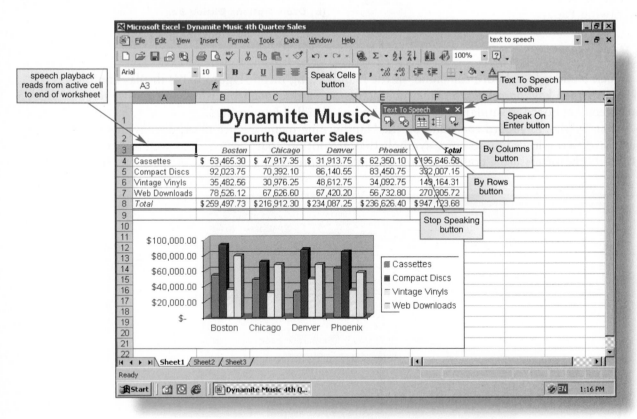

FIGURE B-15

Customizing Speech Playback

You can customize speech playback by double-clicking the **Speech icon** in the Control Panel window (Figure B-16a). To display the Control Panel, point to Settings on the Start menu and then click Control Panel. When you double-click the Speech icon, the Speech Properties dialog box displays (Figure B-16b). Click the Text To Speech tab. The Text To Speech sheet has two areas: Voice selection and Voice speed. The Voice selection area lets you choose between a male and female voice. You can click the Preview Voice button to preview the voice. The Voice speed area contains a slider. Drag the slider to slow down or speed up the voice.

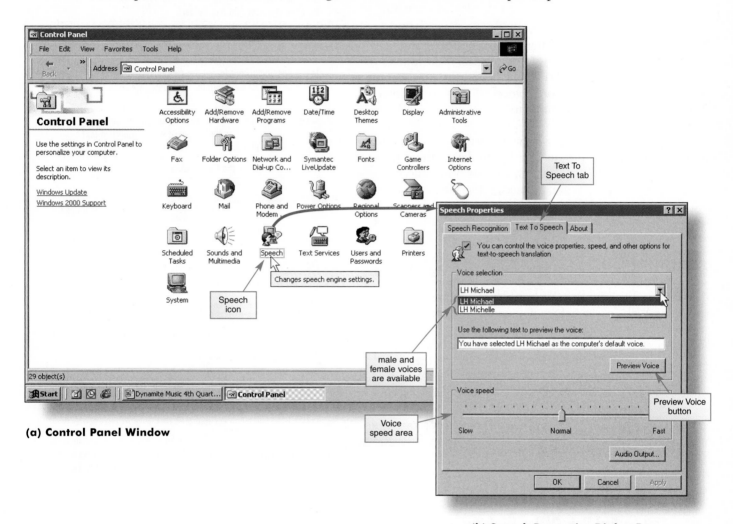

(a) Control Panel Window

(b) Speech Properties Dialog Box

FIGURE B-16

APPENDIX C

Publishing Office Web Pages to a Web Server

With the Office applications, you use the Save as Web Page command on the File menu to save the Web page to a Web server using one of two techniques: Web folders or File Transfer Protocol. A **Web folder** is an Office shortcut to a Web server. **File Transfer Protocol** (**FTP**) is an Internet standard that allows computers to exchange files with other computers on the Internet.

You should contact your network system administrator or technical support staff at your ISP to determine if their Web server supports Web folders, FTP, or both, and to obtain necessary permissions to access the Web server. If you decide to publish Web pages using a Web folder, you must have the Office Server Extensions (OSE) installed on your computer.

Using Web Folders to Publish Office Web Pages

When publishing to a Web folder, someone first must create the Web folder before you can save to it. If you are granted permission to create a Web folder, you must obtain the URL of the Web server, a user name, and possibly a password that allows you to access the Web server. You also must decide on a name for the Web folder. Table C-1 explains how to create a Web folder.

Office adds the name of the Web folder to the list of current Web folders. You can save to this folder, open files in the folder, rename the folder, or perform any operations you would to a folder on your hard disk. You can use your Office program or Windows Explorer to access this folder. Table C-2 explains how to save to a Web folder.

Using FTP to Publish Office Web Pages

When publishing a Web page using FTP, you first must add the FTP location to your computer before you can save to it. An **FTP location**, also called an **FTP site**, is a collection of files that reside on an FTP server. In this case, the FTP server is the Web server.

To add an FTP location, you must obtain the name of the FTP site, which usually is the address (URL) of the FTP server, and a user name and a password that allows you to access the FTP server. You save and open the Web pages on the FTP server using the name of the FTP site. Table C-3 explains how to add an FTP site.

Office adds the name of the FTP site to the FTP locations list in the Save As and Open dialog boxes. You can open and save files using this list. Table C-4 explains how to save to an FTP location.

Table C-1 — Creating a Web Folder

1. Click File on the menu bar and then click Save As (or Open).
2. When the Save As dialog box (or Open dialog box) displays, click My Network Places (or Web Folders) on the Places Bar. Double-click Add Network Place (or Add Web Folder).
3. When the Add Network Place Wizard dialog box displays, click the Create a new Network Place option button and then click the Next button. Type the URL of the Web server in the Folder location text box, enter the folder name you want to call the Web folder in the Folder name text box, and then click the Next button. Click Empty Web and then click the Finish button.
4. When the Enter Network Password dialog box displays, type the user name and, if necessary, the password in the respective text boxes and then click the OK button.
5. Close the Save As or the Open dialog box.

Table C-2 — Saving to a Web Folder

1. Click File on the menu bar and then click Save As.
2. When the Save As dialog box displays, type the Web page file name in the File name text box. Do not press the ENTER key.
3. Click My Network Places on the Places Bar.
4. Double-click the Web folder name in the Save in list.
5. If the Enter Network Password dialog box displays, type the user name and password in the respective text boxes and then click the OK button.
6. Click the Save button in the Save As dialog box.

Table C-3 — Adding an FTP Location

1. Click File on the menu bar and then click Save As (or Open).
2. In the Save As dialog box, click the Save in box arrow and then click Add/Modify FTP Locations in the Save in list; or in the Open dialog box, click the Look in box arrow and then click Add/Modify FTP Locations in the Look in list.
3. When the Add/Modify FTP Locations dialog box displays, type the name of the FTP site in the Name of FTP site text box. If the site allows anonymous logon, click Anonymous in the Log on as area; if you have a user name for the site, click User in the Log on as area and then enter the user name. Enter the password in the Password text box. Click the OK button.
4. Close the Save As or the Open dialog box.

Table C-4 — Saving to an FTP Location

1. Click File on the menu bar and then click Save As.
2. When the Save As dialog box displays, type the Web page file name in the File name text box. Do not press the ENTER key.
3. Click the Save in box arrow and then click FTP Locations.
4. Double-click the name of the FTP site to which you wish to save.
5. When the FTP Log On dialog box displays, enter your user name and password and then click the OK button.
6. Click the Save button in the Save As dialog box.

APPENDIX D
Resetting the Word Toolbars and Menus

Word customization capabilities allow you to create custom toolbars by adding and deleting buttons and to personalize menus based on their usage. Each time you start Word, the toolbars and menus display using the same settings as the last time you used it. This appendix shows you how to reset the Standard and Formatting toolbars and menus to their installation settings.

Steps **To Reset the Standard and Formatting Toolbars**

1 **Click the Toolbar Options button on the Standard toolbar and then point to Add or Remove Buttons on the Toolbar Options menu.**

The Toolbar Options menu and the Add or Remove Buttons submenu display (Figure D-1).

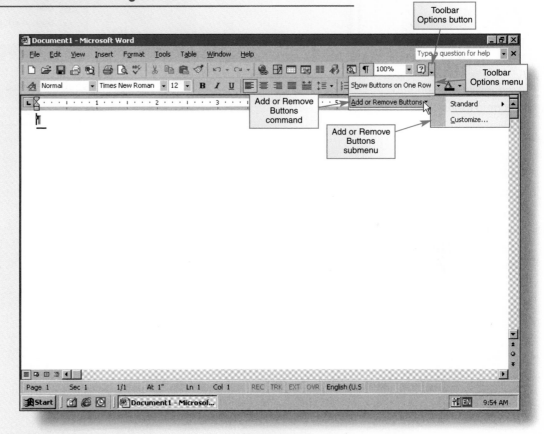

FIGURE D-1

2 **Point to Standard on the Add or Remove Buttons submenu. When the Standard submenu displays, scroll down and then point to Reset Toolbar.**

The Standard submenu displays indicating the buttons and boxes that display on the toolbar (Figure D-2). Clicking a button name with a check mark to the left of the name removes the check mark and then removes the button from the toolbar.

3 **Click Reset Toolbar.**

Word resets the Standard toolbar to its installation settings.

4 **Reset the Formatting toolbar by following Steps 1 through 3 and replacing any reference to the Standard toolbar with the Formatting toolbar.**

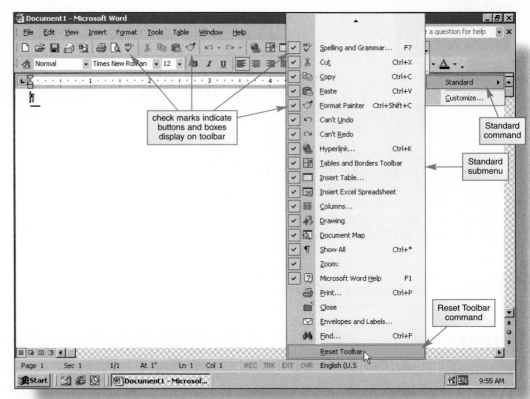

FIGURE D-2

Other **Ways**

1. On View menu point to Toolbars, click Customize on Toolbars submenu, click Toolbars tab, click toolbar name, click Reset button, click OK button, click Close button

2. Right-click toolbar, click Customize, click Toolbars tab, click toolbar name, click Reset button, click OK button, click Close button

3. In Voice Command mode, say "View, Toolbars, Customize, Toolbars, [toolbar name], Reset, OK, Close"

To Reset Menus

1 **Click the Toolbar Options button on the Standard toolbar and then point to Add or Remove Buttons on the Toolbar Options menu. Point to Customize on the Add or Remove Buttons submenu.**

The Toolbar Options menu and the Add or Remove Buttons submenu display (Figure D-3).

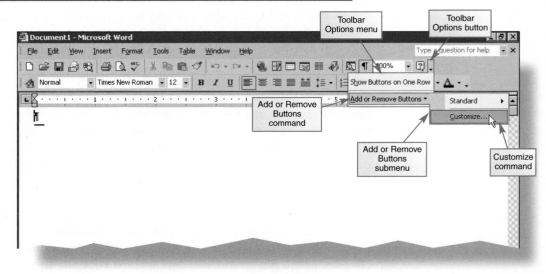

FIGURE D-3

2 **Click Customize. When the Customize dialog box displays, click the Options tab and then point to the Reset my usage data button.**

*The Customize dialog box displays (Figure D-4). The **Customize dialog box** contains three tabbed sheets used for customizing the Word toolbars and menus.*

3 **Click the Reset my usage data button. When the Microsoft Word dialog box displays, click the Yes button. Click the Close button in the Customize dialog box.**

Word resets the menus to the installation settings.

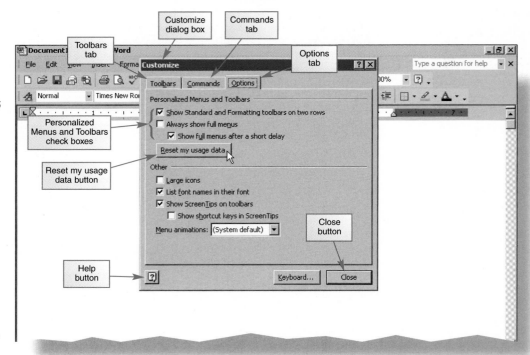

FIGURE D-4

Other Ways

1. On View menu point to Toolbars, click Customize on Toolbars submenu, click Options tab, click Reset my usage data button, click Yes button, click Close button

2. In Voice Command mode, say "View, Toolbars, Customize, Options, Reset my usage data, Yes, Close"

In the Options sheet in the Customize dialog box shown in Figure D-4 on the previous page, you can turn off toolbars displaying on two rows and turn off short menus by removing the check marks from the two top check boxes. Click the Help button in the lower-left corner of the Customize dialog box to display Help topics that will assist you in customizing toolbars and menus.

Using the Commands sheet, you can add buttons to toolbars and commands to menus. Recall that the menu bar at the top of the Word window is a special toolbar. To add buttons, click the Commands tab in the Customize dialog box. Click a category name in the Categories list and then drag the command name in the Commands list to a toolbar. To add commands to a menu, click a category name in the Categories list, drag the command name in the Commands list to the menu name on the menu bar, and then, when the menu displays, drag the command to the desired location in the menu list of commands.

In the Toolbars sheet, you can add new toolbars and reset existing toolbars. If you add commands to menus as described in the previous paragraph and want to reset the menus to their default settings, do the following: (1) Click View on the menu bar and then point to Toolbars; (2) click Customize; (3) click the Toolbars tab; (4) click Menu Bar in the Toolbars list; (5) click the Reset button; (6) click the OK button; and then (7) click the Close button.

APPENDIX E
Microsoft Office User Specialist Certification Program

What Is MOUS Certification?

The Microsoft Office User Specialist (MOUS) Certification Program provides a framework for measuring your proficiency with the Microsoft Office XP applications, such as Word 2002, Excel 2002, Access 2002, PowerPoint 2002, Outlook 2002, and FrontPage 2002. The levels of certification are described in Table E-1.

Table E-1	Levels of MOUS Certification		
LEVEL	*DESCRIPTION*	*REQUIREMENTS*	*CREDENTIAL AWARDED*
Expert	Indicates that you have a comprehensive understanding of the advanced features in a specific Microsoft Office XP application	Pass any ONE of the Expert exams: Microsoft Word 2002 Expert Microsoft Excel 2002 Expert Microsoft Access 2002 Expert Microsoft Outlook 2002 Expert Microsoft FrontPage 2002 Expert	Candidates will be awarded one certificate for each of the Expert exams they have passed: Microsoft Office User Specialist: Microsoft Word 2002 Expert Microsoft Office User Specialist: Microsoft Excel 2002 Expert Microsoft Office User Specialist: Microsoft Access 2002 Expert Microsoft Office User Specialist: Microsoft Outlook 2002 Expert Microsoft Office User Specialist: Microsoft FrontPage 2002 Expert
Core	Indicates that you have a comprehensive understanding of the core features in a specific Microsoft Office XP application	Pass any ONE of the Core exams: Microsoft Word 2002 Core Microsoft Excel 2002 Core Microsoft Access 2002 Core Microsoft Outlook 2002 Core Microsoft FrontPage 2002 Core	Candidates will be awarded one certificate for each of the Core exams they have passed: Microsoft Office User Specialist: Microsoft Word 2002 Microsoft Office User Specialist: Microsoft Excel 2002 Microsoft Office User Specialist: Microsoft Access 2002 Microsoft Office User Specialist: Microsoft Outlook 2002 Microsoft Office User Specialist: Microsoft FrontPage 2002
Comprehensive	Indicates that you have a comprehensive understanding of the features in Microsoft PowerPoint 2002	Pass the Microsoft PowerPoint 2002 Comprehensive Exam	Candidates will be awarded one certificate for the Microsoft PowerPoint 2002 Comprehensive exam passed.

Why Should You Get Certified?

Being a Microsoft Office User Specialist provides a valuable industry credential — proof that you have the Office XP applications skills required by employers. By passing one or more MOUS certification exams, you demonstrate your proficiency in a given Office XP application to employers. With over 100 million copies of Office in use around the world, Microsoft is targeting Office XP certification to a wide variety of companies. These companies include temporary employment agencies that want to prove the expertise of their workers, large corporations looking for a way to measure the skill set of employees, and training companies and educational institutions seeking Microsoft Office XP teachers with appropriate credentials.

The MOUS Exams

You pay $50 to $100 each time you take an exam, whether you pass or fail. The fee varies among testing centers. The Expert exams, which you can take up to 60 minutes to complete, consists of between 40 and 60 tasks that you perform online. The tasks require you to use the application just as you would in doing your job. The Core exams contain fewer tasks, and you will have slightly less time to complete them. The tasks you will perform differ on the two types of exams.

How Can You Prepare for the MOUS Exams?

The Shelly Cashman Series® offers several Microsoft-approved textbooks that cover the required objectives on the MOUS exams. For a listing of the textbooks, visit the Shelly Cashman Series MOUS site at scsite.com/tdoff/cert and click the link Shelly Cashman Series Office XP Microsoft-Approved MOUS Textbooks (Figure E-1). After using any of the books listed in an instructor-led course, you will be prepared to take the MOUS exam indicated.

How to Find an Authorized Testing Center

You can locate a testing center by calling 1-800-933-4493 in North America or visiting the Shelly Cashman Series MOUS site at scsite.com/tdoff/cert and then clicking the link Locate an Authorized Testing Center Near You (Figure E-1). At this Web site, you can look for testing centers around the world.

Shelly Cashman Series MOUS Web Page

The Shelly Cashman Series MOUS Web page (Figure E-1) has more than fifteen Web sites you can visit to obtain additional information on the MOUS Certification Program. The Web page (scsite.com/tdoff/cert) includes links to general information on certification, choosing an application for certification, preparing for the certification exam, and taking and passing the certification exam.

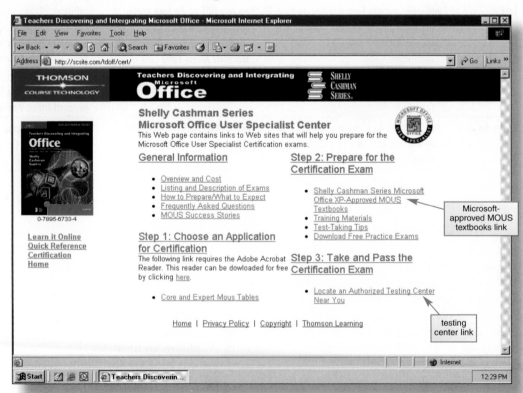

FIGURE E-1

Index

Microsoft Office XP
Quick Reference Summary

In the Microsoft Office XP applications, you can accomplish a task in a number of ways. The following five tables (one each for Word, Excel, Access, PowerPoint, and Outlook) provide a quick reference to each task presented in this textbook. The first column identifies the task. The second column indicates the page number on which the task is discussed in the book. The subsequent four columns list the different ways the task in column one can be carried out. You can invoke the commands listed in the MOUSE, MENU BAR, and SHORTCUT MENU columns using Voice commands.

Table 1   Microsoft Word 2002 Quick Reference Summary

TASK	PAGE NUMBER	MOUSE	MENU BAR	SHORTCUT MENU	KEYBOARD SHORTCUT
Bold	WD 1.45	Bold button on Formatting toolbar	Format | Font | Font tab	Font | Font tab	CTRL+B
Center	WD 1.38	Center button on Formatting toolbar	Format | Paragraph | Indents and Spacing tab	Paragraph | Indents and Spacing tab	CTRL+E
Center Vertically	WD 1.39		File | Page Setup | Layout tab		
Clip Art, Insert	WD 1.46		Insert | Picture | Clip Art		
Close Document	WD 1.58	Close button on menu bar	File | Close		CTRL+W
Delete (Cut) Text	WD 1.54	Cut button on Standard toolbar	Edit | Cut	Cut	CTRL+X
Font	WD 1.36	Font box arrow on Formatting toolbar	Format | Font | Font tab	Font | Font tab	CTRL+SHIFT+F
Font Size	WD 1.20	Font Size box arrow on Formatting toolbar	Format | Font | Font tab	Font | Font tab	CTRL+SHIFT+P
Formatting Marks	WD 1.24	Show/Hide ¶ button on Standard toolbar	Tools | Options | View tab		CTRL+SHIFT+*
Full Menu	WD 1.14	Double-click menu name	Click menu name, wait few seconds		
Help	WD 1.59 and Appendix A	Microsoft Word Help button on Standard toolbar	Help | Microsoft Word Help		F1
Italicize	WD 1.41	Italic button on Formatting toolbar	Format | Font | Font tab	Font | Font tab	CTRL+I
Language Bar	WD 1.18	Language Indicator button in tray	Tools | Speech		
Open Document	WD 1.56	Open button on Standard toolbar	File | Open		CTRL+O
Print Document	WD 1.54	Print button on Standard toolbar	File | Print		CTRL+P
Quit Word	WD 1.55	Close button on title bar	File | Exit		ALT+F4
Repeat Command	WD 1.39		Edit | Repeat		
Resize Graphic	WD 1.51	Drag sizing handle	Format | Picture | Size tab	Format Picture | Size tab	
Restore Graphic	WD 1.53	Format Picture button on Picture toolbar	Format | Picture | Size tab	Format Picture | Size tab	

MICROSOFT OFFICE XP QUICK REFERENCE SUMMARY

Table 1   Microsoft Word 2002 Quick Reference Summary *(continued)*

TASK	PAGE NUMBER	MOUSE	MENU BAR	SHORTCUT MENU	KEYBOARD SHORTCUT
Right-Align	WD 1.37	Align Right button on Formatting toolbar	Format | Paragraph | Indents and Spacing tab	Paragraph | Indents and Spacing tab	CTRL+R
Redo Action	WD 1.39	Redo button on Standard toolbar	Edit | Redo		
Ruler, Show or Hide	WD 1.13		View | Ruler		
Save Document – New Name	WD 1.54		File | Save As		F12
Save Document – Same Name	WD 1.53	Save button on Standard toolbar	File | Save		CTRL+S
Save New Document	WD 1.30	Save button on Standard toolbar	File | Save		CTRL+S
Select Graphic	WD 1.50	Click graphic			
Select Group of Words	WD 1.44	Drag through words			CTRL+SHIFT+RIGHT ARROW
Select Line	WD 1.40	Point to left of line and click			SHIFT+DOWN ARROW
Select Multiple Paragraphs	WD 1.34	Point to left of first paragraph and drag down			CTRL+SHIFT+DOWN ARROW
Select Word	WD 1.42	Double-click word			CTRL+SHIFT+RIGHT ARROW
Spelling Check as You Type	WD 1.28	Double-click Spelling and Grammar Status icon on status bar		Right-click flagged word, click correct word on shortcut menu	
Task Pane, Close	WD 1.10	Close button on task pane	View | Task Pane		
Task Pane, Display Different	WD 1.49	Other Task Panes button on task pane			
Toolbar, Show Entire	WD 1.16	Double-click move handle on toolbar			
Underline	WD 1.43	Underline button on Formatting toolbar	Format | Font | Font tab	Font | Font tab	CTRL+U
Undo Command or Action	WD 1.39	Undo button on Standard toolbar	Edit | Undo		CTRL+Z
Zoom Page Width	WD 1.19	Zoom box arrow on Formatting toolbar	View | Zoom		

Table 2 Microsoft PowerPoint 2002 Quick Reference Summary

TASK	PAGE NUMBER	MOUSE	MENU BAR	SHORTCUT MENU	KEYBOARD SHORTCUT
Check Spelling	PP 1.56	Spelling button on Standard toolbar	Tools | Spelling		F7
Delete Text	PP 1.58	Cut button on Standard toolbar	Edit | Cut	Cut	CTRL+X or BACKSPACE or DELETE
Design Template	PP 1.19	Slide Design button on Formatting toolbar	Format | Slide Design	Slide Design	ALT+O | D
Display a Presentation in Black and White	PP 1.58	Color/Grayscale button on Standard toolbar	View | Color/Grayscale | Pure Black and White		ALT+V | C | U
Font	PP 1.25	Font box arrow on Formatting toolbar	Format | Font	Font	ALT+O | F
Font Color	PP 1.25	Font Color button arrow on Formatting toolbar, desired color	Format | Font	Font | Color	ALT+O | F | ALT+C | DOWN ARROW
Font Size, Decrease	PP 1.25	Decrease Font Size button on Formatting toolbar	Format | Font	Font | Size	CTRL+SHIFT+LEFT CARET (<)
Font Size, Increase	PP 1.27	Increase Font Size button on Formatting toolbar	Format | Font	Font | Size	CTRL+SHIFT+RIGHT CARET (>)
Help	PP 1.62 and Appendix A	Microsoft PowerPoint Help button on Standard toolbar	Help | Microsoft PowerPoint Help		F1
Italicize	PP 1.26	Italic button on Formatting toolbar	Format | Font | Font style	Font | Font style	CTRL+I
Language Bar	PP 1.18	Language Indicator button in tray	Tools | Speech | Speech Recognition		ALT+T | H | H
New Slide	PP 1.32	New Slide button on Formatting toolbar	Insert | New Slide		CTRL+M
Next Slide	PP 1.46	Next Slide button on vertical scroll bar			PAGE DOWN
Open Presentation	PP 1.53	Open button on Standard toolbar	File | Open		CTRL+O
Paragraph Indent, Decrease	PP 1.40	Decrease Indent button on Formatting toolbar			SHIFT+TAB or ALT+SHIFT+ LEFT ARROW
Paragraph Indent, Increase	PP 1.34	Increase Indent button on Formatting toolbar			TAB or ALT+SHIFT+RIGHT ARROW
Previous Slide	PP 1.46	Previous Slide button on vertical scroll bar			PAGE UP
Print a Presentation	PP 1.61	Print button on Standard toolbar	File | Print		CTRL+P
Quit PowerPoint	PP 1.52	Close button on title bar or double-click Control icon on title bar	File | Exit		ALT+F4 or CTRL+Q
Redo Action	PP 1.23	Redo button on Standard toolbar	Edit | Redo		CTRL+Y or ALT+E | R
Save a Presentation	PP 1.29	Save button on Standard toolbar	File | Save		CTRL+S
Slide Show View	PP 1.48	Slide Show button at lower-left PowerPoint window	View | Slide Show		F5 or ALT+V | W
Task Pane	PP 1.11		View | Task Pane		ALT+V | K
Toolbar, Reset	PP D.01	Toolbar Options button on toolbar, Add or Remove Buttons, Customize, Toolbars tab		Customize | Toolbars tab	ALT+V | T | C | B
Toolbar, Show Entire	PP 1.12	Double-click move handle			
Undo Action	PP 1.23	Undo button on Standard toolbar	Edit | Undo		CTRL+Z or ALT+E | U
Zoom Percentage, Increase	PP 1.45	Zoom box arrow on Standard toolbar	View | Zoom		ALT+V | Z

Table 3 Microsoft Excel 2002 Quick Reference Summary

TASK	PAGE NUMBER	MOUSE	MENU BAR	SHORTCUT MENU	KEYBOARD SHORTCUT
AutoFormat	E 1.33		Format | AutoFormat		ALT+O\A
AutoSum	E 1.23	AutoSum button on Standard toolbar	Insert | Function		ALT+=
Bold	E 1.29	Bold button on Formatting toolbar	Format | Cells | Font tab	Format Cells | Font tab	CTRL+B
Center Across Columns	E 1.32	Merge and Center button on Formatting toolbar	Format | Cells | Alignment tab	Format Cells | Alignment tab	CTRL+1 | A
Chart	E 1.37	Chart Wizard button on Standard toolbar	Insert | Chart		F11
Clear Cell	E 1.51	Drag fill handle back	Edit | Clear | All	Clear Contents	DELETE
Close All Workbooks	E 1.45		SHIFT+File | Close All		SHIFT+ALT+F | C
Close Workbook	E 1.45	Close button on menu bar or workbook Control-menu icon	File | Close		CTRL+W
Font Color	E 1.31	Font Color button on Formatting toolbar	Format | Cells | Font tab	Format Cells | Font tab	CTRL+1 | F
Font Size	E 1.30	Font Size box arrow on Formatting toolbar	Format | Cells | Font tab	Format Cells | Font tab	CTRL+1 | F
Full Screen	E 1.12		View | Full Screen		ALT+V | U
Go To	E 1.36	Click cell	Edit | Go To		F5
Help	E 1.52 and Appendix A	Microsoft Excel Help button on Standard toolbar	Help | Microsoft Excel Help		F1
In-Cell Editing	E 1.49	Double-click cell			F2
Language Bar	E 1.16	Language Indicator button in tray	Tools | Speech | Speech Recognition		ALT+T | H | H
Merge Cells	E 1.32	Merge and Center button on Formatting toolbar	Format | Cells | Alignment tab	Format Cells | Font tab | Alignment tab	ALT+O | E | A
Name Cells	E 1.36	Click Name box in formula bar and type name	Insert | Name | Define		ALT+I | N | D
New Workbook	E 1.52	New button on Standard toolbar	File | New		CTRL+N
Open Workbook	E 1.46	Open button on Standard toolbar	File | Open		CTRL+O
Quit Excel	E 1.45	Close button on title bar	File | Exit		ALT+F4
Redo	E 1.51	Redo button on Standard toolbar	Edit | Redo		ALT+E | R
Save Workbook – New Name	E 1.41		File | Save As		ALT+F | A
Select All of Worksheet	E 1.52	Select All button on worksheet			CTRL+A
Select Cell	E 1.16	Click cell			Use ARROW keys
Split Cell	E 1.32	Merge and Center button on Formatting toolbar	Format | Cells | Alignment tab	Format Cells | Alignment tab	ALT+O | E | A
Task Pane	E 1.08		View | Task Pane		ALT+V | K
Toolbar, Reset	E D.01	Toolbar Options, Add or Remove Buttons, Customize, Toolbars		Customize | Toolbars	ALT+V | T | C | B
Toolbar, Show Entire	E 1.14	Double-click move handle			
Undo	E 1.52	Undo button on Standard toolbar	Edit | Undo		CTRL+Z

MICROSOFT OFFICE XP QUICK REFERENCE SUMMARY

Table 4   Microsoft Access 2002 Quick Reference Summary

TASK	PAGE NUMBER	MOUSE	MENU BAR	SHORTCUT MENU	KEYBOARD SHORTCUT
Add Record	A 1.21, A 1.27	New Record button	Insert | New Record		
Close Database	A 1.25	Close Window button	File | Close		
Close Form	A 1.36	Close Window button	File | Close		
Close Table	A 1.25	Close Window button	File | Close		
Create Database	A 1.11	New button	File | New		CTRL+N
Create Form	A 1.35	New Object: AutoForm button arrow | AutoForm	Insert | AutoForm		
Create Report	A 1.41	New Object AutoForm button arrow | Report	Insert | Report		
Create Table	A 1.15	Tables object | Create table in Design view or Create table by using wizard	Insert | Table		
Delete Field	A 1.19	Delete Rows button	Edit | Delete	Delete Rows	DELETE
Field Size	A 1.18	Field Size property box			
Field Type	A 1.19	Data Type box arrow | appropriate type			Appropriate letter
Key Field	A 1.18	Primary Key button	Edit | Primary Key	Primary Key	
Move to First Record	A 1.26	First Record button			CTRL+UP ARROW
Move to Last Record	A 1.26	Last Record button			CTRL+DOWN ARROW
Move to Next Record	A 1.26	Next Record button			DOWN ARROW
Move to Previous Record	A 1.26	Previous Record button			UP ARROW
Open Database	A 1.25	Open button	File | Open		CTRL+O
Open Table	A 1.21	Tables object | Open button		Open	Use ARROW keys to move highlight to name, then press ENTER key
Preview Table	A 1.29	Print Preview button	File | Print Preview	Print Preview	
Print Report	A 1.46	Print button	File | Print	Print	CTRL+P
Print Table	A 1.29	Print button	File | Print	Print	CTRL+P
Quit Access	A 1.49	Close button	File | Exit		ALT+F4
Save Form	A 1.36	Save button	File | Save		CTRL+S
Save Table	A 1.20	Save button	File | Save		CTRL+S
Select Fields for Report	A 1.43	Add Field button or Add All Fields button			
Switch Between Form and Datasheet Views	A 1.39	View button arrow	View | Datasheet View		